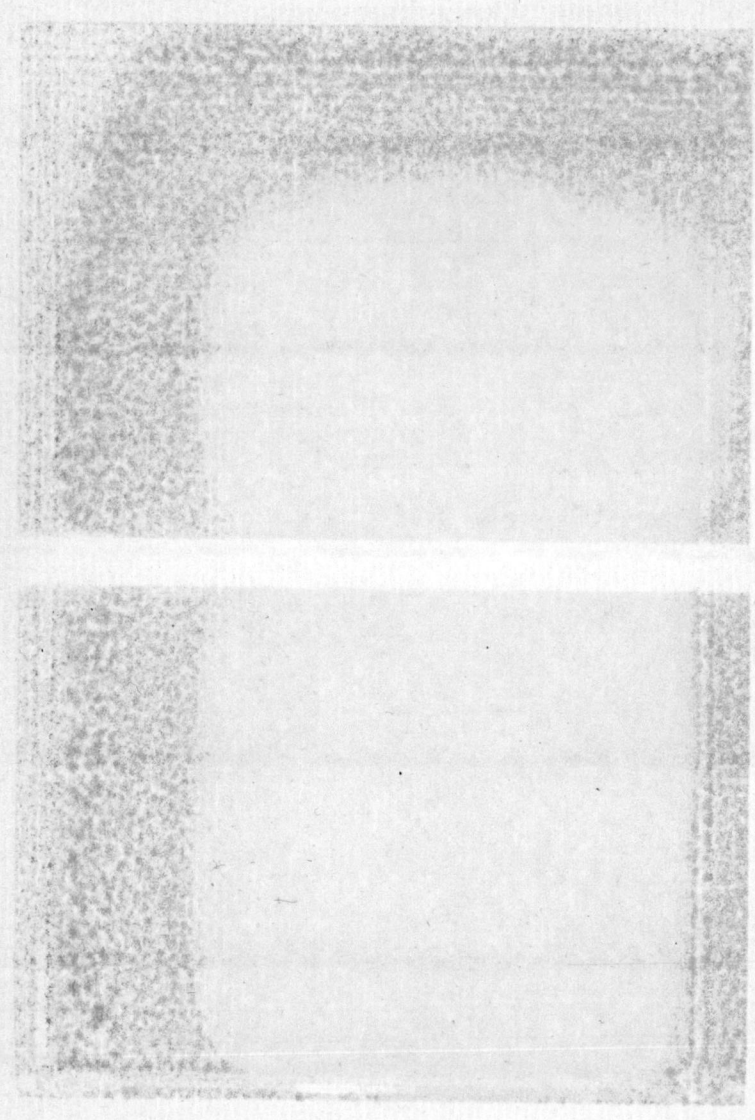

ENGLISH RECUSANT LITERATURE
1558–1640

*Selected and Edited by*
D. M. ROGERS

Volume 281

REGINALD POLE
*A Treatie of Iustification*
*1569*

RICHARD BROUGHTON
*The First Part of the*
*Resolution of Religion*
[*1603*]

# REGINALD POLE

*A Treatie of Iustification*

*1569*

The Scolar Press
1976

ISBN 0 85967 282 4

*Published and printed in Great Britain by*
*The Scolar Press Limited, 59-61 East Parade,*
*Ilkley, Yorkshire and*
*39 Great Russell Street,*
*London WC1*

*NOTE*

The following works are reproduced (original size) with permission:

1) Reginald Pole, *A treatie of iustification*, 1569, from a copy in Cambridge University Library, by permission of the Syndics.

*References:* Allison and Rogers 657; STC 20088/[24245].

2) Richard Broughton, *The first part of the resolution of religion*, [1603], from a copy in the Bodleian Library, by permission of the Curators.

*References:* Allison and Rogers 162; STC 3896.

# A TREATIE of Iustification.



Founde emong the writinges of Cardinal Pole of blessed memorie, remaining in the custodie of M. Henrie Pyning, Chamberlaine and General Receiuer to the said Cardinal, late deceased in Louaine.

Item, certaine Translations touching the said matter of *Iustification*, the Titles whereof, see in the page folowing.

*Prouerb. 4.*

*Ne declines neque ad dexteram, neque ad sinistram.*

Turne not aside to the right hande, nor to the lefte.

LOVANII,
Apud Ioannem Foulerum. Anno. 1569.
CVM PRIVILEGIO.

*Beside the Treatie of Iustification, in this Volume are comprised these Translations.*

First, the Sixte Session of the Generall Councell of Trent, whiche is of Iustification, with the Canons of the same Session.

Item, a Treatie of S. Augustine that famouse Doctour, by him entituled: Of Faith and VVorkes.

Item, a Sermon of S. Chrysostome, Of Praying vnto God.

Item, a Sermon of S. Basil, Of Fasting.

Item, certaine Sermons of S. Leo the Great, of the same Argument.

Last of al, a notable Sermon of S. Cyprian that blessed Martyr, Of Almes deedes.

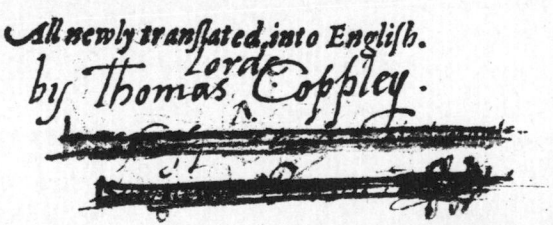

*All newly translated into English.*

by Thomas Lorde Coppley.

[redacted]

# *The Preface to the Reader.*

A*S all Scripture inſpired by God is profitable to* 2.Tim.3.
*teache and inſtructe in rightuouſenes, to the*
*ende that a godly man maie be perfecte, inſtru-*
*cted to al good woorkes:* ſo is there no pointe
or article thereof more expediente for a
Chriſtian man to ſeeke, more neceſſary to find and know,
more comfortable rightly to vnderſtand, and more profitable to remember and practiſe, then is the trewe and
right knowledge of his Iuſtification, and the maner how
the ſame is atteined. We are ſure by the Scripture, that *a*
*wicked man and his wickednes* bothe like *are hateful vnto* Sap.14.
*God:* Neither can there be looked for any other thing,
then heauy puniſhement and iuſt damnation, where the
anger and diſpleaſure of God is vnpacified once iuſtely
deſerued, and not taken awaie by ſome meanes to his contentation. We doubt not alſo, but that all men are borne
*naturally the children of anger*, that is to ſaie, in Gods diſ- Epheſ.2.
pleaſure and indignation, as branches of a condemned
ſtocke, a thral kinde and bonde race of one man, *by whom* Rom.5.
*ſinne entred into the world, and by ſinne death, and ſo wente*
*through all, in whome all haue ſinned.* And what can be ſo
pleaſaunt to a captiue, as to vnderſtande truely the way
and meanes of his deliuerance, or ſo comfortable to a perſon bonde and thrall, as to know, not onely how he maie
be made free, but alſo how he maie be brought in ſpeciall
fauor with his Lorde, by whom onely he muſt liue, or els
periſh? Finally how he maie be made a childe, *a ſonne, and* Epheſ.2.
*heire to him*, vnto whom he was a ſtranger before.

And bicauſe no man, be he neuer ſo rightuouſe and 1.Ioan.1.

Aug. de ciuitate Dei. li. 21. cap. 16. Galat. 5. Ioan. 5. Cypria. de Eleemos.

iuste, *liueth here without sinne*, and fewe there are of that happy estate, that fal not into damnable and mortal sinne, *the doers whereof shall not possesse the kingdome of God*: sith also a law is appointed vs by our Physition, that once made vs hole, who saied: *Thou arte made hole, nowe sinne no more*: *We were*, as S. Cyprian saieth, *driuen to a narowe straite, hauing a precise lawe of innocency prescribed vnto vs, neither coulde the weakenesse of mannes frailtie, tell what to do, if God of his mercy had not appointed a waie and meane, how man, that by sinne falleth from iustice after his Baptisme, may be restored to rightuousnes and iustice againe*. Further it suffiseth not a Christian man to be made rightuouse, and to be set in the state of iustice, vnlesse he contine we and perseuere in the same: *for he shal be saued, that continueth vnto the ende*. Also he muste increase in rightuousenes: for so the Scripture teacheth vs: *Let him that is iuste, be yet iustified*: for trewely is it saied: *Quantumlibet quisque iustificatus sit, habet tamen dum in hac vita est, quo probatior esse posit & melior: Qui autem non proficit, deficit: & qui nihil acquirit, nonnihil perdit*. Euery man, be he neuer so much iustified, yet maie he while he is in this life be more tried and better: and who so encreaseth not, faileth and goeth backeward, and he that getteth nothing, loseth somewhat. For whiche causes it behoueth vs, not onely to knowe how we are made iuste and rightuouse, but also how we be restored to Iustice when we fal: and how we maie continewe and increase in rightuousenes, when we be restored: and finally attaine to saluation and glory, which is the ende of Iustification, and without the which all Iustification in this life auaileth nothing, but rather turneth to a heape and increase of our damnation: bicause

Matth. 24

Apoca. 22 Leo Sermon. 8. de passio. Do.

bicause as Oecumenius saith, *Like vnprofitable seruantes we receiue our maisters mony, and make no gaine thereof:* that is to saie, *we receiue his grace in vaine.* *Oeco.in 2. cap.Iaco.*

This being vnderstanded, how necessary and profitable the knowledge of this Article is, and seing also, that a man, runne he neuer so fast, yet if he runne out of the way, he neuer commeth to the right end of his iourney, to the intente thou be not induced to iudge amisse in so greate a matter, and to thee so necessary, I haue (Christian Reader) with the hope of Gods helpe indeuoured my selfe to laie before thine eies particularly as briefely and plainely as I coulde, the maner of our Iustification in Christ with the circumstances belonging to the same. Grounding my selfe chiefely in al pointes through the Treatie vpon the Scripture and holy Worde of God. And bicause the same *neither is, nor ought to be of any mannes priuate interpretation,* (*for he that goeth abowt to drawe it to his owne priuat sense, shall be depriued of it*) I haue taken suche construction thereof, as the holy Ghost hath deliuered and taught his Church, and suche as the auncient Fathers of sundry ages and places agreeing togethers haue lerned in the Church and vttered in their writinges to teach other. Emong whom I haue especially and moste of all other folowed the auctoritie of S. Augustine, as wel for that he hath written most largely of this matter, as also bicause suche as be of the contrary parte in moste credite, and haue written in this time, confesse, *that in the Doctrine of the Churche he is a moste faithefull declarer of antiquitie:* Intending therby to discharge my selfe, as teaching nothing but that I haue learned *in Goddes Church the staie and piller of truthe*, and geeuing thee thereby good occasion I *2.Cor.16.* *2.Petr.1.* *Aug.lib. Confess.12. cap.25.* *Luthe. Philip. Melan. Calui.Institut. cap.18.* *1.Tim.3.*

 truste,

truſt, readily to beleue that thou ſhalt heere reade.

But as I haue declared vnto thee, that the right knowledge of this pointe concerning our Iuſtification, is to a Chriſtian man moſt neceſſary and comfortable: ſo muſt I aduertiſe thee, that the miſtaking and wrong vnderſtanding thereof, is moſt dangerouſe. For as the Philoſophers ſaie, that euery vertue is beſette of eche ſide with a vice contrary to it: ſo S. Auguſtine writeth, that *the true Doctrine of Iuſtification, hath of eche ſide of it, a deepe and dangerouſe fall, ſo that who ſo goeth out of the ſtreight waie thereof on the right or lefte hand, falleth downe hedlong, and caſteth awaie him ſelfe.*

*Ariſto. Ethic.*

*Aug. in Præfa. Pſal. 31.*

Into the one danger, and of the one ſide they fall, that preſume of them ſelues, thinking to be iuſtified by them ſelues, by their owne ſtrength and rightuouſnes, without the helpe and grace of God. Of them he ſaith: *Si ſe in audaciam quandam, &c.* If a man lift him ſelfe vppe vnto a boldenes of preſumption, *and preſume of his owne ſtrength and iuſtice, and purpoſe in his minde to fulfil iuſtice, and to doe all that is commaunded in the lawe, offending in nothing, and thinke to haue his life in his owne power, that he ſlide no where, faile no where, ſtumble no where, ſee darcke and dymme no where, and attribute this to the power of his owne will, although peraduenture he fulfil al things that ſeeme iuſt in mennes ſight, ſo that nothing be founde in his life that may be blamed of menne, yet God condemneth the very preſumption and vaunting of pride.*

*Auguſt. ſupra.*

The other hedlong fall is on the contrary ſide, and into it ſuche men fall, as pretending their owne infirmitie and weakenes do no good deedes, and truſt and preſume onely to be ſaued by Gods grace and mercie though they liue vngodly, of whome alſo S. Auguſtine ſaith in the ſame

place

place: *Si se infirmitati, &c. If a man yelde him selfe vppe to his owne weakenesse fully and wholy, and bende him selfe to this cogitation to say, bicause the mercy of God is readie for all sinners vnto the ende, in what so euer sinnes they continue, if they beleue that God delivereth, God forgeueth, so that no wicked men that haue faith and beleue, shal perish, that is to say, none of them shall perish, that say to them selues, what so euer I doe, with what so euer outrages and shamefull dedes I be distained, sinne I neuer so much, God of his mercy delivereth mee bicause I haue beleued in him: he then that saith no such menne perish, by that euil thinking is moued to sinne freely. And the iust God, vnto whom mercy is songe and iudgement, not mercy onely, but iudgement also, findeth man yll presuming of him selfe, and abusing Gods mercy to his owne destruction, and of necessity such a one must be damned.* And somewhat after that he saith: *Quid igitur fit?* What shall we then doe? *If a man iustifie him selfe, and presume of his owne iustice, he falleth. If a man considering and thinking vppon his owne weakenesse, and presuming of the mercy of God, haue no care to cleanse his owne life of his sinnes, and drowne him selfe in all the goulfe of lewd doinges, he falleth also. Presumption vppon his owne iustice, is as it were the right hand. The thinking that sinnes escape vnpunished, is like the left hand. Let vs heare the voice of God saying to vs: Turne not aside to the right or left hand. Presume not to come to the kingdome by thine owne iustice, presume not to sinne through the mercy of God.* August. vbi suprà. Prouer. 4.

These be, good Christian Reader, the two perilouse and deadly daungers, that men may fall into, if they doe not rightly vnderstande the true doctrine of Iustification. Whiche falles being so dangerouse, God graunt all men carefully

carefully to eschew. Wherin to helpe thee iudge vprightly, I haue taken in hande this trauaile, trusting by Gods grace, so to leade thee *Via Regia*, that is, in the true and high waie, that thou shalt not nede to fall of either side, if thou wilt vprightly waie, and with the feare of God consider such thinges, as thou shalt finde here alleaged.

And bicause I can not hope to atteine any good, much lesse so great a good, but by his geuing of whom commeth al good, I wil beginne with the prayer, which S. Augustine intending to preache of the same matter made, desiring thee to pray for mee, as he did his hearers for him selfe. *Primùm infirmitatem meam, &c.* First of al saith he, I commende my weakenesse *to your prayers, as the Apostle saith,* Ephes. 6. *that woordes may be geauen me in opening my mouth, so to speake vnto you, as it be not perilouse for me to speake, and may be holesome for you to heare.*

And this request I make vnto thee, Gentle Reader, not onely for mine owne sake, who neede the same, but for thine also, that thou maist perceiue, howe great helpe and asistance thou needest at Gods hand for thy parte, if thou wilt profitably reade or speake of this matter, of whiche so vertuouse and excellently learned a Bishop thought him selfe not able nor meete to speake, without the healpe of godlie prayers.

# A BRIEF TREATIE OF MANS IVSTIFICATION.

## THE FIRST BOOKE.

VVhat is meant by the worde of Iuſtification. And what degrees perfect Iuſtification and ſaluation hath in it.

### THE FIRST CHAPTER.

RIGHT order of teaching requireth, that ſithens mine intent is, to ſhew how a man is iuſtified, I ſhoulde firſt declare what is meant by the worde of Iuſtification, of which the holy Scriptures ſeme to ſpeake after three ſortes and manners.

Three degrees of Iuſtification in Scripture.

The firſt kinde is called the Iuſtification of a ſinfull or wicked man, of which S. Paul ſpeaketh, ſaying: *Credenti in eum qui iuſtificat impium reputatur fides ad iuſtitiam.* Faith is reputed for iuſtice vnto the partie that beleueth in him which iuſtifieth the wicked. Whiche wordes S. Auguſtine expounding, ſaith: *To iuſtifie the wicked, is as much to ſaie, as to make of the wicked a godly man.* And in an other place he ſaith: *When a wicked man is iuſtified, of wicked he is made iuſt.* And ſith all Iuſtification commeth of God, *Deus eſt qui iuſtificat*, It is God that iuſtifieth: of theſe places, and manie other that might be alleaged to this purpoſe, we may gather and ſaie, that Iuſtification in this kind, is the gifte of God, whereby a wicked or ſinfull man is made godlie and rightuouſe.

Rom.4.

*In expoſi. quarund. propoſ. ex epiſtola ad Rom.*

*Aug. in Pſal.7. & in ep.120.*

Rom.8.

2. An other degree or manner of Iuſtification, the Scri-
*Apoc.22.* pture alſo acknowlegeth, ſaiyng: *Qui iuſtus eſt, iuſtificetur adhuc.* Let him that is iuſt, be iuſtified yet. *And let him that is holie, be yet made holier.* And in an other place:
*Eccle c.18* *Non impediaris orare ſemper, & ne veteris vſque ad mortem iuſtificari, quoniam merces Dei manet in æternum.* Let nothing let thee to praie euer, and let nothing forbid thee to be iuſtified vnto thy death, bicauſe Gods rewarde abideth for euer. By which wordes it is not meant, that a wicked man, in whome no goodneſſe is, ſhould be made rightuouſe and godlie, but that a good and a iuſte man ſhould be made iuſter and better. For as we ſaie truely, that water is warmed, not onely when it is of colde made luke warme, but alſo when it is of warme made hotter: ſo ſaith the Scripture, that a man is iuſtified when he increaſeth in iuſtice, and of good and rightuouſe is made iuſter and better.

3. Of a thirde degree of Iuſtification it is ſaid: *Non audi-*
*Rom.2.* *tores legis iuſti ſunt apud Deum, ſed factores legis iuſtificabuntur.* The hearers of the lawe be not iuſt before God, but the doers of the lawe ſhall be iuſtified. Where the worde of iuſtifiyng dothe neither ſignifie the comming to iuſtice, which maketh a wicked man rightuouſe and iuſte, neither the increaſe of iuſtice, whereby a good man is made better: but an ende and perfection of iuſtice, whereunto by Gods iuſt iudgement (of the which S. Paul there ſpeaketh) ſuch ſhal atteine, as keping them ſelues in the ſtate of iuſtice once receiued, or recouering the ſame by penance, continue and perſeuer in doing iuſtice vnto the ende.

This is the ful and perfect Iuſtification of man who being

ing borne in ſinne, is called to the ſtate of iuſtice: and increaſing therein by continuance, is at thende perfited in iuſtice in life euerlaſting. For neither doth it auayle him to beginne wel, if he doo not continue and increaſe, neither is it ynough to continue for a tyme, if afterwarde he fall away. For then doth he loſe the ende and perfection of his iuſtice, without the which the beginning and middle auayleth not.

In this ſorte doth S. Auguſtine ſpeake of mannes Iuſtification: For concerning the twoo firſt degrees thereof he ſayth thus: *Iuſtificatio in hac vita &c. Iuſtification is geuẽ vnto vs in this life by theſe three things: firſt by the waſhing of regeneration, whereby al ſinnes are forgeuen: after that by fighting with vices, from the gylte wherof we were diſcharged and aſſoyled. Thirdely while our prayer is heard, wherein we ſay: forgeue vs our offences.* *Aug. contra Iulia. lib. 2. Et de ciuita. Dei li. 21. cap. 16.*

In which wordes is compriſed not onely the entry and beginning of our Iuſtification, which he calleth Baptiſme, but alſo the increaſe of vertuouſe and godly lyfe, whiche he termeth a conflicte and fighting with vice, wherevnto he ioyneth prayer for the forgeueneſſe of ſinne, when we fal. And this calleth he our Iuſtificatiõ in this life, ſaying further in an other place: *Quiſquis cupit &c. Whoſo euer deſireth to eſcape the paynes euerlaſting, lette him not onely be baptiſed, but alſo be iuſtified in Chriſte.* We doubt not, but that ſuche as are baptiſed, be alſo iuſtified. For where S. Paule ſaith: *Abluti eſtis*: ye are waſhed cleane, he ſaieth alſo: *iuſtificati eſtis*: ye are iuſtified. And yet ſaieth S. Auguſtine, that beſide Baptiſme, a man muſte be iuſtified, meaning by Iuſtification, the continual conflicte with vice, wherein conſiſteth a godly and a vertuouſe *Lib. 21. de ciuit. Dei cap. 16.* *1. Cor. 6.*

lyfe, and increase of iustice.

Of the third degree, whiche is the ende and perfiting of our iustice, he saith: *Complebitur spes nostra &c. Our hope shalbe fully accomplished in the resurrection of the deade: and when our hope shalbe fulfilled, then shal our Iustification be fulfilled and accomplished.*

*Aug epist. 106 Et sermo.61. de ver. Dom.*

Thus doth our Iustification rightly vnderstanded, as it is cōplete and perfect, comprise in it selfe a beginning of iustice, an encrease, and an ende. In this sort do the Scriptures in sundry places speake of it. For this cause, I haue in al this Treatie, to make the matter playner to vnderstande, deduced three degrees of Iustification, comparing the same with S. Augustine to a perfecte buylding, which beside a foundation, hath lodging to dwel in. And to a fruiteful tree, which hath not onely a roote, but fruit also comming of the same.

Note the Authours Intente.

And albeit al these three degrees make but one absolute and perfecte Iustification in euery man that is saued, yet doth the Scripture in sundry places speake seuerally and in diuers maner of wordes: sometyme of the beginning and entree, sometyme of the increase, sometyme of th'ende and perfection of our iustice: whereof may grow obscuritie and occasion of errour to suche as vnderstand not, nor marke not this diuersitie in degrees of iustice.

For it is not one thing that God requireth of him that first commeth to his seruice, and of him that continueth his seruant, and in th'ende trusteth to be rewarded by his seruice. By meane of which difference it is truly sayd in the Scripture, *a man is iustified by faith without woorkes*, and also it is truly said, *a man is iustified by workes*. For as a synner is called and set in the state of iustice by grace, without

Marke this diuersitie.

*Rom.3.*
*Iacob.2.*

without any deserte of woorkes done before: So no man can continue in Christ, increase in iustice, and comme to the perfection thereof in life euerlasting, without good workes, as in processe of this Worke more plainely shal appeare.

VVhat is meant by the name of faith, and how many kindes of faith there be.

## THE II. CHAP.

BIcause in al this discourse of Iustification, I shalbe occasioned often tymes to speake of faith, I thinke it necessary, as I haue already shewed what is meant by the worde of Iustification, so likewise to declare briefly, what is meant by the name of faith, to th'intent that when the Reader shal see any thing alleged concerning faith, he may the better iudge of it.

S. Augustine saieth there be twoo kindes of faith: one, whereby we beleue that whiche is said to vs: An other, whereby we keepe promisse in that we say to other. *De hac fide nunc loquimur, quam adhibemus, cùm aliquid credimus: non quam damus, quum aliquid pollicemur. Nam & ipsa dicitur fides*. We speake nowe of the faith which we vse, when we beleeue any thing, not of the faith whiche we geue when we promyse any thinge. For that also is called faith. *But it is one thing when we say, he gaue no fayth nor credite vnto me, and an other when we saye, he kepte not faith with me. For the one is as muche to saie, He beleeued not that which I said: the other, he did not that which he said. By this faith, whereby we beleue, we be faithfull vnto God: by the other, whereby that is perfour-*

*August. de spirit. & lit. ca. 31.*

Tvvo kindes of faith.

*med which is promised, God also is faithful vnto vs. For so saith the Apostle: God is faithful, who doth not suffer you to* 1. Cor. 10. *be tempted further then you are able.*

Seing therefore, there be but two kindes of Faith, to witte, the faith of God towarde man in keeping his promise, and the faith of man towarde God in beleeuing his worde, and seing also that of Gods faith there is no question nor doubt: it foloweth, that when so euer mention is made in the Scripture of mans faith, alone and in his owne kinde, that faith is vnderstanded, whereby man is faithful vnto God: that is, as S. Chrysostome saith, *Whereby man geueth credite vnto his saiyngs and wordes.* For expounding these wordes: *Credidit Abraham Deo*, Abraham beleued God, he saith: *Credidit dictis Dei*, He gaue credite to Gods wordes and sayinges. In this sense S. Augustine saith: *Ad fidem quid pertinet? Credere.* What appertaineth to faith? To beleue. And bicause a man might aske also, what it is to beleeue, to put that out of doubt, he saith in an other place: *Quid est enim credere, nisi consentire verum esse quod dicitur?* What is it els to beleeue, but to consent, that the thing which is saide is true? By this rule as many in al ages, as haue beleued the Gospel after the right and true vnderstanding of the Catholique Churche, keeping them selues within the same Churche, haue ben called faithful and Catholiques. *Ille est verus & Germanus Catholicus, qui veritatem Dei, qui Ecclesiam, qui Christi corpus diligit, &c.* He is a true and right Catholike, saith *Vincentius Lyrinensis*, that loueth the truth of God, that loueth the Church, that loueth the body of Christ, that estemeth nothing more then Gods religion and the Catholike faith, no not the authoritie and loue

*Chrysost. hom, 31. in Gen.*

*August. de verb. Apostol. serm. 16. De spiri. & lite. cap. 31.*

*Vincent. Lyrinen. aduers. hæres.*

Who is a true Catholique.

loue of any man, father, husband, or whatsoeuer, not wit, eloquence, nor philosophie, not welthe, riches, or honour, but despising al these things and remayning fast and stable in faith, what soeuer he shall knowe that the Catholique Church hath holden from auncient time vniuersally, doth determine to holde and beleeue only that. Such then are faithful and Catholikes, that beleeue the Catholike and auncient faith vniuersally receyued, as Vincentius saieth, that beleue God and geue credite to his words, as S. Augustine, and S. Chrysostome say. And if they be also of life good and vertuouse, then be they called *boni Catholici*, good Catholikes: if they be of yl conuersation, they be called *fideles iniqui*, vniuste faithful, *mali Catholici*, yll Catholiques: faithful and Catholikes, bicause they haue faith: yll bicause their life is vngodly: if they forsake the faith as Iulianus did, they be called Apostates. But as long as they keepe the Catholike faith of Christes Churche, thoughe their lyfe be wicked, and they damnable, yet be they not called infideles, but faithful and beleeuers. And sith no man can be called faithfull, but he that hath faith, and it is faith, to beleeue, and to beleeue, is but to assente vnto trewth: by this it is proued, that the propertie of faith in his owne kinde, is to beleue the Gospel, and to assente vnto the trewth of God. S. Augustine saith: *A man doth learne by the Crede, what is to be beleeued: by the Pater noster, what is to be hoped: and by the commaundementes, what is to be loued.* And albeit faith and charitie must be both in a good man, yet as he saieth: *Quod credit, fidei est: quod operatur, charitatis est*, it is the property of faith that a man beleueth, and of charitie, that he worketh.

*August. in Præfatio. Psal. 31. & Ser. 31. de verb. Apost.*

Note.

*Enchiri. cap. 6. 7. 9. 117.*

Faith in his ovvne nature.

*August. in Præfatio. Psal. 31.*

Faith in his owne kinde may be alone and parted from

charitie,

Iacob.2. charitie and hope. For not onely euil men, but euen *Di-*
Enchirid. *uels doo beleue and tremble*, but as S. Augustine saith: *They*
cap.8. *neither hope nor loue*. And Leo saith: *Multis quibus au-*
Ser.4. de *ferre non potuit fidem, sustulit charitatem.* From many
Collect. hath the Diuell taken awaye Charitie, from whome he could not take awaye Faith. In this sorte doth the Scripture many tymes speake of faith, as it is in it selfe and in
Heb.11. his owne nature, saying: *Fides est substantia rerum sperandarum.* Faith is the substance of thinges that are to be ho-
Prima. in cap.11. ad Heb. ped for. It is called the substance of them, saieth *Primasius*, bicause *vnto such thinges as be taught by the worde of God, though they be not sene, yet faith geueth a being in our soule assenting vnto them, and beleeuing them as well to be true, as though they were seene with our bodily eyes.* In the same place it is saied: *By faith we vnderstande, that the worlde was sette in order by the woorde of God.* And this is faith in his owne kinde, that is to say, a beleeuing and assenting vnto truth.

Somtime the Scripture speaketh of faith as it is accompanied and ioyned with other vertues, and geeueth vnto faith the properties of such vertues as are ioyned with it:
Heb.11. So is it said, that, *by faith Abel offered Sacrifice, Noe feared God, Abraham obeyed, Moyses suffred affliction*, not that these
Faith ioyned with other. are the properties of faith in his owne nature, but bicause the Fathers beside faith had these vertues also: Abell the vertue of religion, Noe the feare of God, Abraham obedience, Moyses patience. So it is likewise said of charitie: *Omnia suffert, oīa credit, oīa sperat.* She suffreth al things, beleueth al things, hopeth al things. And yet saith S. Austine
In Præfa. truly: *Quod credit, fidei est.* It cometh of faith that a man
Psal.31. beleueth. And likewise of patience, that he suffereth, and of cha-

of .charitie, that he loueth and worketh wel.

Trewe it is, that none of these vertues alone and by it selfe maketh a good man. For it is a rule in Philosophie, that vertues be linked together. And yet as trewe it is, that euery vertue hath her owne natural property wherby she worketh somwhat in a good man, So faith beleueth, hope trusteth, charitie loueth, prudence chooseth, fortitude beareth, temperance refraineth: whose properties ioined together with other like, make vppe an absolute and perfecte goodnes. But bicause both faith and also the Scriptures were giuen to men, *to thintente they should haue life euerlasting by them, knowing and doing the wil of God*, S. Paule commendeth specially the faith, that doth not only reste in opinion and beleuing of truthe, but that is actiue and working through charitie toward that ende, saiyng: *In Christe Iesu, neither circumcision, nor to be without circumcision auaileth ought, but faith that worketh through charitie:* declaring thereby, that faith of it selfe is not able to worke the effecte of saluacion for which purpose it serueth, vnlesse it be accumpanied with *charitie the Mother of al vertues:* of which wordes S. Austine gathereth a rule, that when we find in the Scriptures faith commended for Iustificacion or saluacion, we should euer vnderstād it meant of faith which worketh through charitie: saying. *Hanc fidem definiuit Apostolus. &c.* This faith hath the Apostle defined and determined to be it. And in that sense both S. Augustine and other auncient fathers cal that many times, *the trewe faith, the Christian mannes faith, and the faith in deede.* The trewe faith in respecte of the ende whiche is saluacion, not bicause the faith whereby we onely beleue the Scriptures is not a

Ioan. 5. Gala. 5. Leo ser. 7. de Epipha. A notable Rule. De fide & oper. c. 14 De spiri. & lit. ca. 32. Epistola. 105. Enchir. cap. 8. De Gra. et lib. arbi. cap. 7.

trewe Faith. For we saie in the Creede of *Athanasius*, that the Catholique Faith is *a full, perfecte and inuiolable Faith*.

A beleeuing faith and a sauing faith.

But it is perfecte in beleuing, not perfecte in sauing. And therefore it is not saide in the ende, who so beleueth it, shalbe saued, but vnlesse a man beleue and keepe it inuiolable, he shal without doubte be damned. For though he beleue the Scriptures in profesſion, and keepe them not in deede, that is, if he beleue them in worde and mouth, and trangresse them in acte and deede, he shall not be saued. Faith alone and of it selfe maie be perfecte for beleuing, but the faith that is trewe and perfecte for sauing, is euer accompanied, neuer alone. It is one thing then to haue trewe faith in assente and opinion, which is faith in his owne nature, and an other thing to haue faith in obedience of harte and affection, which is faith accompanied with charitie and other vertues: of whiche difference I onely putte the Reader in remembrance, bicause I will more largely speake thereof in the. 7. Chapter of the second booke, to the whiche I referre him.

*August. de Trinitate. Lib. 15. cap. 18. & in Enchirid. cap. 8.*

Thus haue I thought good to open vnto the Reader, what is properly meante by the name of faith alone, and what it taketh of other vertues: *Sine quibus esse potest, sed prodesse non potest*. Without the whiche it may be, but it can not auaile nor attaine to the life euerlasting.

Faith properly is to beleue, and to beleue is to assente to trewth. This faith the age of S. Augustine, S. Chrysostome and Vincentius Lirinensis did knowe and teache, willing men for their saluation to ioyne vnto it charitie with other vertues. If any man deuise an other faithe beside this, he bringeth vs not the consent of Antiquitie,

but an

but an inuention of noueltie.

As concerning the faith whereby miracles and wunderous actes are wroughte, it is none other but the Catholique faith, whereof I haue spoken, which to aduance and commende, God doth miracles in some that professe it, through his name. Whiche faith as both a good and ill man may haue, so may both a good and ill man doo miracles, as appeareth plainely by the wordes of Christe in S. Mathew and by S. Paule to the Corinthianes. thone saying, that *many hauing done miracles shalbe shutte owt of the kingdome of heauen:* The other affirming, that a man maie be able *to remoue mountaines, and yet lacke charitie*, without the whiche he is nothing.

*Ioan. 20.*

*Math. 7.*

*1. Cor. 13.*

VVherein the controuersie of Iustificacion resteth, and what is the rediest way to know how the same is wrought in vs.

## THE III. CHAP.

THERE is emong parties at this time no greate controuersie touching the original cause of our Iustificacion. For the Scriptures plainely shew, and al men agree, that it is God that iustifieth. But the controuersy resteth specially in two pointes: first what our Iustification is, and wherein it standeth: whether it be onely a forgeuenes of sinnes paste, or whether there be also required in it a change of the man and a newnes of life. The other pointe is, how our Iustification is wrought in vs, to witte, albeit God iustifie vs, yet how he worketh it in vs, and by what meanes we comme to it, by faith alone, or by faith ioined with other vertues and Sacramentes: which

*Rom. 8.*

the first point.

the secōd point.

doubtes I thinke ſhalbe much cleared, if we conſider our owne corrupte and ſinfull eſtate, and the cauſe thereof: whiche is our carnall Birthe and deſcente from Adam:
Rom. 5. *By whom ſinne entred into the worlde, and by ſinne death, and ſo wente through all, in whom all haue ſinned.* Seing then that his fall was our fall, and the cauſe of our vniuſtice, if we vnderſtande, in what caſe he was created, and what was in him loſte, wounded and weakened by
Ariſtotle. ſinne (cōtraries being knowen by one rule and teaching) we know alſo what our Iuſtification is. For, the repairing of that which was in him loſte, is our reſtoring, and the ſaluing of that which was in him wounded, is our health: the changing of the olde eſtate, wherein through him we were borne, is our renewing: And our reſtoring,
Eſai. 53. healing and renewing is our Iuſtification. For Chriſt that
Luc. 19. came to iuſtifie ſinners, *came to ſeeke and ſaue that which was loſte, and to make whole that which was wounded.*

VVhat was loſte in Adam by ſinne, and what is reſtored by Chriſte in our Iuſtification: the comparing of Chriſt with Adam: And in what thinges our Iuſtification ſtandeth.

## THE IIII. CHAPTER.

IT is a matter of vndoubted trewthe, and confeſſed of all right beleuers, that God created Adam in moſt excellent and perfecte eſtate. For the Scripture ſaith in
Gen. 1. the perſon of God: *Faciamus hominem ad imaginem & ſimilitudinem noſtram.* Lette vs make manne after our image and lykenes. Wherefore as God him ſelfe is wiſedome, trueth, rightuouſenes, temperance, loue, ſtrength, vertue,

vertue, and in goodnes moste free: so made he manne wise, trewe, rightuous, and iuste, temperate, strong, indued with perfecte loue, vertuous, and to all goodnes willinge and free. *But man vnderstanding not when he was in honor*, abusing his libertie to ill, and transgressing Goddes commandement, did not onely lose that perfect estate and beautie of vertues, but broughte him selfe also into a base, mortall and miserable condition, fell into vices contrarie to the former vertues, and became displeasant and hatefull vnto God: his bodie condemned to death, and his sowle, vnlesse mercie had deliuered him, to endlesse damnation. And albeit it might suffise to say that he loste all the vertues, wherewith he was by God indued, yet to expresse, some parte thereof particularly, Prosper Aquitanus sayth: *Perdidit primitus fidem*, &c. He loste first and chifely faith. *He loste continence, he loste charitie, he was berefte of wisedome and vnderstanding. He was lefte without counsell, and strength, he dranke the poison of all vices, and with the dronkennesse of his intemperance wetted through and soked the whole nature of man*: he loste profitable and effectual faith: for he beleued not God, nor kepte that faith whiche S. Cyprian calleth, *fidem mandati*, the faith of his commandement. It was said vnto him by God him selfe of the tree of knowlege of good and ill: *Thou shalt not eate, what day soeuer thou eate of it, thou shalt assuredly dye*. He disobeied that commandement, and did the contrary.

*Psal. 48.*

*Contra Collatorē. cap. 10.*

*De simplicitate prælator.*

He waied so lightely the souereigne loue which he owed vnto God aboue all things, that *either for his owne pleasure, or for the contentation of his wife, he was soone induced to folow his owne wil*, and to leaue Gods wil vndone.

*Aug. de Ciuit. Dei lib. 14. cap. 13.*

Gen.3. He cast aside the hope that he should haue reposed in God, and beganne to put affiance in him selfe, harkening to the serpentes woordes: *Eritis sicut Dij*, ye shalbe like Goddes.

He lost the vertue of temperance, desiring the meate that was forbidden, and therby vnlawful for him to eate.

And hereby was he berefte of wisedome and vnderstanding, falling into such ignorance, that of him selfe he was not able to knowe the highest and trewe good. *He was lefte without counsell and strength*, and fel into such weakenes, that where by his creation he was of so free and strong will, *that it was in his power to continewe in grace, if he had would, and not to sinne, excepte he would*, thorough his faull he was made weake and vnhable of him selfe to doo any good. Thus dranke he the poyson of all vices, infecting and poisoning his owne nature, and thereby all that descended of him. *Per vnum hominem peccatum:* for by one man sinne came into the world, and by sinne death, and so wente it through all men in whom all sinned. Thus were al men by birth made *naturally the children of angre*. And *by sinne, the enimies of God*.

*Prosper vbi suprà. Aug. de Corrept. & grat. cap.11. Rom.5. Ephe.2. Rom.6.*

Seing therefore that this is mannes estate and condition of his owne nature, and sithens also we knowe, that *the Sonne of man came to seeke and saue that was loste*, to repaire that was in man decaied, to renewe and restore him againe to the estate of iustice, if we wil dispute, what thinges are requisite in him that is to be iustified, we must of consequence say, that *he is made iust and righteouse, vnto whom firste God pardoneth sinne*. And further vnto whom of his bountifull mercie he restoreth the good and heauenly qualities that were planted in Adam:

*Luc.19. Rom.4.*

Adam: vnto whom he inspireth faith, continencie, charitie, wisedome, and vnderstanding, counsel and strength, with other vertues which Adam lost: in whom God restoreth his image and likenes, which by sinne was defaced and decaied.

To make the matter more plaine, let vs lay before our eies the example of a man deadly sicke in al the principal partes of his body, as the harte, the head, the liuer and the lunges: whom if a physition cure of the payne in his head, and of the pasion of the harte, yet can he not be called a whole man, vnlesse the other partes be cured also. For he maie els die neuerthelesse by obstruction of the liuer, or putrifaction of the lunges. Euen so the sowle being generally infected and mortally wounded in all her principall partes and powers, requireth likewise a perfect cure of eche parte, without the which it can not be said vnto man touching his sowle: *Ecce sanus factus es*: Lo thou arte made a whole man.

A Similitude.

Ioan. 5.

There be emong others two principall and souereigne powers of the sowle, the one called reason and vnderstanding, the other will, by the which the image of God is specially represented in man, for that he hath them singularly and alone aboue all beastes and other creatures: so long as the same be rightly ordered, that is to say, so long as he vnderstandeth without error, and willeth nothing but good, all his doinges be godly, and him selfe a heauenly creature, and a liuely Image of God.

Tvvo povvers of the soule.

Bothe these were infected and corrupted in Adam: his reason and vnderstanding yelded to thinke it good for him, to take his pleasure of a vaine and corruptible meate forbidden by God, though he shoulde die for it: his will assenting therevnto strake the stroke and put it in execution.

Bothe the same therefore muste be healed in man, before he can be recouered of that plage. For neither can he doo good, vnlesse he be rightely informed and taught to knowe what is good, neither is it ynough for him to knowe what is good, vnlesse he haue a righte and good will to doo it.

See the 2. Chapter. Hovv the Image of God is restored in man.

The medicine to heale mannes corrupte reason and vnderstanding is right faith. For if reason be subiecte to faith, and the vnderstanding ruled by it, there can be no error in his iudgement. But the salue to cure mannes wil and affection, is specially right loue, which is called Charitie. *Quia rectus est amor eorum, omnes affectiones rectas habent*, sayth S. Augustine. Bicause their loue is right, they haue all affections righte. For sithe mannes will and affection *naturally desireth good*, if it can be induced to loue that whiche is trewely good, it is made perfecte and straight: if it loue amisse, it is crooked and ill. For as S. Augustine saith: *Ita corpus pondere, sicut animus amore fertur, quocunque fertur*. So the body is caried with weight, as the minde is caried with loue, whether so euer it is caried. For what he loueth, he willeth: and what he willeth, being not inforced or lette, that he doth.

*Aug. de Ciuitat. Dei li. 14. cap. 9.* *Ethic. 1. cap. 1.* *Aug. de Ciuita. Dei. li. 11. cap. 28.*

Neither can it be trewely saide, that reasón and vnderstanding being healed by faith, maketh the will whole. For we know by the wordes of Christ, that *a seruant may know the wil of his Master, and yet doo it not*. And the cause why he doth it not, knowing it, is but the lacke of will to doo it. *Neque enim vir bonus meritò dicitur qui scit quod bonum est, sed qui diligit*. Neither is he worthely called a good

*Luca. 12.* *Aug. de Ciuitate Dei. li. 11. cap. 28.*

good man, whiche knoweth that is good, but whiche loueth it. And thereby doe we see, that will and affection may be diseased and disordered, when reason and vnderstanding is healed. And so the man not whole, when reason by faith is healed.

If I should saie no more then is alreadie said, yet might the Reader wel perceiue, what is required to the Iustification of a sinner. I haue declared that Adam being created in perfect iustice, by his sinne loste the same, and *al other men in him*, and that *Christ as a newe Adam* to satisfie for the offence of the olde, *came to seke and saue that was loste*, and to repaire that was by him decayed. And then as *Adam loste Faith, Continence, Charitie, Wisedome and vnderstanding, Counsell and strength*, hope and humilitie: so must all that companie of vertues with other by him lost be restored in such as Christ of his especial grace reneweth and iustifieth. For as Christ saieth of one man whome he healed, so is it true in al whom he restoreth, that he healeth not one part, *but the whole man. His workes are perfecte*, and neither lacketh he power to *cure all our griefes* being God, neither wil to doe it, who *for that cause became man.*

*Rom. 5.*
*1. Cor. 15.*
*Luc. 19.*
*Prosp. supra.*
*Ioan. 7.*
*Deut. 32.*
*Esai. 53.*

And as a man diseased deadly in al the principal partes of his body, is not called a sound and whole man, vntil the partes be al cured: So the soule corrupted and made olde in Adam, decayed in grace, and bereft of Iustice, can not be called a new creature, vntil the salues of these vertues by the hand of our Phisition be laid vnto it and shew their operation in it.

For it is not said, *as many of you as haue ben baptised in Christe*, haue beleeued in Christe, thought vppon him, or

Galat. 3. heard of him, but it is said: *Christum induistis*, ye haue put on Christ, that is to saie, haue taken into you the vertues of Christ, as before ye had the qualities and conditions of Adam. For that, saith S. Paule, is the true receiuing of Christ and his Gospel, *to put of the olde man* and olde conuersation, and *to be renewed in spirite and minde, putting on the newe, which was created after the Image of God in iustice and holines.* Christe, saith S. Augustine, *Dat sui spiritus occultissimam fidelibus gratiam*, Geueth vnto his faithful a most secrete grace of his spirite, which priuily he powreth euen into babes, As Adam by a secret infection of carnal concupiscence infected and consumed, all that came of his race. He saith in the same booke. *Legimus iustificari, &c. We read that such be iustified in Christ, as beleue in him through a secrete geauing and inspiring of spiritual grace, whereby who so euer cleaueth vnto our Lord, is made one spirite with him.*

Ephes. 4.

Libro. 1. cap. 9. de pec. meri. & remiss.

Ibid. c. 10.

What Iustification is.

By all this we vnderstande, that our Iustification importeth not onely an assente of minde and faith to beleue the Gospell of Christe, neither standeth onely in remission of sinnes past, which God mercifully forgeueth, but requireth also *a renewing of spirit and minde*, a change of lyfe and conditions, that as in Adam *we were disobedient, seruinge sundrie lustes and pleasures, leading our lyfe in malice and enuie, hatefull, hating one an other*: So in Christe *forsaking vngodlines and worldely desires, we must liue soberly, iustly and godly, putting on vs as the chosen of God holie and beloued, the bowels of compassion, mercie and gentlenes, humilitie, modestie and patience.* This it is to leaue of Adam, and put on Christe, which is our renewing and Iustification.

Tit. 3.

Tit. 2.

Coloss. 3.

The

*The kingdome of heauen is like vnto leauen, whiche a woman taketh and hideth in three measures of flower vntil the whole be leauened.* But as the whol paste is not leauened as long as any parte thereof remaineth in his olde tallage and taste, euen so is not man translated from death to lyfe, nor *made a newe creature*, vntill the whole estate of his soule be refourmed. And surely vntil he be made a newe creature, he is not iustified. *Sicut fuit vetus Adam, &c.* As the olde Adam was *powred through the whole man, and possessed the whole: So nowe lette Christe haue the whole, who hath created and redeemed the whole, and shall glorifie the whole, who in the Sabboth daie cured all the whole man.* Matth.13. 1.Ioan.3. Galat.6. 2.Cor 5. Bernard. serm.5.de Aduent.

*The olde man was sometime in vs that transgressour of Gods commaundemente, he was in vs, as well in hande and woorke, as in mouth and heart. But nowe if there be any newe creature in him, the olde is past, and contrarie to lewdnes in hande, there is innocente life: in the mouth contrary to arrogante pride, there is the woorde of confession: in the heart contrary to fleshly lustes, there is charitie: contrary to worldly glorie, there is humilitie.* By which wordes of Sainct Bernarde we see sette before vs a true description of our Iustification, by comparing togeather the corrupte estate of man in Adam, and the repairing of the same through *the Mediator of God and menne, the man Iesus Christe.* 1.Timo.2.

For this repairing of mans corrupt estate Christe is often times in the Scripture compared with Adam, and called *an other Adam and the last man.* Not an other Adam like vnto the firste, but an other contrary to the firste: suche as came to restore that which was lost by the Rom 5. 1.Cor.15.

Rom.5. first. For *as by the disobedience of one man many were made sinners, so by the obedience of one many shall be made iuste. And as in Adam all men die, so in Christe all shalbe relieued. And as by the synne of one, all men came to damnation: so by the Iustice of one, all come to the Iustification of lyfe.*

But as we were all condemned in Adam, bicause we were naturally borne of him, and thereby tooke his conditions: so to be saued by Christe, we must also be newe borne in him, and put on vs his qualities. And so do we see, that our true Iustification, is the recouering of that which we lost in Adam, and what that was, I haue shewed before. The whiche Christe hath fully restored in such as truely take a new birth of him, as I shall shewe toward the ende of this woorke, where place shal serue to speake of the vertue and strength of our Iustification by Christe. It is now to be shewed particularly, how such as are borne in synne, come to be iustified in Christ, what the causes of our Iustification be, by what meane God worketh it in vs, and how we receiue it.

In the secōd boke the .xviij. Chapter.

## Of the causes of our Iustification.

### *The V. CHAPTER.*

THE chiefe and principall cause of our Iustification is the great loue that God beareth vnto man, *who so tendred the worlde, that he gaue his onely begotten Sonne.* And to make vs his children, *sent the spirit of his Sonne into our hartes:* that is, the holy Ghoste, wherewith

Ioan.3.

Galat.4.

*he hath*

*he hath sealed vs vp, and geuen it as a pledge of our inheritance.* And this hath he wrought, *not for the workes of iustice that we did, but according to his owne mercie.* Ephes.1. Tit.3.

The cause that deserued this owre Iustification at his handes, was the death of his sonne Iesus Christe, who *when we were synners, died for vs, and when we were enimies, reconciled vs, pacifying him by his owne bloude, and paying our raunsome, in whome God accepted vs to his fauoure.* Rom.5. Coloss.1. 1.Timo.1. Ephes.1.

The meane and instrumente whereby God woorketh Iustification in vs, is the Sacramente of Baptisme, *by the washing whereof and renewing of the holy Ghoste, we are saued.* Tit.3.

Through these causes there is wrought in vs the iustice of God, by the whiche we be and are trewly called iuste. *Qui facit iustitiam, iustus est*: for he that doth iustice, is iuste. It is not the iustice of God, whereby he him selfe is iuste: neyther is it our owne as of our selues, but oures comming from him. *Cùm ero iustus, in tua iustitia erit &c.* When I shalbe iuste, saieth S. Augustine, it shalbe in thy iustice. *For that I shalbe iuste by iustice geuen me from thee, and in suche sorte shall it be myne, that it shalbe thyne also, that is to wit, geuen me from thee.* Which woordes declare, both that there is true iustice in man wrought in his Iustification, and also that the same commeth not of him selfe, but is geuen him from God. 1.Ioan.3. August. in Psal.70.

The final cause and ende of our iustification, is: *vt hæredes simus secundùm spem vitæ æternæ in laudem gloriæ gratiæ Dei*, That by hope we may be inheritors of lyfe euerlasting to the prayse and glory of his grace. Tit.3. Ephes.1.

And thus hauing briefly declared, what the causes of

our Iustification bee, I shal now shewe, howe, and by what meane the same is wrought in vs.

## That the Sacramente of Baptisme is the instrumente and meane whereby God iustifieth vs.

## THE VI. CHAP.

AS God iustifieth synners through suche causes as haue ben rehersed: so hath he appointed the Sacrament of Baptisme as an instrumente and meane, to worke his iustice in them: for whiche cause S. Paule seemeth to take it for al one, to be baptised, and to be iustified,

1. Cor. 6. saying: *Abluti estis, sanctificati estis, iustificati estis.* Ye haue ben washed cleane, ye haue ben made holy, ye haue ben iustified. And in an other place he saieth more playnely:

Tit. 3. *God hath saued vs by the washing of regeneration and renewing of the holy Ghoste.*

And bicause no man should thinke, that he mighte be otherwise iustified or saued, Christe saieth: *vnlesse a man*

Ioan. 3. *be new borne by water and the holy Ghoste, he can not entre into the kingdome of God.* S. Ambrose saieth: *The begin-*

Amb. li. 1. ca. 5. de voca. om. gent. *ning of trewe life and true iustice lyeth in the Sacrament of regeneration, that where a man is newe borne, there also the true vertues should beginne.* And note here by S. Ambrose, not only that Baptisme is the beginning of our iustice, but also that we haue therein a beginning of true

Augu. lib 2 contra Iulian. vertues and true iustice. I haue recited the wordes of S. Augustine before, where he saith, that Iustification is geuen vnto vs in this life by three thinges, whereof he

maketh

maketh Baptisme the firste. And to prooue the same by a reason taken out of the Scriptures: Our iustification standeth specially in twoo pointes, in forgeuenesse of sinnes past, and newnes of life in tyme to come. For as S. Paule saith of such as be iustified: that *God hath pardoned them their former sinnes*: so saith he for the tyme to come, *that they must walke in newnes of life*. In Baptisme al our sinnes be forgeuen. *Prorsus verum est, &c*. It is verely true, *In holy Baptisme al sinnes were put away, wordes, deedes, thoughtes, al were blotted out*. In Baptisme also newnes of life is geuen. For which cause it is called *a newe byrth, the washing of regeneration, and renewing by the holy Ghoste*.

See the 3. Chap. Rom. 3. Rom. 6. Augu. ser. 2. de ver. Apost. Tit. 3.

Wherefore seing that all that apperteineth to Iustification, is wrought in vs by the Sacramente of Baptisme, we may beside the authoritie of Scriptures and auncient Fathers, euen by reason conclude, that Baptisme is the instrumente and assured meane, whereby a synner is iustified.

### Of the Iustification of infantes by the Sacramente of Baptisme.

### THE VII. CHAPT.

BVt as the benefite of Iustification is al one, so it is not receiued of al after one manner. For such as are borne in sinne, and by mercie called to the state of iustice, eyther they be called and christened in theyre infancie, as it is nowe vsed throughowt the Christian worlde: or elles they be called to it in theyre perfecte age, as it was vsed

vsed when the Gospel was preached to them that were borne and brought vp in infidelitie.

The estate of infantes asketh moste fauour and mercie: for as S. Cyprian saieth: *Infans recens natus &c. The infante newly borne hath not offended, but that taking his carnall byrthe after the nature of Adam, he hath drawen into him by his firste byrthe, the infection of the oulde death, who commethe to receyue forgeuenesse of sinnes the more easily for so muche as there be pardoned vnto hym not his owne, but other mennes synnes.* And for that cause as S. Augustine saieth: *Accommodat illis mater Ecclesia:* The Churche our mother lendethe them *other mennes feete to come, other mennes harte to beleue, other mennes tounge to say yea, that forasmuch as their syckenes and griefe commeth by an other mannes synne, they may be saued by the confession of other that be healed.*

Lib. 3 epistol. 8. & Augu. ser. 14. de ver. Apost.

Augu. ser. 10. de ver. Aposto. & sermo. 14.

And albeit they be neyther able to answere nor doo for them selues any thing towarde their owne benefite, yea and so muche as in them is, resiste the same: yet God bringeth them by vertue of that Sacrament *from the power of darckenesse to the kyngdome of his Sonne: powreth into them the secrete grace of his spirite, and maketh them true faithfull, and Christian sowles.* S. Augustine saieth: *Inter credentes. Thou shalte recken and accompte babes that be christened, emong the beleeuing: neither shalt thou by any meanes be so bolde as to iudge otherwise, excepte thou wilt be an open heretique. For yeuen by the auncient canonycall and most suer grounded custome of the Church, Babes once christened are called faithful and beleeuers.* And in an other place speaking of the state of infantes christened if they dye before thage of discretion: *So great,* saieth he, *is the*

Coloss. 1.

Augu. lib 1. ca. 9. de pec. meri. & remiss.

Ser. 14. de verb. Apo.

Aug. ibid.

*mercie*

*mercie of God toward the vessellles of mercie, that euen the first age of man, to witte infancie: &c. If it haue receiued the Sacramentes of the mediator, though it ende his life in those yeares, for that it is taken out of the power of darknes and brought to the kingdome of Christ, is not onely not appointed paines euerlasting, but shall not so much as suffer any purgatory tormentes and paines after death. For the only spirituall regeneration suffiseth, that so much as the carnall generation intermedled with death, be not preiudiciall nor doo it any harme.*

Aug.li.21 cap.16. de Ciuit.Dei.

Colo.ca.1.

Purgatorie paines.

By which sayings we see, first that infantes haue sinnes 1.
to be forgeuen them. Nexte, that they enioie remission 2.
thereof by their baptisme. Thirdely, that they enioie 3.
that benefite in most free manner: Nothing being required for that purpose, but onely that other Christian men bring them to the Church to be baptized, and answere for them. And the cause why: For that they are gilty only of originall sinne, and none other trespasse committed by them selues.

This is the graciouse and most free Iustification of infantes, which they atteyne vnto, not onely without any good doing of their owne, but also without any consent. Yea though they striue against it, through the free mercie of him, *that came to seeke and saue that was loste.* Luc. 19.

And hereby doo we not only see the happie estate of al such as be borne in Christian regions, who by and by after their byrth be baptized and thereby iustified: but also we perceiue, how nedelesse it is, to dispute of the beginning and entree of our Iustification, which is wrought in vs freely by grace without our selues, before we be able to vnderstand how great the benefite is.

And therefore concerning the Iustification of al men that liue this daie in Christian contries, there is nothing so needeful as to vnderstande, how such as fall after Baptisme may be reconciled to God, and restored to the estate of iustice againe, whereof I shall speake hereafter.

## Of the Iustification of suche as were christened being of perfite age, and what was required of them.

## *THE VIII. CHAPTER.*

BVT of such as borne and brought vp in infidelitie, and being of perfect age came to be iustified, and of wicked made rightuouse, bicause they be not onely giltie of originall sinne, but also of many actuall sinnes committed by their owne thought, worde and deed, more is required, and an other order appointed vnto them, whereby they prepare the way to receiue the iustice of God. It is required of them first to beleue. For *he that Hebr. 11. commeth to God, must beleue*. So Christ beganne to preach Marc. 1. vnto such: *Pœnitemini, & credite Euangelio*: Repent and beleue the Gospel. And forasmuch as beleuing the Gospel there is Rom. 1. *reueled and opened vnto them the anger of God from heauen vppon all wickednes and iniustice*: They are stricken with a good and profitable feare of Gods iudgement, as they were that heard S. Peter his preaching, Act. 2. and of that feare they conceiue, and as it were *trauaile Esai. 26. and bring forth the spirite of health*. Yet doo they not rest in that feare, but learning that Christ *came to saue sinners 1. Tim. 1. and died for such as were his ennemies*: Hearing him also say:

ſo ſay: *Confide fili:* be of good comforte ſonne, *thy ſinnes be forgeuen*: They conceiue hope of mercie: and thereby beginne to loue him, by whoſe mercie they truſte to enioy ſo greate a benefite. And for the loue of him deteſte and abhorre their former ſinfull life. And bicauſe it is ſaid vnto them: *Pœnitentiã agite & baptizetur vnuſquiſq; veſtrûm:* Doo penance, and be baptized eche of you, they willingly and hartely repente their former ſinnes, which is al the penance that the Church of God requireth before Baptiſme. And ſo diſpoſing them ſelues they receiue the Sacrament of Baptiſme, and therewith according to the promiſe of God made by S. Peter, *remiſsion of their ſinnes and the gifte of the holy Ghoſt*, to keepe Gods commaundements, which is their Iuſtification.

Rom.6. Matt.9. Act.2. Matt. 28. Act.2.

And this is the order whereby a ſinner, being of perfect age, is iuſtified, that is to ſay, called to the eſtate of iuſtice, and of wicked made rightuouſe.

The firſt and principall cauſe thereof is the loue and mercie of God: thorough the merite of Chriſtes death. Iuſtice is wrought in vs by grace: and atteined by faith with the feare of Goddes iudgement, hope of his mercie, loue of his goodnes, and by penance thorough the Sacrament of Baptiſme.

All which are ſo neceſſarie to the accompliſhing of our iuſtice, that where any of them faileth, trewe iuſtice alſo doth faile. For as *without faith it is vnpoſsible to pleaſe God, and he that beleueth not is already iudged:* So *he that is without feare, can not be iuſtified.* He that hopeth not, deſpeireth. *Neither can any man loue that he hopeth not.* And who ſo lacketh hope and loue, can not be iuſtified by faith. *Nam & Dæmones credunt.* For

Hebr.11. Eccleſ.1. Aug. Enchi. ca. 8.

*euen the Diuelles beleue and tremble, and yet doo they neither hope, nor loue, but rather by beleuing, are afraied that that ſhall come which we hope and loue.*

Such as wilbe iuſtified, muſt not only beleue the Goſpel, but *do penance*, and ſuch as *will not do penance* are aſſured *al to periſh.* Finally who is not baptized, *putteth not on Chriſte*: and therefore is *neither renewed, nor iuſtified.*

*Mar. 1.*
*Luc. 13.*
*Gal. 3.*

This manner of Iuſtification is not onely teſtified by the Scriptures, but alſo expreſſed in th'ancient vſage of the Church, by ſuch order as was exerciſed vppon them that receiued baptiſme, when they were of perfect age, euen from the Apoſtles time, whiche thinge we maie perceiue by the wordes of S. Paule, where he ſaith: *Intermittentes inchoationis Chriſti ſermonem. &c.* Leauing aſyde the wordes of our yong beginning in Chriſt, *Lette vs drawe to a perfectenes, not layinge againe the foundation of penance from deade workes, and of faith towarde God, of the teaching of Baptiſme, and alſo of laying on hands, of the reſurrection of the dead and iudgement euerlaſting,* al which thinges (ſaith S. Auguſtine) *apperteyne to thadminiſtration of Baptiſme*: whereby we vnderſtande, that of ſuch as were baptized in perfect age, there was not only required faith, in profeſsing tharticles of the Crede, but alſo they were required to doo penance from deade workes of ſinne. And to ſhewe ſome outwarde token thereof, there was appointed vnto them before theire baptiſme, a time to faſte and praie: As is teſtified by ſuch as liued nigh vnto the Apoſtles time. *Iuſtinus Martyr* ſaith: *After what ſorte we haue offred and dedicated our ſelues vnto God being newe made throughe Chriſte, we will declare. As many as be perſuaded and beleue,*

*Hebr. 6.*

*Aug. in expo. ad Ro. incho. & de fid. & oper. cap. 11.*

*Apolo. 2. pro Chriſtian.*

*leue, that the thinges are trewe which be taught and saied by vs, and promise that they be able so to liue, they be taught to praie, and by fasting to aske at Goddes handes forgiuenes of former sinnes committed by them.* Tertullian expresing the same custome saith further, that they made also a confesion of their former sinnes. *Ingressuros baptismum. &c.* Suche as wil come to Baptisme, *must by often petitions, fastinges, kneelinges and watching, and with confession of all their former sinnes vse praier.* S. Augustine declaring the order of his time, saith, *that such as intended to take baptisme, certeine daies before gaue their names in writing, and were purged and cleansed, by abstinence, fasting, exorcismes, forbearing the companie of their laweful wiues.*

*Tertullia. De Bapti.*

*De fide & oper. ca. 6.*

And by these doo we vnderstande, that suche as were christened being of perfect age, were not only instructed in faith, but also taught to doo penance, to faste, to praie, to promise that they would liue according to Christ his teaching, to feare God, to loue him, and to hope in him, al which thinges were conteined in their instruction and doctrine of Baptisme, whereof S. Paule maketh mention. And being in this wise prepared, they receiued that Sacrament, and therewith their Iustificacion. If any would not professe amendemente of life, but continewe in damnable vice, or in any vngodlie kinde of liuing, beleued they neuer so wel, they were not admitted to be christened, as S. Augustine saieth, *Meretrices.*&c. *Common harlottes, and stage plaiers, and other what so euer occupiers of common lewde doinges, vnlesse they vndoe and breake suche bandes, be not suffered to come to the Sacramentes of Christ.* But this the Reader maie see at large in the booke it selfe of S. Augustine intituled, of faith and workes, which is

*Hebr. 6.*

*De fide & oper. ca. 18*

translated into englishe, and sette furthe herewith. The cheefe argumente whereof is to declare, that it suffiseth not him that wil be baptised and iustified, to beleue, vnlesse he haue faith that worketh by charitie, and vnlesse his life be agreable to that holy Sacrament. For *where any of bothe faileth*, saith he, *there neither ought nor can any promise be made of life euerlasting.* And thus haue we seene, how they receiued their Iustificacion, who came to be christened and iustified, when they were of perfecte age.

Cap. 26.
Cap. 15.
Cap. 16.

That our Iustification and the vertues whereby we receiue it, be the giftes of God, and come of grace.

## THE IX. CHAP.

*Of Grace.*

BVT as a sinner is brought to the state of iustice, by faith through feare of God, hope, loue, penance, and the Sacrament of Baptisme: so is it trewely to be said, and faithfully to be acknowleged, that it is the free grace of God that worketh al these vertues in him, without the whiche he is not able of him selfe to atteine, not only to the state of iustice, but not so muche as to right faith and loue of God, or any other gifte perteining to his saluation. *Cùm sine gratia Dei. &c. For seeing that mannes nature was not able to keepe saluation whiche it receiued without the grace of God: how can it be able to repaire that it hath loste, without the grace of God?* As many then as are made members of Christe by the Sacrament of Baptisme, or falling afterward be restored by penance, are moued and stirred therevnto, not by their owne desertes but by the free mercie and grace of God, whose gifte both trew penance

Concil. Arausica. Cap. 19.

nance and also Iustification is.

And therefore although it be said to sinners: *Agite pœnitentiam:* doo penance. And, *Conuertimini ad me*: Turne yee to me: Yet as S. Augustine saith: *Pœnitentia meritum gratia præcedit, quòd neminem peccati sui pæniteret, nisi admonitione aliqua vocationis Dei.* Grace goeth before the merite of penance. For no man would repent him of his sinne, were it not by some admonition of Gods calling. The wastefull sonne said: *Surgam & ibo ad patrem meum.* I will rise and go to my Father. *Quam cogitationem bonam quando haberet, nisi & ipsam illi in occulto pater misericordissimus inspirasset?* Whiche good thought when should he haue had, vnlesse his most merciful Father had inspired it into him?

*Acto 2.* *Zacha. 1.* *Exposi. Episto. ad Ro. incho.* *Aug. Episto la 106.*

As many as sinne, seuer them selues and straie from God; and sure we are, it can not be false that trewth said: *Nemo venit ad me nisi fuerit ei datum à patre meo*: no man cometh to me, vnlesse it be geuē him of my Father. What thing so euer man thinketh, heareth or seeth, whereby he is moued to good, that motion commeth of God. *Visorum suasionibus agit Deus*: God worketh in vs, saith S. Austine by persuasion of suche thinges as we see, *not only to Will, but also to beleue: he Worketh it either outwardely by exhortacions of the gospel, or inwardly. For that no man can chuse What shal come into his mind, but it is in his owne Wil to consent or disagree.* Without this helpe of grace *no man is able so much as to thinke any thing that maie please God.* As this commendacion of grace is plainely sette forth in the Scriptures, so hath it ben in all ages faithfully tought by the Church: Bicause as S. Augustine saith: *Hæc cogitatio sancta. &c.* This holy thinking *keepeth the children of men vn-*

*Ioan. 6.* *De spiri. & Lit. Cap 34.* *2. Cor. 3.* The Churches sound doctrine, of Gods grace. *De spirit. & Lit. Cap. 7.*

*der the defence of Goddes wynges, this thought bringeth no pride.* The Church commendeth good workes, but it setteth grace before them, saying: *Debetur merces. &c.* Rewarde is due *to good workes if they be done, but grace that is not due, goeth before, that they maie be done.* It teacheth that mannes Iustificacion is the effecte of grace. *Per ipsam gratiam iustificatur. &c.* By grace man is iustified *freely: that is to saie, no merites of his workes going before. Otherwise grace is not grace.* It teacheth, that no man dothe good workes before he haue receiued grace, thereby to deserue Gods grace, but that God geueth his grace first, whereby man doth good workes afterwarde, whiche thing S. Augustine declareth by two apte similitudes. *Non vt ferueat, calefacit ignis.* The fier doth not heate, to be made hote it selfe, *but bicause it is hote. Neither doth the whele runne well thereby to be made rounde, but bicause it is rounde. Euen so noman worketh well, that he maie thereby receiue grace, but bicause he hath receiued it. For how can he liue iustely that is not iustified, but grace doth iustifie, that a iustified man maie liue iustely.* And further to shewe, how necessary Gods helpe and grace is to euerie man and at all times, the Church teacheth, that God doth not giue his grace onely once, and then leaue man to him selfe, but assisteth him in euery good acte that he doth: *fateantur, gratiam Dei & adiutorium etiam ad singulos actus dari*: Lette them confesse, that Gods grace and helpe is geuen euen to euerie good acte and deede.

*Concil. Arausi. cap. 8.*

*De spiri. et lit c. 10.*

*Li. 1. ad Simplicia. Quaest. 2.*

*Aug. Epistola. 106. de Cōcil. Palest.*

I doo more willingly recite the wordes of S. Austine in this pointe, bicause the moste learned in all ages since, haue folowed the same iudgement and manner of teaching, not onely *Prosper Aquitanus* in Italie, *Fulgentius* in Africa, and S. *Bede* in this our country of Englande, but alſo the moſte learned ſchole menne: As *Hugo de ſancto Victore, S. Thomas, Bonauentura*, and other. Whereby the Reader maye vnderſtande, what hath benne the teaching of the Church in all ages concerning the grace of God. The teaching of the Churche cõcerning the grace of God in al ages.

As this grace of God is it whereby man is moued to al thinges that he doth wel, ſo it is alſo the cauſe that worketh in him true penance, and thereby Iuſtification. For ſhyning vppon the ſoule of a ſinner and geuing lighte to that darcknes, it moueth the ſame to prepare him ſelfe and to receyue the working of God in ſuch manner, as I haue ſhewed before.

By grace God inſpireth faith into our hartes, whiche no man can haue without his ſpeciall gifte. *No man can comme vnto me*, ſaieth Chriſte, *vnleſſe it be geuen him from my Father*. Of whiche woordes S. Auguſtine gathereth: *Ergo, & credere datur nobis*. Then euen faith is geuen vnto vs. When S. Paule preached in Macedonia, *God opened the harte of a woman called Lydia to geue heede vnto ſuche thinges as were ſaid by him*. Many other heard S. Paule as wel as ſhee, but God gaue her the grace to beleue his woordes: *To you it is geuen*, ſaieth S. Paule, *for Chriſtes ſake, not onely to beleue in him, but alſo to ſuffer for him*. *Ioan. 6.* *Auguſtin. Tract. 27. in Ioan.* *Act. 16.* *Philip. 1.*

And as theſe and other ſayinges prooue that faith is Gods gyfte, ſo of the feare of God, it is ſayd by the Prophete: *Timorem meum dabo in corde eorum, vt non recedant à me*. I will geue my feare in their harte, to thende they ſhall not goe from me. Dauid knowing that it is the gyfte of God, prayeth for it, ſaying: *Configе timore* *Ierem. cap. 32.* *Pſal. 118.*

*tuo carnes meas*: Pearce my flesh through with thy feare. If hope were not the gifte of God, it should not be saide: Psal. 4. *Tu Domine singulariter in spe constituisti me.* Thou Lorde haste placed me in hope singulerly. Neither woulde S. 2. Thes. 2. Paule haue said: *God our father hath loued vs, and geuen vs* 1. Ioan. 4. *comforte euerlasting and good hope in grace.* Charitie com- Rom. 5. meth of God, *powred abrode in our hartes, through the holy Ghoste which is geuen vs.* What shal I say of penance, 2. Tim. 2. *whiche God geueth vnto sinners to knowe the treuth, and to amende and gette out of the snares of the Diuel, of whome they be holden captiue at his pleasure.* It is God that *geueth a newe harte, and putteth a newe spirite in the middest of vs, that taketh away the harde stonie harte, and geueth a* Ezec. 36. *softe harte and tender as fleshe.* And what is that greate change of harte and minde from euil to good, but repentance? And to commende his grace and make it appeare as it is very grace in deede, he saieth: *non propter vos ego faciam.* This wil I doo not for your sakes, *but for my holy names sake.*

A doubte. Here it may be said. If our Iustification, and what so euer apperteineth vnto it, be the gyfte of God, and procede of grace, what parte hath man therein, and what is there lefte for him to do? To this question I shal answere in the next chaptre.

And hereby maye the Reader vnderstande, that the grace of God is neither hydden, nor obscurely preached by the Churche in the Doctrine of Iustification, seing that both our Iustification it selfe, and the meanes wherby we comme vnto it, be truely ascribed specially vnto grace.

That

## That man hath free wil which being holpen by grace worketh in our Iustification: and what it worketh.

### *THE X. CHAPTER.*

God worketh mannes saluation by his grace, but he worketh it in him by hĩ selfe, that is to say, with his own cõsent and by his free wil. He workethin al his creatures causing the earth to bring forth grasse: the trees theyr leaues and fruite: the beastes to doo according to their kinde. But these effectes he worketh in them by his owne power without them, that is, without any consente of them. And this is the difference betwene beastes that wante reason, betwene the insensible creatures, and man: *Man*, as S. Augustine saith, *Nec vt pecora factus est*, was neither made as beastes were, *nor made lyke a tree, nor made lyke a stone, but was made after the Image of his Creator*. That is as I shewed before, indued with reason and wil: And therefore although there may be in man corrupte wil and deceyued reason, yet whatsoeuer he doth, he woorketh it thorough will and reason. *Liberum eum fecit Deus ab initio*: saieth the aunciente Father Ireneus: God made man free euen from the beginning *hauing aswell his owne power, as his owne soule, to doo Goddes will and minde voluntarilie and willingly, not compelled by God. For there is no force vsed of Goddes parte*. The wooman when she had offended, framing an aunswere to excuse her selfe, sayde not: *Serpens coegit me*, the serpente forced me, and I eatte: but what sayde shee? *The serpente deceyued me, there is no necessitie nor violence,*

*Of free will.*

*Serm. 11. de verb. Aposto.*
*Iren. li. 4. cap. 72.*
In the 4. Chapter.
*Iren. li. 4. cap. 71.*
*Chrysosto. Hom. 17. in Genes.*

August. de grat. & lib. arbit. cap. 2. *lence, but will and arbitremēt*. And bicause no man should doubte hereof, *Reuelauit nobis per Scripturas suas sanctas*: God him selfe, saith S. Augustine, hath reueled vnto vs by his holy Scriptures, *that there is free will in man. And howe he hath reueled it I put you in remembrance, not by mannes saying but by Goddes woorde. Firste bycause the very commaundementes of God, coulde doe man no good, vnlesse he had free will, by the whiche he might doo them, and atteyne to the rewardes that be promysed*. And in the same place. *Further there be so many commaundementes, whiche doo in a manner by name speake*
Rom. 12. *unto our will: as that: Noli vinci à malo*. Will thou
Psalm. 31. not be ouercomme of yll. *Be not made lyke a horse and a*
Prouer. 1. *mule, in whome there is no vnderstandinge. Forsake not*
Prouer. 3. *the counselles of thy mother. Be not wise in thyne owne conceyte*: and after manye other Scriptures there alleged, he concludeth thus. *Surely where it is saied: will not thus, and will not that, and where in the admonitions that God geueth, the worke of mannes will is required, to doo somewhat, or not to doo it, mannes free will is sufficiently prooued*. If I saied no more, this place of S. Augustine mighte suffice. For what man woulde not rather confesse free will, then say either that God hath geuen his commaundementes in vayne, or that so many Scriptures be voide and vntrue?

Mannes wil then is euer free from compulsion and ne-
Bernar. de gratia & lib. arbit. cessitie, though it be not euer good: *Manet libertas voluntatis &c.* The wil remaineth free, *euen where the mind is captiue, as full in the euil, as in the good, but more orderly in the good*. A woorse man, and a greater enemie of Gods people is not found in the Scripture, then Pharao

And

And yet was not he without free wil, saith S. Augustine. *Nec ideo auferatis, &c.* Take not away *free wil so muche as from Pharao, bicause in many places God saith: I haue hardened Pharao, or I haue or wil harden Pharao his heart: for it foloweth not therefore, that Pharao himselfe did not harden his owne heart. For of him this is read also: When the dogged flie was taken awaie from the Aegyptians, the Scripture saith, Pharao made his owne heart heauy.* If Pharao thē had free wil, and that proued by the Scripture, what man is without it? *Si nō est liberū arbitriū, quo modo iudicat, &c.* If there be no free wil, how doth God iudge the worlde? For if men doe nothing but by compulsion and force, neither is it Iustice to punish their vices, nor to reward their well doinges and vertues. If there were no free will in sinners, what came Christe to saue? He came to saue sinners, and no man sinneth but by his wil, and therefore S. Bernard saieth: *Tolle liberum arbitrium &: non erit quod saluetur.* Take awaie free will, and there shal be nothing to be saued. And this much I haue said to lette the Reader vnderstand, what inconueniences come by deniyng free wil, which who so denyeth, doth as we see denie in effecte Gods iustice and iudgement, denie the fruicte of Christe his coming to saue vs, denie a number of plaine Scriptures affirming it. And sith mans free wil is as well his owne as his soule, he would haue man without a soule. Finally, he maketh man that was created after the Image of God, no better then an vnreasonable beast, or vnsensible stocke.

*De gratia & li. arbi. cap. 23.*

*August. epist. 46.*

*De grat. & liber. arbit.*

The cause of their errour is, that they can not, or will not discerne and make a difference betweene a free wil, and a wil strong and able of it selfe to doe good. Al men be thei good or il, haue free wil, but he that hath wil without grace, is weake and vnable to doe well. *We doe not saie, that free Will was lost and perished out of mans nature by the sinne of Adam. But We saie, that in men subiect to the Diuel, it is of force inough to sinne. Marie to liue Well and godly it is not strong inough, vnles the Wil of man be deliuered, and made free by grace, and holpen to all good, in dede, Worde, and thought.* If free wil then, was not loste by the sinne of Adam, as S. Augustine saieth, it was neuer lost. But as it was made weake and feeble by his sinne, so is it by grace in our Baptisme, made whole and stronge againe. *The freedome of Wil, Whiche in the first man Was made Weak, can not be repaired, but by the grace of baptisme. That Whiche Was loste, can not be restored, but by him that could geue it. Whereuppon trueth it selfe saith: If the Sonne make you free, then shal you be free in dede.* By this we see, that as free wil by sinne was made weake and feble, so was it neuer lost by sinne, and was also made strong againe by our baptisme. For strength in goodnes it was, and not freedome of wil, that Adam loste. Thus doth the Churche teache vs to speake of free wil, not to denie it, but to acknowledge, that without grace, it is not able to do good. That as by sin it was made weake, so by grace in the Sacrament of Baptisme, it is repaired. That as many, as by the Sonne of God are made free, that is to saie strong and able to doe good, as al good Christian men be, are no longer bounde, but truely and in dede free.

*Aug. cont. epist. Pel. lib. 2. c. 5.*

*Concil. Arausic. cap. 13.*

*Aug. De Ciuit. Dei li. 14. c. 11*

*Ioan. 8.*

1. 2. 3.

And hereby may the Reader iudge, what ground they haue, who contrary to the manifest Scriptures, and authoritie of al auncient writers, haue turned the terme of free wil, vnto bond and thrall wil. Let al men concerning this point,

point, kepe the high waie. Let no man goe to farre on the left hande, and saie that there is no free wil: Let no man turne to farre on the right hande, and thinke that freewill without grace may suffise him to liue well. Manicheus toke on the left hand, Pelagius on the right. But a Councel of Bishops assembled in Palestina against Pelagius kept the high waie, geuing out this rule for him to folow: *Fateatur esse liberũ arbitrium, etiam si diuino indiget adiutorio.* *August. epist. 106* Let him confesse that there is free will, although it haue nede of Gods helpe. And here note, that albeit Pelagius did attribute to muche to free will, and the Bishops contrarying him said, that free wil without grace suffised not, yet did they neuer saie, man had no free will. Whereby we perceiue, that it was euer a trueth receiued in the Churche, that man had free wil, and they would not pull downe one ttueth to set vp an other.

This Decree of theirs made in Asia, was allowed by S. Augustine and the Bishops of Africa: confirmed by Innocentius, Zozimus and Bonifacius Popes, with the Bishops of Europa: and so is one of the thinges, as S. Augustine saith there, *Quæ semper tenet Catholica Ecclesia.* Whiche *August. epist. 106.* the Catholique Churche hath euer holden.

It remaineth now to shew, what free wil (whiche no man can with reason and trueth denie) woorketh in our Iustification. Which to resolue, it is truely said: First, that *Bernard. De grat. & liber. arbit.* free will is saued: Nexte, that free will once healed by Christe, and holpen by his grace, is stronge and able to doe all good, and to worke togeather with Christe in our Iustification. As it is God that by his grace iustifieth, so *Rom. 8.* doth he iustifie no man, but by his owne wil and consent. S. Augustine saith: *Esse potest iustitia Dei sine volũtate tua.*

The

Serm. 15. de verb. Aposto. & in Psa. 44

The iustice of God may be without thy wil; *But in thee it can not be, but by thy will: he that hath made thee without thy selfe, doth not iustifie thee without thy selfe. He made thee without thy knowledge, he iustifieth thee by thy wil.*

And in an other place he saith further. That Christes worke in our Iustification is our woorke. That Christe woorketh it not without vs, that we woorke togeather with Christ our owne Iustification and saluation: *Credenti in eum qui iustificat impium.* To the beleuer in him that iustifieth the wicked, *faith is accompted for iustice. In this woorke we doe the woorke of Christe: For the very beleefe in Christe, is Christ his worke. This he worketh in vs, but assuredly not without vs.* And alleaging the place of S. Paule, that willeth vs *with feare and tremblinge to worke our owne saluation,* he saith: *Operante in se Christo.* By Christes working in man, *togeather with Christe, man worketh his owne saluation euerlasting and Iustification.*

Tract. 72. in Ioan.

Philip. 2.

Eusebius Emisse. ho. 9. de Pasc.

And this God worketh in vs, not onely to commend his mercie, but also to shewe his iustice: *Iusto ordine, qui per calliditatem,* Iust order requireth, saith Eusebius, *that man who by the subtil crafte of the malitiouse serpent was not forced, but seduced to his destruction, should be againe by the wisedome of a louing redemer not compelled, but lead to saluation: and he that semed to haue fallen by his owne wil, should be repaired againe by his owne will, that there might be place for vertue and rewarde. Therefore he pulleth him not awaie by force, but rather by iust good will inuiteth and instructeth him to lyfe: for the louing gentlenes of the prouoker, longeth for the merite of the agreer: and the fauour of the most curteouse Physition requireth the consent of his sicke patient.*

What

What can be more plainely saied then this? Man is iustified by his owne free will. He geueth his assente and agreement vnto it. He getteth merite and rewarde by his assente.

This is the righte teaching of Christes Churche, neither to derogate from Goddes grace, nor to pull away mans seruice in our saluation. The holy Ghost saith, *it is God that worketh in you both to will, and to doo.* The holie Ghost saith also in the same place, *with feare and trembling worke your owne saluation.* *Non est volentis, neque currentis. &c.* It is not in the willer nor in the runner, *but in God that taketh mercy.* And yet saith S. Augustine. *Proculdubio si homo. &c.* Without doubt if a man *be of suche age, that he is once able to vse reason, he can not beleue, hope, nor loue, vnlesse he will: neither can he come to winne the price of the high callinge of God, vnlesse he runne with his will. How is it then neither in the willer, neither in the runner, but in God that taketh mercy, but after this sorte, bicause the very wil it selfe, as the Scripture saith, is prepared by God?*

Philip. 2.

Rom. 9.

Enchiri. cap. 32.

By this order is our saluation wrought. Neither God worketh it alone without man, neither man without God can atteine to any degree thereof: God firste prepareth the will and maketh it meete to serue him, and the will directed and holpen by grace, is able to doo all good. And by this rule, faith and workes, saith S. Augustine, are both the giftes of God, and faith and workes are both the doinges of men: *Vtrumque nostrum est propter arbitrium voluntatis, & vtrumque tamen datum per spiritum fidei & charitatis: vtrumque ipsius est, quia ipse præparat voluntatem, & vtrumque nostrum, quia non fit, nisi volentibus nobis.*

Retract. Li. 1. ca. 23

*bis*. Either of bothe is ours for free willes ſake, and yet either of bothe is geuen by the ſpirite of faith and charitie. Either of bothe is his, bicauſe he prepareth the wil, and either of both is ours, bicauſe it is not done but by
Pſal.134. our will. Though God by him ſelfe *doo all that liketh him in heauen and in earth*, yet hath it pleaſed him to aduance man to that dignitie, as to make him *a worker together*
1.Cor.3. *with him* in his owne ſaluation.

Aug. in Pſal.77. *Non ſolùm operatur remiſsionem peccatorum.* The grace of God doth not onely worke remiſsion of ſinnes, *but alſo maketh the ſpirite of man a worker with him ſelfe in the doing of good workes:* Quando enim cum ſpiritu Dei operante. &c. *For when with the working of Gods ſpirite the ſpirite of man worketh together, then is that fufillled which God hath commaunded.*

And by this doo we ſee, what free will worketh in Iu-
1. ſtification. Firſt it is ſaued, deliuered, and prepared by
2. grace. Then doth it ioine and worke together with God.
3. It worketh the ſame thing that God worketh. It beleueth.
4. It hopeth. It loueth. It runneth and getteth the price of
5. the heauenly calling. It fulfilleth the lawe.
6. *God ſtandeth at the dore knocking, and it openeth. God ope-*
Aug. de *neth the eare, and it doth not gaineſaie him nor goeth backe-*
ſpiri. & *warde:* God inſpired good thoughtes, and willingly it
Lit. ca.30. executeth them. *God prepareth good workes*, and it wal-
Apoca.3. keth in them, *It liueth not nowe vnto it ſelfe, but Chriſte*
Eſai.50. *liueth in it, and it liueth vnto him that died to ſaue it.*
Epheſ.2.
2.Cor.5. And thus farre haue I ſpoken of Iuſtification, which is the reconciliation of a ſinner, whereby as S. Paule ſaith, *We haue acceſſe to God*, and of wicked are made rightuouſe eſpecially by grace, through the Sacrament of Baptiſme

and

and other giftes of God before rehearſed, *without any workes of iuſtice* going before to deſerue the ſame.

That ſuche as fall into ſinne after Baptiſme, be iuſtified by penance againe, and what penance is required of them.

## THE XI. CHAP.

IF ſuch as haue receiued the Sacrament of Baptiſme, and thereby remiſsion of all ſinne, coulde keepe them ſelues in that happie eſtate of innocency and vprightnes, there were no neede to ſay any more in this argument. For al men that liue this day in Christian Regions, were chriſtened in their infancie, and by their Baptiſme made *heires in hope of euerlaſting life.* But if there had ben none other prouiſion made for man, but once to ſaie vnto him: *Ecce ſanus factus es,* Lo thou arte made whole, *nowe ſinne not, leſte ſome worſe happe fall vnto thee.* We had ben driuen to a narowe ſtraite, neither coulde mannes frailety tel what to doo, who being *prone to ill euen from his youth,* was in daunger by ſinne to loſe Gods grace, and then to ſtande without hope of remedie. For this cauſe God hath prouided penance. *Quam humano generi noſtro ob ineffabilem miſericordiam ſuam conceſsit.* Whiche throughe his vnſpeakeable mercy, ſaith Chryſoſtome, he hath graunted vnto mankinde, which benefite he accompteth ſo greate, that in an other place he reckeneth it emong the moſt excellent giftes, that euer God beſtowed vppon man, ſaying: *God hath deliuered his Sonne for our ſinnes, he hath graunted the*

*Of Penance.*

*Tit. 3.*

*Ioan. 5.*

*Cypria. de eleemo*

*Gen. 8.*

*Chryſoſt. Ho. 27. in Gen.*

*Chryſoſt. Ho. 34. in Gen.*

*gyftes of Baptiſme, he hath geuen remiſsion of our former ſinnes, he hath opened vnto vs the waie of Penance.*

By this remedie ſuch as fall into ſinne after Baptiſme, may be reſtored againe to the ſtate of iuſtice. For to ſuch as do penance, God hath promiſed grace and reconcilia-
Ezech. 18. tion, ſaying by the Prophete: *Si impius egerit. &c.* If the wicked man *doo penance for all his ſinnes that he hath committed, he ſhall aſſuredly liue and not die.* The like promiſe
Acto 3. he hath made in the newe Teſtament by S. Peter. *Pœnitemini & conuertimini, vt deleantur peccata veſtra* Doo penance and turne, that your ſinnes maie be blotted owt. But vnto ſuche as falle and will not doo penance, God threateneth damnation. *Si impius nō fuerit conuerſus à via*
Ezech. 33. *ſua. &c. Ipſe in iniquitate ſua morietur.* If the wicked be not turned from his waie, in his wickednes ſhall he die.
Luca. 13. And in the newe Teſtamente Chriſte him ſelfe ſaith: *Niſi pœnitentiam egeritis, omnes ſimiliter peribitis.* Vnleſſe ye doo penance, ye ſhall periſh all after like ſorte. By which wordes putte together we vnderſtande, that as penance is the ſure and vndoubted waie to reſtore a ſinner againe: ſo without the ſame there is no hope of his reconciliation. As this order is commanded by the Scriptures, ſo hath it in all ages ben practiſed by the Churche of Chriſt, that ſinners ſhould be reconciled and iuſtified by
Clem. lib. penance. Clement S. Peters ſcholer and ſucceſſor, com-
2. ca. 45. pareth penance with the Sacrament of Baptiſme, ſaying
Conſtitu. to the Biſhoppe: *Quemadmodum gentilem per lauacrum.*
Apoſt. *&c.* As thou receiueſt the heathen by Baptiſme *after that*
Tit. 3. *he is inſtructed, ſo ſhalt thou reſtore this man that is the penitent to his olde eſtate, when he is cleanſed by laying handes on him as by penance, all men praying for him,*

*and*

*and the laying of handes shalbe in steade of Baptisme.* He saith that penance standeth in steade of Baptisme, bicause, as by Baptisme the sinner is saued, euen so by penance his sinnes be forgeuen: for Christe hath saide: *Quorum remiseritis peccata, remittuntur illis.* Whose sinnes you forgeue, they be forgeuen them. S. Augustine making the same comparison, saith: *Quæ autem Baptismatis, eadem reconciliationis est causa.* The like respecte is to be had of reconciliation and absolution, as of Baptisme, *if it happen the penitent to fall in daunger of death: for the Churche our mother ought not by her will to suffer them passe out of this life without the pleadge of their peace.* He calleth absolution the pleadge of our peace, as whereby our sinnes be forgeuen and conscience quieted. He maketh penance as necessary to a sinner after Baptisme, as Baptisme it selfe to him that is heathen. S. Leo saith: *Peccata Baptismi aquis et pœnitentiæ lachrymis abluũtur.* Sinnes are wasshed away by the water of Baptisme and by the teares of penance.

*Ioan.20.*

*De adulter. cõiug. li.1.ca.28*

*Ser.11. de quadrag. & ser.9. de Pasch.*

And as men entre into the Church and be made members of Christe by Baptisme, so if they fal away againe by sinne, *they may returne,* saith S. Cyprian, *by penance. Nam cùm scriptum sit.* &c. For sith it is written, *God made not death, neither is delited to haue the liuing cast away, vndoubtedly he that willeth none to perish, desyreth that sinners should doo penance, and by penance returne to life againe.* Pacianus saith, that *God hath prouided this remedie for men.* And in the same sentence: *Idem stantibus præmia, qui iacentibus remedia largitus est.* Euen he hath giuen rewardes to them that stand, who hath graunted remedies to such as lie and are fallen.

*Cypria.li.4.epist.2.*

*Pacia.epi.1.ad Sympronia.*

And thus we see it proued by authoritie of Scriptures and auncient Fathers, that the right and assured remedy to heale a sinner after Baptisme, is penance. And that the Sacrament of penance by the promise of Christe hath vertue to reconcile and iustifie a sinner. For which cause it is compared with the Sacrament of Baptisme, and cal-
1. led by S. Cyprian *a returning to life*: by S. Clement, *a re-*
2. *storing and cleansing*. By S. Augustine, *a pleadge of our*
3. *peace and quiete of conscience*: by S. Leo, *a wasshing away of*
4. *sinne*: by Pacianus, *the remedy of such as are fallen*. And to
5. make vppe the matter S. Chrysostome calleth it, *the cure*
6. *of our woundes*, and by the plaine terme, *Iustification*. *Contritionem vult cordis*: God will haue, saith he, *contrition of harte, remorse of minde, confession of the fall, a continuall care and diligence, and geueth not onely the curinge of woundes, and cleanseth from sinne, but euen him that was before laden with innumerable burdens of sinnes, he maketh a iust man.*

*Chrysost. ho. 20. in Genes.*

And hereby also may the Reader perceiue, how good cause the auncient Bishop Pacianus, and S. Ierome had, to cal penance *a borde to saue him that had suffred wreack, or a seconde borde after wreack*, that is to say, a second refuge, when the firste helpe is loste. And also he may see how litle ground they haue, who against authoritie, trewth, and reason, mislyke that manner of speache, seeinge that by penance a sinner may be reconciled and saued, which without the same should perish, as hath ben proued.

*Pacia. epi. 2. ad Sympronia. Hiero. ad Pamma. & Ocea.*

How a sinner commeth to trewe penance, and by what meanes he receiueth his Iustification, I haue declared before, and shall for the Readers remembrance onely

*Cap. 8.*

onely repete the ſame here.

It is grace firſt that moueth him to amendement,and
to ſay: *Surgam, & ibo ad patrem meum.* I will riſe and *Luc. 15.*
go to my father: through which grace faith being ſtirred
to beleeue the Scriptures, and the threatninges of God
vttered therein againſt ſinners, ſtriketh into him a feare
of Goddes iuſt iudgement: and further bicauſe he ſhould
not diſpaire,moueth him to conceiue hope of mercie,for
that God *is full of compaſsion and mercie, and came to ſaue* *Pſal. 102.*
*ſinners*, and that hope being once entred,engendreth a *1.Tim.1.*
loue of God, as S.Auguſtine ſaith: *Quia credidiſti, ſpe-* *Aug. in*
*raſti, quia ſperaſti, iam dilexiſti:* Bicauſe thou haſt bele- *Pſal. 114.*
ued, thou haſte hoped, bicauſe thou haſte hoped, nowe
haſt thou loued. Charitie taking roote in the harte,brin-
geth forth a louing feare and care, loth to offende God,
and ſuch as maketh all penance, be it neuer ſo ſharpe,to
ſeeme eaſy and light. And theſe be the fiue pointes ap-
perteining to trewe penance: faith, a dreadfull feare of 1.
God, hope, Charitie, and a louinge feare, or carefull 2.
loue, which thing may not onely be noted in the *Nini-* 3.
*uites, in Marie Magdalene, Zacheus*, and ſuche as the 4.
Scripture declareth to haue ben turned from ſinne to 5.
iuſtice, but alſo are expreſſed in the wordes of S. Paule, *2.Cor.7.*
who ſpeaking of the Corinthians repentance, ſaieth,
*Lo, euen this godly ſorowe how great a care it worketh*
*in you, yea a defence, yea an indignation and diſpleaſure,*
*yea a feare, yea a deſier, yea an emulation, yea a re-*
*uengement.* The grace of God working in them, made
them to beleeue S. Paules wordes, and ſo to ſee their
ſinne, wherein they ſhewed faith, they conceiued 1.
thereof not onely a feare, but alſo a deſier to be acqui- 2.

3. ted whiche was not without hope. They were carefull
to auoide like occaſions : they had an indignation againſt
4. them ſelues : and were ready to reuenge in them ſelues
5. their owne ſinne, wherein they ſhewed theire loue towarde God, and the reuerent feare they had to offende
him.

To applie the ſame by mo examples: The Niniuites
through grace beleued the preaching of Ionas, and vpon
Ion. 3. feare which they conceiued, *they proclaimed a generall
faste*, they were not without hope of Gods mercie, ſaying: *Who can tell whether God wilbe turned and forgeue?*

Luc. 15. The waſtefull ſonne had ſuch a reuerente loue toward
his father, that he was ready to ſuffer more penance for
his miſbehauor then his father would lay vpon him, ſaying: *Iam non ſum dignus vocari filius tuus, fac me ſi-
cut vnum de mercenariys tuis.* I am no longer worthy
to be called thy ſonne, make me as one of thy hired
ſeruantes.

Luc. 7. I doubte not but that the Reader can apply the rule
in like manner to the example of *Marie Magdalene*, in
which woman there ſhineth as it were a glaſſe and mir-
rour of trewe penance.

But as it is trewe that no man is iuſtified without penance, ſo is it not one manner of penance, that is required of him that cōmeth to be chriſtened, and of him that
after his chriſtendome committeth mortall and deadly ſinne. Of him that is of perfect age and to be chriſte-
Ambro. in ned, no ſtraight or painefull penance is required : for as
cap. 11. ad S. Ambroſe ſaith : *Gratia Dei in Baptiſmate non quærit*
Rom. *gemitum, aut planctum, aut opus aliquod, niſi ſolam ex
corde profeſsionem.* The grace of God in Baptiſme requireth

reth not sighing or mourning, or any woorke, but onely a profession from the harte. Bicause the partie not hauing enioied, any benefite of Christ his grace, wherunto he was not yet called, his sinne and vnkindenes is the lesse. But suche as haue benne *once broughte to the lighte and haue tasted the heauenlie gifte, and benne made partakers of the holie Ghoste*, beeing called to adorne and sette foorth the doctrine of our Sauiour in all thinges: if they be vngodly, firste they be *vnkinde to God*, whose grace they receiue in vaine. Secondlye, they *doe wronge to the holy Ghoste*, whome they greue. Thirdly, as the Prophet said vnto Dauid: *Blasphemare fecisti inimicos nomen domini*. Thou hast made the enimies blaspheme the name of the Lorde: So may it be said vnto them: *Nomen Dei per vos blasphematur inter gentes*. By your meanes the name of God is blasphemed emong the Heathen.

Heb. 6. Tit. 2. 2. Cor. 6. Ephes. 4. 2. Reg. 12. Esai. 52. Rom. 2.

For these and other causes, a greater penaunce is and euer hath ben required of such offenders in the Churche.

And that according to the iuste rule of Christe, who saith: *Omni cui multum datum est, multum quæretur ab eo: & cui commendauerunt multum, plus petent ab eo*. To whom so euer much is geauen, muche shalbe required of him, and to whom they haue committed much, they wil aske the more of him. Luc. 12.

After this rule, saith Theodoretus: *Sunt ergo medicabilia etiam quæ post baptismum fiunt vulnera*. Euen such woundes as are made after Baptisme be curable. *Marie curable, not by forgeuenes geuen by faith onely as once it was: but by many teares, weaping and wailing, fasting, praying, and labour, measured after the quantitie of the sinne commit-*

Theodor. Epito. Diuino. Decreto. c. de pœniten.

G ted:

*ted: for such as be not so disposed, we haue not learned to admitte nor receiue.*

In which wordes we see the difference of penance appointed by the Church to both sortes of men. Suche as came to be christened were cured, saith he: by onely beleuing, which S. Ambrose calleth *a profession only from the heart*, without either good workes going before, or painful penance for sinne past, of them that were christened before, and then fel into great sinne, there was required weeping, wailing, fasting, praier, and other labour, according to the quantitie of the sinne, which vnlesse they would doe, they were not receiued into the Churche.

*In cap. 11. ad Rom.*

Of such penitentes S. Augustine saith: *Qui agunt pœnitentiam in sordibus agunt, si tamen intelligunt, & veraciter agunt.* They that doe penance, do it vgly and mournfully, if they haue vnderstanding and doe it truly. Whereby we learne, that such as for great sinne doe light penance, or none: neither haue vnderstanding of their owne estate, nor doe penance truely. For as S. Cyprian saith: *Dominus longa & cōtinua satisfactione placandus est.* Our Lorde must be pacified by long and continual satisfaction. And in an other place he saith: *Orare oportet impensius & rogare, &c. iustis operibus incumbere, quibus peccata purgantur, eleemosinis frequenter insistere, quibus à morte animæ liberantur.* Such must praie earnestly and aske, they must applie iuste workes, wherby sinnes are purged, they must often times geue almes, whereby sowles are deliuered from death. And a litle after: *Pœnitēti, operanti, roganti, potest clementer ignoscere.* God can mercifully pardon him that doth penāce, him that worketh, him that prayeth. This streight and paineful penaunce the Church learned to enioyne for

*Serm. 31. de verb. Dom.*

*Lib. 1. epistola. 8.*

*Cyprian. de lapsis.*

*Tob. 4.*

great

great ſinne cōmitted after Baptiſme, by the example of S. Paule, *Who deliuered* the Corinthian that had abuſed his fathers wife, *to the Diuel, the body to be puniſhed and pinched, that the ſowle might be ſaued.* And bicauſe that he ſaith, that he did it in *the name of Chriſte, and by the holy Ghoſt that ſpake in him*, we knowe, that ſtreight penance practiſed in the Church, is not the inuention of men, but the teaching of the holy Ghoſt. And where he ſaith: he woulde haue his body *pinched and puniſhed*, we knowe what penance God iudgeth due vnto great ſinne Whereupon Pacianus alleaging theſe wordes of S. Paul, ſaid vnto ſuch as were in penāce: *Quid dicitis pœnitentes? Vbi eſt veſtræ carnis interitus?* What ſaie you that be penitents? Where is the pinching of your bodie? And albeit this penance ſeme to the fleſh heauie and ſtreight, yet doth faith, with the feare and loue of God, make it eaſie and light: eſpecially, bicauſe we are ſure to eſcape the heauie and puniſhing hand of God. For ſo S. Paul ſaith: *Si nos ipſos diiudicaremus, non vtiq; iudicaremur.* If we would iudge (that is to ſay) puniſh our ſelues, we ſhoulde not be iudged.

1. Cor. 5.

1. Cor. 7.

Pacia. de Pœniten. & confeſſ.

1. Cor. 11.

Thus haue I ſhewed, that ſuche as fall after Baptiſme into greate and deadly ſinne, are reſtored againe and iuſtified by penance, whiche hath that vertue, by the woorde and promiſe of Chriſte. I haue alſo declared howe a ſinner is brought vnto true penance. And further, I haue ſhewed the difference betweene penance, that is required of ſuche as being of age, come to be chriſtened, and of ſuch as fal after Baptiſme, wherin it hath ben proued, that ſinners after Baptiſme, are reſtored again to the eſtate of iuſtice, by doing the worthie fruits of penance, and not by Faith onely. And ſeing that al Chriſtian

Ioan. 20.

Theodor. ſup. Paul. 2. Cor. 7.

men now liuing, were baptised in their infancie. This is the Iustification that we ought specially to loke vnto, by knowledge to learne, and to practise by dede. As for the Iustification of faith alone, how so euer it serue for suche,
In the viij. Chap. of the secōd booke. as are to be christened, whereof I shall speake hereafter, it serueth not for vs that are christened alreadie.

Of the increase and perfiting of our Iustification, wherein it is truely said, that we be iustified by good workes, and not by faith onely.

## THE XII. CHAP.

IT is not inough for the obteining of lyfe euerlastinge, that sinners be iustified, and made of wicked righte-
*Psal.* 83. ouse, vnlesse they continue also and increase in iustice,
*Tit.* 2. goe from vertue to vertue, and liue soberly, iustly, and godly. For as S. Cyprian saith: *Parum est adipisci aliquid po-*
Cyprian. li. 1. ep. 5. *tuisse.* It is a small matter to be able to get a thing. *It is more to be able to kepe that is once gotten: as in faith it selfe and the healthfull byrth, it is not the receiuing, but the keping of it, that geaueth lyfe, neither is it by and by the attaining, but the perfiting, that preserueth a man to God.* This
*Ioan.* 5. *our Lorde taught by his owne instruction, when he saied: Lo thou art made a whole man, nowe sinne not, least some worse happe fall vnto thee. Christe gaue him selfe for vs,* saieth S. Paule, *to the intent he might redeeme vs from*
*Tit.* 2. 2. *Cor* 6. *all iniquity, and cleanse vnto him selfe a singular and special people, a folower of good workes.* If this effect folowe not, *in vaine hath Christe geauen him selfe to death for vs, in*

vaine

*vaine doe we receiue his grace* and Iuſtification. And not onely in vaine, but to our great daunger and peril. *Better* 2. Pet. 2.
*were it for them*, ſaith S.Peter, *neuer to haue knowē the way* Luc. 11.
*of iuſtice, then after the knowlege of it to turne backe againe* Auguſtin.
*from the holy cōmandement that was deliuered vnto them.* epiſt. 106.
He that is iuſtified, is ryd of *the vncleane ſpirite*, and his harte lyke *to the ſwepte houſe*. But if the ſame ſtande emptie, not inhabited by the holy Ghoſt, nor filled with the fruites of iuſtice, *the vncleane ſpirite doth not onely returne agayne, but alſo bringeth with him ſeuen other worſe then him ſelfe*, who entre and dwel there, and *the later doinges of that man becomme worſe then the firſte were*.
For as *to him that hath, there ſhalbe geuen and he ſhall haue* Math. 25.
*aboundance: ſo from him that hath not, euen that he ſeemeth to haue, ſhalbe taken awaye. To haue the gyftes of God*
*is to vſe them*, as Theophilacte writeth vpon that place. Theophil.
And he vſeth Goddes grace, that doth good workes, to in ca. 25.
the which ende grace is geuen. Chriſte ſente his Apoſtles Math.
*to chriſten all Nations, and to teache them to keepe all that* Math. 28
*he had commaunded them*. He woulde not onely haue a
people to knowe him; but ſuch a people as ſhoulde *ſerue* Luc. 1.
*him in holynes and iuſtice*. He ſaith to his Apoſtles: *Ego* Ioan. 15.
*elegi vos, & poſui vos, vt eatis, & fructum plurimum afferatis, & fructus veſter maneat*. I haue choſen you, and placed you, to thintent you ſhould go and bring forth fruite, and to thintent your fruit ſhould remaine. And in the ſame
chaptre he ſaith: *in hoc glorificatus eſt pater, vt fructū plurimū afferatis & efficiamini mei Diſcipuli*. Hereby is my Fa- Ioan. 15.
ther glorified, that you may bring forth much fruit, and be made my ſcholers: geuing vs to vnderſtande, that they be Chriſtes ſcholers, that ſhew the fruite of his teaching,

and that God is glorified, not onely in our calling, but also in the fruite that commeth of our calling. For this cause the Scripture saieth to such as are already called to
Apoca. 22 the state of iustice: *Qui iustus est, iustificetur adhuc.* Let
Eccle. 18. him that is iuste, be iustified yet. And also: *Let nothing*
Math. 5. *let thee from continuall prayer, and let nothing forbid thee to be iustified vnto thy death: for Goddes rewarde abydeth for euer. Blessed are they that hunger and thyrst after iustice*, saieth our Sauiour. *Apertissimè nos instituens, &c.*
Beda in solen. om. Sancto. Most euidently teaching vs, *that we should neuer thinke our selues iuste inough, but euer more loue and desire a daylie increase of iustice.* For true it is that Leo saieth:
Leo ser. 8. de Passio. & Aug. ser. 15. de verb. Apo. *Quantumlibet quisque iustificatus sit, &c.* Be a man neuer so much iustified, *yet while he is in this life, he may be better and more tryed: but he that increaseth not, decayeth and goeth backewarde, and he that getteth nothing, loseth somewhat.*

Why increase of Iustice is called Iustificatiō.

And bicause, as in al artes vse maketh the artificer more skilful, then he was: so the continuance and practise of iustice maketh a good man readyer, and more able to do well, and thereby iuster then he was, the Scripture calleth it Iustificatiō: that is to say, an increase of iustice, and declareth in sundry places, howe the same is obteyned.
Iacob. 2. S. Iames saieth: *videtis, quòd ex operibus &c.* You see, that *a man is iustified by workes, and not by faith onely.* And
Eccles. 18. he that saieth: *lette nothing staye thee from continuall prayer, nor forbid thee to be iustified to thy death*, teacheth, that prayer is a meane to iustifie, whiche Chrysostome
Chrysost. Tom 5. de orand. expresseth in more playne woordes, saying: *vitam piam ac cultu Dei dignam miris modis oratio conciliat, conciliatam auget:* Prayer doth meruelously winne and gette a good

good life, and increaseth it when it is a gotten. Christ him selfe calleth prayer, fasting and asmosedeede, *our iustice*, and sure we are, *that he is iuste, who doth iustice.* Math.6. And so muche the iuster, the more iustice he doth. By 1. Ioan. 3. the same rule *Leo* speaking of almose, saieth: *Hoc pio impendatur operi, &c.* Let that be bestowed vpon godlie woorke, *that can iustifie the harte and washe the conscience.* And in an other place: *Goddes will is,* saieth he, *to iustifie the poore by patiente suffring of labour, and trauaile, and the riche by the woorke of charitie. Abraham was iustified by woorkes, offering vp his sonne*: by woorkes, I say, of obedience, bicause he obeyed the voice and commaundement of God. The Scripture saith of Moyses: *In fide & lenitate ipsius sanctum fecit illum.* God made him holy, by faith, and mildenes. S.Bernarde saith as much of humilitie: *Sectamini illam, quæ sola potest saluare animas vestras*, folow her, which alone is able to saue your soules.

Leo.ser.3. de ieiun. mensis.7. Leo ser.8. de ieiu. men.10. Iacob. 2. Gen.22. Bernard. ser.1. in die natal.

Finally, al good workes done in faith bring with them a Iustification: *Quia hac quæ per se sunt vilia, fides efficit pretiosa: & quæ ab infidelibus ministrantur, etsi fuerint sumptu magna, omni tamen iustificatione sunt vacua*: faith maketh those thinges pretiouse, which of them selues be litle worth. And such as are done by infideles, though in coste they be great, yet be they voide of al Iustification. If the workes of infideles be voide of Iustification, bicause they be done without faith: then Christian mennes woorkes done in faith may iustifie.

Leo ser.6. de Quadrages.

By these places of the Scripture, and aunciẽt Fathers, it is proued, that good works done in faith iustifie the doers. And bicause no man can doo such workes, vnlesse he be him selfe

*Aug de fide & ope. ca.14.* him selfe a good man (*Sequuntur enim iustificatum, nō præcedunt iustificandum*, for they follow him that is made iust, they go not before him that is to be iustified) we must cōfesse, that beside the Iustification of the wicked, whereby a synner *of vngodly is made righteouse*, there is an other degree of iustice, which both the Scripture and Fathers, as I haue shewed, call Iustification: that is, an increase of iustice, whereby a iuste man is made iuster. Whiche to make the thing more playne, I cal the seconde kynde or degree of Iustification: bicause it commeth after the Iustification of a sinner, whiche is the firste degree of iustice. And this kinde of Iustification, whiche is an increase of iustice, *is obteyned and gotten by godly life, by fighting with vice*, saieth S. Augustine, *by workes of faith, without the whiche after baptisme faith auayleth not, but maketh vs also gyltie of greater sinne, receyuing the talente, and bringing no gayne of it.*

Rom. 4.

The secōd Iustification.

*Lib. 2. cōtra Iulia. supra ca. Oecom. in c. 2. Iaco.*

By this meane it is truely said, that a wicked man is iustified, that is, reconciled to God by grace through faith, hope, charitie, penaunce, and the Sacramente of Baptisme, without anye woorkes of merite goyng before. And truely is it saied also, that suche as be already iuste, may be yet iustified, that is, increased in iustice by good workes. So is it true that faith without workes iustifieth, and true also, that a man is iustified by workes, and not by faith onely: the one being meant of man not yet baptised, the other of suche, as are baptised or christened.

And further, woorkes of faith doo not onely increase a good mannes iustice in this life: but also procure vnto the dooers life euerlasting. Whiche S. Paule calleth *our ende.*

*Rom. 6.*

*ende*. And S. Augustine *the perfiting of iustice*, saying: *Complebitur spes nostra*, our hope shalbe fully accomplished *in the laste resurrection of the deade, and when our hope shalbe fulfilled, then shal our Iustification be fully accomplisshed*. And bicause our iustice, be it neuer so well begonne and continued here, yet before that time is neuer perfect, and without that ende, auaileth not, I call that with S. Augustine the perfiting of our Iustification, or the thirde degree and ende of our iustice. To the which the Scriptures plainely declare that we must comme by workes of faith: *Reddet vnicuique secundùm opera eius*: God shall render vnto euery man according to his workes. *What thinges a man soweth, the same shall he reape: for he that soweth in flesh, of flesh shall reape corruption. But he that soweth in spirite, of spirite shall reape euerlasting life*. Our sowing is our workes, of which if they be ill, we shall reape damnation: if they be good, we shall receiue life eternall.

*Ser.61. de ver.Do. et ep.106.*

*Rom.2. Psal.61.*

*Gala.6.*

And bicause it is said in sundrie places of the Scripture, that God will *render life euerlasting to good workes, and that as a iuste iudge*: we gather with S. Augustine, that *life euerlasting is the rewarde of good workes*: whereof I shall haue occasion to say more, when I come to speake of that matter. *Lib.2 cap. 13.*

*2. Tim.4. Epist.105. & lib de gra.& libe. arbi. ca.8.& 9.*

In the meane time we see, that as a man is called to the state of iustice by faith without workes, which is Iustification: so can he neither be increaced, nor perfited in iustice, but by faith and good workes, which is also called, Iustification: So can he neither comme to the beginning, but by faith, hope, and charitie, as hath ben shewed, neither to the middle, nor th'ende, but by faith and good

Where is then faith alone?

workes ioined together. And this difference marked and rightely applied, doth not only geue light to sundrie Scriptures seeming otherwise darcke, but also taketh away the difference imagined, to be betwene S. Paule, and S. Iames, S. Peter, and S. Iohn, concerning the doctrine of Iustification, whereof I shall speake more largely in an other place.

In the 10. chap. of the 2. booke.

## VVhat good workes be, and howe they be called ours.

## THE XIII. CHAPTER.

Three kindes of vvorkes in Scripture.

THE greate commendation and price which the Scripture geueth to good workes, moueth me briefly to declare, what workes they are that we call good, where with God is so highly pleased. We finde in the Scriptures three kindes of workes named, whereof some are called *workes of the flesh*, other *the workes of the lawe*. The third kinde, *the workes of God; and the fruites of the holy Ghost*. The workes of the flesh are *fornication, vncleanes, vnchast life, and other like, the doers whereof shall not enioie the kingdome of God*. The workes of the lawe, be such as a man doth by him selfe, *presuming of his owne power and strength without the helpe of God, by commandement of the lawe for feare of punishement, and not for loue of iustice*. Of which S. Paule saith: *I take them all as hinderance and losse, and accompte them as durte, so that I may gaine Christ*. Leauing then aside these twoo kindes of workes, whereof th'one is damnable, and the other vnprofitable: there remaine the workes which the Iewes called *the workes of God*, saying to Christ: *Quid faciemus, vt operemur opera Dei?* what shal we doo, to worke the workes

*Gala. 5.* *Ioan. 6.* *Gala. 5.* *Gala. 5.* *Aug. ser. 15. de ver. Apost.* *Philip. 3.* *Ioan. 6.*

workes of God? These workes be such as be done by the motion and inspiration of God. Christ saith: *Qui facit veritatem,* He that doth vprightely and trewly, *commeth to the light, that his workes may be shewed, bicause they are done in God,* that is, by the inspiration and helpe of God. These workes S. Paul calleth *the fruites of the holy Ghost,* bicause the holy Ghost bringeth them forth. Such are *charitie, ioy, patience, gentlenes, sufferāce, mildnes, faith, modestie, continence, chastitie.* These workes as al Christian men are willed to doo, so no man doth them without the grace of God preuenting him and mouing his wil to mind them, and folowing and working with him to doo them. Neither doth the Scripture and the Church of God teach vs, that faith is Gods gifte, and charitie with good workes our owne, as of our selues. Al are the giftes of God: of al and singuler it is said: *Sine me nihil potestis facere,* without me ye can doo nothing. *What haste thou that thou receiuedst not? We knowe not what to pray, as we ought to doo, but the holy Ghost doth aske for vs, that is to say, doth teach vs, and make vs to aske.* S. Paule calleth almose *the grace of God.* And briefly of all good workes he saith: *We be made and framed in Chriiste Iesu, to doo good workes. Quæ præparauit Deus, vt in illis ambulemus:* which God hath prepared for vs to walke in. Whereuppon S. Augustine saith: *fingimur ergo &c.* we be made and fashioned, *that is, we are fourmed and shaped in good workes, which we haue not bene the preparers of, but God hath prepared them for vs to worke in.* By this rule S. Augustine saith: our good life is nothing els, but the gifte of God. *Quisquis tibi enumerat vera merita sua, quid tibi enumerat, nisi munera tua?* Whosoeuer reckeneth vppe vnto

Ioan. 3. Gala. 5. Aug. epist. 105. Ioan. 15. 1. Cor. 4. Rom. 8. Aug. epist. 105. 2. Cor 8. Ephes. 2. De grat. & lib. arbit. cap. 8. Aug. confess. lib. 9. cap. 13.

thee (o Lorde) his trewe merites, what doth he recken vp, but thy giftes?

Howve good vvorkes are called oures.

Here it may be ſaid: what parte haue we then in our good workes, and why be they called ours, if they be the giftes of God? I anſwere: God worketh all that is good in vs, but as S. Auguſtine ſaith, *not Without vs.* And therfore as they be the workes of God who inſpireth them, ſo be they the workes of man that doth them. *Dei adiutores ſumus*, we be the helpers and workers with God. *Dei ſunt proculdubio munera, tam noſtra opera, quàm eius præmia: ad quæ tamen condenda merita, dignatur ſibi adhibere creaturarum miniſteria*: without doubt they are Gods giftes, as wel our workes, as his rewardes: and yet to make them merites, he vouchesafeth to vſe the ſeruice of his creatures. And bicauſe he vſeth mannes ſeruice in the doing of good workes, he calleth them in the Scripture our workes. So doth S. Auguſtine ſay of faith and good life: *vtrunq; ipſius eſt*, Eche of bothe is his, *bicauſe he prepareth our Will: and either of bothe is ours, bicauſe it is not done, but by our Will.* Although much might be ſaid in this place, yet I ſhall take one place of S. Auguſtine in ſtede of many, who expounding the wordes of Dauid, ſaith in this manner: *In Deo laudabo ſermones meos:* In God will I praiſe my wordes. *Si in Deo, quomodo meos. &c. If in God, how mine? Both in God, and yet mine: in God, bicauſe they come from him: mine, bicauſe I haue receiued them. He that gaue them, Would haue them mine, bicauſe I loue him Whoſe they are: bicauſe they comme to me from him, they are made mine: for Whence cōmeth this? Geue vs this day our daily bread? How call We it ours, and how ſay We, geue? If thou cal it not thine, thou haſt not receiued it: againe if thou*

*Aug. in Ioan. tractat. 72.* *1. Cor. 3.* *Bernar. de grat. & lib. arbit.* *Retract. li. 1. ca. 23* *Pſal. 55.* *Aug. in Pſa. 55. ib.* *Matt. 6.*

*if thou call it thine after that ſorte, as though it came of thy ſelfe, when thou calleſt it thine owne, thou loſeſt that thou haddeſt receiued: bicauſe thou arte vnkinde to him, at whoſe hande thou haddeſt receiued it.*

There needeth no more to be ſaid. Good workes, if we doo them, be ours, bicauſe we haue receiued them. They be Gods, bicauſe he giueth them. They be not ours as of our ſelues, they be not ours to be prowd of: for then we loſe them, bicauſe we be vnkinde to the giuer. But they be ours, when meekely we doo them, and acknowlege the geuer of them. They be ours, *to ſhine before men, that they maie ſee them, and glorifie our Father that is in heauen*. Finally they be ours, bicauſe God ſo calleth them. Matth. 5.

S. Paule knewe, that faith, charitie, praier, and good workes were the giftes of God, and yet writing to the Coloſsians, and Theſſalonians, *he commendeth their faith and their charitie*, deſired the Romaines *to remember him in their praiers*, and praied for Timothee in his owne: He ſaith to the Hebrues: *God is not vniuſte to forgette your worke*: He was not ignorant, that it was the grace of God that wrought with him, and yet he ſaith: *I haue wraſteled well for the game. I haue finiſhed my race, I haue kepte my faith.* Coloſ. 1. 1. Theſ. 1. 2. Theſ. 1. Rom. 15. 2. Tim. 1. 1. Cor. 15. 2. Tim. 4.

As he that hath an hundred pounde landes giuen him by the Prince, hath landes, and yet hath none of him ſelfe, but of the Princes gifte, and were well worthy to loſe them, if he would bragge of his poſſeſsion againſte the giuer, and ſaie he gaue him none: euen ſo the godly and faithfull haue good woorkes, not of them ſelues, but of Goddes geuing, not to be prowde and vante them ſelues, but humbly to ſerue him that gaue them, to doo good to

*Aug. in Psal. 85.* them selues and others by them. *Arguens superbiam Apostolus*, The Apostle rebuking pride, *doth not saie, thou haste not, but he saith, What haste thou, that thou receiuedst not?*

These be the workes that we commende and sette forth in Christian men, not the workes of the lawe, not suche as men doo of them selues, or through vaine glorie to please men, but the workes of God, the fruites of the holy Ghost done onely for Gods sake, suche as God by his inspiration and helpe worketh in men, wherein men are workers together and helpers with God. To these we geeue commendation, and that none otherwise, then the holy Scriptures and auncient Fathers doo.

The Catholike doctrine slaūdered. And hereby the Reader maie see, how vntrewly it is saide, that the Catholike Doctrine teacheth men to presume of their owne workes, or to thinke they be able to doo well without the grace of God: yea howe farre they are, that so saie, from knowing what good and godly workes are.

## A briefe rehersall of so much as hath ben hitherto saide, in this Treatie of Iustification.

## *THE XIIII. CHAPTER.*

IN the Preface of this treatie, after that I had shewed, howe profitable and necessary the trewe knowledge and doctrine of Iustification was: I did by the wordes *In Psal. 31.* of S. Augustine put the Reader in minde of two great daungers, which that most learned and godly Father calleth

leth *hedlong falles, sayinge: that who so speaketh of this matter, vnlesse he keepe the streight high waie, going neither to farre on the righte hande, nor on the lefte, may easily fall him selfe, or bringe his hearer into one of them.* The one perill is, the presumption of mans owne iustice, to thinke, that he maie be iustified, and liue godly, without the helpe of grace: which danger he saith is *as it were on the right hande.* The other perill is, the presumption vppon Gods mercy, to thinke, that a man though he liue ill, dooing no good workes, yet shal be saued by faith: that peril, he saith, is *as it were on the lefte hande.* To shewe the good Christian Reader, who desireth to go the streight way, howe he may auoide bothe daungers, the falling into either whereof is the losse of life euerlasting, I haue taken this trauaile in hande, wherein I trust I haue nowe saide inough to keepe him from the daungerouse fall on the righte hande, hauing declared at large, howe litle cause man hath to presume of his owne iustice: who descending of the corrupte race of Adam, borne in sinne and in daunger of the diuell, hath no hope to aspire
to the state of iustice, whiche Adam loste to him selfe, 1. Timo. 1.
and for all vs, but onely by mercie of *the mediatour of God and menne, the man Iesus Christe*, who *gaue him selfe a raunsome for all*, by whose grace we are freely iustified, *without respecte of any good woorkes* going Rom. 3.
before, or deseruing that mercy at his handes. Ephes. 2.

I haue shewed, that the chiefe and original cause of our Iustification was the exceding loue of God, who *when* Ephes. 2.
*we were deade in sinne, gaue vs life againe in Christe.* The cause that procured vnto vs the benefite of our Iustificatiõ, to be the merit of Christs death, who died for vs when Rom. 6.

Colos.1. we were sinners, *pacifiyng by the bloud of his Crosse all that is in heauen or in earth.* I haue declared, that our Iustification is wrought in vs by grace, and atteined by faith through the feare of God, hope, charitie, penance, and the Sacrament of Baptisme. And this much haue I said

Ro.5. of the first degree of our Iustification, whereby *we haue accesse to comme to this grace*: making with the Scripture and aunciente Fathers, for plainer vnderstanding three degrees of our Iustification and saluation.

The seconde and thirde degrees of our Iustification, whiche are increase of iustice in this life, and perfiting thereof in the life to comme: I haue proued to be gotten and obteined by faith and good workes. I haue also declared, that not only faith, the feare of God, hope, charity, and penance, but also our good workes, and all thinges any waie helping to our Iustification, be the giftes of God, and made ours by the assent and working of our free will, which is first healed and made strong by grace and the speciall helpe of God.

And bicause no man liueth without sinne, and fewe without greate and mortall crimes, whereby the grace of Iustification is loste, I haue shewed, that the waie to recouer it againe, is by the Sacrament of penance, which is also the gifte of God, for that he moueth a sinner to

Math.3. change and amende his life, *and to doo the worthy fruites of penance*: without the whiche motion no man euer did profitable penance.

And thus haue I proued, that all Iustification in euery mãner commeth from God, and is receiued and wrought

1.Cor.3. in man through grace, by his owne will and consent, whom it hath pleased God to haue *a worker together with*

*With him*, not empeyring thereby, but muche auancing
his owne glorie, for that he is *meruelouse*, not onely in him Psal. [illegible].
selfe, but also *in his holie*. And so haue I truely and faithfully excluded al boasting of man in him selfe, *geuing glo-* Rom. 3.
*ry to God*. For I haue so set forth the free wil of man, and
commended good workes, that the indifferent Reader may truly say: *Omnia ex Deo*. All is 2. Cor. 5.
of God: to thende that *who so*
*vanteth and boasteth,* 1. Cor. 1.
*may vante and*
*boaste in*
*God.*

I THE

# THE SECOND BOOKE DECLARING THE SECOND DANGER.

## Howe daungerouse it is for a man to presume only vpon Gods mercy, and to doo no good workes.

### THE I. CHAPTER.

*August. in præfatio. Psalm. 31.*

*Augu. de fid. et operib. c. 14.*

HAVING thus shewed the waye to auoyde the one daunger whiche is on the righte hande, and playnely declared that no man is iustified by him selfe, nor hath to presume of him selfe, bicause it auayleth a man nothing to eschewe one peril, and to perishe by an other contrarie to it, that is, as the Poete saieth, to escape Charibdys, and be drowned in Sylla: *Iam illud videamus, &c.* Let vs nowe consider *that other pointe, whiche muste be shaken owt of good and religiouse hartes, leaste putting cocke in the hoope by an yll securitie and carelesnes, they lose their saluation, if they thinke faithe onely sufficiente to obteyne it, and take no care to holde them selues in Gods waye by doing good woorkes.* By whiche woordes S. Augustine moneth vs to auoide the other daunger on the lefte hande, of presuming in Gods mercy alone. Willing no man to thinke, he may be saued by faith and beleeuing onely, if hauing tyme thereunto, he neyther

lyue

lyue godly, nor doo good woorkes.

And this perill is so muche the more to be wayed, and carefully to be eschewed, bicause as he saieth in the same woorke, *that is the moste daungerouse opinion of all,* August.de *Whereby menne are made beleeue, that lyue they neuer so* fid.& ope. *lewdely and shamefully, yea, and continue in that kinde* ca.27. *of lyfe, yet if they doo no more but beleeue in Christe, and receyue his Sacramentes, they shall come to euerlasting life.*

I cal this with S. Augustine the moste daungerouse opinion of al, bicause it is the greateste enemy of godly life and good woorkes, without the whiche no man shalbe saued. For he that putteth affiance in good life, and thinketh he is able to atteyne vnto it of him selfe, albeit he neuer reacheth thereunto, and loseth the hope of al August.in his trauayle, bicause he presumeth of him selfe, and God præfation. condemneth euen that presumption: yet hath he a desire Psal.31. to lyue wel, and a care to doe good workes. But who so is persuaded, that faith onely suffiseth to obteyne both Iustification and saluation, let him be well ware, leste he Aug.ibid. falle into the goulfe, and saye: *Faciam ergo quicquid volo.* I will doo then what I liste, *for though I haue no good Woorkes, and doo no more but beleeue in God, my faith shall be reputed to me for iustice. If he haue so saied and determined With him selfe he is fallen in, and drowned. If he be yet but thinking thereof and Wauering, he is in daunger.*

Further, if it be true that the Philosopher saieth, that Aristote. of twoo vices contrarie to one vertue, the more daun- Ethic.lib. gerouse and greater vice is that, whereunto menne are 2. cap.8. more geuen: We doubte not but the greater number

of men is rather prone and contente of them ſelues to beleue only, and put the reſte in Gods mercie, then deſirous to leade a ſeuere and ſtrayte life, and payne them ſelues with good workes. Which thing the diuel wel knowing, hath in ſundry ages gone about to put this opinion in the
Ca. 12. heades of ſuch as he could abuſe, as I ſhal ſhewe hereafter. Wherefore to auoide this goulfe, whiche is moſt perillouſe, I wil declare, that faith alone ſuffiſeth not in any ſorte of true vnderſtanding, to our Iuſtification or ſaluation. That is to ſay, that faith alone is neither able to
1. iuſtifie and bring to the ſtate of iuſtice, him that is a ſinner: nor alone able to keepe and increaſe our Iuſtification, when it is gotten:
2. nor able alone to bring him that
3. is iuſtified to the perfection of iuſtice in life euerlaſting. In which three degrees conſiſteth the abſolute and perfecte Iuſtification of man, as I haue ſhewed before. (In the firſt Chap.)

VVhence the opinion came, that onely faith iuſtifieth: and of diuers kindes of mainteyning the ſame.

## THE II. CHAPTER.

1. *Auguſt. de gratia & liber. arbit. c. 7. Rom. 3. Gal. 3.*

THE opinion that moued ſome menne to thinke onely faith ſufficiente to ſaluation, tooke his firſte grounde of miſconſtruing the wordes of S. Paule: *Homines enim non intelligentes. &c.* For men, ſaieth S. Augustine, not vnderſtanding *theſe wordes of the Apoſtle, we thinke a man is iuſtified by faith without workes of the law, thought he ſaid, that it is ſufficient for a man to haue faith although*

*though he liue yll,and doe no good vvorkes.But God forbid the
choſen veſſel ſhould be of that opinion.*

And vppon this,and other places of Scripture, whiche *Aug. in*
alſo they miſconſtrued,they perſwaded them ſelues, that *præfat.*
a Chriſtian man needed not to doe any good woorkes, *Pſa.31. &*
for that he might be ſaued by faith, though he liued vn- *de fid. &*
godlie. *oper.c.14.*

Others, when they ſawe the Scriptures ſo euidently 2.
commending good workes, and ſetting foorth the neceſ- *Caluin. in*
ſitie of doing them, being aſhamed to mainteine that they *inſtit. ca.*
were nedeleſſe to be done,haue ſaied: *that men muſt liue* *de iuſtific.*
*godly, to teſtifie and declare their faith, but yet that their* *ca. 10.*
*good vvoorkes deſerue no rewarde of lyfe euerlaſting, neither* *Brent.in*
*can ſtand in the iudgement of God.* *confeſſ.*
*VVirtēber.*
And to minſe this matter more finely, ſome haue yet *de bonis*
gone further: And whereas the Catholike Churche folo- *operibus.*
wing the manifeſt Srciptures,hath euer taught,that a ſin- 3.
ner is iuſtified through the merite of Chriſt and his Sacramentes, by faith, hope, charitie and penance: they haue
taught that he is iuſtified by faith only,and although they
graunt,that he muſt haue both hope and charitie,that ſhal
be iuſtified,yet is it faith onely, ſaie they,that ſtriketh the
ſtroke in the acte of Iuſtification, hope and charitie ſtan-
ding by as lookers on, but working nothing.

Into theſe three kindes of dangerous errours,men haue
fallen by teaching and beleeuing the Iuſtification of faith
alone, not onely barring the neceſsitie of doinge good
woorkes and penance, but alſo abaſing the worthines of
hope and charity,and th'eſtimation and dignitie of Chriſt
his Sacramentes.

Againſt the firſt opinion, S. Auguſtine both preached 1.

and disputed in sundrie places of his learned woorkes, and namely, wrote his booke of faith and woorkes against the same, which thou hast here (gentle Reader) together with this Treatie translated vnto thee.

2. Concerning the seconde, which the Authors would faine haue appeare different from the firste, and yet in effecte seemeth all one: I haue saied somewhat before, and plainely proued, that good woorkes doe not onely keepe and increase our iustice here, but shalbe rewarded also in the ende with life euerlasting, whereof I shall saie more hereafter.

In the. 12. Chapt. of the firste booke.

In the. 13. Chapter.

3. To the thirde opinion I shall nowe answere, and euidently shew, that it is not faith alone, that worketh th'acte of our Iustification, but that hope, charitie, and the Sacramentes, haue their partes in working it also. And by this shall the Reader perceiue, that after their meaning it can in no wise be truely said, that faith alone iustifieth.

And here must I aduertise the Reader, that this thirde opinion is newe and lately come out of the forge, neuer heard of to my knowledge, before these our daies. For as there hath ben in sundrie ages, carnal men, which thought them selues, and went about to perswade others, that faith and the Sacramentes of Christ, might saue a man without good workes, so haue I not read of any, that plainely said, faith without hope, charitie, and the Sacraments of Christ, can iustifie a man. And therfore, as diuers, or rather al the auncient Fathers, haue in some places of their woorkes, gone about to pul the one opinion out of mennes heades, so do I not finde, that they make any mention of th'other, and much lesse, that any one of them before this our age, hath affirmed it to be true.

*August. de fid. & oper. c. 27*

That

## That Faith excludeth not Charitie in our Iustification, that is to saie, Faith alone iustifieth no man, without the helpe and woorking of Charitie.

### *THE III. CHAPTER.*

AND nowe to beginne with the moste excellente vertue that is in a Christian man, Faith alone iustifieth no man, without the helpe and working of charitie. It hath ben declared before, that our Iustification in Christe, is but the restoring of that whiche was lost by Adam. And as Adam sinned, not onely by lacke of faith, but rather and much more, by lacke of good wil and right loue, so is not a man once fallen, restored againe by recouering onely righte faith, vnlesse he recouer also righte loue. The sinne of Adam was chiefely a peruerse desire and luste, through a loue settled where it should not be, pulled from God and delyte heauenly, and settled on him selfe and thinges transitorie. And as that peruerse loue, which is called *luste*, made him of good and righteouse, euill and sinnefull: so in all that descende of his race, yll loue and *luste* maketh an yll man: and good loue, which is called *Charitie*, maketh a good man. *Interoget se quisque quid amet, & inueniet vnde sit Ciuis.* Lette euery man aske of him selfe what he loueth, and he shall finde whereof he is a Citizen. That is to saie, whether he be of the Citie of God, or of the Diuell. Charitie yt ys that altereth and chaungeth the hearte, and the hearte is it that chaungeth the woorkes. *Muta cor & muta-*

*Of Charitie.*

In the. 4. Chapter.

*August. in Præfat. Psal. 31.*

*August. in Titul. Psal. 64.*

August. Serm. 12. de verb. Dom. *mutabitur opus.* Change the heart, saith S. Augustine, and the woorke will be changed. And howe the hearte is changed, it foloweth: *Extirpa cupiditatem, planta charitatem.* Roote out luste and ill desire: plante charitie, *for as luste is the roote of all yll, so is charitie the roote of all good.*

No man is iustified, but he that is made a good man, and charitie it is that maketh a man good. (Aug. Enchi. c. 117) For *when the question is asked, whether any one be a good man, it is not demaunded what he beleueth, or what he hopeth, but what he loueth. For who so loueth rightly, without doubt he beleueth rightly.* Al men wil confesse, that no man can be iu-
1. stified, vnlesse he know God, be new borne of God, tran-
2. slated from death of the sowle to lyfe, fourmed of newe,
3. and graffed in Christe, and finally, made a new creature.
4. For who so euer remaineth without knowledge of God,
5. and continueth in the olde estate of Adam, is the childe of anger, in the state of iuste damnation, and farre from iustice. If then it plainely appeare, that all these fiue pointes be wroughte in vs, especially by charitie, wee must needes confesse, that charitie doth not onely worke, but singularly worke in the acte of our Iustification.

To proue the firste and seconde pointe, S. Iohn saith: (1. Ioan. 4.) *Euerie man that loueth, is borne of God, and knoweth God. He that loueth not, knoweth not God, for God is charitie.* (1. Ioan. 3.) The thirde pointe he proueth by these wordes: *Nos scimus*: We knowe, *that we are translated from death to lyfe, bicause we loue our brethren: he that loueth not, remaineth in death.* (August. in expo. epist. ad Galat.) Of the fourth point, S. Augustine saith: *formatur Christus in eo qui formam accepit Christi.* Christ is formed in him, that hath receiued the fourme and shape of Christe,

Chriſt,but he it is that receiueth the ſhape of Chriſt,who cleaueth faſte to Chriſte by a goſtely and ſpirituall loue. The fifte pointe is proued by S.Paule,who taketh it for al one *to be made a newe creature* and to haue *faith that worketh throughe charitie.* For as he ſaieth: *In Chriſte Ieſu neither circumciſion, nor to be without circumciſion auaileth ought, but faith that worketh through charitie.* So he ſaith: *Neither circumciſion nor to be without circumciſion auaileth ought, but the newe creature.* This being proued, that man knoweth God, is borne of God,tranſlated from death to life, newe fourmed in Chriſte, and finally made a newe creature by Charitie, it is alſo proued conſequentely, that man is iuſtified eſpecially through Charitie. Galat.5. Galat.6.

I go not abowte here to abaſe the excellente gifte of faith nor to ſaie, charitie onely iuſtifieth,excluding faith, which is the foundation of all rightuouſenes. my intente is onely to ſhewe, howe ſhamefull a diuorce they make, that parte theſe ſo wel agreeing vertues in the acte of our Iuſtification, whiche God hath ioined together. For trewely it is ſaied.*Charitas robur eſt fidei,fides fortitudo eſt charitatis.*Charitie is the force of faith,faith is the ſtrength of Charitie,*and then is the name trewe,and trew fruite of bothe,when eche remayneth ſure and faſte knitte to other.* Seing then that Iuſtification is the greateſt fruite that can come of faith, it foloweth, that the ſame can not be had without thaid of charity.Faith may be in a man without charitie, but it maketh no man rightuouſe and iuſte, but by charitie.S.Auguſtine ſaith,A man may beleue that Chriſt is Chriſt, by faith without hope and charitie: but he can not beleue in Chriſte,whiche is as muche to ſaie, Matth.19 Leo ſerm. 7.de quadrag.

as to be vnited and made a member of Christe, without
Aug. Ser. 61. De ver. De. hope and charitie. *Qui credit in Christum. &c.* who so beleueth in Christe, *by his beleuing, Christe commeth vnto him, and by some meanes he is made one with Christ, and a member of his body, which can not be done, vnlesse hope and charitie be ioined also.*

1. In which place three thinges are to be noted: first he saith, that faith alone is sufficiente for vs to beleue that
2. Christe is Christe. Next, he saith, that faith alone is not inough to make a man the member of Christ. Thirdely
3. he saith, that faith, hope and charity ioined together make a man the member of Christ. Wherefore seing that to be iustified is nothing els but to be made a member of Christ: it is a plaine matter with S. Augustine, that faith only can not iustifie, bicause it can not make a man the member of Christe. And for as muche as that effecte is wroughte by the three vertues ioined together, it foloweth also that hope, and charitie worke in the acte of our Iustification, as well as Faith.

Faith can not onely iustifie no man without charitie, but as S. Bernarde saieth, dieth, if charitie be pulled from
Bernar. Ser. 24. super Canti. it. *Mors fidei est separatio charitatis.* It is the death of Faith to be parted from charitie. *And he that diuideth them,* saith he, *is fideicida,* a murtherer of Faith.

A deade faith can not geue life to the sowle. *Mortuam*
Iaco. 2. *Apostolus definit eam esse.* And the Apostle S. Iames determineth that faith to be deade, *that worketh not by loue.*
Bernar. Epist. 42. *Quasi non habens animam ipsam dilectionem.* Bicause she hath not loue whiche is her very sowle. If faith when she is without charitie, wanteth her sowle and life, without the which she can doo no acte, howe should she without

charitie worke that greate acte of our Iustification?

To make the matter plaine, we shall neede but one argument grounded vppon the wordes of S. Paule. *In Christ Iesu neither circumcision, nor to be without circumcision auaileth any thing, but faith that worketh through charitie.* If that be the Faithe that auaileth, whiche worketh through charitie, then faithe alone destitute of charitie auaileth nothing. If it auaile nothing, muche lesse dothe it worke our Iustification: For that is not onely somewhat, but it is as S. Augustine and Prosper Aquitanus say, *a greater worke, then to make heauen and earth, or to bring a deade man to life againe.* The argument is not mine, but suche as S. Augustine vseth, and repeteth almost as often as he speaketh of Iustification: Saying that S. Paule by these wordes hath decided and determined the matter: *Non quamlibet fidem qua in Deum creditur. &c.* It is not euery Faith whereby a man beleueth in God, *that the Apostle determineth to be healthfull and Euangelicall, but that is the Faith, saith he, which worketh through charitie: whereuppon he auoucheth that the Faith, which some take to be sufficiente for their saluation, auaileth nothing: in so muche that he saith: If I haue all Faith, in suche sorte that I be able to moue hilles owt of theire places, and haue no charitie, I am nothing.*

*Gala. 5.* *Aug. tra. in Ioan. 72. Prosper de promis. part. 2. cap. 30. De fide & oper. cap. 14. De gratia & lib. arbit. cap. 7. Epist. 107. Enchi. c. 8. Aug. de fide & oper. ca. 14*

I woulde seeke a plainer decision, if any thing coulde be more plainely spoken. He saith, S. Paule hath defined, that there is but one Faithe auailable, to witte, the faithe that worketh through charitie. He saith, all other Faithe what so euer it be, auaileth nothing. He saith, and that verie often, that *Faith destitute of charitie maie be not onely in euill men, but also in the diuell him selfe.* And

*Ser. 15. de ver. apost. De fide & oper. c 14.*

calleth it *fidem dæmoniorum*, the faith of diuelles.

And leste any man should saie, that albeit good workes are done by charitie, yet is all to be imputed to faithe, Note vvel which is the cause that worketh al, S. Paule saith on the other side, that faith it selfe taketh her doing and working of charitie. For as they know that vnderstand the Greke tongue, ἐνεργουμένη is a participle of pasiue significatiō, and rightely shoulde he translate the wordes of S. Paule, who shoulde saie, *That faith in Christ Iesu is auailable, which e is made actiue and doing thorough charitie.* For if we will speake of the nature of faithe as it is by it selfe, it is vndoubtedly, to vnderstande and assent vnto trewth, as hath ben shewed before.

In the 2. Chapt.

And bicause all knowledge be it of the Scriptures, or the articles of our Crede, maie be, not onely in il men, but in diuels also: Faith is not able of her selfe to make a man iuste and righteouse, vnlesse shee take vnto her hope, and charitie, and so be made actiue and doing: by the one to hope in God, by the other to loue God and man. whiche conclusion concerning charitie S. Augustine maketh. *Ergo si nihil mihi prodest fides sine charitate. &c.* If faithe then auaile me nothing without charitie, *and charitie wheresoeuer it be, muste needes be working, faithe it selfe by charitie hath her working.*

*In Præfa. Psal. 31.*

Reason in man is the thing that maketh the difference betwene him and al brute beastes: which be called brute, bicause they lacke reason. For which cause, Reason, as the principal power of the sowle is called of the Philosopher ἐντελέχεια, the forme and perfection that maketh a man.

In like manner charitie is the thing that maketh the difference betwene faith and faith, betwene the faith of

a good

a good and an ill man, betwene the faith of good Christians, and vncleane diuelles. As S. Augustine saith at large in a learned and godly Sermon able to satisfie any indifferente Reader, not onely in this point, but in the whole matter of Iustification. *Quid pertinet ad fidem? Credere.* What belongeth to faith? to beleue: *But lette there yet further be a difference made betwene this faith, and the faith of vncleane Diuelles. For the Apostle S. Iames saith, the Diuelles also beleue and tremble: if thou doest but onely beleue, and liuest without hope, and haste no charitie, the Diuelles beleue also and tremble.* And a litle after, *first therefore make a difference betwene thy faith, and the Diuelles faith. Whereby wilte thou make the difference? The Diuelles said, Christ was the sonne of God, through feare. S. Peter said it through loue: Put hope then to faith. And what hope is there, without some good conscience? put vnto hope it selfe, charitie.* And somewhat after that: *Therefore make a difference of your faith, then are ye of the predestinates of the called, and of the iustified.* And in the same Sermon to conclude, he saith: *Therefore if there be in you faith that worketh through loue, now belonge you to the predestinates, to the called, and to the iustified. Let that faith therefore growe in you that is working by charitie: for faith working by charitie can not be without hope.*

*Aug. ser. 16. De ver Aposto.*

*Iaco. 2.*

*Mar. 1. Matt. 8. Luc. 4.*

*Gala. 5.*

Now if charitie be it, that maketh the difference betwene faith, and faith, as S. Augustine proueth, and if that which maketh the difference betwene any one creature and al other, be the perfection, life, and sowle, of that creature: Then is charitie not an instrument to serue faith, but the life and sowle of faith, without the helpe and mouing whereof, faith neither iustifieth, neither worketh any good acte in the beleuer.

Ioan.12. The Euangelist saith: *Ex principibus multi crediderunt in eum, sed propter Pharisæos non confitebantur, vt è synagoga non eijcerentur: dilexerunt enim gloriam hominum magis quàm gloriam Dei.* Many of the chiefe rulers beleued in him, but they confessed him not, bicause they would not be caste out of the Synagoge. For they loued the glory of men more, then the glory of God. The scripture saith, they had faith, and yet no man I thinke will say they were iustified, who neither confessed Christe, and also loued the worlde better then God. And what lacked there in them, to make them belonge to the predestinates, to the called and iustified, as S. Augustine saith, *but onely right loue, to make that faith actiue and stronge* to loue the glory of God more then the glory of men, whiche vnlesse God gaue them afterwarde, that faith nothing auailed them.

Thei had faith, vvithout right loue

Wherefore if a man were disposed to make a diuorce betwene faith, hope, and charitie, which no good man euer did, he might say by these and other reasons, that charitie alone rather iustifieth, and haue S. Augustine to say with him, whose wordes these are: *Charitas inchoata, inchoata iustitia est, &c.* An vnperfect charitie, is an vnperfect iustice: *a well increased charitie, is a well increased iustice: a great charitie, is great iustice: perfect charitie, is perfect iustice.* And in the same booke he saith of charitie: *Qua vna verè iustus est, quicunque iustus est.* By the which onely he is trewly iuste, who so euer is iust. But to declare, that his minde was not to make any such separation, he saith, *it is the charitie that commeth from a pure harte, a good conscience and vnfained faith.*

Ser.16. de ver. Apos.

Only charitie rather then only faith.

De natura & gra. cap.70.

Ca 38.ib.

Ib.cap.70.

He

He might allege for him th'authoritie of S.Ihon th'Euangelist, who being required by his scholers a litle before his death, to teach them some perfecte lesson, whereby they might liue well and haue cause to remembre him, said: *my children, loue one an other.* And when they looked for more, he repeted the same againe, and said: *It is our Lords commaundement, and if there be no more done but that, it is inough.* He should haue Prosper to say for him: *Charitie is a summarie and abbridgement of all good doings, of the which euery good worke taketh his life, without the which neuer man pleased God.* S.Bede would say, *Charitie is the principall vertue, in so muche that without that vertue, other principall vertues can not be.* Leo would call her *the mother of all vertues*, and Chrysostome *the mother of all goodnes.* And thus haue I proued, not only that faith without charitie iustifieth no man, but also that charitie hath a souereine working in the acte of our Iustification, without the which faith auaileth nothing, and so doth not faith alone iustifie, nor exclude charitie.

*Hier. li.3. com. in epist. ad Galat. cap.6.*

*De vit. contēpla. li.3. ca.13*

*Homi. æstiua in lita. maio.*

*Ser.7. de Epipha.*

*Chrysost. tom.1. fol. 176.*

An answere to obiections that be made, to proue that faith alone iustifieth without charitie

## *THE IIII. CHAPTER.*

BVT leste the mainteiners of Iustification by onely faith should seeme to be without all ground, and to exclude charitie without colour of reason, they frame one especiall argument, which for the readers better satisfaction, I will put forth and answere here. The argument is this.

We be iustified by faith without all workes of the Lawe.

Charitie is a worke of the Lawe.

*Ergo*, we be iustified by faith without charitie.

To the which I answere with S. Augustine, that their second proposition deceiueth them, for that charitie is not onely a worke of the lawe, but also the gifte of the holy Ghost in the newe testament. S. Paule saith, *the charitie of God is powred abrode in our hartes through the holy Ghost that is geuen vs.* And S. Iohn saith: *Moste dearely beloued, let vs loue one an other, for loue commeth of God.* Vppon which wordes S. Augustines answere is: *Cùm dicitur, diligamus inuicem: lex est. Cùm dicitur, quia dilectio ex Deo est, gratia est.* When it is said: Lette vs loue one an other, it is the lawe: when it is said, for loue commeth of God, it is grace. He maketh this the greatest differēce betwene th'old and new testament, that where as in the old, God lead his people by terror and feare, in the newe he geueth them plenty of his charitie and loue. *Hæc est breuissima, &c.* This is the shortest *and plainest difference of both testaments: feare, and loue. Ibi in tabulis lapideis. There the holy Ghost wrought in tables of stone, here in mens hartes. And what be the lawes of God writen by God him self in mennes hartes, but the presence of the holy Ghost who is the finger of God, by whose presence charitie is powred abrode in our hartes, which is the fulfilling of the law.* Thus doo we see, that charitie is not onely a worke of the law, but also the fruite of the holy Ghost, the speciall token of the new testament, wrought in our hartes by the holy Ghost. And so hath S. Augustine answered this argument xi. hundred yeares before they were borne that lately haue made it.

*Rom 5.* — *1. Ioha. 4.* — *De grat & li. arb. cap. 18.* — *Contr. Adiman. cap. 17.* — *De spirit. & lit. cap. 17. Item cap. 21. ca. 16.*

And

And whereas it is saied, that faith onely iustifieth, bicause faith onely apprehendeth Christe: I aske, what is meant by the terme of Apprehension? If it be to beleue onely that Christ died for sinners, that alone iustifieth no man, for *the Diuelles beleue it, and tremble*, bicause they hope not to be partakers of that benefite, nor loue him that purchased it: If to apprehend Christe be vnderstanded, to dwell in Christe, and to haue him dwell in vs, it is not true that Christe is apprehended in that sorte, by onely faith without charitie. For it is saied: *God is charitie, and he that dwelleth in charitie, dwelleth in God, and God in him.* And Christ him selfe saith: *Si quis diligit me, sermonem meum seruabit, & Pater meus diliget eum, & ad eum veniemus, & mansionem apud eum faciemus*: If a man loue me, he will kepe my saying, and my Father wil loue him, and to him will we come, and make our abode with him. By these woordes let the Reader learne, what it is truely and profitably to apprehend Christe.

What it is truely to apprehēd Christe.

Iacob. 2.

1 Ioan 4.

Ioan. 14.

He apprehendeth Christ truly, *that is vnited and made a member of Christe*, whiche as I haue proued in the last Chapter, can not be done without hope and charitie. He apprehendeth Christ truely, *that cleaueth vnto Christ, and the glue whereby the sowle is fastned vnto Christe*, saith S. Augustine, *is charitie*: *Ipsum gluten est charitas*: If it be said, that faith apprehendeth the promise: Christ hath promised lyfe euerlasting *to suche as become his friendes.* And they be his friendes *that keepe his commaundements. He is made a cause of life euerlasting*, but, *to such as obey him.* The promise is made *to the children of Abraham*, that is to suche as haue the faith and obedience of Abraham, whereof I shall speake at large hereafter. And so is it

Aug. ser. 61. de ver. Dom. & tract. in Ioan. 29.

In Psal. 62

Ioan. 15.

Heb. 5.

Chapt. 23.

true, that faith alone neither apprehendeth Christe, nor his promise profitablie, vnlesse hope and Charitie be ioyned vnto it.

## That Faith excludeth not Hope in the acte of our Iustification.

## THE V. CHAPTER.

*Of Hope.* As God requireth of such as come to his seruice, that they stedfastly beleeue in him, and with all their heartes loue him: So doth he also require of them, to repose al hope and affiance in him onely, saying by his
*Iere.17.* Prophete: *Maledictus homo qui confidit in homine.* Cursed is the man that putteth his trust in man. And by the
*Iere.9.* same Prophete: *Let not the wise bragge in his wisedome,*
*1.Cor.1.* *neither lette the strong boast in his strength. Nor lette the*
*Psal.107.* *riche glorie in his riches: But lette him that boasteth, boast*
*Psal.33.* *in our Lorde.* Wherefore, *as mans power to saue is vaine, and he vnhappie that trusteth in it:* so happie *is the man, that trusteth in God.* Of so great force is a right and constant hope in God, that nothing perteining to saluatiō, can
*Aug. Enchi.cap.8.* be auaileable to him that wanteth it. *No true charitie can be without it.* No faith can iustifie, but by the helpe and direction of it. A good mans *faith is the substance of things*
*Hebr.11.* *that are to be hoped.* Take awaie hope then from faith, and faith must nedes fainte and quaile. The thing that kepte the Fathers, of whome S. Paule speaketh, so faithfull to God, was, that they had a strong hope and trust to enioye his promises. And that which was said of Moyses, may be

be truely ſaid of them al: *Aſpicicieбat ad remunerationem.* They looked to the rewarde, which can not be without hope. *The Diuelles beleue and tremble, but* as S. Auguſtine ſaith, *they neither hope, nor loue.* In like manner euil Chriſtians may beleue, and yet remaine ſtil vngodly, and voide of iuſtice, bicauſe they want hope and loue. Hebr. 11. Aug. Enchi. cap. 8.

I haue proued before, that faith without charitie iuſtifieth no man: *Propter quod Apoſtolus Paulus,* For which cauſe the Apoſtle Paule *commendeth the faith, which hath her woorking through charitie. Quæ vtique ſine ſpe eſſe non poteſt.* Which can in no wiſe be without hope. For ſith a man may beleeue, that whiche he hopeth not for: what auaileth him to beleeue, that Chriſte is *the Sauiour of all men*, vnleſſe he hope alſo to be partaker of that ſaluation? Or howe ſhoulde he be moued to loue him for the benefite of our redemption, if he truſt not to enioy it? And therefore ſaith S. Auguſtine: *Nec amor ſine ſpe, nec ſine amore ſpes, nec vtrumque ſine fide.* Neither is there loue without hope, nor hope without loue, nor both without faith. And ſo doth faith woorke our Iuſtification through hope and loue. So is it true, that *fides, ſpes, charitas, ad Deum ducunt,* faith, hope, and charitie leade vs to God, to whom we are aſſured not to come, if either of the three want in vs. And therefore as it is ſaied, *by grace are ye ſaued through faith*: So is it alſo ſaid: *Spe ſalui facti ſumus.* By hope are we ſaued. Hope ioyning with faith and charity, ingẽdreth an affiance in God, and maketh a ſtrong hoping faith, vnto whiche affiance euerlaſting life is promiſed: *Qui habet fiduciam mei, hæreditabit terram, & poſſidebit montem ſanctum meum.* He that hath affiance in me, ſhall inherite the earth, and poſſeſſe my holie Hill. Aug. ibid. 1. Timo. 2. Ench. c. 8 Auguſt. epiſt. 121. Epheſ. 2. Rom. 8. Eſai. 57.

Heb.6. So dothe S. Paule call hope *the safe and sure anker of the sowle*. Wherunto as many as flee for refuge, haue a most strong comforte. For as the ancor staieth the shippe, so doth hope the sowle: faith would be weake, and charitie colde, if hope mainteined and staied them not. S. Paule Coloss.1. saieth to the Colossians: *Gratias agimus Deo & Patri*. We geue thankes to God and the Father *of our Lorde Iesus Christe, euer praying for you. For that we heare of your faith in Christe Iesu, and of the loue you beare towarde all the holie. Propter spem quæ reposita est vobis in cælis*. For the hopes sake that is laid vppe for you in heauen. He maketh the ende of our hope the marke, wherevnto both faith and charitie haue their respecte. And if the Philosophers sayinges be true, that *the ende is it whiche is last done, and first in our intente*, a man may reason vppon this place, that in the acte of our Iustification, Hope dothe not onely worke, but hath the chiefe place and principal woorking. Bicause his obiecte is the ende, wherevnto faith and charitie referre all their dooinges, and consequently, the cause that moueth faith to beleeue, and charitie to loue: without the direction of hope, faith and loue may be fruitlesse. A man may haue faith and doe good woorkes, and yet lacking a right hope, he shall not be a goodman: For saith S. Augustine: *Quid si de ijs omnibus bonis operibus, &c.* What if by all these good woorkes, *either thou hope for that is to be hoped, but not at his hande of whom it shoulde be hoped, or hope after that is not to be hoped, though it be at his hande of whome euerlasting life is to be hoped. To put an Example: For thy good workes, thou hopest to get thy selfe a worldly felicitie. Thou arte a wicked man. And therfore he saith in the same place: Corrige fidem,*

Hope by some reason, is the principall vvorker in our Iustification

August. in Præfat. Psal.31.

dirige

*dirige fidem*. Correcte thy faith, directe thy faith. And what is the direction of faith, but to referre and applye it to life euerlasting? which we ought to hope and trust for in al our doinges. If faith then can not iustifie, vnlesse it be rightly directed, and direction of faith is hope: howe shoulde faithe iustifie without hope? *Adde ergo fidei spem*: Therefore put hope to faith, saieth S. Augustine. *And what hope is there without some good conscience? put charitie then also to hope*: These three ioyntly together beginne to woorke our iustice: These three increase our iustice. These three bring vs to the rewarde and perfection of iustice: faith, hope and charitie leade vs to God: *fide, spe, & charitate colendus est Deus*. By faith, hope and charitie God muste be serued. *Et nos fide, spe, & charitate cum capite nostro sumus in cœlo*. By faith, hope and charitie we be in heauen with Christe our heade: let vs make no diuorce betwene these vertues, whome God hath so ioyned to worke our iustice and saluation.

*Ser. 16. de ver. apost.*

*Aug. epistol. 121.*

*Ench. ca. 2 & 6.*

*August. in Psalm. 26 enarr. 2.*

But as we be assured, that without hope the acte of our Iustification is not wroughte, so it behoueth vs to vnderstande, howe hope muste be nurisshed and mainteyned. The lesson is shorte, but of greate proffite, vttered by him that had good experience thereof. *Cupiditas refrenetur, charitas excitetur*. Lette luste be brydeled, lette charitie be stirred vp. *The very charitie of a man that worketh well geueth him the hope of a good conscience. For good conscience is it that beareth hope. As an yll conscience is all in dispayre, so the good conscience is all in hope*. We see then that it is charitie and godly life which fostereth and mainteyneth hope. And as without hope faithe suffiseth not, for whiche cause it is saied by S. Augustine:

*August. in præfation. Psalm. 31.*



gustine:

Augu.ser. 16.de ver. Apost.

gustyne: *Putte hope vnto faith*: so hope without charitie wil not be had. For *What hope is there without some good conscience? Put charitie then to hope also*. Thus is faith directed and stayed by hope: hope mainteyned by charitie: and a man made acceptable to God by all three. For *if these be in vs, then doo we belonge to the predestinate, to the called, and to the iustified*. Whiche is also expressed by the woordes of S.Paule, where he saith: *Finis praecepti est charitas, &c.* The perfyting and ending of the commaundement is charitie, *that commeth from a cleane harte, from a good conscience, and an vnfayned faith*. In which place S. Augustine saith: *The Apostle putteth in good conscience in steade of hope*. Wherefore if the commandement be geuen to make man perfect, in such perfection as he may haue in this life, and the ende and perfecting of the cõmandement lyeth in these three vertues: the greatest perfection that man may reache vnto in this life is gotten by faith, hope and charitie. And our greatest perfection in this life is, our Iustification: for our glorifying apperteyneth to the life to come.

Ser.16.de ver.apost. — 1.Tim.1. — De doctr. Christian. lib.1.c.40

That faith excludeth not the working of Sacramentes in our Iustification.

## THE VI. CHAPTER.

*Of the Sacramentes.*

As faith doth not barre hope and charitie from working our Iustification, so doth it not exclude the Sacramentes of the Church instituted by Christ in the newe Testamente. Whiche Sacramentes be not only requisite

quisite to the iustifying of a sinner, but doo worke also in him remissiō of sinne, bring and restore him to rightuousnes, and geue life euerlasting. *Baptisme*, saieth S. Peter, *saueth vs*. Concerning the Sacramentes of the Altar, Christe saieth: *He that eateth my fleshe, and drinketh my bloode, shall lyue for euer*. He saieth also of the Sacramente of Penaunce: *Whose sinnes you forgeue, they be forgeuen them*. The like may be said of the rest, of which S. Augustine maketh this general rule, putting a differēce betwene the Sacramentes of the olde and newe Testament: *Sacramenta noui Testamenti dant salutem, Sacramēta veteris Testamenti promiserunt Saluatorem*. The Sacramentes of the newe Testamente geue saluation: the Sacramentes of the old Testamente promised a Sauiour.

1. Pet. 3.

Ioan. 6.

Ioan. 20.

August. in Psal. 73.

S. Bede, whom I allege for honours sake, both bicause he was a singular lighte of our Country, and also bicause he was in all his writinges an exquisite and moste diligent folower of S. Augustine, saieth: *The Apostles were sente, Qui cunctis per orbem nationibus, &c. Who shoulde both preache the woorde of life to all nationes through the worlde, and minister the Sacramente of faith, by whiche men mighte be saued, and atteyne to the ioyes of the heauenly country*.

Bed. Hom. in feri. 3. Pascha.

The reason why so high and excellente a vertue should be in the Sacramentes, is bicause they take their force of Christ his Death and Passion. *Percussum est latus pendētis de lancea: & profluxerunt Ecclesiæ Sacramenta*: The side of Christ hanging on the Crosse, was stryken with a speare, and the Sacramentes of the Church came flowing out.

August. in Psal 56. et idem in Psal. 103.

And as they issued and flowed out of his side, so doo they applye and geue vnto vs, the benefyte of his bloode

and

Augu. ex posit. epist. ad Roma. inchoat. Such as vvere christened Were signed vvith the Crosse.

and pasſion. *Illud Sacrificium &c. That Sacrifice, to witte, the whole Sacrifice of our Lorde, whiche, after a manner is then offred for euerie one, at what tyme he is christened and signed, if he ſinne againe, can not be offered.* S. Auguſtine ſaith, that the Sacrifice which Chriſte made for all vppon the Croſſe is offred after a ſorte for euery one particularly, when he is baptized. For as he died for al, and paide the price and ranſome of his bloode ſufficiente for all: ſo is his paſsion auayleable and applyed vnto ſuch as receyue the healthful Sacramentes of his paſsion. *Cuius mors non ſic impenſa eſt humano generi*: His death was not ſo beſtowed vpon man kinde, *that euen they that neuer ſhoulde be regenerate or christened, ſhould alſo be partakers of his redemption, but in ſuch ſorte was it geuen, that it whiche was by one onely example and paterne done for al in general, ſhould by a ſpecial Sacramente be celebrated and done in euery one by him ſelfe.* Let no man therefore aſſure him ſelfe of his Iuſtification by faith or other meanes, without the helpe and benefite of the Sacramentes, whiche God hath prouided firſt to applie his death and paſsiõ vnto vs, as we haue ſeene proued: and nexte he hath alſo prouided them to be bandes to bynde and rowle vp our woundes in this life, to ſtaye and eaſe the ruptures and breaches of our ſoule. *Alligamenta medicinalia, &c. The Sacramentes vſed here for the tyme, by which we haue confort, be medicinall bandes of our contrition and rupture. Perfecta ſanitate detrahentur.* When our healthe ſhalbe perfect, which ſhalbe in heauen, they ſhalbe pulled of, *but we ſhould not atteyne and comme to that, were we not rouled and bound vp.*

Augu. ad arti. falsò ſibi impoſit. artic. 1

The Sacramẽt of penance.

Auguſt. in Pſal. 146.

S. Auguſtine ſaith, that the Sacramentes for the tyme of this life be our medicines and ſalues to keepe vs in healthe, health, and for the life to comme so necessarie, that no man should atteine thereunto without them.

Here some man will say, how should the Sacramentes be so necessarie for our saluation? Is it not writen, that by *faith God purifieth and maketh cleane the hartes of men?* Is it not in S. Paule, *by grace are ye saued through faith?* Did not Christ him selfe say, *he that beleueth in me, hath life euerlasting?* With many like sayinges, wherein faith is commended, without any mention made either of hope, charitie, or Sacramentes? Yeas verely, they be all the wordes of God, and al trewe, but these are not onely the wordes of God, nor onely trewe. The holy Ghost hath vttered the trewth of God in the Scriptures, where and by what wordes it liked that diuine wisedome. Al are inspired from God, and all to be beleeued alike: but not all together, nor all in one place. And therefore as we beleeue it is vndoubtedly trewe, *he that beleueth in me, hath euerlasting life:* so doo wee likewise beleue it to be trewe: *If I haue all faith, and haue no charitie, I am nothing:* as trewe doo we thinke that also: *by hope are we saued*: and no lesse true: *Vnlesse a man be borne againe by water and the holy Ghost, he shall not enter into the kingdome of heauen.* As true doo we take that to be: *vnlesse ye doo penance, ye shall all perish, after a like sorte.*

Obiectioa

Act. 15.

Ephe. 2.

Ioan. 6.

Answere

Ioan. 6.

1. Cor. 13.

Rom. 8.

Ioan. 3.

Luc. 13.

After this manner doth the Scripture somtime speake of faith, and attribute Iustification vnto it, making no mention of hope, charitie, or penance. Sometime it seemeth to geue the like preeminence to charitie, mentioning neither faith, nor any of the rest, sometime to hope, sometime to Baptisme or penance without the rest: somtime it promiseth rewarde of life euerlasting to faith

Note wel.

without mention of good workes: ſometime to good workes, ſaying nothing of faith: and yet is there no one of them meant to be excluded or left out. And therefore the godly reader wiſely meeke, and meekely wiſe, when he ſeeth life euerlaſting promiſed to euery one of theſe particularly, remembring that euery woorde of God is like true, ioyneth them al together, and truely beleueth, that to the perfiting of our Iuſtification and Saluation there is required grace, faith, the feare of God, hope, charitie, together with the Sacramentes of Baptiſme and penance, and alſo good workes, as hath ben ſhewed before.

A rule for the right vnderſtāding of the Scriptures.

It is not the manner of the holy Ghoſt, nor of the Catholike Church by affirming of one treweth, to deny or take away an other, but to ioine all trewth together. S. Paule the true and earneſt commender of faith, preached in Aſia publickly and priuately. *Teſtificans Iudæis atque gentibus in Deum pœnitentiam, & fidem in Dominum noſtrum Ieſum Chriſtum.* Proteſting to the Iewes and Gentiles penance towarde God, and faith in our Lorde Ieſus Chriſt, and there ioined he faith and penance together. S. Auguſtine often times teacheth, that we are ſaued by Baptiſme, intending not to exclude faith in ſuch, as be of perfecte age: and therefore ſaith: *Baptiſmus, qui ſemel adhibetur, per fidem mundat:* Baptiſme that is geuen but once, cleanſeth by faith. If this rule were marked and put in vre, we were at a point, not onely in this matter, but in many other.

*Act.* 20.

*Ser.* 30. *de ver. Do.*

Note.

The Euchites waying the greate commendation that Chriſt in the Goſpell geueth vnto praier, ſaying: *Petite & dabitur vobis.* Aſke, and it ſhalbe geuen you: *And what ſo euer thinges ye aſke in praier, beleue ye ſhall haue them,*

*Matt.* 7.
*Luc.* 11.
*Mar.* 11.

*and*

*and they shall come to passe vnto you*, were of opinion, that praier alone was sufficient for a Christian man. They did sette light by Baptisme, and said *the holy Sacrament of the altare did neither good, nor harme*. Whereby they tooke no fruit of theire praier, and loste the benefit of the Sacramentes, and theire owne saluation. Lette them be taught by this example, who seeming to extolle faith, make light not onely of hope, charitie and good workes, but also of the very Sacramentes ordeined by Christ for our saluation. Lette them take heed, leste beside losing the benefite of Christes Sacramentes, they be not founde voide of true faith also. For what faith can we say that they haue, or howe doo they beleue Christe, who being taught by his owne wordes *to be Baptized*, if they be Hethen, and by the wordes of S. Paule, and S. Peter, after Baptisme *to doo penance*, when they haue sinned, be carelesse to doo the one, or the other?

*Theodor. li. 4. here. fabul. et hist. eccle. li. 4. ca. 11.*

*Matt. 28. 2. Cor. 12. Act. 8.*

It hath ben declared before, that sinnes be forgeuen and we iustified by the Sacraments of Baptisme and penance. It hath ben shewed also, that faith is one of the partes of true penance, and therefore penance can not exclude faith, neither faith, if it iustifie, exclude penance.

In the 6. chapter.

In the 11. chapt.

For faith is either vnfained, liuely and profitable, such as S. Augustine termeth, *fidem Christianorum*, Christian mennes faith, or els it is naked and deade, such as bicause the Diuel may haue, he calleth, *fidem Dæmoniorũ*, the Diuels faith. The naked and bare faith iustifieth no man: for if it could, the Diuel might be iustified. The liuely and Christian mans faith beleuing al scripture to be true, and seing penance not only cõmended, but also cõmanded, can not passe it ouer, but by praier obteineth it, and so iustifieth.

*De fid. et oper. ca. 16*

*Iaco. 2.*

*Aug. de trinit. lib. 4. cap. 3.* Penance is the reuiuing of a ſowle that is dead by ſinne. *Anima Deo deſerente, moritur*, the ſoule dieth when God forſaketh it: *Reſuſcitatur per pænitentiam*: It is raiſed vp againe by penance. And bicauſe penance is the meane to receiue Goddes grace, Chryſoſtome ſaith, *that vppon contrition of harte, remorſe and confeſsion, God doth not onlygeue the healing of wounded, but maketh him a iuſte man that was before loded with innumerable burdens of ſinnes.* *Ho. 20. in Gen.*

*Conſtitu. Apoſt. lib. 2. ca. 23.* Seing therefore, the holy Ghoſt hath ſo prouided for vs, that as S. Clement ſaith, *the Church of God is our peace, and a quiet and calme hauen, vnto the which ſinners may be reſtored, by abſolution*: Seing alſo that Chriſt hath made that fauorable promiſe, ſaying, *whoſe ſinnes you forgeue, they be forgeuen them*: *Ioan. 20.* whereby as S. Auguſtine ſaith, *Per claues regni cælorum non dubitatur fieri remiſsio peccatorum*: *De adulter. cõiug. li. 2. ca. 9.* There is no doubte, but through the keies of the kingdome of heauen ſinnes be forgeuen: Lette no man preſume through Iuſtification by faith, to miſpriſe or contemne the Sacrament of penance. Lette no man leaue the ſure for the doubtefull and vncerteine. For as in caſe of neceſsitie men may enioy the inuiſible grace of God, without the viſible Sacramentes, ſo is not the viſible Sacrament to be diſpiſed when it may be had. *Aug. ſuper Leuiti. Quæſt. 84.* *Nam contemptor eius ſanctificari nullo modo poteſt*. For the diſpiſer of it can by no meanes be ſanctified inuiſibly. Faith can not onely iuſtifie no man, where the contempte of Chriſtes Sacramentes is, but furder, that very contempt maketh a man prophane and wicked, as S. Auguſtine ſaith. *Contr. Fauſt. lib. 19. cap. 11.* *Sacramentorum vis inenarrabiliter valet plurimum, & ideo contempta facit ſacrilegos: impiè quippe contemnitur, ſine qua nõ poteſt perfici pietas.* The vertue of Sacraments is of greate

greate and vnſpeakeable force, and therefore if it be diſpiſed, it maketh men profane and wicked. For wickedly is it diſpiſed, without the whiche godlines and pietie can not be perfited.

Seing then that the Sacramentes by the death of Chriſt haue that ſingular vertue whereby ſinnes be forgeuen, the paſsion of Chriſte applied vnto vs, our woundes and ruptures tied vppe and rowlled by them, as by medicinall bandes, without the whiche we coulde not atteine to perfecte health: how can it be ſaid, that faith alone can iuſtifie, or exclude the vertue of them in our Iuſtification?

VVhat is the trewe meaning of theſe wordes in the Scripture: *vve are iuſtified by faith*, or *ſaued by faith:* with other like.

## THE VII. CHAPTER.

BVT ſeing that all wordes of the Scripture be the wordes of God, writen by inſpiration of the holie Ghoſt, and therefore vndoubtedly trew, if Faith can not worke our Iuſtification without charitie and other vertues, howe is it then ſaied that, *the iuſtice of God commeth through faith of Ieſus Chriſt into al, and vppon al that beleue in him?* And in an other place. *By Faith God iuſtifieth the gentiles?* What is meant by theſe wordes of Chriſt? *He that beleueth in me, hath life euerlaſting. Thy Faith hath ſaued thee*, with many other like? Whereunto I anſwere. There be two cauſes why it is ſaied, through faith, and by faith we are iuſtified.

*Of faith Iuſtifing.*

Rom. 3. Galat. 3. Ioan. 6. Luca. 7.

Tvvo Cauſes vvhy faith is ſaied to iuſtifie.

To beginne with the firſt, Faith is the beginning of iustice, the roote of good workes, the foundation where-vppon godly life is builded: *Ex fide aũt ideo dicit iustificari hominem*, For this cause S. Paule saith a man is iustified by Faith, *not by workes, for that Faith is first geuen, whereby other which properly are called good workes (by the whiche men liue iustely) maie be obteined.* *Aug. de prædesti. Sanct. c. 7.*

Without the direction of Faith no man can liue well, nor doo good workes. *Nisi præcedat fides, vita bona sequi non poterit. &c.* vnlesse Faith goo before, good life can not folowe, *for what so euer a man shall doo with shewe of well doing, excepte it be done for pietie and duties sake towarde God, it can not be called righteouse nor good.* *Ianua & via in vitam fides est.* *Faithe is the gate and waie to entre into life.* Faith is the foundation whereuppon the whole building of a Christian and godlie life is laide. *Si autem Christus, proculdubio fides Christi. &c.* If Christe be the foundation, vndoubtedly the Faith in Christ is the foundation, *for by Faith Christ dwelleth in our hartes.* For that cause the Bisshoppes assembled at Magunce to reforme the state of the Churche, and to directe the people to a Christian and godly life, saide: *Initium actionis nostræ de fide esse decreuimus. &c.* We haue determined, that the beginning of our doing is of Faith, *whiche is the foundation of all good: for without Faith we can not please God. By Faith it is that we haue accesse to Christ.* Faith is a meane to obteine and gette our Iustification. *Iustificatio autem ex fide impetratur. &c.* Iustification is obteined by Faith. And by what meane, S. Augustine doth there expresse. *Per fidem impetratio gratia contra peccatum: Per gratiam sanatio animæ à vitio peccati.* By Faith grace is obteined against sinne, and by grace the sowle is healed of that is amisse by sinne.

*Aug. de fide & operib. cap. 7.* *Cyril. in Ioan. li. 4. cap. 9.* *1. Cor. 3.* *Augu. de fide & operib. c. 16* *Concil. Magun. cap. 1.* *Rom. 5.* *Ephes. 3.* *Aug. de Spiri. et Lit. ca. 29* *Aug. de Spiri. & Lit. ca. 30.*

Bicause

Bicause therfore Faith is the gate and entrie to life, the roote of good workes whereof all iustice taketh his beginning, the foundation whereupon godly life is builded, the meane to obteine Iustificatiō and good workes, without the which nothing pleaseth God, the Scripture saith, that by Faithe a man is iustified: for of Faithe it maie be saide: *Hæc porta Domini, iusti intrabunt in eam*. This is our Lordes gate, the iuste shal entre into it. *Psal. 117.*

And here the Reader must be aduertised, that by faith is vnderstanded the trewe Catholique faith, *whiche holdeth and beleueth onely that, that the Catholique Churche hath holden from Auncient time vniuersally. And what so euer it shall vnderstande to be brought in, afterwarde of any one beside or against all the holy, it accompteth that not to perteine to religion, but to temptation*. To this Faith is all promise made and preeminence geuen in the Scripture. This faith is the foundation of iustice. If any other be brought in contrarie or diuerse from this, *Nō est fides, sed perfidia*. It is not faith, but falsehod: not the foundation of iustice and gate of life, but the waie to destruction. For we sing in the Creede: *Vnlesse a man holde the Catholique Faith sounde and inuiolable, he shal without doubt be loste for euer.* The Catholike Faith. *Vincentius Lyrinēsis. Cyril. suprà. Symbol. Athan.*

Another cause why the Scripture so speaketh, is, that wheresoeuer it is said a man is iustified by faith: there is not meant a bare, naked, or solitarie faith, but that faith that worketh through Charitie. And therefore S. Augustine, where he saith, that faith is the foundation wherby Christe dwelleth in our hartes, immediatly after addeth these wordes: *Porrò fides Christi illa vtiq, &c.* But that *is verely meant the faith of Christ, which the Apostle determined* *Aug. Enchi. cap. 8. De fide & ope. ca. 14. Epist. 105. De spiri. et Lit. cap. 32. Aug. de fide et oper. c. 16.*

Iaco.2. *mined, that hath her working through Charitie. For it is*
Mar.1. *not the Faith of diuels, though they also beleue and tremble,*
Luca.4. *and confesse Iesus to be the Sonne of God, that may be taken*
Matth.8. *for the foundation: and why so? but bicause, it is not the Faith that worketh through Charitie, but suche as is wroong owt through feare. The Faith then of Christe, the Faith of Christian grace, that is to witte, the Faith that hath her working through charitie, if it be laied in the foundation, suffreth*
1. *none to perish:* by which wordes it appeareth, that Faith maie be without charitie, but suche a Faith can not make
2. Christ to dwell in vs. Againe, that Faith voide of charitie
3. is not the Christians, but the diuels Faith. Thirdely, that the Faith of Christ, the Christians Faith, and the Faith of grace is that which worketh through Charitie, and that is it that muste be laide for the foundation in al that shal not perish: And seing that no man will saie, that Faith can iustifie other then suche as is the faith of Christ, the faith of grace, the Christian, and not the diuels faith: it remaineth, that when it is saied in the Scripture, a man is iustified or saued by faith, we must vnderstand that faith onely that worketh through Charitie. Charitie maketh the difference betwene good men, and wicked diuels. Charitie is the cause, why a Christian man may be iustified by faith, and the diuell maie not. *Illa quippe fides est Christia-*
Aug. Epistola. 105. *norum, non dæmoniorum*: That whiche worketh through
Iacob.2. Charitie, is the Christian, and not the diuels faithe: *for*
Mar.1. *diuels also beleue and tremble: but doo they likewise loue? If*
Luca.4. *they had no belefe, they woulde not haue saied, thou arte*
Matth.8. *the Holie of God, thou arte the Sonne of God: had they loue, they woulde not haue saied, what haue we to doo with thee?* Other faith then this S. Augustine commendeth not, as able

able to iustifie: *Illa est laudabilis fides, ipsa est vera gratiæ fides, quæ per dilectionem operatur.* That is the praise worthie faith, that is the true faith of grace, whiche worketh through charitie. *August. serm. 13. de verb. Apostol.*

That faith it is that Christe requireth of vs, whiche if we haue not, we shal die in our sinne. They be his owne woordes: *If you beleeue not that I am, ye shall die in your sinne.* And *let vs not thinke*, saith Cyrillus, *that God made this threat onely vnto the Iewes*: *Eadem enim nos quoque manet damnatio si non in Christum fide per per dilectionem operante crediderimus.* For the like damnation remaineth for vs also, if we beleue not in Christ by faith that woorketh through charitie. To teache vs this difference of faith and beleeuing, Christe saith in an other place: *Qui credit in me sicut dicit scriptura, flumina de ventre eius fluent aquæ viuæ.* He that beleeueth in me, in such sorte as the Scripture saith, fluddes of liuely water shall flowe out of his belie. By fluddes of liuely water, as there S. Iohn saith, is meant the holie Ghoste, *which they should receiue that beleeued in him.* Christe said not, who so beleeueth in me, but he that beleueth in me as the Scripture saith: for that is the true pointing of the sentence, as *Theophilactus* noteth there. And who doubteth, but that the Scripture beside faith, teacheth vs also to loue Christe, to hope in him, to doe penance, to receiue his Sacramentes, and to liue godly? If no man then be iustified without the holie Ghoste, who powreth charitie into our heartes, seeing the holie Ghoste is geuen to suche onely, who beleue in Christe as the Scripture saieth, the Scripture bidding vs not onely to beleeue in Christe, but also to loue him, it foloweth that they onely be iustified, who haue faith

*Ioan. 8.* *Cyril. in Ioan. li. 5. ca. 23.* *Ioan. 7.* Note.

Theophil. ibi. in cap. 7. Ioan. working through charitie. *Multi enim se putant credere, sed non vt dicit Scriptura, &c.* For many thinke they beleue, but they beleue not as the Scripture saieth. *And so haue they folowed their owne sectes, such as all heretikes be: but he saieth, the riuers shall flowe out of his belie, that is the true faithful beleuer.*

Although this place alone might suffice, to teache the indifferent Reader, what faith it is that pleaseth God, yet do other Scriptures in sundry places put vs in minde, that a bare and solitarie faith sufficeth not. As Christe saied to Marie Magdalene: *Fides tua te saluam fecit*, Thy faith hath saued thee, so said he there of her also, *synnes be forgeuen her, bicause she hath loued much*. And what is that to saye, but that shee was saued by faith through charitie? Beside that, she shewed by her teares a greate penance, and by comming to Christ being so notable a synner shee declared a greate hope. The woman that was healed of the blooddy flyxe, had not onely a faith, but also so earneste hope, that shee trusted shee shoulde be whole, might she *but once touch the skyrte or hemme of Christes garment*. Christe commended in an other woman faith, but a great faith, saying: *O Woman great is thy faith, bicause*, saieth Chrysostome, *he sawe in her such a constancie and perseuerance that coulde not be Wearied.* And as S. Augustine saith: *He that looketh into the hart, sawe that shee Was chaunged and become a new Woman: and therefore Whereas he had before called her dogge, he saied not then: O dogge, but ô Woman, greate is thy faith:* Cyrill saieth, that *they be the faithfull Who by sincere faith are graffed in Christe as branches in the vine*. And to declare what he meaneth by sincere faieth, he saieth: *It is not inough for our sanctifi-*

Luc. 7.

Math. 9.

Math. 15.

Hom. 34. in Gene.

De fide & oper. c. 16.

In Ioan. li. 10. c. 16.

*ſanctification, vnleſſe we cleaue ſtyll faſte vnto Chriſte by charitie.* Oecomenius requireth in our Iuſtification a faith in deede: λέγω τὰρ ὄντι πίσιν: a true faith, ſuche as can not be in an vncleane man, a faith not only in aſſente, whiche reſteth in beleeuing trueth, but a faith in affection that ſtandeth in loue. S. Hierome ſaieth, that both in the woman that was healed, and in the petie captayne or Centener, *Deuota Deo ſuo anima approbata eſt.* A deuoute ſoule to their God was allowed, *ſuche a faith as is hardely founde in them that beleeue well. Be it vnto thee, ſaith God, according to thy faith: that ſaying would not I heare, for if it be done to me according to my faith, I ſhal periſhe. And yet ſurely I beleeue in God the Father, I beleeue in God the Sonne, I beleeue in God the holy Ghoſte.* By whiche woordes we vnderſtande, that S. Hierome thinketh it not inough to beleeue, but requireth alſo with faith a greate and earneſte deuotion, whiche can not be without a greate and earneſt loue.

*In cap. 2. Iacob.*

*Math. 9.*

*Aduer. Luciferianos*

S. Paule aduancing faith with ſingular commendation, and ſaying, that *al the Fathers were allowed and pleaſed God thereby*, commendeth that faith, wherewith not onelye charitie, but all other vertues were ioyned. *By faith Abel offered ſacrifice, Enoch liued godly, Noe feared God. Abraham obeyed God, forſooke his countrie, and offered vp his ſonne. Moyſes was content to ſuffer affliction, Raab receyued the meſſengers ſente to ſpie. By faith the holy did woorke iuſtice, ſuffred ſcorning, and whipping, yea chaynes and priſon, were ſtoned, cutte in peeces, and dyed by the ſworde.* Suche a faith doth S. Paule commende, a faith ioyned with religion and dutie towarde God, with feare of God, with obedience of Gods commandement, with pacience,

*Heb. 11.*

*Ambulauit cum Deo.*

with iustice, with suffring of al griefe and paine, yea death it selfe for Gods sake.

According to the same rule our Crede requireth *a sound and Catholique faith.* S. Augustine, *the faith of Christe, the faith of christian grace, a faith of Christian* men, not such as may be in Diuelles. Cyril, a *sincere faith.* S. Hierome, *a faith full of deuotion.* Oecumenius, *a true faith,* not onely in opinion, but in hearte and affection.

All whiche thinges are comprised by S. Augustine in these fewe woordes. It is the faith that hath her woorking through charitie, that maketh a iuste and a good manne. *Hæc est fides, ex qua iustus viuit:* This is the faith whereby the iuste man liueth, *this is the faith wherby men beleeue in him that iustifieth the wicked. This is the faith whereby vaunting and boasting is shut out. This is the faith whereby abundance and largesse of the holy Ghoste is obteined. This is the faith whereby they are saued, to whome it is saied, by grace ye are saued through faith. Finally, to conclude, this is the faith that woorketh through charitie.* In whiche woordes beside other thinges it is to be noted, that the faith whereby we are saued, and the faith whereby the iuste man liueth, is none other but the faith that worketh through charitie. Which vertue, saith Leo, *by her mixture and tempering, geueth life euen to very faith, whereby the iuste man liueth.* For the iuste man liueth by faith, saith S. Bede, *not by that faith that is vttered onely by confession of the lippes, but by that faith that woorketh through charitie.*

*Abac. 2. Rom. 1. August. de spirit. et. li. c. 32*

*Ephe. 2. Galat. 5. Abach. 2. Rom. 1.*

The true meaning of those vvoordes, *The iust mā liueth by faith.*

*Leo ser. 5. de collect. Bed. in die natal. Do. ad Sum. Miss.*

And thus may we truely vnderstande, what the Scripture meaneth, as often as it is said, by faith we are saued, or through faith we are iustified.

That

## That S. Paule teacheth not Iustification by onely Faith, excluding charitie, &c. And in what sense the Fathers sometime saie, Faith alone iustifieth.

### *THE VIII. CHAPTER.*

BVT yet this satisfieth not all men. For some thinke still we are iustified by faith alone, for that S. Paule saying, *We are iustified by faith*, and putting to it, *Without Woorkes of the Lawe*, semeth to them, to saie as much, as we are iustified by faith alone. And that opinion they inforce the more, bicause diuerse of the auncient Fathers haue vsed these woordes: *Faith alone iustifieth*. To the whiche I answere, that neither S. Paule, nor any of the Auncient Fathers euer meant it in that sense which they haue taken it, that is, to exclude from Iustification Charitie, hope, penance, or any vertue and gifte of God. S. Paule his wordes by them alleadged, be in the Epistles to the Romaines and Galathians. The Argument and intent of his whole Epistle to the Romains, as S. Augustine saith, is this: *Vt de ipsorum meritis nemo glorietur, &c*. That no man boast nor vaunt him selfe of the merite of his workes, *of Which the Israelites Were bolde to make their boaste that they serued the Lawe Which Was geauen them, and thereby had receiued the grace of the Ghospell as a debt due vnto their desertes, bicause they serued the lawe, for Which cause they would not haue the same grace geuen to the Gentils as vnworthy of it, vnlesse they Would receiue the Iewish Sacramentes.*

*An Obiection.* *Rom. 3. Galat. 3.* The Answere. *Aug. ad Simplicia. li. 1. qu. 2. Et in exposit. epist. ad Rom. inchoat.* Primas. *in Praefa. epist. ad Rom.*

The Galathians, to whome the Gospell had ben preached, were moued and solicited by Iewes, whose desire

*Aug. in Exposi. 4. ca. ad Gal.*

*Aug. in Exposi. 4. ca. ad Gal. Prima. in argu. ep. ad Galat.* *Rom. 4. Galat. 3.*

was to bring them to carnal obseruances of the Lawe, as though saluation laie in the same. To answere vnto bothe these, boasting of them selues, and of the woorkes of the law, and exacting them of other, as necessary to saluation, In bothe these Epistles S. Paule saith, *no man is iustified by the lawe*, proouing the same by Abraham, who was iustified before circumcision was commaunded, and long before the law was geuen, and therby doth barre and put of al workes of the Lawe from our Iustification, as nothing auailing towarde the same.

*August. de spirit. et. li. c. 29*

But what the woorkes of the lawe be, it is not a matter so plaine to all men. Beside the rites and ceremonies commaunded by Moyses, S. Augustine calleth all suche the woorkes of the Lawe, as a man presumeth to doe of him selfe, of his owne power and strength, without faith and the helpe of God: *Adhuc dubitamus, quæ sunt opera legis, quibus homo non iustificatur, si ea tanquam sua crediderit, sine adiutorio & dono Dei, quod est ex fide Iesu Christi?* Doe we yet doubt what the woorkes of the Lawe are, by whiche no man is iustified, if he take them as his owne without the helpe and gift of God, which cometh by the faith of Iesus Christe? These be the workes of the lawe, which in an other place he calleth also the iustice of the law: *Lege Dei proposita, &c.* When the lawe of God is laid before vs, *Who so euer is proud and thinketh he is able to fulfil it by his owne power and strength, if he do that the lawe commaundeth, not for the loue of iustice, but for feare of punishment: this man concerning the iustice of the lawe, is a man without blame.* In both places, he calleth al suche the workes of the lawe, and the iustice of the lawe, that a man doth of him self presuming of his owne strength without

*Serm. 15. de verb. Apostol.*

grace

grace and helpe of God. *Ex lege, quia in mandatis: sua tanq̃ de viribus suis:* It is the iustice of the law, bicause it is commanded. It is a mans own bicause it cometh as of his own strength. Now as S. Paul doth truly barre and shut out from the procuring of our Iustification al rites and ceremonies of the lawe, and also all morall workes, that we doe of our selues, without faith and helpe of God: So if a man would reason that he barreth likewise charity, hope, penance, and the Sacraments of the Church, bicause a man is iustified by faith without workes of the law, he should shew him selfe ignorant of the Scriptures and of S. Paules meaning. *Aug. ibid.*

These be no workes of the law. For not onely *charitie, ioy, peace, patience, mildenes, and faith*, but briefly al workes of charitie, when they be done by faith, by helpe of grace and the gifte of God, *are fruites of the holie Ghoste*, not workes of the lawe. *Lex spiritus & vitæ.* They be the law of the holie Ghoste, and of life, perteining not to the letter that killeth, but to the spirit that geueth life. *Ad prudentiam carnis terrendam. &c. When the workes of charity are written in tables to make the wisedome of the flesh afraied, it is the lawe of workes, and the letter that killeth the transgressour: but when charitie is powred into the beleuers heart, it is the lawe of faith and the spirit that geueth lyfe to the beleuer.* S. Augustine saith, woorkes that be done for feare onely, by commaundement of the law, are called the lawe of woorkes, and the killing letter: but when they be done by charitie, which through the holy Ghost is powred into our heartes, they be called the Lawe of faith, and geue life to the doers. They be called the lawe of faith, and workes of faith, bicause they are geauen by faith and with faith. *Per fidem impetratio gratiæ contra peccatum, &c.* By faith grace *Galat. 5.* *Rom. 8.* *August. de spirit. et lit. c. 17* *Aug. ibid. cap. 30.*

grace is obteined against sinne, *by grace the sowle is healed from sinne.*

Wherefore, when S. Paule saieth: *a man is iustified by faith without workes of the Lawe*, he saith nothing els, but that a man is iustified by grace, and not by him selfe. For as he saith here, *by faith a man is iustified*, so saieth he els where, *by grace yee are saued*: As he saith in this place, *non ex operibus legis*, not by woorkes of the lawe: So he saieth there: *Non ex vobis, Dei donum est*: Not by your selues, it is the gift of God. So doth he saie: *Abraham was not iustified by his workes*, he deserued not Gods grace and his Iustification by his owne doinges: he was not able to crake against God, nor to presume of him selfe. He had it not *secundùm carnem*, by flesh, and of him selfe: but by promise and by faith from God. And thus it appeareth plainly that S. Paule by Iustification of faith without woorkes of the Lawe, dothe not exclude charitie, hope, penance, nor any vertue or gifte of God geuen by faith, but onely barreth mannes owne presumption and pride, mannes owne doinges without God, with rites and ceremonies taught by Moyses. Otherwise, if it had ben his intent to exclude the giftes of God, vertues and workes of faith, we might saie with S. Augustiue: *Quomodo dicit Apostolus iustificari hominem, &c* How doth the Apostle saie, that a man is iustified *by faith without woorkes, seeing that he saith in an other place, that is the faith which woorketh through charitie: We nede not then set the Apostle Iames against Paule, but Paule him selfe against Paule.*

Rom.3. Ephes.2. Rom.3. Ephes.2. Rom.4. August. in præfatio. Psalm.31.

And this much may suffice concerning the right vnderstanding of S. Paules wordes, who as S. Augustine saith, If he should meane that faith alone iustifieth, he should not

onely

onely ſpeake againſt S. Iames, but againſt him ſelfe alſo.

For euen as God, when he ſaith, *Videte quòd ego ſim ſolus.&c.* See, that I am alone, *and there is none other God beſide me,* ſpake not the ſame in the perſon of the Father onely, meaning therby to exclude the Sonne and the holy Ghoſt, as the Arrians vnderſtoode it, but did exclude onely creatures, and all that is not God: in like manner, when it is ſaied, by faith we are iuſtified, there is no vertue or gifte of God barred: nothing is excluded, that is ioined and geuen with faith, but that onely is ſhut owt, whiche is repugnante, contrary or ſtrange vnto Faith. Deut. 32. A very apte ſimilitude.

That whiche I haue ſaied of S. Paule, ſerueth alſo for the trewe vnderſtanding of the auncient Fathers, who when they ſaie, Faith alone iuſtifieth, exclude ſome one thing, whiche is repugnante, or, in the ſenſe that they meant, not neceſſarie to Iuſtification. S. Baſill writing in the commendation of humilitie, ſaithe: *Hæc eſt perfecta & integra gloriatio in Deo.&c.* This is the perfecte and ſound boaſting in God, *when a man doth not vante him ſelfe of his owne iuſtice, but knoweth him ſelfe to be needy of trewe iuſtice, and iuſtified by onely Faith in Chriſt.* He barreth as S. Paule doth the preſumption of our owne iuſtice, boaſting and vanting of our ſelues, not hope, nor charitie, which be Gods giftes: which plainely to declare, a litle after he ſaith theſe wordes. *Quid extollis te, dic mihi? &c.* Tell me, why doſte thou extoll thy ſelfe, *as it were for thine owne good doinges, whereas thou ſhouldeſt render thankes to the geuer for his giftes?* Faith then iuſtifieth vs without our owne workes as of our ſelues, but not without charity and the workes which God hath prepared for vs to walke in. S. Ambroſe ſaith: *Sublatis omnibus neomenijs.&c.* Baſil. concio. de humilita. Epheſ. 2. In cap. 9. Epiſtola ad. Rom.

*nijs.&c.* Al the festiual daies of the new mone, *the sabboth day and Circumcision, the lawe of meates and offering of beastes taken away, faith alone is placed for our saluation.* He excludeth the rites and ceremonies of Moises, as S. Paule dothe, saying that faith alone without them saueth. The same answere serueth to the wordes of Chrysostom, who expounding the place of S. Paule, where he forbiddeth men to auoid Iewish fables, saith: *Si fidei credis. &c.* If thou credite faith *why bringest thou in other thinges beside, as though faith alone were not inough to iustifie: why doest thou subiect thy selfe to voluntary bondage, and put thy necke vnder the yoke of the lawe?* He saieth not, why doest thou match with faith, hope or charitie, but why doest thou put thy necke vnder the yoke of the lawe? And in an other place he saith: *vt iam neminem fugere possit. &c.* So that no man can now be ignorant, *but that it is declared by these wordes, that saluation euerlasting is geuen to men through faith, not by the workes of the lawe*: he saith by faith, and yet not alone. excluding onely the workes of the lawe.

*Hom. 3. in Epist. ad Tit.*

The Word, *Sola*, Alone, is not in the Greeke.

*Hom. 27. in cap. 8. Matth.*

Arnobius writing vppon the Psalmes, and reprouing the Nouatians heresy, who saied that such as were once christened, if they did fall afterwarde, coulde not be holpen nor restored againe by penance, hath these wordes: *Thou saiste that such as be not yet redemed and Christened, they through penance may attaine to pardon: we saie they obteine pardon by Faith alone. But suche as be redemed and christened come to enioye the mercy of their redemer, not by Faith alone bicause they haue already beleued, but by penance.* Of such as came to the Faith and desired baptisme, the Church required not seuere nor straite penance, such

*In Psal. 106.*

Baptisme is called redemption, bicause ther by vve be partakers of Christ his redemption.

as was

as was vsually inioined to sinners that after Baptisme fell againe, and therfore he saith such were pardoned by faith alone, that is to say, without that kind of sharpe penance. But how there was in them Faith alone, the Reader may knowe by that I haue saied in the eighth Chapter, where it is declared by *Iustinus Martyr, Tertullian*, and *S. Augustine*, that the custome of the Churche, as well before as after Arnobius his time, was to receiue none to Baptisme, but such as asked pardon of their former sinnes, promised a newe life, and for certaine daies before theire Baptisme, vsed fasting and praier: The like wordes, and in the like argumente vseth *Theodoritus*, saying: *Woundes that are made after Baptisme, are curable. Mary curable not by forgeuenes through Faithe onely, as once it was, but by many teares, weping and wayling, by fasting, praier and labour measured according to the quantitie of the sinne committed.* To these I will ioine S. Ambrose, bicause he agreeth with them in wordes and matter: *Gratia Dei in Baptismate. &c.* The grace of God in Baptisme *requireth not sighing or morning, or any worke, but onely a profession with harte*: And in that sense he saith: *Iustificati sunt gratis. They are freely iustified, bicause working nothing, nor making no recompence, they are iustified by Faithe alone thorough the gifte of God. Quemadmodum autem &c.* But howe *can it stretch or apperteine to the person of suche as doo penance, when he saith, Blessed they are whose sinnes be couered, sithe it is a matter well knowen, that penitente persones gette remission of their sinnes by labor and sighing?* Arnobius, Theodoritus, and S. Ambrose saie, that some men are iustified by onely Faithe, that is to saie, without penance: they saie it not of all men, but of suche as

*Ibidem.*
*Iusti. Mar.*
*Tertullia.*
*August.*
*Epito. Diuino Decreto. de pœniten.*
*In ca. 11. ad Rom.*
*In cap. 3. ad Rom.*
*In cap. 4. ad Rom.*

come newely to the Faith and be baptized. Furder their mening is not, that they are iustified without al penance, for then should they gainesaie Christes preaching, which was: *Pœnitemini, & credite Euangelio.* Repente and beleue the Gospell: and I haue shewed before, that trewe Faith can not be without penance: but they saie, in Baptisme such are iustified *without sighing or morning*, that is to say without sharpe and laboriouse penance, *as in the Churche they did who properly were called penitentes*, as S. Augustine saith.

*Mar.1.* In the 6. Chap. of this booke. *Ambros. supra.* *De fide & oper.c.26.*

Therefore, as for our selues to whom all this question muste be referred, being baptized in our infancie, when they saie, that suche as falle after Baptisme, can not be iustified by Faith alone, but by penance, They plainely saie, towching vs already baptised, that no man is nor can be iustified by Faith alone, and so by them is this question ended concerning vs.

Note. Faith alone.

But some man will say, howe may it be plainely vnderstanded, that by Iustification of faith onely, which the auncient Fathers seeme in wordes to affirme, their meaning was not to exclude and barre hope, charitie and workes of faith? To that they shal answere for them selues seuerally eche by their owne wordes. S. Basil asketh: *Quid est proprium Christiani?* What is the peculiar propertie of a Christian man? *fides per dilectionem operans:* faith that worketh through charitie. And toward the ende of the same chapter: *What is the propertie of a Christian man? that his iustice abunde in all pointes aboue the Scribes, and Pharisees according to the doctrine in our Lordes Gospel: What is the property of a Christian man? to loue one an other as Christ hath loued vs.* By S. Basil then faith alone is not inough to

*Sum. Moral.80. cap.22.* *Matth.5.*

make

make either a iuste or a good Christian man.

S. Ambrose declareth his meaning in sundrie places, but of many to take one he expresseth it in these wordes. *Sine fide impossibile est placere Deo &c.* Without faith it is impossible to please God, *but faith alone sufficeth not, it is necessary for faith to worke through charitie, and to vse conuersation worthy to be allowed of God.* Chrysostom saith. *Ne fideles sola fide, &c.* Bicause the faithful *should not truste they might be saued by faith alone, Christe speaketh of the ill mennes paines: so doth he moue the infideles to faith, and the faithful to good life.* And in an other place he saith. *Ad agenda opera festinemus, neque enim aliter saluari nos possibile, &c.* Let vs make haste to doo good workes, for otherwise it is not possible for vs to be saued.

In ca.4. epist.ad Hebre.

Hom.70. in Matt. cap.22.

Hom. in Gen.47.

Theodoritus in like manner saith: *Et post Seruatoris aduentum*, Euen after the comming of our Sauiour *all atteine not to saluation, but such as beleue and frame theire life according to his diuine Lawes.*

Epito. Diuino. Decre. de seruato incarna.

*Christ plainely teacheth*, saith Cyrillus, *that such as go away from him, whether it be, that they fall in faith, or in keeping of his commandements, shal not onely bring forth no fruit, but shall also suffer euerlasting fier.* And further he saith, *if onely faith were inough, the multitude of Diuelles should not perish.* Assure thy selfe good Reader, a whole booke much bigger then this treatie is, could not suffice to holde the sayinges of the auncient Fathers, like vnto these. But seing that *in the mouth of two, or three witnesses, standeth euery worde*: I may say either these witnesses suffise, or I know not what may suffise.

In Ioan. li.10.ca. 17.

Cyril. in Ioan. lib. 10. cap.18.

Matt.18.

The opinion is such as ought to be remoued out of all

 Chri-

*De grati.* Chriſtian hartes: which as S. Auguſtine ſaith, *hath none*
*& lib.ar-* *other grounde but the miſconſtruing of S. Paules wordes*, of
*bit.ca.7.* which he him ſelfe ſaith there: *God forbid, that the Apo-*
*ſtle ſhould be of that minde:* It is ſuch as no man can hold
for true, vnleſſe he wil make many and euident Scriptures
falſe. For grаunting it to be true that onely faith ſuffiſeth,
*Aug. de* *falſa erunt illa quæ obſcuritatem ambiguitatemque non ha-*
*fid.et ope.* *bent, &c.* Thoſe ſayinges of Scripture ſhalbe falſe, which
*cap. 15.* are neither darke nor doubtefull. *If I haue all faith, in ſo*
*1.Cor.13.* *much as I be able to remoue mountaines out of theire place,*
*and haue no charitie, I am nothing: What ſhall it auaile,*
*Iaco. 2.* *my bretherne, if a man ſay he hath faith, and haue no good*
*Matt. 19.* *workes, can faith ſaue him?* And alitle after, *if thou wilt*
*come to life, keepe the commandementes.* Theſe (ſaith S.
Auguſtine) with other there alleged, ſhalbe falſe.

Whiche inconuenience bicauſe no man can beare, I
will applie vnto faith touching our Iuſtification, the
*Chryſoſt.* wordes that Chryſoſtome vttered of praier. *Neque ſola*
*To.5.li.1.* *temperantia, &c.* It is neither temperance alone *that can*
*de orand.* *ſaue a man, if other vertues lacke, neither carefull prouiſion*
*Deum.* *for the poore, nor any other thing that is vertuouſely done:*
*but all muſte concurre and come together into our ſoules.*
*Marie praier is laied vnder all the reſte, as the roote and*
*foundation to beare them vppe:* Euen ſo it may be truely ſaid, faith is the roote of all good workes, and the
foundation that is laid vnder godly life. And yet can
neither faith, nor hope, nor charitie alone iuſtifie. All
muſt concurre and comme together into our ſowles, and
then is that excellent and diuine worke of our Iuſtification accompliſhed, and not otherwiſe.

Howe

## Howe Abraham was iustified. VVhat his faith was, and who be the true children of Abraham.

## *THE IX. CHAPTER.*

THE readiest and plainest waie to open matters doubtefull and to cleare that whiche is darke, is to teach by examples. Seing therefore the Scripture commendeth often vnto vs Abraham for an example and paterne of Iustification, and faith: *Attendite ad Abraham patrem vestrum:* Looke to Abraham your father, there is no better way for vs rightly to vnderstand that matter, then to consider how Abraham was iustified, and howe he atteined to that singuler prerogatiue to be commended by the holy Ghost, and called *the father of all faithful and beleuing, and inheriter of the Worlde*. The Scripture saith of him: *Credidit Abraham Deo.* Abraham beleeued God, *and it was accompted vnto him for Iustice*: but as Abraham was iustified by faith, whiche all menne confesse, so is it to be considered, what faith that was, whereby he was iustified, and so singulerly pleased God. *Primasius* saith: *Abraham quia credidit Deo, &c.* Bicause Abraham beleeued God, *it was accompted vnto him for iustice, and he was called Goddes frende. But this faith is so to be taken, that it be beleeued in heart, confessed in mouth, and garnisshed in workes*. And here it is well to be noted, that the Scripture commending Abrahams faith, saith not, Abraham beleeued there was a God, but: *Credidit Abraham Deo*: Abraham beleued God: that is, as Chrysostome saith: *Credidit dictis Dei*:

Esai. 51. Rom. 4. Gen. 15. Galat. 3. In cap. 11. epist. ad Hebræ. Iaco. 2. Hom. 31. in Gen.

He

Iaco.2. Mar.1. He gaue credit vnto Goddes wordes and sayinges. Many euill men, yea the Diuel him selfe beleueth that there is one God, but neither euill men, neither the Diuelles geue credite to God nor his wordes to obey them. And this is the difference, betwene the good and ill man, yea betwene a good man and the Diuel: the one beleueth the Psal.102. Scripture and obeieth it not, the other *is mindefull of Goddes commaundementes to doo them*. So doth the Scri- Eccl.32. pture teach vs to beleue: *In omni opere tuo crede ex fide animæ tuæ: hoc est enim conseruatio mandatorum. Qui credit Deo, attendit mandatis*: In euery worke of thine, beleue and vse the faith of thy sowle, for that is the keeping of the commaundementes. He that crediteth God, Eccl.33. geueth hede to the commaundementes. *The wiseman doth credite the Lawe of God, and the Lawe is true vnto him*. Then to credite God and the Lawe, is to beleue Goddes wordes to be true, and to obey the commandementes of God and the Lawe. For to him is the Law true, who doth not shewe by his life that he thinketh it false.

So did Abraham beleue and credite God in euery Gen.12. worke of his: God said vnto him: *Egredere de terra tua, &c.* Go out of thy coūtry, *from thy kinred from thy fathers house, and come into the lande that I shall shewe thee*. He Hebr.11. was in yeares, *he wente*, as S. Paule saith, *he knew not whither*, he might haue vsed many excuses, as a man lothe to leaue his natiue country, his kinred and frendes, which Chrysost. hom.31.in Gene. naturally all men loue. But as Chrysostome saith: *Nihil horum vel in mentem, &c.* He thought it not his parte so much as to take any of these thoughtes into his minde, but as a willing seruante obeied, at the onely bidding, and asked no curiouse question. And what was it that made him so to doo?

to doo? *Omnia leuia & facilia. &c. His loue that he bare towarde God, made all thinges appeare light and easy to him.* Chrysost. ibidem. This was Abrahams faith. To beleue God, that is, to credite his wordes, and through a singuler loue to obey his commandement. God promised him a childe, when both his wife and he by course of nature were paste hope of issue, *he beleued the promise hoping againe hope*. Many yeares passed before it was fulfilled, *his faith decaied not*, he still perseuered constantely beleuing it. God bid him offer in sacrifice his onely sonne whome so dearely he loued: without all douting or question asking he obeied the commaundement. *O religiosam animam, &c.* O religiouse sowle (saith Chrysostome) *O stronge hart and minde. O greate desier. O reason passing the nature of man.* He shewed not his faith onely in beleuing Goddes promise, but also in keeping his commandementes. *Credidit suscepturus filium. Credidit occisurus, &c.* He beleued when he shoulde haue a sonne, he beleued when he should kill his sonne. *In all pointes faithfull, in nothing cruell.* He had not onely faith and good beleefe, but, as Chrysostome saith: *Possedit iustus ille omnes virtutes:* That iuste man had all vertues. He noteth in him, *fortitude, magnanimitie, excellente faith, good and godly conuersation, singuler modestie, meruelouse dispisinge of riches.* Worthely is he called *the father of many nations: Sufficit enim vnus ille iustus vt omnes nos erudiat.* For that one iuste man is inough to teach vs all. What faith was in him, that beleued Gods promise concerning his issue against the course of nature? what obedience? who being but once spoken vnto, forsoke his countrie, his inheritance, his frendes and kinred? Yea was

Gen. 15. Rom. 4. Gen. 22. Hom. 47. in Gen. Aug. ser. 72. de tempo. Chrys. ho. 24. ad Hebre. Hom. 42. in Gen. Hom. 36. in Gen. Rom. 4. Gala. 3. Chrysost. hom. 36. in Gen. Gen. 15. Gen. 12.

Gen.22. content to forgo his owne and onely sonne? How constante hope that neuer mistrusted Gods promise, were
Rom.4. it neuer so long delaied? What charitie, almose, and ho-
Gen.18. spitalitie? who vsed to sitte at his dore to wait for straun-
Rom.4. gers, and Pilgrimes? What humilitie, who being inheri-
Gen.23. tor of the worlde bowed and kneled to the heathen peo-
Ibidem. ple of the land? what iustice, that would not take a graue to bury his wife in, before he had paied for the grounde?

This is our paterne, by comparing our selues with him,
Galat.3. we knowe whether we be the children of Abraham, and
Ioan.8. to be blessed with the faithfull Abraham or no. Christ said to the Iewes: *Si filij Abrahæ estis, opera Abrahæ fa-*
Cyril. Hierosol. Cateche. 5. *cite.* If yee be the children of Abraham, doo Abrahams workes: *Quemadmodum ille iustificatus est, & tu iustificeris.* As he was iustified, so be thou iustified.

And here it is to be noted, that God emong al his faithfull and holy, hath chosen him to be our example and paterne, who at his cōmandement forsoke his natiue countrie, kinred and inheritance, to teach vs thereby, that such
Note S. be the true children of Abraham, that deale with the world (when Gods honour or commandement so requireth) as he did with his country and inheritance.

Gen.12. God said vnto him: *Go out of thy countrie and kinred.*
Esai.52. He saith vnto vs: *Exite de medio eorum & separamini:*
2.Cor.6. Goo out of the middle of them, and departe from them.
Chrysost. Abraham with a sincere faith and minde, obeied the
hom.37. commandement: *hunc & nos imitemur:* Lette vs folowe
in Gen. him, *and in readie minde and heart, Let vs get out of the busines of this presente life* (especially when it draweth
Hebræ.11. vs from God) *and go into heauen.* Abraham knewe not
Rom.8. the place whether he should go: *We hope for that we see*

*not*

*not, and by patience looke for it.* By saith Abraham *dwelled like a stranger in the land of promise:* we are required like strangers and Pilgrimes, *to absteine from carnal desiers that warre against the soule:* God said to Abraham, *offer in sacrifice thy only sonne whom thou louest.* Christe saith vnto vs: *If a man come vnto me and do not hate* (that is to say, cā not be cōtent to leaue and to lacke for my sake) *his father and mother, wife and children, brothers and sisters, yea and his own life also, he cā not be my scholer. Discamus et nos obsecro a Patriarcha Dei credere dictis.* Let vs I pray you (saith Chrysostom) learne of the patriarch to credite Gods wordes.

Hebra. 11.
1. Pet. 2.
Gen. 22.
Luc. 14.
Hom. 36. in Gen.

The Prophet Esaie saith of Christ: *Dominus iudex noster, Dominus legifer noster, Dominus Rex noster ipse saluabit nos.* The Lord is our iudge, the Lord is our law maker, the lord is our king, he shal saue vs. He is then not only a promiser and sauiour, but he is also a iudge, a law maker, and a king. As a sauiour he redemeth and promiseth. As a law maker he appointeth orders. As a king he geueth cōmandementes. As a iudge he threateneth malefactors. Who so beleueth him as a sauiour, and beleueth him not as a law maker, as a kinge, and as a iudge, he beleueth one parte of Christ, but not the whole. Abraham beleued his promise *that in his seede all nations should be blessed,* wherein he tooke him for a redemer. He beleued him as a lawemaker, taking circuncision by his appointement. He beleued him as a king, leauing at his commandement his country, kinred and inheritance: he tooke him for a iudge, saying, *Qui iudicas omnem terrā, nequaquam facies iudicium hoc.* Thou that iudgest al the earth, wil not doo this iudgement. Let vs learne to truste his promise. He saith: *I will dwell emong them, I will walke emong them, I will be their*

Esai. 33.
Gen. 15.
Gala. 3.
Gen. 17.
Gen. 12.
Gen. 18.
2. Cor. 6.

Rom. 8. *God, and they shalbe my people: if God be for vs, who shall*
Ioan. 6. *be against vs? He that beleueth in me, hath life euerlasting.* Let vs beleue him as a Lawe maker, receiuing the Sacramentes and rites of the newe testament, as A-
Gen. 17. braham receiued circumcision: Let vs beleue his com-
Matt. 19. mandementes also: he hath said: *If thou wilte come to*
Ioan. 15. *life, keepe the commandementes, you be my frendes if you doo such thinges as I commaund you:* Let vs beleue his me-
Matth. 3. nasses and threateninges. He hath said: *Euery tree that beareth not good fruit, shalbe cutte downe and caste into*
Ser. 16. de ver. Do. *the fier. Non times ne te iudicet Deus? vbi est fides?* Arte thou not afraied saith S. Augustine, that God wil iudge thee? where is faith?

If we beleue his promises, and not his orders, not his commandementes, nor threateninges, that is, beleue him in some thinges, and discredit him in other: we be not the right children of Abraham, who was euerywhere, and in all thinges faithful, but rather bastarde sonnes such as the
Deut. 32. Scripture speaketh of, *infideles filij*, vnfaithful children.
De simpli. Prælato. S. Cyprian wil say vnto vs: *How can he say that he beleueth in Christ, who doth not that Christ hath commanded him to doe? or how shall he come to the rewarde of faith, that wil*
Basil. in consti. exercit. ca. 1. *not keepe the faith of the commandement?* S. Basill will say: *Nos fidem non habemus ipsi:* We beleue him not, *as one not able to reliue, we shunne to take vppon vs that good and light yoke of his: we shunne to entre into the kingdome of God by the narowe gate:* He beleueth not nor crediteth Christe, saith S. Basill, that fleeth his yoke, and will not entre by the strait gate. And yet he may beleue, that Christ is God and man, the Sauiour and redemer of the world: but he beleueth him not as Abraham did, louingly

and willingly to obey him. *Imitare fidem Abrahæ*. Folow Abrahams Faith, saith S. Basill. If a man imagine and frame vnto him selfe a new deuised faith, persuading him selfe assuredly and vndoubtedly, that all his sinnes be forgeuen in Christe and for his sake, for that *he hath taken our sinnes vppon him*, further assuring him selfe, that for this faithes sake he is *the Sonne and heire of God, and heire partener with Christe*, although he *neither suffer with him, to be glorified together with him, nor die with him, to liue together with him*, it may trewely be saied of such a one: *Credit Christum, nō credit Christo*: he beleueth that Christ is, but he crediteth not Christ: he hath a faith of his owne, but he hath not Abrahams faithe: for if he had, he would as well be contente *to crucifie the lustes and vices of his body*, as desire to liue with Christ: as well suffer, as reigne with him. *Fidelis sermo*: It is a trewe saying, *and by all meanes worthy to be imbrased, that Christe Iesus came into this worlde to saue sinners*. *Fidelis sermo*: It is also a trewe saying. *If we haue died with him, we shall liue with him, if we suffer with him, we shall reigne with him, if we denie him, he will denie vs, if we beleue not, he remaineth trewe, he can not denie him selfe*. Who so beleueth one of these Scriptures, and careth not for the other, he hath not Abrahams Faith, nor is his childe. For Abraham beleued God, that is, as Chrysostome saith: *Credidit dictis Dei*. Gaue credite to Goddes woordes, obeying and folowing them, not one, but all. Wilte thou knowe good Reader, what Abrahams Faith was, and how thou maiste be made his childe? Learne by example of him, whom trewth it selfe declared to be the trewe Sonne of Abraham.

*Basil. ibid.*
A nevve Faith.
*Esai. 53.*
*Rom. 8.*
*Gala. 6.*
*1. Tim. 1.*
*2 Tim. 2.*
Marke this vvel.

Zacheus standing before Christ, at what time he came into his house, saied: *Lo I geue the one halfe of my goodes to the poore, and if I haue deceiued any man in ought, I restore him fowre times as muche*, bicause he beleued the wordes of Christe, *Date elemosinam. &c.* Geue almes, *and all is cleane to you.* He said: *I geue the one halfe of my goods to the poore.* And bicause he beleued that *God hateth all vniust dealers*, he saied, *if I haue deceiued any man in ought, I rendre fower for one.* And beleuing these thinges, whiche to a carnall man seeme harde, and doing them so readily for Christe his sake, we doubte not but he beleued likewise all other pointes of Faith as readily. Whereuppon Iesus saied vnto him: *This daie health and saluation is come to this house, bicause he also is the Sonne of Abraham.* And how he was the Sonne of Abraham, S. Cyprian telleth. *Nam si Abraham credidit Deo.* For if Abraham credited God, *and it was accompted to him for iustice, doubtlesse he that according to Gods comandement geueth almes, doth credit God: and he that hath the trewe faith, keepeth the feare of God.*

*Luca 19.* *I sal. 5.* *Luca. 19.* *Cypria. de Elemos.*

Thus haue I shewed, that the Faith which was reputed vnto Abraham for iustice, was that faith whereby he did credite vndoubtedly, and obediently follow, the wordes of God, were they promises, or were they commandementes, as faithefull in the one, as faithefull in the other. By this Faith Abraham was made the Father of the beleuing: by this faith Zacheus was made the childe of Abraham: by the same rule, *Qui ex fide sunt, benedicentur cum fideli Abraham.* As many as be faithefull, by this Faithe, shal be blessed with the faithfull Abraham.

*Gala. 3.*

If all other Scriptures towching this matter were doubtefull and darke, yet might the example of these two men so men so plainely set forth in both Testamentes, suffice the meeke and godly Christian man trewely to vnderstande what apperteineth to Iustification.

That there is no contrarietie betwene S.Paule and S.Iames, concerning the doctrine of Iustification, and howe they are to be vnderstanded.

## THE X. CHAP.

BIcause S.Paule saieth: *Abraham was iustified by faith and not by workes:* And S.Iames writeth, that *Abraham was iustified by woorkes, and not by Faithe onely*, some haue thought ther was a contradiction imploied in the wordes of the two Apostles: but the holy Ghost, who ruled bothe their pennes, and is neuer contrary to him selfe, meante one thing in them both, and by them both vttered one trewth well agreing with it selfe. Rom.4. Iacob.2.

For the plaine declaration whereof it is to be vnderstanded, that our Iustification is compared *vnto a perfecte building, or vnto a fruitefull tree*. For as in building there muste be a foundation to beare vp the house, and the tree muste haue a roote owte of the whiche the leaues and fruite maie spring: and yet it is to no purpose to laie a foundation if a man builde nothing vppon it, neither is it inough in a fruitefull tree to haue the roote without branches, leaues, and fruite: euen so is there in our Iustification, as it were a foundation and roote, and a perfecte building and fruit. The foundation and roote is Faith, whereby *we haue accesse to God, and be made of* 1 Cor 4. Aug. in Præfa. Psal. 31. See the first Chap. of this treatie.

*wicked*

Rom.5. *Wicked rightuouse:* when I say, Faith, I meane not Faithe
Ephes.2. alone, but *accumpanied with charitie* as S.Paule doth. The
Gala.5. building vppe or fruite of our Iustification, is the continuance, increase, and perfection of iustice, whereby such as are once iustified, be made more iuste, and in the ende perfited in iustice, that is to say, saued: Of al which I haue saied sufficientely before.

Of the roote and foundation, which is the entrie and first degree of Christian iustice, S.Paule speaketh. Of thincrease and perfection S.Iames. S. Paule saith, *We are iusti-*
Rom 4. Iaco.2. *fied by Faith*, declaring what he meaneth by Iustification:
Rom.5. *Habemus accessum per fidem in gratiam istam.* We haue ac-
Ephes.2. cesse and comming to this grace throughe Faith. And when he saithe through faithe, he meaneth especially
Ephes.2. through grace and throughe mercie, whereby Faith is
Tit.3. geuen. *It was not for the workes of iustice, that we did, but through his mercy he saued vs.* All men are borne sinners, called when they be sinners, by grace called, by grace iustified, and made of sinners rightuouse. Before our Iusti-
In Præfa. fication, S.Augustine his wordes maie be saied to euery
Psal.31. one of vs: *Attenduntur opera tua: & inueniuntur omnia mala.* Thy workes are loked on, and they be founde all
Rom 6. euill. *If God shoulde rendre vnto these workes that is due, he should condemne thee. For the wages of sinne is death.*

Workes done vvithout Faithe.

So was neither Abraham, nor any man iustified by workes: Neither Abraham, nor any other could deserue Iustification by his workes. For workes done without Faith, and before God geue his grace in some degree, deserue not at Gods hand either grace or reward of life euerlasting. And thus do wee see, in what sense S.Paule saied, *Abrahā was iustified by faith, and not by workes.* He was first called

called by mercie, and by grace, without anie deserte of his woorkes going before. The like he saith generally of al men, that by *grace they are called, and by faith haue accesse to God*, and be planted in Christe, and so iustified by faith, and not by woorkes.

*Rom.5.* *Ephes.2.*

But here let the Reader take hede that he deceiue not him selfe. For as before the grace of God, no man is able to doe any woorke good and profitable towarde the life euerlasting: so as many as are called, receiued to Gods fauour, and iustified, be made able and *meete to doe all good woorkes*. And as God calleth al men without iustice and holines: So doth he call them *to serue him in iustice and holinesse*. And as he found al men of them selues without good workes: so did he suffer, *to cleanse vnto him selfe a people that shouldfolowe good woorkes*. And suche good woorkes, being *the fruites of the holie Ghoste*, woorkes of faith, *done in God*, God working in man, and *man working togeather with God*, through the bountiful and liberal promise of God, are rewarded with increase of grace and iustice here, and in the life to come with perfection of iustice, that is, life euerlasting. And bicause the Scripture calleth *increase of iustice Iustification*, S. Iames saith: *Abraham was iustified by workes*, that is to saie, made more iust then he was, strengthened and increased in iustice by woorkes. In this sense he saith: *you see that a man is iustified by woorkes, and not by faith onely.*

Of vvorks don vvith faith, and after God hath geuē his grace. *2. Timo.3.* *Luc.1.* *Tit.2.* *Galat.5.* *Ioan.3.* *1.Cor.3.* *Apoca.22* *Ecclес.18.* See the 12 Chapt. of the firste booke. *Iacob.2.*

And thus saith S. Paule truely, a manne is called to iustice, hath accesse to God, and is made of wicked righteouse by faith deseruing it not by woorkes. And S. Iames as truely saieth: A man is iustified by woorkes, that is, a manne alreadie iuste, is by woorkes made more iuste, ſtrengthened and increaſed in iuſtice.

Oecom. in ca. Iaco. 2 *There is faith*, ſaith Oecumenius, *that requireth no workes that goeth before Baptiſme. And there is faith that muſt be coupled with good woorkes: and that is faith after Baptiſme, after whiche ſenſe certaine of the Greeke Fathers* (ſaieth he) *understoode S. Paule to ſpeake of faith before Baptiſme, which bringeth a ſinner to Chriſt, and iuſtifieth him without reſpect of any woorkes going before, and S. Iames to ſpeake of faith which is in a Christian man after Baptiſme, which muſt be ioyned with good workes, as Abrahams faith was, or els iuſtifieth no man: Grace goeth before,* ſaith S. Auguſtine, *but good woorkes folowe.*

Aug. ad Simpli. li. 1. quæst. 2. Auguſt. ad Simpli. ib. de fide. & oper. c. 14 Auguſt. ſer. 61. de ver. Dom. Epheſ. 4.

Euerie man that wil be ſaued, muſt be made *a member of Chriſt, whiche is done through faith, hope, and charitie:* and of this incorporation ſpeaketh S. Paule: but it is not inough for vs to be made members of Chriſt, vnles being *knitte in the bodie, we increaſe in all thinges in Chriſt, who is our heade.* Of this increaſe and growing, ſpeaketh S. Iames: It is not inough for vs to be called and iuſtified, we muſt alſo *be glorified*, and that ſhall not be, vnleſſe we be *conformed and made like vnto the Image of Chriſt by godly lyfe*, which S. Iames ſpeaketh of.

Rom. 8.

Al this is compriſed in our perfit Iuſtification. As it is neceſſarie for our ſaluation, that we be made members of Chriſt (which S. Paule calleth our Iuſtification) ſo is it neceſſarie for the ſame end that we do good workes, which S. Iames calleth our Iuſtification. *If Abraham had offred his ſonne without faith*, ſaith S. Auguſtine, *the worke had nothing auailed him, what ſo euer it were. If he had kepte his faith and not offred his ſonne when God bad him, his faith without woorkes had ben dead, and ſhoulde haue remained*

In præfat. Pſalm. 31.

like

*like a roote barren, and drie without fruite.*

When S. Paule had taught that *we are iustified by faith*, meaning thereby as hath ben declared: Suche as vnderstode him not, thought he had said, faith had ben sufficient for a man though he liued yl, and did no good workes. *And bicause this opinion was then sprong vppe, the other Apostles, as S. Iames, S. Peter, S. Iohn, and Iude in their Epistles, directed their intent, specially againste the same, earnestly affirminge, that faith without woorkes auaileth nothing.* So did S. Peter exhorte menne to pietie, and good conuersation against the comming of Christe, warninge them, that there were many thinges in S. Paules Epistles, *darke and harde to vnderstande, which the vnskilfull and vnstable did peruerte to their owne damnation:* sayinge further, that *who so lacketh good conuersation, is blinde and gropinge with his hande.* Therevppon did S. Iames call him *a vaine manne that thoughte faith without woorkes mighte saue him*, and called faith without woorkes, a deade faith, and the Diuelles faith. Therevppon didde S. Iohn speake as muche in the commendation of Charitie, as S. Paule had donne of Faith: saying: *He that loueth not, remaineth in deathe:* not that these Apostles did teache contrary to S. Paule, but bicause that S. Paule was misconstrued: Their preaching was one: For as S. Paule dothe saie, *by faith a manne is iustified, and by grace are ye saued, not of your selues:* So saieth S. Iames: *Euery good thinge that is geauen, and euery perfite gifte commeth from aboue.* And seeing that Faith, Hope, Charitie, and good woorkes be the giftes of God and the fruites of grace, S. Iames saying that we *are iustified by woorkes*, disagreeth not with S. Paule,

[Margin notes: Aug. de fid. et oper cap. 14. — 2. Pet. 3. — 2. Pet. 1. — Iacob. 2. — 1. Ioan. 3. — Rom 3. — Ephes. 2. — Iacob. 1. — Ephes. 2.]

Ephes.2. that saith *we are saued by grace*: And when S. Iohn saieth: 1.Ioan.3. *charitie commeth of God, and we knowe we are translated from death to life, bicause we loue our brothers*, he saieth no Galat.5. more then S. Paul doth, that *in Christ Iesu neither circumcision, nor to be without circumcision auaileth aught, but faith which worketh through charitie*. So did S. Paule, S. Peter, S. Iames, and S. Iohn, being mooued to speake by one spirit, agree in one minde, concerning our Iustification. S. Paule commendeth the foundation, roote, and beginning of it. S. Iames th'increase, the fruite, and perfection of the same, without the which, the foundation should be voide, and the roote barren and drie.

Iacob.2. Galat.3. God graunte vs to beginne with Abrahams faith, and to increase with Abrahams woorkes: that faith may ioyne with our woorkes, and by woorkes our faith may be perfited, that we may be blessed with the faithfull Abraham.

## That Faith alone without good woorkes saueth not. And what it is to be iustified freely by grace.

## THE XI. CHAPTER.

BY this it is euidently declared, that as faith in the beginning of our Iustification and comming to Christe, excludeth not hope, charitie, penance, nor baptisme: so in our continuance, and growing in Christe, and saluation, it excludeth not good woorkes, but must haue them ioyned

ioyned with it, as time and oportunitie may ſerue the beleuer to do them: or els the hope of his ſaluation is preſumptuouſe and vaine.

For if *Abrahams faith, excepte he had offered his ſonne, when he was byd, ſhould haue ben deade lyke vnto a baren and withered roote*, as S. Auguſtine ſaith, he being the example and paterne of our Iuſtification: what can we looke for, if we haue faith and care not to doo good woorkes, which God commaundeth? *He that heareth my wordes, and doth them not, ſaith our Sauiour, ſhalbe lykened to a foole that hath buylded his houſe vpon the ſande.* They are the dooers, not the knowers, whom he calleth happye. *If you knowe theſe thinges, you ſhalbe happie, when ye doo them. They are not the hearers of the lawe, that are iuste before God, but the dooers ſhalbe iustified.* If faith woulde ſerue without good workes, they ſhould not be reiected, who ſhal ſay at the daye of iudgement: *Lorde in thy name we haue preached, in thy name we haue caste out diuelles, and in thy name we haue done many greate wounders*, whiche can not be done without faith. Neither ſhoulde the fiue fooliſhe virgins be ſhutte out at the mariage: and therefore ſaieth Cyril: *Trust not vppon that thou haste a lampe onely, but keepe it burning: truste not vpon this alone that thou haste faith, but keepe thy faith burning, that thy lighte may ſhyne before men through good workes, leſte for thy ſake Chriſte be blaſphemed.* And a litle before: *Howe ſhall we gette*, ſaieth he, *into the kingdome of heauen? I was hungry, ſaieth Chriſte, and thou gaueſte me meate to eate. Learne the way, for here needeth no allegory: If thou doo theſe thinges, thou ſhalt reigne, if thou do not, thou ſhalt be condemned: beginne therefore nowe to doo theſe woorkes*,

*Auguſt. in præfation. Pſal. 31.*

*Math. 7.*

Ioan 13.

Rom. 2.

*Math. 7.*

*Math. 25.*

Cyril. Cateche. 15.

Leo. Ser. 3. de Epiphan. *and continue in faith: by right faith and good workes we attaine to the kingdom of God,* saith Leo. *Factis, non verbis operandum, &c.* We must worke by deedes, not by woordes, saith S. Cyprian, *for the kingdome of God standeth not in talke, but in vertue. Omnes mali Catholici, &c.* Al euil Catholikes *confesse Christ in wordes, and deny him in deedes: therfore be not ye as men carelesse bicause ye haue faith, ioyne good life to right faith.*

Cypria. ad Quiri. lib. 3. cap. 96.

Aug. Ser. 31. de ver. Apost.

And to vnderstand the more plainly, what iustice it is, to haue faith without good workes, let vs take the aduertisement of S. Augustine. Christ said: *Nisi abundauerit iustitia vestra, &c.* Vnlesse your iustice be more abundant *then is the Scribes and Pharisees, ye shall not entre into the kingdom of God: Iustitia eorum est dicere, & non facere. &c.* Their iustice is to say, and not to do, *and hereby he would haue our iustice surmount and be more abundant then theirs is both to say and to do. If that be not, there shalbe no entrye into the kingdom of heauen.* S. Augustine maketh this difference betwene the Pharisee and the good Christian man: The Pharisee saith wel and doth it not, he beleueth, and worketh not, the good Christian man doth both.

August. de fid. et ope. cap. 26.

The Phariseis iustice.

If it be true that the Scripture saith: *faith without workes is deade, Quousq; falluntur, qui fide mortua sibi vitam perpetuam pollicentur?* How longe wil they be deceyued, that promise them selues euerlasting life by a faith that is deade? But here it may be said: *we are iustified freely and by grace. And if it be by grace, then is it not by workes, otherwise grace is not grace.* I answere: We are called to faith, reconciled, planted in Christe and so iustified, by grace without respecte of anye woorkes going before, as hath bene saied: So saith S. Ambrose, *Iustificati sunt gratis &c.* Men

Iacob. 2.

August. de fid. et ope. cap. 14.

Rom. 3.

Rom. 11.

In the 10. Chaptre.

Ambro. in cap. 3. ad Rom.

&c. Men are iustified freely, *bicause woorking nothing, nor making no recompence they are iustified by faith alone, through the gifte of God.* He calleth the gifte of God our calling ad comming to faith, and our Baptisme, which as he saith in an other place, *requireth not sighing or moorning, or any woorke but onely a profession with the harte.* In the same sense saieth S. Augustine: *Per ipsam gratiam iustificatur gratis, id est, nullis suorum operum precedentibus meritis:* By grace is a synner iustified freely, that is to saye, no merites of his owne woorkes going before: And note that he termeth his owne workes, and workes going before. By his owne woorkes he vnderstandeth suche as a man dothe hym selfe, without Goddes helpe. He calleth suche woorkes going before, as a heathen or synnefull man dothe, before he hath receyued the grace of God: withoute these woorkes, S. Paule saieth a man is iustified freely, and by grace: that is to saye, *called to faith, planted in Christe, and made of wicked rightuouse.*

Ambro. in cap. 11. ad Rom.

August. de spirit. & lit. ca. 10.

What is to be iustified freely.

Note

But how is the iust man made more iuste and iustified yet? for so must he be, or els he loseth his iustice. How is he saued? Verely by grace, and yet not without good workes: for of them that haue receyued the faith and be iustified, it is saied: *Reddet vnicuique secundùm opera sua.* God shal render vnto euery man according to his workes. Howe then doth S. Paule saye? *Gratia Dei vita æterna.* Euerlasting life is the grace of God. Howe may these twoo stande together, a man to be saued by grace, and yet by good woorkes? I answere with S. Augustine: They stand well together: *Lyfe euerlasting is the grace of God, and lyfe euerlasting is geuen as a rewarde to good woorkes:*

Rom. 2.

Rom. 6.

Obiection

Answvere.

August. de gratia & lib. arbit. cap. 8.

*bicause*

*bicause our good woorkes perteyne to the grace of God:* that is to say, be the grace of God: and so being saued by good woorkes, we are saued by the grace of God: the woordes of S. Augustine be these: *Ipsa vita æterna, quæ vtique in fine sine fine habebitur, & ideo meritis præcedentibus redditur, tamen quia eadem merita quibus redditur, non à nobis parata sunt per nostram sufficientiam, sed in nobis facta per gratiam, etiam ipsa gratia nuncupatur, non ob aliud nisi quia gratis datur, nec ideo meritis non datur, sed quia data sunt & ipsa merita, quibus datur.* The very life euerlasting, whiche in the ende shalbe had without ende, and therefore is rendered vnto merites that go before, yet bicause the same merites, whereunto it is requited, were not prepared of vs by our owne habilitie, but made in vs by grace, euen it selfe is called grace, for none other respecte, but bicause it is freely geuen. And yet it is geuen to merites, bicause the very merites them selues, whereunto it is geuen, were also geuen. The like resolution he hath at large in his booke intituled of grace and free wil.

*Aug.epist. 105.*

Merites.

*Ca.8.&.9*

So is it true concerning the entrye and beginning of our Iustification, that *we are iustified freely by grace without any woorkes going before*: for our workes before grace coulde not be good. And in the continuance, and perfyting of iustice, whiche is life euerlasting, we are also iustified and saued freely by grace, and yet not without woorkes, bicause our workes be not onely made good by grace, but be also them selues the very grace of God.

*Rom.3.*

Note Wel

And here let the Reader learne of S. Ambrose, and S. Augustine, what it is, truly to be iustified, freely and by grace to the commendation of mercye whiche God geueth

ueth, not to the derogation of good workes which God alſo geueth.

Wherefore if faithe withoute good woorkes can ſaue no man, that hath tyme to doo them, as hath benne proued, it is no where true (as they meane it) that faithe alone iuſtifieth. It is not true in the entry of our Iuſtification and firſte comming to Chriſte, that faith alone, without hope, and charitie iuſtifieth. If it were, then might the Diuel be iuſtified, *who beleeueth, but neyther hopeth, nor loueth*: then ſhoulde this Scripture be falſe: *If I haue all faithe, and haue no charitie, I am nothing.* It is not true in the continuance and increaſe of our iuſtice that faith may ſerue without good workes: for if it mighte, then were all the Scriptures falſe, whiche a lytle before I alleaged. It ſhall not be in the perfyting of our iuſtice and ſaluation, that faith alone may ſaue: for then ſhoulde it be falſe, that *God ſhall render vnto euerie man according to his woorkes*: then were the ſentence, that God ſhall geeue, falſe, wherein he ſhall ſaye: *Come vnto me you bleſſed of my Father, receyue the kingdome prepared for you*. And he will ſhewe the cauſe, for that they haue done the woorkes of mercie there rehearſed. But bycauſe neither all theſe Scriptures, nor anye one ſyllable of them can be falſe, therefore it is falſe, that fayth alone iuſtifieth, meaning by fayth alone, to ſhutte out eyther hope, charitie, penaunce, the holye Sacramentes, or vertuouſe life, and good workes, from our perfyte Iuſtification.

The iuſtification of faith alone.

*Iacob. 2.* *Aug. Enchi. cap. 8.* 1. Cor. 13. *Math. 7.* *Ioan. 13.* *Rom. 2.* *Math. 25.* *Rom. 2.* *Matt. 25.* *Chryſoſto. Hom. 41. in Gene.* *Auguſt. Serm. 49. de verb. Dom.*

## VVhat they were, who in sundrye ages haue taught, that men should be saued without good workes.

## THE XII. CHAPTER.

IF nothing els could make vs think, that godly life were necessarily required in a Christian man, and workes of faith a greate and singular helpe to the atteyning of our saluation, the diligente practise of the Diuel were sufficiente to make vs beleue it: who beside his particular trauayle and persuasion whiche he vseth seuerally with euery man to turne him from wel doing, hath also in sundry ages moued such as by his sleyghtes he coulde abuse, to teach and openly persuade in derogation of good workes, that the same were not auayleable, or not necessary for a Christian mannes saluation.

*August. de fid. & ope. cap. 14. De prædest. sanct. cap. 7. Euseb. Ecclesi. histo. lib. 2. ca. 1 & cap. 13. Theodore. here fabu. compen. lib. 1. Iren. li. 1. cap. 20.*

When S. Paule was most diligent to sowe the good seede teaching the right faith of true Iustification, the Diuel was as busie to intermengle his cockle and darnel emong it, making men that vnderstode not S. Paule, beleue, *that he sayde it was sufficiente for a man to haue faith, though he lyued yll, and dyd no good woorkes*: Symon Magus who was taken for a God, taught his followers, *to care litle for the Prophetes, nor to feare the threatninges of the lawe, but bad them like free men to doo what them lysted, for they shoulde atteyne saluation, not by good doing, but by grace*. Whereupon *suche as were of his secte, boldelye gaue them selues to all luste and intemperate life*.

Carpo-

Carpocrates ſaied, *men ſhould be ſaued by faith and loue, as for all other thinges, they were of them ſelues indifferent, and by opinion of men ſometyme were taken for good, ſometyme for yl, but nothing was naturally euill.* Theodo. ib. Iren. li. 1. cap. 24.

Valentinus and his ſcholers ſay, *they neede no works, for that, knowlege may ſuffice to ſaluation,* and therefore, *ſuch as be emong them moſte perfite, without all care, and feare, doo what ſo euer is by Gods lawe forbidden.* Theod. vbi ſuprà. Iren. li. 1. cap 1.

It is ſaied of Eunomius, that *he was ſo farre an enemy to good conuerſation, that he plainely auouched, no man ſhoulde take hurte by any ſinne what ſoeuer he committed or continued in, ſo that he were partaker of the faith that he taught.* Auguſt. de here. ad Quodvult De. ca. 54.

Euen in S. Auguſtines tyme th'enemy of good life perſuaded carnal and diſſolute men to think, that *liued they neuer ſo il, continuing in great ſinne, and not ſo much as profeſſing amendement, yet if they beleued in Chriſte and receiued his Sacramentes, they ſhould be ſaued.* Note. Auguſt. de fid. & ope. cap. 1. & cap. 27.

But as the ſerpente in all theſe tymes wente aboute *by his craſte to ſeduce*, whome he coulde, ſo did *not the holy Ghoſte withdrawe his care and helpe from the Churche,* mouing at the firſt S. Peter, S. Iames, and S. Iohn to redreſſe by their Epiſtles the errour, which vnſtable heades had falſely gathered of S. Paules true preaching: and afterwarde inſpiring the learned Biſihoppes of euerye age to note and condemne the heretiques aboue named: moued alſo S. Auguſtine againſte the corrupte opinion of ſundry in his age to write this learned Booke, *Of faith and woorkes*, whiche is delyuered thee herewith, to put thee in remembrãce of the enemies craftes, and ſleightes. For as *by enuye of hym, deathe came into the woorlde,* 2. Cor. 11. Ioan. 17. 18. Rom. 5.

 ſo by the

so by the same enuye to turne Christian men from life
Ephes.2. euerlasting, he hath gone aboute in sundrye ages and yet doth, to pul from them good workes, which *God hath prepared for vs to walke in.* His desyer is specially to take from vs faith and the professing of Christe, but bicause he dareth not attempte that by playne and open mea-
Leo. ser. 4 de collect. nes: *Sciens Deum non solùm verbis: &c.* Knowing that God *is denyed, not onely by woordes, but also by deedes, he*
Note. *hath taken charitie from many men from whom he could not take awaye faith.* He vnderstandeth to well, that as charitie is the life and strength of faith, so pulling awaye the one, he shalbe able, either to drawe the other after, or els to make it deade and vnprofitable to him that keepeth it. Which if he may obteyne, and make vs beleue that faith alone iustifieth, taking away hope, charitie, penance and the vertue of Christes Sacramentes from woorking our Iustification, and good workes, from helping our saluation: what doth he els but bring the Gospel, which S. Paule cal-
Rom.1. leth *the stronge and mightie power of God*, to a naked and bare name?

Therefore seing we knowe his slyghtes, and haue lear-
2.Cor.2. ned them not only by report of other ages, but also by the lamentable experience of our owne, let vs to resiste him
Ephes.6. *put on al the whole armor of God, that we may be able to*
1.Thess.5. *stand against him that lyeth in wayt for vs.* Let vs not only take in hande for our defence, *the buckler of faith*, but also to saue the whole body, *put on the Iacke of faith and charitie*, and take *for an helmet hope of saluation*, not lea-
Ephes.6. uing of the *breaste plate of iustice, nor the gyrdle of truth.* For he that goeth to that fraye, hauing but a buckler, maye take a deadely wounde, for lacke of a helmet or breast

breastplate : and if he so doe, he may be founde giltie of his owne death, bicause he was warned to arme him selfe in all partes, and to put on a complete harnesse.

The cause whye good woorkes are donne, and that they are rewarded in this life with increase of grace, and in the worlde to come with life euerlasting. And why they be so rewarded.

## THE XIII. CHAPTER.

AS I haue shewed that good workes must necessarily be done of such as wil be saued: so wil I now declare for what ende they should be done, and what fruite and profite they bring to the doers. *Vt curent bonis operibus praesse qui credunt Deo.* To the intent that suche as beleue God, may haue a care to be chiefe doers of good woorkes. Tit. 3.

The holie Ghost saith of them: *Haec sunt bona & vtilia hominibus.* They be good and profitable for men. If we aske to what ende, he saith: *Pietas ad omnia vtilis est, promissionem habens vitae quae nunc est, & futurae* : Godlinesse is profitable to al purposes, hauing promise of the life that nowe is, and the lyfe to come. In this life godlinesse hath promise to directe faith and leade her to the vnderstanding of the Ghospell. *If a manne will doe his will that sente me*, saieth Christe, *he shal knowe of my doctrine, whether it be of God, or I speake of my selfe.* Good woorkes make faith perfite. *Thou seest*, saieth S. Iames of Abraham, *that faith was ioyned with his woorkes, and by his woorkes faith was perfited.* They confirme and

Tit. 3.
1. Tim. 4.
1.
Ioan. 7.
Iacob. 2.
Eccles. 7.
2.
3.

 streng-

4. ſtrengthen charitie. *Be not lothe to viſite the ſicke, for*
Ecclеſ.7. *by ſuche doinges ſhalte thou be made ſtrong in loue.* Good
woorkes breede in vs a ſtronge hope and affiance in God.
Tobi.4. *Almes ſhall be a greate affiaunce before God the higheſt,*
*vnto all that doe it.* He ſaieth not, it ſhall be onely a declaration of faith before menne, but a greate affiance be-
1. Tim. 3. fore God. *Deacons that ſerue well, gette them a good degree, and muche affiance in faith, whiche is in Chriſte Ieſus.*
Whereby we vnderſtande, that good workes do not onely nurriſhe hope, but alſo ſtrengthen faith. And as S. Au-
Ser.16. de ver. Apoſ. guſtine ſaith: *Quæ ſpes, niſi de aliqua conſcientiæ bonitate?* What hope can there be, but vppon ſome goodneſſe of conſcience? So a conſcience vſed and confirmed in well doing, is full of affiance and hope. S. Paule ſaieth to the Hebrewes, who had ben charitable to ſuche as were imprisoned, and alſo loſte their owne goodes for Chriſtes
Hebr.10. ſake: *Loſe not your confidence and affiance which hath great rewarde.* He ſaith, that their good woorkes had not onely bredde a ſtronge hope and affiance to them, but alſo that the ſame ſhould haue a great rewarde.

And here let the Reader learne, how ſtrong hope and affiance in God is to be gotten. Prayer is but one of the woorkes commended by Chriſte, of which Chryſoſtome
5. Chryſoſt. Tom.5. de orād. Deū ſaith: *vitam piam oratio conciliat: conciliatam auget.* Prayer bringeth a godly life, and increaſeth it when it is gotten: faſting, watching, and prayer, make vs ſtande and perſeuer in goodneſſe, and defende vs from yll. *Hæc ſunt no-*
6. Cyprian. lib.1.ep.1. *bis arma cœleſtia, &c.* Theſe be vnto vs heauenly armour *that make vs ſtande and perſeuer ſtrongly, theſe be ſpirituall municions and weapons geauen of God, whiche defende vs.* Almes, an other of the workes which Chriſte commendeth,

deth, is a bulwarke and defenſe bothe of faith and hope: *Solatium grande credentium, &c.* Holeſome woorking is 7.
a great comforte of the beleeuing, *a forte of our ſafetie, the* Cyprian.
*buckler of hope, the defence of faith, the medicine of ſinne:* de elemo.
Faſting, almes, and prayer ioyned togeather, be meanes to heale our ſores, to get the fauour of God, to put away the penaltie due to ſinne, to auoide the Diuell. *Curandis læſionibus quas ſæpe, &c.* To cure the hurtes which often they fal into, that *with the inuiſible enemie haue conflict the medicine of three remedies is ſpecially to be laide. In earneſt prayer, in chaſtiſment of faſting, in liberal almes. When theſe be exerciſed togeather, God is made fauourable, gilte and fault is put out, and the tempter is beaten downe.* Theſe auncient Fathers ſaid not thus much of their owne heades: but as they had learned of the Scripture, ſo they ſpake. Daniel ſaid to Nabuchodonoſor: *Peccata tua eleemoſynis redime: & iniquitates tuas miſericordijs pauperum.* Ranſome thy ſinnes with almes, and thine iniquities by ſhewing mercy to the poore. *By mercie and faith, ſinnes are purged: by mercie and troth iniquitie is ranſomed: Almes deliuereth from all ſinne and from death, and ſuffereth not the ſowle to goe into darkeneſſe. Geue almes, and all thinges are cleane vnto you.*

8. Leo ſer. 4 de ieiu. 10. men.

Dan. 4.

Prouer. 15. & 16.

Tobi. 4.

Luc. 11.

Neither doth God hereby take away his owne prerogatiue, which is to remitte ſinne, but prouideth for mans weakeneſſe many remedies, and by ſundrie waies inuiteth him to enioye remiſsion of ſinne, of all whiche remedies God him ſelfe is the Author and geuer. And ſo haue we not many Sauiours, but one Sauiour, which geueth many helpes and waies of ſaluation.

Note.

To ſuche as doe workes and vſe the grace of God, in-

creaſe

Matth. 25 Theophi-lact. ibid. crease of grace is promised: *Omni habenti dabitur.* To euery man that hath (that is to saie, that vseth his giftes) there shal be geuen. There is no difference noted betwene the good and yll seruaunt, but that the good increased in that he had receiued: The slouthful and yll, had no more at the time of the accompte, then he receiued the firste daie.

10. 2. Pet. 1. By good workes our election and calling is made sure, as in this life it may be assured: *Satagite vt per bona opera, &c.* Earnestly endeuour by good woorkes *to make sure your calling and election.* By good workes we grow and increase in Christe: Ephes. 4. *veritatem facientes, &c.* By doing truth *in charitie, let vs growe in all thinges in him who is Christe our heade.* 1. Pet. 2. *Deponentes omnem malitiam, &c.* Laying aside al malice, *and all guile, false semblance, enuie, and detraction, as children newly borne, couet after reasonable and spiritual milke, that therby ye may grow to saluation.* S. Paule and S. Peter saie, that by true and charitable doing, by leauing vice, and folowing a new and innocent life, we increase in Christe, and grow in saluation.

These be the benefites and commodities that Christian men may take by good woorkes in this life. 1. Direction of faith: 2. Perfiting of the same. 3. Increase of charitie: 4. Strength of hope and affiaunce in God. 5 The getting of a good life, and increase thereof. 6 Strength and defence againste sinne, and the Diuell. 7 Pardone of penaltie due vnto sinne. 8. Turning away of Gods iust and deserued plague. 9 Growing in Christ. 10 Increase of grace to saluation.

The promises that good woorkes haue concerning the life to come, be no lesse then life it selfe euerlastinge.

*Euer*

*Euerie man*, saith our Sauiour, *that shall leaue house, or brothers, or sisters, or father, or mother, or wife, or children, or landes for my names sake, shall haue againe an hundred times as muche, and shall inherite life euerlasting.* God promiseth by his Prophete, that *who so euer keepeth his leage, he will bring him to his holy hill.* And in the Euangeliste Christ saith of his commaundementes: *Hoc fac, & viues:* Doo this and thou shalte liue. He biddeth vs geue almose, saying: *make your selues frendes of the mucke of iniquitie, that when you shall faile, they may receiue you into euerlasting tabernacles. Bid the riche men of this worlde doo wel,* saith S. Paule, *to be riche in good workes, easely to bestowe, to geue parte, to laie vp a good foundation against the time to come, to the intente they maie gette the trewe life.* In all whiche places and many like God promiseth to suche as leaue their frendes or landes, to suche as keepe his commandementes, or geue almose for his sake, life euerlasting.

Matt. 19.
Esai. 56.
Luc. 10.
Luc. 16.
1. Tim. 6.

And to declare more plainely, that he geueth it in respecte of wel doing, and to recompence good workes: *life euerlasting* (saith S. Augustine) *in many places of holie Scripture is called a reward:* Christe saieth to his Apostles, *be glad and reioice, bicause your reward is plentuouse in heauen. And who so euer geueth one of the leaste of these a cup of colde water to drinke, onely in the name of a Disciple, verely I saie vnto you, he shall not lose his rewarde. When thou makest a feaste, call the poore, the feeble, the lame and blinde, and happy shalte thou be that they be not able to requite thee. For it shalbe requited thee in the resurrection of the iuste.* By the worde of requitall, he promiseth rewarde, and by the resurrection of the iuste, the Kingdome of heauen.

Aug epist. 105. De grat. & lib. arbit. cap. 8.
Matt. 5.
Matt 10.
Mar. 9.
Luc. 14.

The sentence that Christe shal geue in the latter day suffreth vs not to doubte, but that the kingdome of heauen shall be geuen as a rewarde for good workes: for he shall saie to them that stande on his righte hande: *Come you blessed of my Father, receiue the kingdome that vvas prepared for you from the beginning of the vvorlde. Quibus meritis*: saithe S. Augustine. *For vvhat desertes?* And Chrysostome: *Cuius gratia, & propter quid?* Why, and wherefore? *For I vvas hungry, and you gaue me meate to eate. &c.* If Christe make good workes a cause of our saluation, and geeueth the kingdome of heauen in respecte of them, who shal be heard speaking to the contrary? *He that commeth to God must beleue that he is, and that to suche as seeke him he is a revvarder.* The waie to seeke him, saie Chrysostome and S. Augustine, *is by deuout praier and good vvorkes.* If we muste then as well beleue that God is a rewarder, as that he is God, sith he rewardeth nothing but vertue and well doing, he that denieth him to be a rewarder of good workes, beleueth not in effecte that he is God. For if he be God, he is trewe of his promes, and then wil he rewarde good workes as he hath promised. And this being so, no man needeth to aske how the workes of a Christian man shoulde come to that estimation with God to be rewarded with life euerlasting. For as Christe saied to his Apostles: *Complacuit patri vestro dare vobis regnum.* It hath pleased your Father to geue you a kingdome, euen so hath it pleased him to promes rewarde of that kingdome for good workes. And he hath promised it that can not lie.

*Matth. 25* — *Aug. Ser. 49. de ver. Dom.* — *Chryso. Hom. 41. in Gen.* — *Hebre. 11.* — *Chryso. hom. 22. ad Hebr. Moral.* — *Aug. in Psal. 76.* — Note vvel — Why good vvorkes be revvarded. — *Lucæ. 12.* — Marke vvel. God promiseth to revvarde good vvorckes.

Vppon this ground standeth al that is saied and taught in the Catholike Church in commendation and rewarde

of good

of good workes. Not that we of our ſelues can claime of him or chalenge him for our debter, bicauſe we haue firſt giuen him, but bicauſe he hath promiſed vs: *Debitor factus eſt.&c.* God is become our debter, ſaith S. Auguſtine *not by taking any thing of vs, but by promiſing that whiche it pleaſed him:* for it is one thing when we ſaie to a man, thou oweſte me ſuche thinges as I haue geuen thee, and an other thing when we ſaie, thou oweſte me bicauſe thou haſte promiſed me: *Non poſſumus ergo ei dicere. &c.* We can not then ſaie vnto God, *rendre that thou haſte receiued, for who gaue him firſte to be requited againe? We can not ſaie: Render that thou haſte receiued, but plainely we ſaie: Render that thou haſte promiſed:* Vppon this promiſe S. Paule ſaied, *I haue wraſteled well for the game, I haue finiſhed my race, I haue kepte my faith: For the reſte the crowne of iuſtice is laide vp for me, whiche our Lorde ſhall render vnto me in that day as a iuſte iudge.* Although it came *of mercie, that God called S.* Paule, and gaue him *grace to doo good workes*, and to keepe his Faithe, yet when S. Paule hath ſo done, he ſaied, that God *of his iuſtice woulde render him the crowne.* Vppon this promes Ezechias, and Nehemias praied God, *to haue reſpecte to their life, and to remember their well doing*: not as prowde men preſuming of them ſelues: but meekely acknowleging, that God *is faithefull and trewe in all his wordes*, and where he *geueth grace*, he will alſo *geue glorie* and rewarde. As he ſaieth vnto the laboroures: *Go into my vineyarde:* So he ſaieth alſo, *that whiche is iuſte, I will geue you.* No man goeth vnleſſe he be called, and yet who ſo euer laboureth faithfully and trewly, when he is ſente, is aſſured of wages, bicauſe

Aug. Ser. 16. de ver. Apoſt. & in Pſal. 32. conci. 1

Ser. 31. de ver. Dom.

Rom. 11.

2. Tim. 4.

Galat. 1.

1. Tim. 1.

4. Reg. 20

2. Eſdr. 5.

Pſal. 144.

Pſal. 83.

Matth. 20

*Leo serm. 4. de Collect.* it was promised: vppon this promise Leo saied: *Cibus egeni, regni cœlestis est pretium: & largitor temporalium hæres efficitur æternorum.* The meate giuen to the needy is the price of the kingdome of heauen, and the geuer of thinges temporal, is made heire of the eternal. S. Cyprian saith, *Matth. 13. Cypria de Elemo.* that Christe by the parable of the merchante who solde all his goodes to bie a preciouse pearle, *teacheth vs, that with the quantitie of our patrimony we should purchase and bye euerlasting life.* And S. Augustine saith: *Viduæ suffecerunt duo minuti nummi. &c.* *August. in Psal. 147.* Two litle peeces of coine were inough for the wydowe *to doo mercie, two peeces of coine were inough to purchase the kingdome of God.* A smalle price, a man mighte saie, for so greate a Iewell, were not the bountie and liberalitie of God the owner: who being Lorde of all, hath sette suche a price vppon it, and by his gratiouse and free promise hath bounde him selfe to performe it.

This is the trewe commendation, which the Scripture and auncient Fathers geeue vnto good workes, and these be the causes why Christian men should doo them. They that say good workes serue to geue testimony and make declaration of our Faith, and be commendable, but haue no rewarde of grace here, nor value of euerlasting life, albeit they exhorte men to liue godly, they maie commende and set forth good workes in wordes, but they hinder the doing of them in deede.

*Note.* Nouatus his heresy was, that suche as fell into deadely sinne after their Baptisme, coulde not be absolued by the prieste, neither restored to the Church againe, but muste be lefte vnto Gods iudgemente: and yet did he exhorte men to doo penance and satisfaction, to waile and weepe *Cyprianus lib. 4. Epistola. 2.* night

night and day for theire sinnes. S.Cyprian saith of him, that he was *Misericordiæ hostis : interfector pœnitentiæ.* The enimie of mercie, the killer of penaunce, bicause, though he exhorted men to satisfaction and penance, *yet,* saith he : *He tooke away the medicine and remedie that came of satisfaction. Operari tu putas rusticum posse? &c.* Thinkest thou the husbandman can worke, *if thou say to him. Trimme thy ground with all skill of husbandry, plie thy tillage diligently, but thou shalte reape no corne at haruest, thou shalt haue no vintage, thou shalt take no profite nor fruite of thy oileyearde, thou shalt gather no apples of the trees.* As suche an exhortation to husbandrie were inough to discourage the good husband from his trauaile : And *as they killed penance,* saith S.Cyprian, *that tooke away the fruit of it* : euen so doo they hinder nowe a daies the dooing of good workes, that commend them in wordes, and take away the rewarde of them in deed: *Nemo enim sine fructu imperat laborem :* for no man (saith Pacianus) enioineth labor without profite. Neither is there any profite or rewarde that a true Christian man passeth vppon, if it perteine not to life euerlasting : for this life and all that belongeth vnto it, he is taught to sette litle by.

Cypria.li.1.epist.1.

Cypria.li.4.epist.2.

Note.

Pacia.epistol.1.ad Sympronia.

Therefore the Church exhorteth al men to doo good workes, but it keepeth not backe the liberall promise of life eternal which Christ hath annexed to them. S.Paule saith, *be ye stedfaste and vnmoueable, euer plentifull in euery worke of our Lord.* And why? *Scientes quòd labor vester non est inanis in Domino.* Knowing that your labour is not idle in our Lorde: And when he saith, *in our Lord,* he meaneth no temporall nor worldely rewarde : *It is*

1.Cor.15.

Chrysost. ho. & 8. in Gen. *not onely a comfortable saying, but a trueth taught by the Scripture, that a Christian man should directe all his doinges to serue God in hope of life euerlasting: Lette vs not fainte and be wearie of well doing*, saith S. Paule, *for we shall reape it in his time, without fainting.* Gala. 6.

Heb. 11. This cogitation maketh men quietly and contentedly to beare aduersitie. *Moyses did chose rather to suffer affliction with the people of God, then to haue a pleasure of sinne for the time.* But what made him content so to doo? *Aspiciebat enim in remunerationem.* He loked to the rewarde: *Ita quando quisque aduersi aliquid patitur.* Euen so euery man when he suffereth any aduersitie, *should call to remembrance, what rewarde he shall receiue thereby at Goddes hande.* Prima ib. in cap. 11. ad Hebr.

The lacke of this cogitation maketh vs many times to fainte in well doing. *Omnia nobis difficilia videntur.* All thinges seeme heard to vs, saith Chrysostome, *bicause we haue not the remembrance of God.* Chrysost. hom. 22. ad Hebr.

This cogitation maketh men contente to take vppon them a painefull kinde of life, whiche otherwise, they would flee. S. Augustine saith, *that diuers being sodeinly taken and required to be Preestes, whereby they muste liue chaste all theire liues, were contente to doo it. Sperantes se illustrius in Christi hæreditate fulgere. Trusting to shine the brighter in Christes inheritance.* De adulter. cõiug. lib. 2. cap. 20. Note.

This cogitation caused Martyrs willingly to susteine all paine and tormente: Confessours, to leade a vertuouse and straite life: Virginnes, to dispise worldelie pleasures: of all whiche it may truelie be saied: *Aspiciebant in remunerationem:* They looked to the rewarde: This hope maketh seruauntes doo good and true

true seruice to theire maisters, in which sense S. Paule saith: *Quodcunque facitis, ex animo operamini, &c.* What so euer ye doo, doo it hartelly *as it were vnto our Lord, and not to men, knowing that of our Lorde you shall receiue the rewarde of inheritance.* And when I speake this muche of good workes, and of the rewarde due vnto them: what workes I commende, thou knowest good Reader, by that which I haue saied in the 13. Chapter of the first Booke. Coloss. 3.

## An answere to certeine obiections made against the rewarde of good workes.

## *THE XIIII. CHAPTER.*

BVT all this notwithstanding, yet some lette not to say, that the workes of faith, which Christian men doo, can not deserue rewarde of life euerlasting,
neither stande in Goddes iudgemente, as well bicause 1.
they be vnperfite, as also bicause no man liueth here 2.
withoute sinne, and fewe without greate sinne, and breache of some of the commaundementes, and then is it written: *Who so offendeth in one, is made giltie of all*: and thereby say they: all our workes be infected, and consequentely excluded, from that greate rewarde. Iaco. 2.

To the firste pointe I answere. There be two kindes of perfection in iustice, the one such as is in God, the Angelles, and that happie company of men, who being presente with God, enioy the sighte of the Deitie: Note vvel these tvvo kindes of perfection in iustice.

An

2. An other, such as may be founde in men being yet Pilgrimes from God and liuing in this worlde. In comparison of the first kinde of perfection, no man is iuste, neither any iustice of man, be it neuer so exquisite and perfite, can stande in the iudgement of God. In that respecte it is true: *Ecce inter Sanctos eius nemo immutabilis: & cæli nō sunt mundi in conspectu eius.* Lo emong his Saints and holy none is immutable, and the heauens in his sight be not cleane. *So is it vnderstanded,* saith S. Augustine: *Nemo bonus, nisi vnus Deus: quia omnia quæ creata sunt, &c.* No man is good, but onely God, bicause all thinges that be created, *though God haue made them very good, yet if they be compared with the Creator and maker, they be not good, with whom if they be compared, they be not.* In the same sense is it said: *Non intres in iudicium, &c.* Entre not into iudgement *with thy seruaunt, bicause no man liuing shalbe iustified in thy sight: This is meant by it,* saith S. Augustine, *entre not into iudgement with thy seruant. Noli me iudicare secundùm te, qui es sine peccato: Iudge me not after thy selfe, who arte without sinne.* And where he saith, no man shalbe iustified: he referred it to that perfection of iustice, which is not in this life. In the same manner doth S. Hierome expounde the place.

*Iob. 15.* *Mar. 10.* *August. de perfect. iustitia.* *Aug. vt suprà.* *Li. 1. dialo. cont. Pelagia.*

But as no man is iuste in comparison of that excellent iustice of God, of the Angelles, and Sainctes: so yet saith S. Augustine: *Dici potest quædam iustitia minor huic vitæ competens, qua iustus ex fide viuit, quamuis peregrinus à Domino:* It may be said, that there is a lesser iustice, meete for this life, whereby the iust man liueth through faith, though he be yet a Pilgrime from God.

*De spiri. & lit. cap. 36.*

S. Basil expounding these wordes of the Psalme: *Indica*

*me*

*me Domine ſecundùm iuſtitiam meam.* Iudge me Lord ac- *Pſal. 7.*
cording to my iuſtice, ſaith: *Eſt quædam Angelorum iuſti-*
*tia humanam trangreſſa, &c.* There is a iuſtice of Angels *Baſil. in*
that paſſeth mannes iuſtice. *And if there be any power* *Pſal. 7.*
*aboue Angelles, it hath an excellencie of iuſtice, anſwerable* *Ibidem.*
*to his greatenes, and there is the iuſtice of God him ſelfe, that*
*excedeth all vnderſtanding of minde, being vnſpeakeable*
*and incomprehenſible to all mortall nature: Iudge me ther-*
*fore Lorde according to my iuſtice, that is to ſay, according*
*to that iuſtice which men may atteine vnto, and which* Note.
*is poſſible to ſuche as liue in fleſh.* No thing can be more
plainely ſpoken, to proue, both that there is a iuſtice in
God and his Angelles, which ſurmounteth mannes nature, and alſo that there is a iuſtice that man may atteine
vnto: And ſo be all good mennes workes and theire iuſtice vnperfect, if they be compared with God and his
Angelles, and yet perfite according to the eſtate and nature of man. It is ſaid: *Diliges Dominum Deum tuum, ex* *Matt. 22.*
*toto corde, &c.* Thou ſhalt loue thy Lorde God with all
thy harte, with all thy ſoule, with all thy minde. And
yet ſaith S. Auguſtine: *Neque ſi eſſe non dum poteſt tan-* *De ſpirit.*
*ta dilectio., &c.* If the loue of God can not yet be ſo *& lit.*
greate, *as vnto that full and perfite knowlege of heauen, is* *cap. 36.*
*due, it is not now to be taken for a faulte.*

Note Reader: he ſaith, although mannes loue towarde
God wante of that perfection that ſhalbe in heauen, yet it
is not accompted a ſinne nor faulte. S. Paule ſpeaking in
his owne perſon, as he confeſſeth he wanted one of theſe *Philip. 3.*
perfections, ſo doth he ſignifie, that he was not without
the other. *Non quòd iam acceperim, aut iam perfectus ſim:*
Not that I haue already receiued it, or am alreadie per-

fite,&c. And in the same place: *Quicunque ergo perfecti sumus, hoc sentiamus:* As many of vs then as be perfite, let vs be of this minde: he saieth he was not perfite, and yet that both him selfe and others were perfite: which wordes S. Augustine expounding, saith: *Si secundùm hominis mortalis capacitatem pro huius vitæ modulo perfecti sumus, ad ipsam perfectionem hoc quoque pertinere intelligamus, vt Angelica illa, quæ in Christi manifestatione nobis erit iustitia, nondum nos perfectos esse sapiamus.* If we be perfite after a mortall mannes capacitie, according to the measure of this life, let vs vnderstande this also to be one pointe of perfection, not to thinke our selues perfite after that Angelicall iustice, whiche we shall haue when Christe shall shewe him selfe. And in an other place declaring the same wordes he saieth: *Perfecti, & non perfecti: perfecti viatores, nondum perfecti possessores: & vt noueritis quòd perfectos viatores dicat, qui iam in via ambulant perfecti viatores sunt:* We be perfite, and not perfite: perfite waifarers, not yet perfite possessours: and to th'intente ye may knowe he calleth waifarers perfite, they that nowe trauell by the way, be perfite waifarers.

*Aug. contra. 2. epi. Pelagia. li. 3. ca. 7.*

*Ser. 15. de verb. Apost.*

And here I may admonishe the Reader to consider with him selfe, howe well such as nowe a daies do condemne all mannes good workes for imperfection, doo agree, first with S. Paule, and then with S. Basill, S. Augustine, S. Hierome, with others that I might here allege. They say: All our iustice and good workes can not helpe towarde the kingdome of heauen bicause they be vnperfite. S. Paule saith: *As we lacke one perfection, so haue we an other.* S. Basill saith, *We lacke suche iustice as is in*

God

*God and Angelles, but haue a iustice which mannes nature may atteine vnto, and may be iudged thereby*: S. Augustine saith, *we may be perfite after the capacitie of mortall men, and after the measure of this life, though after that Angelicall iustice whiche we shall haue in heauen, we be not nowe perfite*: he saith, *we be perfite as waifarers, but not perfite as possessours*, bicause we be not yet in heauen. They say, bicause our loue is vnperfite, it is sinne. S. Augustine saith, *although it wante of the heauenly perfection, yet it is neither accompted sinne, nor faulte*: They say, no good workes may stande and abide Goddes iudgement, for that no man liuing shalbe iustified in the sighte of God. S. Basill saith: *Lorde, iudge me according to my iustice, not like an Angell, but like a man.* S. Augustine and S. Hierome say: *It is not meant thereby, that there is no iustice in man, but that man may not be iudged after the rule of God, who is without all sinne*: and that no man liuinge here shalbe iustified *in Goddes sighte*, that is to say, founde iuste after suche perfecte iustice, as is in heauen.

And thus may the Reader also perceiue, that such as condemne all mannes good workes as vnperfite vnder coloure of an heauenly perfection, go about to take away all perfection, suche as may be in earth. And bicause Note. men in this worlde can not be Angelles, they would not haue them so much as iuste men: And where Christe hath saied, *Estote vos perfecti*: Be you perfite, they Matt. 5. say, no man is perfite: And where as he calleth fasting, Matt. 6. praier, and almoes *our iustice*, and promiseth rewarde to the same, they say there is no iustice in vs, that can deserue any such rewarde, If no good workes Rom. 2.

may ſtande in the iudgement of God, how ſhall he in his laſte and iuſte iudgement *render vnto euery man according to his Workes?* Or howe is it true: *Opera illorum ſequuntur illos?* Theire workes folowe them? To what ende doo the good mennes workes folowe them, if there be no rewarde for them? And this much concerning the firſt parte of the obiection.

*Iacob.3.* To the ſecond I ſay: although it be true: *In multis offendimus omnes,* In many thinges doo we all offende, bicauſe as S. Auguſtine ſaith, *fight We neuer ſo manfullie againſt vice, We are men,* yet God of his goodnes hath prouided a remedie: the remedy, I ſay, of penance, wherby ſuche as falle, may riſe againe, and be reſtored to the eſtate of Iuſtice: *Habet Eccleſia maculas & rugas: ſed confeſsione ruga extenditur, confeſsione macula abluitur.* The Church hath ſpottes and wrinkles, but by confeſsion the wrinkle is ſtretched forth and made ſmothe, by confeſsion the ſpot is waſſhed out. Penaunce doth not onely helpe and releaſe a ſinner in the iudgment of the Church, but alſo taketh away the offence in the iudgement of God. For as S. Leo ſaith: *Non remanet iudicio condemnandum, quod fuerit in confeſsione purgatum.* That, that is purged by confeſsion, remaineth not to be condemned in the iudgement. S. Auguſtine ſaith, that Baptiſme or penaunce is able to ſalue adultery, in ſo muche that the partie afterwarde ſhall not be taken for an adulterer: *Cur enim adhuc deputamus adulteros, quos vel Baptiſmate ablutos, vel pœnitentia credimus eſſe ſaluatos?* Why doo we yet ſtill take them for adulterers, whome we beleeue to be either waſſhed by Baptiſme, or healed by penaunce? And as by true penaunce a ſinner is diſ-

*Aug. contra Iulia. lib. 2.*

*Aug. ſer. 29. de ver. Apoſto.*

*Leo. ſer. 11. de Quadra.*

*De adulter. cõiug. lib. 2. cap. 6.*

is discharged of his sinne, euen in Goddes iudgement, so a iuste man falling into sinne, and rising againe by penance, loseth not the name of a iuste man. *Septies cadit iustus, & resurgit: si cadit quomodo iustus? Si iustus, quomodo cadit? Sed iusti vocabulum non amittit, qui per pœnitentiam semper resurgit:* Seuen times falleth the iuste man and shal rise againe, If he falle, howe is he iuste? If he be iuste, howe dothe he falle? But he loseth not the name of a iuste man that euer riseth againe by penance. God saieth by his Prophete: *Impietas impij non nocebit ei in quacunque die conuersus fuerit ab impietate sua.* The wickednes of the wicked shall not hurte him what daie so euer he shall be turned from his wickednes: he that thinketh there can be no iustice acceptable to God, where any sinne is committed, doth not vnderstande the Scriptures. For as it is saied: *Nemo mundus a peccato.* No man is cleane from sinne. And if we say, we haue no sinne, we deceiue our selues, and there is no trewth in vs: So it is saied: *Sunt iusti, & sapientes, & opera eorum in manu Dei.* There be iuste men and wise, and theire workes in the hande of God. It is saied by God him selfe of Noe: *Te vidi iustum coram me.* Thee I haue sene a iuste man before me. Zacharie and Elizabeth were both iuste, not onely after mennes iudgement, *but before God.* Christe calleth Abell, *a iuste man.* And yet, saieth S. Augustine, *neither Abell, nor any man or woman, whom the Scripture calleth iuste, excepte the Virgine Marie, that bare Christe, was without sinne.* Dauid committed, not a smalle sinne, suche as weakenesse can not auoide, but adulterie and murder: yet dyd God vppon penaunce not onely pardone his sinne and restore him to iustice,

*Proue. 24.*

*Hiero. To. 1. Epistola ad Rusticum.*

*Ezech. 33.*

*1. Ioan. 1.*

*Eccles 9.*

*Gen. 7.*

*Luca. 1.*

*Math. 23.*

*De natur. et gra. ca. 36. ca. 38.*

*2. Reg. 12.*

4 Reg.19 but for his ſake benefited a whole citie. *Protegam vrbem hanc & ſaluabo eam propter me, & propter Dauid ſeruum meum.* I will defende this citie and ſaue it for mine owne ſake, and for Dauid my ſeruantes ſake. Therefore albeit the iuſte man be not without all ſinne, yet if he doo trewe penance for his ſinne, he maie not onely ſtill be called a iuſte man, but alſo atteine to a perfection of iuſtice ſuche as is in this life, and his good workes acceptable and pleſant in the ſight of God. *Quamuis ſcriptum ſit, quis gloriabitur caſtum ſe habere cor?* Although it be writen, ſaieth Leo who ſhall crake that he hath a chaſte harte, *or that he is cleane from ſinne, yet is not th'atteining of a pure life to be deſpeired, whiche, while it is euer deſired, is euer receiued: neither doth that remaine to be condemned in the iudgemente, that is by confeſsion purged.* Wherefore if the ſinne of a iuſte man be purged by confeſsion, and pardoned by trewe penaunce what remaineth then, (his ſinne being forgeuen) but that, *Iuſtitia eius manet in ſeculum ſeculi:* His iuſtice abideth for euer, and euer?

Note.

Prouer.20

Leo.Ser. 12. de Quadrag.

## VVhat aſſurance of his Iuſtification and ſaluation a Chriſtian man maie haue in this life.

## *THE XV. CHAP.*

Matth.5. CHriſte ſaied vnto his Apoſtles: *Beati qui eſuriunt & ſitiunt iuſticiam.* Bleſſed are they that hunger and thirſte after iuſtice. And S. Paule willeth vs

Philip.2.

*with*

*With feare and trembling to woorke our saluation*: whereby as we are taught euer to desier increase of righ- tuousenes, fearefully and carefully to worke, so doo we not learne to assure our selues of our iustice and saluation: for he that hungreth and thirsteth, confesseth, that he is not satisfied of that he thirsteth after. And fearefull trembling, can not stande with securitie. Nothing can be more daungerouse to a Christian man pasing through the perilles of this life, *whiche is it selfe a tentation*, then to thinke him selfe owte of danger, and to conceiue a carelesse securitie, that he is vndoubtedly in Goddes fauour, and suer of his saluation. For as S. Leo saieth: *Hæc est perfectorum vera iustitia, vt nunquam præsumant se esse perfectos, ne ab itineris nondum finiti intentione cessantes, ibi incidant deficiendi periculum, vbi proficiendi deposuerint appetitum*: This is trewe iustice of them that be perfite, neuer to presume them selues to be perfite, leste while they leaue the intente to goo on their iourney, that is not yet ended, they falle in danger of failing euen there, where they leaue the desire of going forewarde. What greater perfection can there be in this life, then for a man to beleue without all doubte, and to be able to assure him selfe that his sinnes be forgeuen, that he is iuste, that he is the heire of God, and an heire partener with Christe? How then can any man stande assured thereof, if this be the trewe iustice of the perfite, neuer to presume of suche perfection? With Leo S. Augustine agreeth, saying: *Quantumcunque hic vixerimus. &c.* Liue we neuer so long here, *profite we neuer so muche here: let no man saie, I haue ynoughe, I am iuste. He that so saieth, staieth*

*Iob.7.*

*Leo. Ser. 2 de Quadrage.*

*Aug. in Psal. 69.*

*by the*

*by the waie, he can not come to the iournies ende. Looke* 
1 Aug. Ser. 5. de ver. Aposto. *where he saieth, I haue inough, there he sticketh faste.* And in an other place he saieth. *Semper tibi displiceas quod es, si vis peruenire ad id quod nondum es.* Euer mislike in thy selfe that thou arte, if thou wilte come to that which yet thou arte not. *For where thou haste liked thy selfe, there hast thou stand still. But if thou say I haue inough thou arte loste. Increase euer, euer go on, euer profite:* In
Philip. 3. bothe places he alledgeth the wordes of S. Paule, saying of him selfe: *Fratres, ego me non arbitror comprehendisse.*
Aug. Ser. 15. de ver. Apostolo. Brothers I doo not thinke that I haue atteined and gotten to it: *Ne forte surrepat vobis, quia vos aliquid estis, qui seipsum putat aliquid esse. &c.* Leste it creape into your
Gala. 6. heades, that you are somwhat: he that thinketh him selfe to be somewhat *when he is nothing, seduceth him selfe,*
1. Cor. 8. *and he that thinketh he knoweth somewhat, doth not yet knowe after what sorte he muste knowe:* Thus doo we see by the wordes of S. Leo and S. Augustine, yea and of S. Paule, howe daungerouse the opinion is for men to put them selues in assurance of iustice and saluation. They saie it is the meane to make vs falle from iustice, to staie by the waie and neuer to come to the ende of our iourney. S. Augustine saithe, that S. Paule was
Math. 24 not of that minde, nor woulde any of his scholers to be. Our Sauiour saith, *he that holdeth owt to the ende, shalbe saued.* Whereby we knowe there is no hope of saluation
Aug. de bon. perse ne. cap. 1. without perseuerance. And as S. Augustine saieth: *Vtrum quisquam hoc munus acceperit, quamdiu hanc vitam ducit, incertum est.* Whether any man hath receiued this gifte as long as he liueth here it is vncerteine. It appereth by him in the same booke, that it is not Gods pleasure, that men

should

shoulde be put in that suertie, his woordes be these: *Deus aũt melius esse iudicauit, miscere quosdam non perseueraturos, certo numero sanctorũ suorum vt quibus non expedit in huius vitæ tentatione securitas, non possint esse securi: multos enim à pernitiosa elatione reprimit quod ait Apostolus: Quapropter qui videtur stare, videat ne cadat.* God hath thought it better, to mingle some that woulde not continewe emonge the certaine number of his holie, that for as muche as it is not expediente for them in the tentation of this life to be in securitie, they should not be without care. For that sayinge of the Apostle: Lette him that seemeth to stande, take heede he fall not, stayeth many from a perniciouse pride. If it be S. Paules counsell, that *suche as thinke them selues to stand, should take hede they fall not*, of like suche as stande may fall, and if they may fall, seeing that the risinge againe by penance is the gifte of God, howe can manne either assure him selfe to stande still, or promise him selfe Gods grace to rise againe at his pleasure, when he is fallen? And therefore as Chrysostome saieth: *Omnes nos vigilare & sobrios esse oportet, & nunquam in securitate esse*: We must al watch and be sober, and neuer be without care, for thoughe we stande nowe, yet are we mutable, and not assured so to continewe. S. Augustine saieth; *Licet de perseuerantiæ præmio certi sint, de ipsa tamen perseuerantia sua reperiuntur incerti. Quis enim hominum se in actione profectúque iustitiæ perseueraturum vsque in finem sciat, nisi aliqua reuelatione ab isto fiat certus?* Though men be assured of the rewarde of perseuerance, yet of their owne perseuerance be they founde vncertaine. For what manne can knowe that he shall continewe in the dooing

Aug. De bon. perseueran. c. 8.

1. Co. 10.

1. Cor. 10.

Note:

Hom. 22. in Gen.

Aug. De Ciuit. Dei li. 11. c. 12.

and increase of iustice to the ende, vnlesse he be certified from God by some reuelation? He saieth menne be assured, that suche as continewe to the ende shall be rewarded, but whether he him selfe shall so continewe, no manne can tell, vnlesse he vnderstande it by speciall reuelation from God. For the reuelation of the Scripture is generall and onely this, that suche as continewe to the ende shall be saued. If it be Gods predistination that maketh vs presume of this assurance, heare what S. Bernarde saieth: *Quis potest dicere, ego de electis sum? &c.* Who is able to saie, I am one of the electe? *I am one of them that are predestinate to life? I am of the number of the children? Who is able to saie these things? Seeing the Scripture cryeth to the contrary, a man can not tell whether he be woorthy of loue, or hatred. Certaine assurance we haue not, but an affiance of hope dothe comforte vs, bicause wee should not vtterly be grieued with the perplexitie of this doubte.* No man, saith he, can assure him selfe that he is electe, that he is predestinate, we haue no certaine assurance of our saluation, affiance and hope we haue to comforte vs.

*Math. 24* *Bernar. in septuages.* *Eccles. 9.*

An easie matter is it for a man to deceiue him selfe, and as the Ciuile Lawe saieth: *that a man often times trusteth his goodes to be more worth then he findeth them*, so commeth it many times to passe, that a man thinketh him selfe to be better and stronger in good, then he is. S. Peter said vnto Christ: *though I should die with thee, I will not deny thee.* But as S. Augustine saieth: *Nemo se comprehendit, nemo de se præsumit: Nunquid comprehendit corde suo cor suum Petrus, qui dixit tecum vsque ad mortem ero? in corde erat præsumptio falsa, in corde latebat timor verus. No-*

*Institut. quibus ex causis manumittere nõ licet* *Mar. 14.* *Aug. in Psal. 39. &. 41.*

*uerat*

*uerat .in illo Deus, quod ipse in se non nouerat.* No man conceiueth nor comprehendeth him selfe. No man presumeth, of him selfe. Did S. Peter with his owne hearte, conceiue his owne hearte, who saied: I will be with thee to the deathe? There was in his hearte a false presumption, there laie hidden in his hearte a trewe feare. God knewe in him, that whiche he knewe not in him selfe. And in an other place generally of all men he saith: *Plarumque homo putat se posse, quod non potest. Aut putat se non posse quod potest. Accedit ad illum interrogatio ex* *Aug. in*
*Diuina dispensatione, & per interrogationem notus fit sibi.* *Psal. 43.*
Commonly a manne thinketh him selfe able to doe that whiche he is not, or thinketh he is not able to doe that he is able. A tryall commeth vnto him by Gods ordering, and by the tryall, he knoweth him selfe. Howe dothe man then take vppon him to iudge and pronounce of him selfe, if he neither conceiue nor knowe him selfe, nor vnderstande what is in him selfe? If he wil saie true, he may saie with S. Augustine: *that he knoweth him selfe* *Aug. in*
*better then other men, but what he is in dede, God knoweth* *Psal. 36.*
*better then he.* *concio. 3.*

When Christe saied to his Apostles: *vnus vestrum me tradet*: One of you will betraie me: they were all sadde. *Leo ser. 7*
*Contristati sunt non de conscientiæ reatu, sed de humanæ* *passio Do.*
*mutabilitatis incerto, timentes ne minus verum esset, quod in se quisque nouerat, quam quòd ipsa veritas prauidebat.* They were sadde (saieth S. Leo) not for any gilte of conscience, but for the vncertaine state of mannes mutabilitie, fearing that mighte rather be false, which euery man knew in him selfe, then that which trueth it selfe did forsee. Out of what schoole commeth this assurance,

which neither other Apostles, neither S. Iohn that was in Christes bosome, had learned? Vppon this vncertaintie and bottomelesse depth of mannes hearte, S. Paule saied: *Nihil mihi conscius sum, sed non in hoc iustificatus sum: qui*

1. Cor. 8. *autem me iudicat, Dominus est.* I knowe not my selfe giltie of any thinge, but I am not thereby iustified: it is God that iustifieth me.

If then S. Peter knew not his owne estate, but promised more of him selfe then was true, if God knowe more of man, then he doth of him selfe, if the Apostles finding them selues not giltie of the minde to betraie Christe, were yet sadde, fearing least it might be: if no man commonly knowe him selfe but by tryall, whiche may euer alter and change while he liueth, if S. Paule would not be his owne iudge, touchinge his conscience: what manne shoulde presume to assure him selfe of his iustice and saluation, vnlesse, as S. Augustine saith, *he be certified thereof by some reuelation?* When S. Paul biddeth vs with *feare and trembling to woorke our owne saluation*, he sheweth a cause of that saying, which is well to be considered: *for* saith he, *it is God that woorketh in you, both to will, and to*

Leo ser. 8. *woorke. Et hæc sanctis causa est tremendi atque metuendi,*

De Epiph. *ne ipsis pietatis operibus elati deserantur ope gratiæ, & remaneant in infirmitate naturæ.* And this, saith S. Leo, is cause for the holy to tremble and feare, leaste while they be proude of the very woorkes of pietie, the helpe of grace forsake them, and they remaine in the weakenesse of nature. A man may assure him selfe of that whiche is in his owne power, so farre as he is not inforced nor lette: but of that whiche dependeth of God, as well willinge, well woorking, iustice, and saluation doth, no man without his

reue-

reuelation doth aſſure him ſelfe,but he that is diſpoſed to deceyue him ſelfe.

The Angelles who were created moſt perfite,had not the aſſurance to continue in that happie eſtate of good Angelles: For, as we knowe, a greate number of them fell from it. *In ſummo bono permanentibus cæteris vt de ſua ſine fine permanſione certi eſſent, tanquam ipſius præmium permanſionis dedit:* God gaue vnto the reſte, who remained in the higheſte good,euen as a rewarde of their remayninge, that they ſhoulde be certayne, of theyr continuance without ende. S. Auguſtine ſaith,that God hath geuen it as a ſpecial rewarde vnto Angells to be aſſured of their eſtate, and that vnto ſuche as remained with him when the reſte fell: And albeit ſuche as ſhalbe compted worthy of that worlde and the reſurrection, ſhalbe equall vnto Angelles,and then conſequently in aſſurance without feare, yet bicauſe earthe is not heauen, while we lyue here, S. Auguſtine ſaieth: *Adhuc in via ſumus.* We be yet in the waye, and therefore it is ſaied to vs: *Seruite Domino in timore*, Serue God in feare. He ſaieth in an other place, there be two wayes to bring vs in danger,to muche hope, and to litle. *Ex vtraque parte periclitamur, & ſperando, & deſperando.* Of both ſides we fall in danger,by hoping, and by deſpairing. To kepe vs therefore from preſuming in hope, it is ſaied: *Serue the Lorde in feare And with feare and trembling worke your owne ſaluation.* To keepe vs from deſpaire S. Bernarde ſaieth: *An afficiance of hope doth comforte vs, to the ende we ſhould not be vtterly perplexed and doubtefull.* And S Paule ſaieth: *Tribulatio patientiam operatur, &c.* Trouble worketh patience, *and patience trial, trial woorketh*

*De ciuita. Dei lib. 22 cap. 1.*

*Luc. 20. Math. 22.*

*Aug. Ser. 12. de ver. Apoſt.*

*Ser. 47. de ver. Do. et Ser. 59.*

*Pſal. 2. Philip. 3.*

*Bernar. in Septuage.*

*Rom. 5.*

*keth hope, and hope confoundeth not*. By which wordes we learne, not onely that hope keepeth vs from despayre and confusion, but also, how true hope is gotten: that is to say, by trial and patience, ioyned with charitie, as is there expressed: And therefore the more euery man is tried by patience, and the greater his charitie is, the greater also and surer his hope is: and such as be perfite, though they haue no certayne assurance, yet haue they a greate and strong hope of Gods grace and their saluation.

Hovve true hope is gotten.

Wherefore leauing the perfection of Angelles, which is all in assurance, to the worlde to comme, let vs speake of our selues, as of men that be yet *Pylgrimes from God*, trauayling in the waye, besette on euery side with tentation, euer praysing God: that emong so many dangers, we may say with the Prophete: *Factus est mihi Dominus in refugium*: &, *Deus meus in adiutorium spei meæ*: The Lorde is made my refuge, and my God the healpe of my hope. *Quamdiu enim hîc sumus, in spe sumus, nondum in re*: For as longe as we be here, we be in hope, not in thing it selfe: Let euery man *be renewed from daye to day, put of the olde man, and put on the newe*, forsake Adam, and flee to Christe. But as S. Augustine saieth: *no man ought to assure him selfe, that he is passed from the one to the other, but when he shalbe there, where no tentation shalbe*.

2. Cor. 5.

Psal. 93.

Aug. ibid. in Psal. 93

Ephes 4. Colos. 3.

De ciuita. Dei lib. 21 cap. 15.

Of the fruites and ende of our Iustification, and what strength in wel doing God geueth thereby, where it is truly receyued, and effectually put in vre, and the way to come to it.

THE

## THE XVI. CHAPTER.

AS all thinges naturally are done to some ende and purpose, so is not our Iustification wrought of God vayne, but to the intente we shoulde enioye the fruite and ende thereof. What that is, S. Paule expresseth in these fewe woordes written to the Romaines, who as long as they were heathen, lyued vngodly, but after that they were turned to Christe and iustified, he saieth vnto them: *Nunc verò liberati à peccato, serui autem facti Deo, habetis fructum vestrum in sanctificationem, finem verò vitam æternam.* Rom. 6. Nowe that ye are delyuered from sinne and made seruantes to God, ye haue for your fruit holinesse, and for your ende life euerlasting. Whereby we vnderstande, that the true fruit of Iustification, is to leade a godly and vertuouse life here, and the ende, to enioye life euerlasting. To woorke this effecte Christe *gaue him selfe for vs, to ransome vs from all iniquitie, and cleanse to him selfe a speciall people, that should followe good workes.* Tit. 2. To this ende was his grace shewed *vnto al men, teaching vs to renounce wickednesse and worldely desyres, and to liue soberly, iustely, aud godly in this worlde, looking for the blessed hope and comming of our Sauiour.* Ibid. This effecte was wrought not onely in Christes Apostles, who at his calling through grace, forsooke all that before they looued in the worlde, but also in sundrie others, Math. 4. Math. 19. mentioned in the Scripture: of whome it maye truely be sayd, that being once brought to Christe, and made his, *they crucified theire fleshe, with the vices and concupiscences*, Gal. 5. liued to Christ, and Christ in them. Gal. 2.

Marie Magdalene, of an vnchaste wooman was made

made so vertuouse and constant in God, that when Christ his Apostles forsoke him, she went not awaye. And after his ascension, as probable histories testifie, as wel she, as Lazarus, Ioseph of Arimathia and others forsaking Iudea sayled into other countries, where they did continually

Tit. 2. leade a solitary, seuere, and strayte life, *looking* (as S. Paule saieth) *for that blessed hope, and comming of our Sauiour.*

*The multitude of the beleuing* (which were as we know

Act. 4. thousandes) *agreed all in one harte and one minde*: Were so full of charitie and true loue, that suche as were possessioners, solde theire landes and houses, to helpe them that had neede.

The fruit of Iustification was so great, and wrought so

1. Pet. 4. great a chaunge generally in Christian menne, as S. Peter saith, that such as remained stil heathen *maruayled at them that they would not do as they did, in banketting, dronkenes, and confusion of ryot.*

Euse. li. 3. Eccles. histor. c. 32. Plinius in epist. *Plinius secundus*, being a heathen man and Lieutenant in a prouince where he sawe many Christian men martyred, was by the good example of their life, moued to write to the Emperour, and to signifie: *that there was none offence founde in them, other then that they songe Hymnes early before daye to Christ their God: but as for whoredome and other like crimes*, he said, *they tooke them for vnlawfull, and vtterly eschewed them.*

Tertullian writing in the defence of Christian men in his tyme against the heathen, saith in sundry places of that boke, that the magistrates being heathen, neither did nor could charge the Christians with murder, inceste, adultery, sorcery, conspiracie againste Princes, or other notoriouse crimes, but onely laide to their charge, that they were Christians: *Bonus vir, Caius Seius, sed malus tantùm quia Christianus:* Such a one is an honeste man, but he is nought, onely bicause he is a Christian. And alitle after: *Quæ mulier? quàm lasciua, quàm festiua? Qui iuuenis? Qui Lucius, quàm amasius facti sunt Christiani? ita nomen emendationi imputatur:* What a woman, howe wanton, howe pleasante, what a yong man? What a Lucius, howe amorouse, are become Christians? So the very name is accompted for amendement. S. Augustine saith, it was seene in his tyme, *that common harlottes and stage players, sodenly conuerted, prooued suche, that they passed the colde Christians, not onely in patience and temperance, but also in faith, hope, and charitie.* By al which examples, we see, that the grace of Iustification, where it is truely and vnfaynedly receiued, is that *Leauen* whereof Christe spake, *Which being put into three measures of meale, leueneth the Whole,* that is to say, geueth it a newe tallage and taste other then it had before: *Qui enim mortuus est iustificatus est à peccato:* for he that is deade, is iustified from sinne, *and he that is iustified, is deade from sinne.* By these examples, we see it true that S. Paule saieth: *The Gospell is the power and might of God:* for that the Gospel wherein Iustification is preached, being truely and effectually receyued, maketh them that so receyue it, strong: and so strong, that as S. Augustine maketh the comparison, *many Martyrs haue shewed them selues to haue more perfite faith, hope, charitie, better and more stronge freedome of Will, then Adam had:* for he had receyued the power not to sinne, vnlesse he would, neyther to forsake God, vnlesse he would, but he had not the perseuerance nor will to continewe in any of both: and therefore he forsooke the

Tertulli. in Apolog.

Tertul. ibi.

Ad Simplician. li. 1. Quæst. 2.

Math. 13.

Rom. 6.

1. Pet. 4.

Rom. 1.

August. de correp. & grat. c. 11. & 12.

good, and became ſinnefull. Theſe receyued by grace not onely the power to reſiſte ſynne, but alſo the perſe-
Aug. ibid. cap. 12. uerance and will ſo to continue. *Denique ille Adam, & terrente nullo &c.* Finally Adam when no man put him in feare, *yea and againſte the commandemente of God that did put him in feare, vſing his free Will, ſtoode not faſte in ſo greate felicitie, in ſo greate facilitie and eaſe of not ſinning. Theſe Martyres, When the Worlde did (I Will not ſaye) put them in feare, but cruelly rage that they ſhould not ſtande, ſtoode faſte in faith. Whereas Adam ſawe preſent before him the goods that he ſhould leaue, theſe did not ſee the goods that they Were to receyue.*

This is the ſtrength in well doing, whiche the grace of Iuſtification truely receyued and faithfully putte in vre, geueth vnto Chriſtian men, by the whiche Chriſte is ſtronge in vs. Seing therefore that *Chriſte Ieſus is all*
Heb. 13. *one yeſterday, and this daye, and for euer*: howe is it, that we finde not in our ſelues the ſtrengeth in well doing whiche we commende in them? Neyther the fruite of Iuſtification, whiche S. Paule commendeth in the Romaines, that is, holineſſe and vertuouſe life: ſuche as Plinie being a heathen man, and Tertullian euen by the confeſsion of the heathen ſaieth was commonlye founde in Chriſtian menne? What ſhall we ſaye, but that God offereth it, and we will not receyue it. *We*
2. Cor. 6. *receyue the grace of God in vaine*, we geue not the cre-
See the 7. chapt. of this. 2. Booke. dite to Gods woordes that they did: we haue not the faithe of Abraham faithfully to beleeue, and obediently
Cypria. de ſimplicit. Prælator. to doo all that God biddeth vs to doo. We beleeue his promiſes, and care not for his commaundementes, and therefore be faynte in faith, and without hope and cha-

ritie.

ritie. To redresse this, let vs firste beginne with the foundation, and beleeue concerning our Iustification as they did. Tertullian saieth, that onely Christian menne were the innocente and godly lyuers, and sheweth the cause. *Nos ergo soli innocentes, quid mirum si necesse est? Enimuerò necesse est, innocentiam à Deo edocti & perfectè eam nouimus, vt à perfecto magistro reuelatam, & fideliter custodimus, vt ab incontemptibili dispensatore mandatam*: We alone be the innocente lyuers, what maruayle if it muste needes be so? In deede it muste of force be so. We that haue learned of God innocencie and good life, bothe knowe it perfectely, bycause it is reueled by a perfyte Maister, and we keepe it faithfully, bicause it is commaunded by an officer that maye not be despised. Take this lesson, Christian Reader, learne of Christ for thy Iustification, not onely to beleeue, but also to lyue godly and vertuously, whiche lesson, as thou seeste they kepte, whom thou canst not but commende, and so shalte thou be like them whome thou doeste rightely commende. Tertull.in Apologe.

Thou knowest by that which hath benne saied before, in the twelth chaptre of this second Booke, what a false and dissolute doctrine concerning Iustification is able to doo. When Simon Magus, Carpocrates, and Valentinus had taught, that menne might be saued by grace, fayth, and knowledge, without good woorkes, theyre scholers gaue them selues to luste and licentiouse lyfe. To auoyd that mischiefe beleue assuredly this godly and learned saying: *Non dormiẽtibus prouenit regnumcælorum, sed in mandatis Dei laborantibus, atq; vigilantibus. vt si dona illius irrita nõ fecerimus, per ea quæ dedit, mereamur accipere* Leo.ser.2. in Epipha. & ser.5. ibid.

*quod promisit*. The kingdome of heauen commeth not to sleapers, but to such as labour in Gods commandementes, and watche to th'ende that if we make not his giftes ydle and voide, by such thinges as he hath geuen, we may deserue to receiue that which he hath promised.

The right and assured way to come to this fruite of Iu-
Miche. 6. stification, is to followe the counsel of the Prophete: *To do iustice, to loue mercie, to walke carefully in Gods sight. Circũ-*
Leo. ser. 1. de Quadrag. *spiciat se omnis anima Christiana.* Let euery Christiã soule, saith S. Leo, looke about it selfe, *and by straite examination discusse the inwarde thoughtes of her harte, let it see that no debate cleaue there, that no couetousnes settle, let chastitie driue away incontinencie, let the light of truth driue away the darckenesse of lying. &c. Let pride asswage, let humilitie be taken in, let anger amende, let vengeance cease, and wronges*
Aug. Ser. 15. de ver. Apost. *be forgotten.* The like counsel geueth S. Augustine: *Proficite fratres mei. &c.* Increase my bretherne, *serche your selues euer without guyle and flattery.* Especially folow one shorte rule which he maketh for euery man, saying: *In-*
Augustin. Tract. 6. in epistol. Ioan. *terroga cor tuum si est ibi dilectio fratris.* Examine thy harte whether the loue of thy brother be there: *Si inueneris te habere charitatem, habes spiritũ Dei.* If thou finde that thou haste charitie, thou haste the spirite of God: And then, *if*
Rom. 8. *his spirite that raysed Iesus from the deade dwell in you, he that raysed Iesus from the deade, will also geue life to your mortall bodies.*

And thus do we see, that the way to examine and trie our selues, and thereby to iudge of our Iustification, is not only to serche whether we haue faith, but also whether
2. Cor. 7. we loue, and liue godly. *Perficientes sanctificationem in timore Dei.* Doing holinesse in the feare of God.

The

## The Conclusion and ende of the VVoorke.

THVS haue I nowe by Gods helpe, finished the second parte of this Treatie, wherein mine intente hath ben to aduertise the Christian Reader, how to eschewe the second great, or rather most dangerouse fal, on the lefte hande, whiche S. Augustine willeth all that teache or speake of Iustification, to beware of. *The perill is for men to presume only of Goddes mercie, dooing nothing them selues, towarde their owne saluation*: whiche opinion, he saieth, *if any man folowe, leadeth him vndoubtedly to euerlasting ruine of sowle and bodie*. See the Preface. Aug. in præfat. Psal. 31.

And bicause the onely or readiest meane to leade a man to that fall, is, to thinke that faith alone may suffise to iustifie and saue vs: I haue at good length prooued, that faith alone is not inough to bring a sinner from sinnefull estate to Gods fauour, nor of wicked to make him righteouse, without the woorking and helpe of hope, charitie, penance, and the Sacramentes of Christ: wherein I haue ben the longer, bicause this opinion is lately crepte into the worlde, and nowe spred farre and wide. For albeit in times past, some thought they might be saued without good woorkes, yet did they not saie, they might be saued without the Sacramentes: As by this booke of S. Augustine thou maiest see. And so all be it they waded deepe inough to drowne them selues, yet wente they not so farre into the bottomelesse goulfe, as sundrie haue done in this our age, who saie, that nothing woorketh in the acte of our Iustification, but onely faith. And therevpon haue brought in, this proposition, and made it a com- *De fide & oper. c. 27* mon ſpeache emong them ſelu es an d theirs, *Faith alone iuſtifieth*, excluding therby fro m the acte of our Iuſtification, not onely hope, charitie, and penance, but alſo the very Sacramentes. For if faith alone iuſtifie a ſinner, and make him of wicked rightuouſe, then is there none of theſe requiſite or neceſſary for that effecte, whiche neuer anie auncіente man learned, that I haue ſeene, didde maineteine.

I haue further declared, that faith alone can continue no man in the ſtate of grace, muche leſſe increaſe him in iuſtice, and leaſt of all, bring him to the ende and perfectiō of iuſtice in life euerlaſting without the helpe of good woorkes. And ſo is the opinion of Iuſtification by onely faith in trueth and deede diſprooued, and founde vntrue, in no ſenſe maintenable, as they take it: I ſaie as they take it. For although certaine auncіente Fathers ſometime vſed theſe woordes, *Faith alone iuſtifieth:* yet doe they not meane thereby, as theſe doe, to exclude any of the vertues afore named, or Sacramentes, as I haue plainely ſhewed.

In the. 18. Chapt. of this ſecōd booke.

I haue according to my promiſe, in this whole Treatie affirmed nothing of my ſelfe: that whiche I haue ſaied, I haue prooued by euidente Scriptures, folowing euery where the interpretation of ſuche as God *hath placed in his Churche, to be Paſtours and Doctours, to the perfiting of the holie, and to the building vp of Chriſtes body, which is his Churche.*

Epheſ.4.

The labour hath ben beſtowed, to the ende that the godly man, whiche is the Chriſtian man, *might be perfite and ſownde, readie and inſtructed to all good Woorkes.* Whiche God graunte thee, and mee with thee good Reader.

2.Timo.3.

der: Once the beste exhortation and righte encouragemente to doe good workes, is truely to thinke and beleeue, that no man hauing time and opportunitie to doe them, shal be saued without them. See the .23 chapter.

*Thus endeth the Seconde Booke of this Treatie of Mans Iustification.*

## *The Praier of the Churche.*

Omnipotens sempiterne Deus, da nobis fidei, spei, & charitatis augmentum, & vt mereamur assequi quod promittis, fac nos amare quod præcipis.

*Almightie euerlasting God, geue vs increase of faith, hope, and charitie: and to the intent we may deserue to come to that which thou promisest, make vs loue that, that thou commaundest, through Iesus Christe our Lorde. Amen.*

# TO THE READER.

TO the intente, Christian Reader, thou maiest vnderstande, both that, the doctrine of Mans Iustification, declared vnto thee in this Treatie, is consonant and agreable to the assured and vndoubted doctrine of Christes Catholique Churche, by long and mature deliberation, by most exact and diligent * trauaile, expressed and sette forth to the worlde, in the late General Councell holden at Trent: and also that the saied moste Reuerende and Learned Assemblie of Bisshops, Doctours, and Fathers, defined nothing in this matter, but suche as most expressely agreeth with the holy Scriptures, and consent of the Auncient Fathers, here in this Treatie laied before thee: to this intente I saie, and for these causes, thou haste here to this Treatie annexed, the Sixt Session of the saied Councell, with the Canons of the same, translated into English, worde for worde: In the which, the whole doctrine of Iustification, is most exactly, plainely, and withal shortly, taught, declared, and comprised.

* Aboute this onely mater, the Bisshops and Doctors, had lxxx. seuerall meetinges and conferences, before they concluded.

The

# THE SIXTH SESSION OF *THE GENERAL COVNCEL OF TRENT HOLDEN THE THIRTENTH DAIE OF IANVARIE, IN THE YEARE OF OVR LORDE 1547.*

## A DECREE TOVCHING Iuſtification.

### *The Preface.*

FOR ſo muche as there is at this preſent a certaine erroneous doctrine ſowen in diuers and ſundrie places concerning Iuſtification, not without the loſſe of many ſowles and greuous decaie of vnitie in the Church: to the praiſe and glorie of Almightie God, tranquillitie of the Church, and ſaluation of ſowles, the Holie, Oecumenicall, and Generall Councell of Trent, lawfully aſſembled in the Holie Ghoſt, the right Reuerend Lordes *Iohn Maria de Monte*, Biſſhop of Preneſte, and *Marcellus* Prieſt by title of the holie Croſſe in Hieruſalem, Cardinals of the holie Churche of Rome, and Legates Apoſtolike *de Latere*, being in it Preſidentes, in the behalfe of our moſt holie Father in Chriſte and Soueraine Lorde *Paulus* by the prouidence of God the third Pope (of that name) intendeth to ſet out to all the Faithfull of Chriſte, a true and ſound doctrine of Iuſtification, which Ieſus Chriſt the Sonne of iuſtice, the beginner and ender of our Faith hath taught, the Apoſtles haue deliue- *Heb.12.*

red, and the Catholike Church, by suggestion of the holy Ghost, hath continually kept: streightly forbidding, that no man from hence foorth be so bold as to beleue, preach, or teach otherwise, then is ordeined and declared in this present Decree.

### Of the insufficiencie of our nature and of the Lawe towardes Iustification.

### *THE I. CHAP.*

FIRST of all, the holie Councell declareth, that to vnderstand the doctrine of Iustification wel and sincerely, it behoueth euerie man to acknowledge and confesse, that, after what time all men had in the preuarication of Adam lost their innocencie, and were made vncleane, and (as the Apostle saieth) *by nature the Sonnes of Wrath* (as it is expressed before in the Decree concerning originall sinne:) they were so muche the bondslaues of sinne, and in such subiection to the deuil and death, that they could not be deliuered or rise againe out of it, neither the Gentiles by the strength of nature, neither yet the Iewes them selues by the letter of the law of Moyses: albeit that free will was not vtterly quenched in them, though the strength of it were much weakened and decaied.

*Rom. 5.* *Ephes. 2.*

### Of the dispensation and Mysterie of the coming of Christe.

### *THE II. CHAP.*

WHerevpon it came to passe, that the heauenly Father, the Father of mercies, and God of all comfort,

comfort, when that blessed fulnes of time was come, sent vnto men Christ Iesus his owne Sonne, who was declared and promised vnto manie holie Fathers, both before the law, and in the time of the lawe: to the ende that he should redeeme the Iewes, which were vnder the lawe: and that the Gentiles, which folowed not iustice, might laie hand on iustice, and that all men might receiue the adoption of Sonnes. *This Iesus, hath God set foorth an appeacer by Faith in his owne bloud for our sinnes, and not only for our sinnes, but also for the sinnes of the whole worlde.*

Galat. 4.
Rom. 9.
Ephes 2.
1. Ioan. 2.

VVho they are, that are iustified by Christe.

## THE V. CHAPTER.

HOwbeit, although he died for all men, yet do not al men receiue the benefite of his death, but they only, to whome the merite of his passion is communicated. For as in deede, men should not be borne vniust vnlesse they were descended and borne of the seede of Adam: for so much as in that descente they do gather by him an vnrighteousnes of their owne, whiles they are conceiued: euen so they should neuer be iustified, except they were borne againe in Christ: bicause in that second birth, by the merite of his passion, grace is geauen vnto them, by the which they are made iust. For this benefite the Apostle exhorteth vs to geaue thankes at all times to the Father, which *hath made vs woorthie to be partakers of the lotte of Saintes in light, and hath deliuered vs from the power of darkenes, and hath transposed vs into the kingdome of his welbeloued Sonne, in whome we haue redemption and remission of sinnes.*

Colos. 3.

## THE SIXT SESSION

### A description of the Iustification of the wicked, and the manner of it in the state of grace.

### THE IIII. CHAPTER.

BY the which wordes is described and declared the Iustification of the wicked, that it is, a translation from that state, in which man is borne the sonne of the first Adam, into the state of grace and adoption of the sonnes of God by the second Adam *Iesus Christ* our Sauiour: The which translation, after the publishing of the Gospel, can not be made, without receiuing the water of Baptisme, or the purpose to receiue it, as it is written: *Except a man be borne againe by water and the Holie Ghost, he can not enter into the kingdome of God.*

*Ioan. 3.*

### That it is necessarie for such as be of age to prepare them selues to receiue Iustification, and from whence Iustification commeth.

### THE V. CHAPTER.

THE holie Councell declareth moreouer, that the beginning of Iustification, in such as be of age, is to be taken of the preuenting grace of God through Christ Iesus, that is to say, of his calling, whereby they are called without anie their owne merites: that they, which were turned away from God through sinnes, may, by his stirring and helping grace, be disposed to conuerte them selues, vnto their owne Iustification, by yealding their

their consent freely, and woorking together with the grace of God: in such sort, that, when God toucheth the harte of man by geuing vnto it the light of the Holie Ghost, neither may the man him selfe do nothing at all, when he receiueth that inspiration (for he hath power also to caste it away, and refuse it) neither yet can he without the grace of God, of his owne free will, moue him selfe to iustice before God. Whereupon in the holie Scriptures, when it is said: *Be you turned vnto me, and I will be turned vnto you*: We are put in minde of our libertie. When we answere, *Turne vs, O Lord vnto thee, and we shalbe turned*: we do confesse, that we are preuented by the grace of God.

*Zacha. 1.*

*Thren. 5.*

The manner of our preparation.

## *THE VI. CHAPTER.*

VNTO this same iustice are men disposed, whiles, being stirred vp and holpen by the grace of God, they conceiue faith by hearing, and are freely moued towardes God, beleeuing such thinges to be true, as are by God reueled and promised: and that especially, that the wicked is iustified by God through his grace, through the redemption, which is in Christe Iesus. And when they vnderstand them selues to be sinners, turning them selues from the feare of Gods iustice (wherewith they are profitably shaken) to cōsider the mercie of God, they are raised vppe into hope, trusting, that God wilbe mercifull vnto them for Christes sake: and so beginne they to loue him, as the fountaine of al iustice, and therfore are moued against sinnes, through a certeine hatred

and deteſtation, that is, through ſuche penaunce, as is behouefull to be done before Baptiſme: finally when they purpoſe to receiue Baptiſme, they are moued to beginne a new life, and to keepe the commaundementes of God.
Hebr.11. Of this diſpoſition it is writen, *he that commeth vnto God, muſt beleeue, that he is, and that he is a rewarder to thoſe*
Matth.9. *that ſeeke him.* Againe: *Be of good comfort ſonne, thy ſinnes*
Eccle. 1. *are forgeuē thee.* Againe: *The feare of God driueth out ſinne.*
Actor.2. Againe: *Do you penance, and let euerie one of you be Baptized, in the name of Ieſus Chriſte, to the remiſsion of your ſinnes, and you ſhall receiue the gifte of the holie Ghoſt.* A-
Luc.24. gaine: *Go ye therefore and teach all nations, Baptizing them in the name of the Father, and of the Sonne, and of the holie Ghoſt, teaching them to keepe what ſo euer thinges I haue*
1.Reg.7. *commaunded you.* Finally: *Prepare your hartes vnto God.*

VVhat the Iuſtification of the wicked is, and what the cauſes of it are.

## THE VII. CHAPTER.

AFter this diſpoſition or preparation, the Iuſtification it ſelfe foloweth: which is not onelie the remiſsion of ſinnes, but alſo a ſanctifying and renewing of the inward man through the voluntarie receiuing of grace and giftes, whereby man is made, of vniuſt, iuſt: of an ene-
Epheſ.1. mie, a friend: that he maie *be the heire of life euerlaſting according to hope.*

The cauſes of Iuſtification 1. Of this Iuſtification the cauſes are theſe. The cauſe final is the glorie of God and of Chriſte, and life euerlaſting. The cauſe efficient is our mercifull God, who doth freely

freely clenſe and ſanctifie, ſealing and annointing vs with the holie ſpirite of promiſe, which *is the pleadge of our inheritance*. The cauſe meritorious, is his moſt deere the onlie begotten ſonne, our Lord Ieſus Chriſt: who when we were ennimies, *for the exceding great charitie, wherewith he loued vs*, hath deſerued Iuſtificatiõ for vs, through his moſt holie paſion on the tree of the Croſſe, and hath made ſatisfaction vnto God the father for vs. The cauſe instrumental is the Sacrament of Baptiſme, which is the Sacrament of faith, without the which no man euer atteined Iuſtification. Laſt of al, the only cauſe formal is the iuſtice of God: Not that iuſtice, by the which God him ſelfe is iuſt, but that, by the which he maketh vs iuſt: by the which, when it is geauen vs frõ God, we are renewed in the ſpirite of our mind, and we are not onely reputed iuſt, but we are named iuſt, and are iuſt in deede, receiuing iuſtice in our ſelues, eche man his, according to the meaſure, which the holie Ghoſt geaueth to ech particular man, as his will is, and according to the proper diſpoſition and working of euerie man together with the holie Ghoſt. For although no man can be iuſt, but he, to whom the merites of the paſion of our Lord *Ieſus Chriſt* are communicated, yeat in this Iuſtification of a wicked man it is done, whiles by the merite of the ſaid moſt holie paſion, through the holie Ghoſt *the charitie of God is powred abroade in the hartes* of thoſe, that are iuſtified, and cleaueth faſt in them. Wherupõ in Iuſtificatiõ, man receiueth with the remiſion of ſinnes all theſe thinges, faith, hope, and charitie powred in him together by Chriſte, in whom he is ingraffed. For faith, vnleſſe hope come vnto it and charitie, neither doth it perfectely vnite a man

Ephes. 1. 2. 3. 4. Rom. 5.

vnto

vnto Christe, neither doth it make him a liuely member of his bodie. By reason whereof, it is most truly saied: that
Iacob. 2. *Faith without woorkes is dead* and idle. Againe *In Christ*
Gal. 5. *Iesus neither to be circumcised, nor to be without circumcision auaileth any thing, but Faith, that worketh by charity.* This Faith do the Catecumens require of the Churche according to the tradition of the Apostles, before they receiue the Sacrament of Baptisme, when they require that Faith, that geaueth life euerlasting: the whiche life faith can not geaue without hope and charitie. Whereupon they heare this saying of Christe, foorthwith pronounced vnto them:
Math. 19 *If thou wilt enter vnto life, keepe the commaundementes.* And thus do they receiue a true and Christian iustice: the whiche, being geauen vnto them by Christ Iesus as the first stole, in place of that, which Adam lost both to him selfe and to vs, through his disobedience, such, as are regenerated in Baptisme, are by and by commaunded to keepe white and vnspotted, that they maie bring it before the iudgement seate of our Lord *Iesus Christ*, and so receiue life euerlasting.

### How it maie be vnderstanded, that the wicked is iustified by Faith, and freely.

### THE VIII. CHAP.

Rom. 5. Gratis. NOVV whereas the Apostle saieth, that *man is iustified by faith, and freely*: those wordes are to be taken in that sense, which the continual agreement of the Catholike Churche hath alwaies holden and expressed,

pressed, which is: that, we be said to be therfore iustified by faith, bicause faith is the beginning of mannes saluation, the foundation, and roote of all Iustification: *Without which it is impossible to please God*, and to come vnto the felowship of his children: And that we be said, to be therefore iustified freely, bicause none of those thinges, whiche go before Iustification, whether it be faith, or woorkes, deserueth the grace of Iustification. *For if it be grace, then is it not by woorkes: otherwise*, as the same Apostle saieth, *grace were not then grace.*

*Hebr. 11.*

*Rom. 11.*

Against the vaine affiance of Heretikes.

## THE IX. CHAPTER.

AND although it be necessarie to beleeue, that sinnes neither are, neither haue ben at anie time forgeuen, otherwise then freely, by the mercie of God for Christes sake: yet muste we say, that sinnes neither are, nor haue ben forgeuen to anie man, that boasteth of an affiãce and certaintie of the forgeuenes of his sinnes, and resteth vpon it only: For so much as this affiance (which is vaine, and farre wide from all godlines) maie be, and is in our time emõgest heretikes and schismatikes, set foorth and mainteined against the Catholike Church, yea and that with earnest contention. Neither is that opinion to be holden, that such, as are truely iustified, must without all doubte in the worlde make them selues assured, that they are iustified, and that no man is absolued from his sinnes and iustified, but he, which beleeueth certainly, that he is absolued and iustified, and that absolution and Iustification is made perfecte by this belefe onely, as though he that beleeued this,doubted of the promises of God,and of the efficacie of the death and resurrection of Christ. For as no godlie man ought to doubt of the mercie of God,of the merite of Christ,and of the vertue and efficacie of the Sacramentes: so euerie man,when he looketh vpon him selfe,and considereth his owne weakenes and indisposition, maie stand in doubt and feare of his owne grace, for so much as no man is able to know by certaintie of faith (such as is infallible)that he hath atteined the grace of God.

Of the increase of Iustification,after it is receiued.

## THE X. CHAPTER.

*Ephes.2.* *Psal.83.* *2.Cor.4.*

THEY therefore, that are thus iustified and made *the frendes and of the houshold of God, going from vertue to vertue,are renewed*, as the Apostle saieth, *from daie to daie*: that is to say, by mortifying the members of their flesh, and by yelding them,as the armour of iustice to sanctification,by keeping the cōmaundementes of God and of the Churche, they growe in this iustice, which they receiued by the grace of Christ, faith woorking together with good woorkes, and so they are iustified more and more,as it is writen: *He that is iust,let him be further iustified.* and againe: *Be not ashamed to be iustified euen vnto death.* and againe: *You see, that man is iustified by woorkes,and not by faith only.* This increase of iustice doth the holy Church aske of God, when she praieth thus: *Geaue vs,O Lord,increase of faith,hope,and charitie.*

*Apoc. 22.* *Eccles.18.* *Iacob.2.*

Of the

## Of the obseruation of the commaundementes. Of the necessitie and possibilitie thereof.

## THE XI. CHAPTER.

NO man, be he neuer so much iustified, ought to thinke him selfe to be discharged from the keeping of the cõmandementes: no man ought to vse that talke (which is both rash and forbiddẽ of the holy Fathers vnder paine of excõmunication) that the cõmandements of God are impossible to be kept of a man being iustified. For God cõmaundeth not thinges impossible: but by cõmaunding, he warneth thee both to do, what thou canst, and to aske of him, what thou canst not do, and so doth he helpe, that thou maist be able to do, *whose cõmandementes are not heauie, whose yoke is sweete, and burden light.* For they, that are the sonnes of God, do loue Christ: and *such as do loue him, do* (as he him selfe witnesseth) *keepe his wordes*, the which thing vndoubtedly they are able to performe with Gods helpe. For although men in this mortal life, be they neuer so holy and iust, do some time fal at the lest into certaine light and dailie trespasses, which are also called *veniall sinnes*, yet do they not for that cease to be iust. For this is the voice of iust men, both humble and true: *forgeaue vs our trespasses.* Wherfore the iust ought to thinke them selues so much the more bownd to walke in the waie of iustice, to the end that being now deliuered from sinne, and made seruantes vnto God, they maie *liue soberly, iustly, and godly*, and so go foreward by Christ Iesus, by whome they haue had accesse into this grace. For God forsaketh not such as are once iustified by his grace,

Note. 1. Ioan. 5. Matth. 11. Ioan. 14. Matt. 6. Tit. 2.

vnlesse he be first forsaken of them. No man ought therfore to flatter him selfe in onlie faith, thinking that he is made an heire, and that he shall obteine the inheritance for faith onlie, although he suffer not with Christ, that he
Hebr.5. maie be glorified with Christ. For euen *Christ him selfe* (as the Apostle saieth) *for all that he was the sonne of God, yet did he learne, by such thinges as he suffered, obedience: and when he was perfited, he was made to all suche as were obedient vnto him, the cause of euerlasting saluation.* Wherefore the Apostle warneth such as are iustified, say-
1.Cor.9. ing: *Know you not, that suche as runne in the race, they runne all together, but one receiueth the price? So runne ye, that you maie laie hand on the game. I therefore do so runne, not as for an vncertaintie, I do so fight, not as one that beateth the aier: but I do chastice my bodie, and bring it into bondage: lest peraduenture, when I haue preached vnto other men, I maie become a castaway my selfe.* In like
2.Pet.1. manner speaketh the chiefe of the Apostles S. Peter: *Do your endeuour to the vttermost, that ye maie by good workes make your calling and election certaine: for in so doing you shall not sinne at anie time.* By the which places it is euident, that those men do impugne the Doctrine of the true and Catholike religion, which saie, that the iust man sinneth in euery good worke at the lest venially, or that he doth (which is more intolerable) deserue euerlasting damnation. It is also manifest, that they do impugne the true and Catholike doctrine, which do determine, that the iust do sinne in all their woorkes, if in the same good woorkes in stirring vp their owne sluggishnesse, and in cheering them selues to runne in the race, they do principally respect this, that God may be glorified, and withal do looke

vpon

vpon the euerlasting reward: for so much as it is writen: *I haue inclined my hart to do thy iustifications, for the rewardes sake.* and the Apostle saieth of Moises, *that he looked vpon the rewarde.* *Psal. 118.* *Hebr. 11.*

That the rash andpresumptuous opinion of predestination is to be eschewed.

## *THE XII. CHAP.*

NO man, so long as he is in this mortall life, ought to presume so far of the secret mysterie of Gods predestination, as to saie assuredly, that he is in the number of the predestinate: as though this were true, that a man being once iustified, either coulde not sinne any more, or els, if he do sinne, that he should assure him selfe of amendement: for (vnlesse it be by special reuelation) it can not be knowen whom God hath chosen vnto him selfe.

Of the gifte of perseuerance.

## *THE XIII. CHAPTER.*

THE like maie be saied of the gifte of perserance, wherof it is writen: *who so perseuereth vntil the ende, he shall be saued*: the whiche thing can not be had from anie other, then from him, which is able to stay him, that standeth, that he maie continually stand, and to set him vp againe that falleth. No man maie promise him selfe any thing of certaintie, with an absolute certaintie, *Matth. 10 & 24.*

 although

although all men ought to ſettle and repoſe a moſt ſure hope in the helpe of God. For God, (excepte they
Philip.1. do not their parte according to his grace) *as he hath begon a good Woorke, ſo Will he ende it, Woorking in them*
1.Cor.8. *to Will, and to make perfecte*. Howbe it *let them, that*
1.Cor.10. *thinke them ſelues to ſtande, take heede, that they fall not:*
Philip.2. And let them *With feare and trembling Woorke their ſaluation*, in labours, in watchinges, in almeſdeedes, in praiers and offeringes, in faſtinges and chaſtitie. For, knowing that they are regenerated in hope of glorie, and not as yet in glorie, they haue cauſe to miſdoubt of the battaile, whiche remaineth with the fleſh, with the worlde, and with the diuel: in the whiche battaile they can not be conquerers, vnleſſe with the grace of
Rom. 8. God they obey the Apoſtle, ſaying: *We be debters, not to the fleſh, to liue according to the fleſh: for if you liue according to the fleſh, you ſhall die: but if you ſhall mortifie the deedes of the fleſhe by the ſpirite, you ſhall liue.*

### Of them, that are fallen, and of their recouer.

### THE XIIII. CHAPTER.

NOW ſuch, as are through ſinne fallen from the grace of Iuſtification, whiche they had receiued, maie be iuſtified againe, if, when God ſtirreth them to riſe, they will procure through the merite of Chriſte to recouer the grace loſte, by the Sacrament of Penance. For this manner of Iuſtification is the recouecouering of him, that is fallen, whiche the holie Fathers aptly termed *the second boord after shipwracke* of grace lost. For in deede, for them that fal into sinnes after Baptisme, *Christ Iesus* hath instituted the Sacrament of Penance, when he saied: *Take ye the holie Ghoste: Whose sinnes ye forgeaue, they are forgeauen them: and Whose ye reteine, they are reteined.* Wherfore it is to be declared, that the penance of a Christian man after his fall differreth verie much from that, whiche is done before Baptisme: and that in this penance is conteined, not only a ceasing from sinnes and a detestation of them, or a contrite and humbled hart, but also a Sacramentall confession of the saied sinnes (at the leste in purpose, and to be made at time conuenient) and the absolution of a Priest. There is also conteined in this penance a satisfaction, by fastinges, almesdeedes, praiers, and other godlie exercises of spiritual life: not for the paine euerlasting, which is forgeauen either by the Sacrament, or els by purposing of the Sacrament together with the offence, but for the temporall paine, the whiche (as the holie Scriptures teache vs) is not alwaies forgeauen wholly (as it is in Baptisme) to suche, as being vnthankefull for the grace of God, whiche they haue receiued, *haue sorrowed the holie Ghost, and haue not ben afraied to violate the temple of God.* Of this penance it is writen: *be mindefull from Whence thou art fallen, do penance, and do the former Woorkes.* And againe: *That sorrowe, Whiche is according to God, Woorketh penance towardes a stable saluation.* And againe: *Do ye penance, and do ye the Woorthie frutes of penance.*

*Ioan. 20.*

*Ephes. 4.*

*Apocal. 2.*
*2. Cor. 7.*
*Matth 3.*
*Luca 3.*

That

## That by euerie mortal ſinne grace is loſt, but not Faithe.

### THE XV. CHAP.

Rom.16. AGainſt the craftie wittes of certaine men, whiche *through ſwete talke and faire wordes do ſeduce the hartes of innocentes*, it is to be holden, that the grace of Iuſtification once receiued is loſt, not only by infidelitie, by the whiche Faith it ſelfe is loſt, but alſo by any other mortal ſinne, although faith be not loſt. Herein do we defend the doctrine of Gods lawe, which excludeth from the kingdome of God, not onely Infidels, but alſo
1.Cor.6. the faithfull, being *fornicatours, adulterrers, wantonnes, buggerers, theeues, couetouſe, drunkerdes, euill ſpeakers, extorcioners*, and al others, which do commit mortal ſinnes: from the which they maie with the aſsiſtance of Gods grace abſteine, and for which they are ſeperated from the grace of Chriſt.

## Of the fruicte of Iuſtification, that is to ſaie, of the merite of good woorkes, and of the conſideration of merite.

### THE XVI. CHAP.

WHEN men therfore are by theſe meanes iuſtified, whether they do continually keepe the grace once receiued, or whether they do leeſe it and recouer it againe, the wordes of the Apoſtle are to be ſet be set before them: *Abound ye in euerie good woorke, knowing that your labour is not void in our Lord. For God is not vniust, that he will forget your woorke and loue, whiche ye haue shewed in his name.* And: *Leese not your affiance, which hath a great reward.* And therefore to such, as woorke well to the ende, and hope in God, we ought to set foorth life euerlasting, both as a grace mercifully promised vnto the Sonnes of God through Christ Iesus, and as a wages faithfully to be paied, according to the promise of God him selfe, to their good woorkes and merites. For this is that *crowne of Iustice* whiche the Apostle saied, *was laied vp for him after his conflicte and running, whiche* he saied, *should be rendered vnto him by the iuste iudge*: And not onely to him, but also *to all them, that loue the comming of Christe.* For seing that the selfe same Christe Iesus doth continually sende downe by influence into them, that are iustified, as the head into the members, and as a vine into his branches, a vertue, the whiche vertue goeth before, accompanieth, and foloweth their good woorkes, without the whiche their woorkes could not posibly be acceptable to God and meritorious: we ought to beleeue, that there lacketh nothing els in such as are iustified, wherfore they maie not be thought, by their good woorkes, whiche are done in God, to haue satisfied the lawe of God, (so muche, as the state of this life requireth) and truly to haue deserued life euerlasting, which they shal enioy, when the time cometh, if so be that, they depart out of this life in grace: for so much as Christe our Sauiour saieth: *If any man shall drinke of this water which I shall geaue him, he shall not thirst for euer: but*

Hebr. 10. 1. Cor. 15. 2. Tim. 4. Ioan. 4.

*it shall be made in him a fountaine of water springing to life euerlasting.* And thus, neither is our owne proper iustice so taken to be our owne, as though it proceded from our owne selues, neither is the Iustice of God either vnknowen, or refused. For that Iustice, which is called ours, bicause we are iustified by it cleauing fast in vs, the selfe same is the Iustice of God, bicause it is powred into vs by God through the merite of Christe.

Neither is that to be omitted in this place, that although there be so much ascribed vnto good woorkes in the holie Scriptures, that Christe promiseth euen
*Matth.10.* to him, that shall *geaue a draught of colde water to one of his litle ones, that he shall not lacke his rewarde:* and the Apostle witnesseth, that *that tribulation of ours, which in*
*2.Cor.4.* *this present life is but short and light, woorketh in vs an euerlasting weight of glorie high aboue measure:* yet God forbid, that a Christian man should either trust, or glorie in him selfe, and not in our Lorde, whose goodnes is so great towardes all men, that he will haue those thinges to be their merites, which are his owne giftes. And bi-
*Iacob.3.* cause *we offende all in many pointes*, euerie man ought to haue before his eies, like as his mercie and goodnes, euen so his seueritie and iudgement: neither ought any man to iudge him selfe, although he knowe nothing by him selfe: bicause all the life of men is to be examined and
*1.Cor.4.* iudged, by the iudgement not of man, but of God: *who shall bring to light the hidden thinges of darkenes, and*
*Matth.16* *make manifest the counsels of hartes:* and then *shall euerie*
*Rom.6.* *man haue his commendation from God, who*, as it is writen, *shall render to euerie man according to his woorkes.*

After

After this Catholique Doctrine touching Iustification, the whiche vnlesse euerie man receiue faithfully and firmely, he can not be iustified, it hath pleased the holie Councell to adioine hereunto these Canons: to the entent all men maie knowe, not onely, what to holde and folowe, but also, what they ought to auoide and flee.

# THE CANONS OF THE SAME SESSION TOVCHING IVSTIFICATION.

## THE FIRST CANON.

Note Reader, the doctrine of the Catholike Churche is not, as heretikes do slaunder it.

IF anie man saie, that a man maie be Iustified before God by his owne woorkes, whiche are done, either by the power of mannes nature, or by the doctrine of the lawe, without the grace of God through *Iesus Christe:* Accursed be he.

## THE SECOND CANON.

IF anie man saie, that the grace of God is geauen through *Iesus Christe* to this ende onely, that man maie with the more facilitie liue iustly, and deserue life euerlasting, as though he were able by free will without grace to persourme both the one and the other: (thowgh hardly and with difficultie) Accursed be he.

## THE THIRD CANON.

IF any man saie, that man is able without the preuenting inspiration of the holie Ghoste, and aide of the same, to beleeue, to hope, to loue, or to repent (so as it behoueth) that the grace of Iustification be geuen vnto him: Accursed be he.

## THE FOVRTH CANON.

IF anie man ſaie,that mannes free will moued and ſtirred of God, woorketh nothing together with him by aſſenting vnto God,ſtirring and calling,whereby he may diſpoſe and prepare him ſelſe towardes the obteining of the grace of Iuſtification, and that he can not diſſent, if he will, but that being as a thing without life, he doth nothing at all, but beareth him ſelſe, as a thinge that ſuffreth only: Accnrſed be he.

## THE FIFTH CANON.

IF anie man ſaie, that mannes free wil is loſt and extinguiſhed after the ſinne of Adam: or that it is a thing of a title only,or rather a title without a thing:finally if any man ſaie, that it is a deuiſe brought into the Church by Satan: Accurſed be he.

## THE SIXT CANON.

IF anie man ſaie,that it is not in the power of man, to make his waies euyll, but that God woorketh euyll woorkes euen ſo, as he doth the good, not only by permiſsion, but alſo properly and by him ſelſe, in ſo much, that the treaſon of Iudas be no leſſe the proper woorke of God,then the calling of Paule: Accurſed be he.

## THE SEVENTH CANON.

IF anie man ſaie, that all woorkes, which are done before Iuſtification, by what meanes ſo euer they be done,are verily ſinnes,or that they deſerue the hatred of

God, or that a man, the more earneſtly he endeuoureth to diſpoſe him ſelfe to grace, the more greuouſly he doth ſinne : Accurſed be he.

## THE EIGHTH CANON.

IF anie man ſaie, that the feare of hell, by the which feare we do flee vnto the mercie of God, in ſorowing for our ſinnes, or els absteine from ſinning, is ſinne, or that it maketh ſinners the worſe : Accurſed be he.

## THE NINTH CANON.

IF anie man ſaie, that the wicked is iuſtified by faith only, meaning thereby, that there is nothing els required, which ſhould worke withall towardes the atteining of the grace of Iuſtification, and that it is in no wiſe neceſſarie, that he be prepared and diſpoſed by the motion of his owne will : Accurſed be he.

## THE TENTH CANON.

IF anie man ſaie, that men are iuſtified without the iuſtice of Chriſte, by which he hath deſerued for vs, or that they are iuſt by the ſame iuſtice [ of Chriſt ] * formally : Accurſed be he.

* *Formaliter.*

## THE ELEVENTH CANON.

IF anie man ſaie, that men are iuſtified, either by the only imputation of Chriſtes iuſtice, or els by the only remiſsion of ſinnes, excluding grace and charitie, which is

powred

powred in their hartes by the holy Ghoſt, and is inherent in them, or alſo that the grace by the which we are iuſtified, is only the fauour of God: Accurſed be he.

## THE TWELFTH CANON.

IF anie man ſaie, that the iuſtifying faith, is nothing els, but an affiance of the mercie of God forgeauing ſinnes for Chriſtes ſake, or that that affiance is the only thing, by the which we are iuſtified: Accurſed be he.

## THE THIRTENTH CANON.

IF anie man ſaie, that, to atteine the remiſsion of ſinnes, it is neceſſarie for euery man to beleeue aſſuredly, and without caſting anie doubt of his owne infirmitie and indiſpoſition, that his ſinnes are forgeauen him: Accurſed be he.

## THE FOVRTENTH CANON.

IF anie man ſaie, that a man is abſolued from his ſinnes, and iuſtified for that, that he beleeueth aſſuredly, that he is abſolued and iuſtified, or that no man is truly iuſtified, but he, which beleeueth him ſelfe to be iuſtified, and that by this beleeſe onlie, Abſolution and Iuſtification is perfited: Accurſed be he.

## THE FIFTENTH CANON.

IF anie man ſaie, that a man being borne againe [by Baptiſme] and iuſtified, is bownd by faith to beleeue, that

he is

he is aſſuredly in the number of the predeſtinate: Accurſed be he.

## THE SIXTENTH CANON.

IF anie man ſaie, of an abſolute and infallible certaintie, that he ſhall aſſuredly haue that great gifte of perſeuerance vntil the ende, vnleſſe he haue learned it by ſpecial reuelation: Accurſed be he.

## THE SEVENTENTH CANON.

IF anie man ſaie, that the grace of Iuſtification cometh not, but only to ſuch as are predeſtinate to life: and that all others, which are called, are onely called, but do not receiue grace, as who were by the power of God predeſtinate to euil: Accurſed be he.

## THE EIGHTENTH CANON.

IF anie man ſaie, that the commaundementes of God are impoſsible to be kept, euen of a man that is iuſtified, and in the ſtate of grace: Accurſed be he.

## THE NINETENTH CANON.

IF anie man ſaie, that there is nothing commaunded in the Ghoſpel beſides faith, that al other thinges are indifferent, neither commaunded, nor yet forbidden, but free: or that the ten commaundementes do nothing apperteine to Chriſtian men: Accurſed be he.

## THE TWENTETH CANON.

IF any man ſaie, that a man being iuſtified, and neuer ſo perfecte, is not bound to the keeping of the commaundementes

dementes of God and of the Churche, but onely to beleeue: as though the Gospell were a bare and absolute promise of life euerlasting, without anie condicion of keeping the commaundementes: Accursed be he.

## THE XXI. CANON.

IF anie man saie, that Christe Iesus was geauen by God vnto men, (onely) as a redeemer, whome they should trust, and not also as a lawe maker, whome they should obeie: Accursed be he.

## THE XXII. CANON.

IF anie man saie, that a man being iustified, either maie without the speciall helpe of God perseuere in the Iustice receiued, or that with the saied helpe he can not [perseuere]: Accursed be he.

## THE XXIII. CANON.

IF any man saie, that a man being once iustified can sinne no more, nor leese grace, and therfore saie, that he, which falleth and sinneth, was neuer truely iustified, or contrariwise, that he maie in all this life auoide al sinnes, euen venial [sinnes] vnlesse it be by special priuilege of God, as the Churche holdeth of the blessed Virgin Marie: Accursed be he.

## THE XXIIII. CANON.

IF any man saie, that iustice receiued is not conserued,

and also that it is not augmented before God by good woorkes, but that the woorkes them selues are the frutes onely and signes of Iustification [already] gotten, and not a cause of the same to be augmented: Accursed be he.

## THE XXV. CANON.

IF any man saie, that the iust sinneth in euerie good woorke, at the least venially, or, (which is more intolerable) mortally, and therefore deserueth euerlasting damnation: and that he is not damned for that onely, bicause God doth not impute those woorkes to damnation: Accursed be he.

## THE XXVI. CANON.

IF any man saie, that the iust ought not, for the good woorkes, whiche haue ben done in God, to looke and hope for the euerlasting reward from God, through his mercie and the merite of Iesus Christ, if they shal continue euen vntill the ende in well doing, and in keeping the commaundementes of God: Accursed be he.

## THE XXVII. CANON.

IF any man saie, that there is no sinne mortall, vnlesse it be [the sinne] of infidelitie, or that grace once receiued is lost for none other sinne, be it neuer so grieuous and enormeouse, excepte it be by the sinne of infidelitie: Accursed be he.

THE

## THE XXVIII CANON.

IF anie man ſaie, that, when grace is loſt by ſinne, faith is alwaies loſt withal: or that faith, which remaineth, is not true faith, although it be not liuelie faith: or, els that he, which hath faith without charitie, is not a Chriſtian: Accurſed be he.

## THE XXIX. CANON.

IF anie man ſaie, that he, whiche hath fallen after Baptiſme, can not riſe againe by the grace of God: or that he maie [riſe againe] but ſo, that he recouer the iuſtice loſte by onely faith, without the Sacrament of penauncee, as the holie, Romaine, and vniuerſall Churche, taught by Chriſt our Lord and his Apoſtles, hath til this daie profeſſed, kept, and taught: Accurſed be he.

## THE XXX. CANON.

IF anie man ſaie, that after the grace of Iuſtification receiued, the fault is ſo forgeauen to euerie penitent ſinner, and the gilt of the euerlaſting paine taken away in ſuch ſorte, that there remaineth no gilt of temporall paine to be paied, either in this worlde, or els in the worlde to come in purgatorie, before the way may be ſet open to the kingdome of heauen: Accurſed be he.

## THE XXXI. CANON.

IF anie man ſaie, that a man being iuſtified ſinneth,

whiles he woorketh well in respecte of euerlasting rewarde : Accursed be he.

## THE XXXII. CANON.

IF anie man saie, that the good woorkes of a man iustified, are so the giftes of God, that they are not also the good merites of him, that is iustified: or that he, which is iustified, doth not, by good woorkes (whiche are done by him by the grace of God, and by the merite of Iesus Christe, of whome he is a liuely member) verely deserue increase of grace, life euerlasting, and the atteining of thesame life euerlasting (so that he departe out of this life in grace) yea and the increase of glorie also: Accursed be he.

## THE XXXIII. CANON.

IF anie man saie, that, this Catholike doctrine touching Iustification, expressed by the holy Councel in this present Decree, doth in any wise derogate from the glorie of God, or from the merites of Iesus Christe our Lord, and doth not rather sett foorth the truth of our faith, and finally the glorie of God, and of Christe Iesus: Accursed be he.

*AMEN.*

# A TABLE OF THE CHAPTERS OF THE TREATIE OF IVSTIFICATION. Wherein the Argumentes and the principal *matters of the whole Treatie are* conteined.

## *In the First Booke.*

## In the Second Booke.



FINIS.

# CERTAINE TREATIES OF THE AVNCIENT HOLY FATHERS, TOVCHING THE DOCTRINE OF *good woorkes.*

*Namely,*

A Treatie of S. Augustine, whiche he Intituled: *Of Faith and VVorkes.*

Item, a Sermon of S. Chrysostome, of Praying vnto God.

Item, a Sermon of S. Basil, of Fasting.

Item, certaine Sermons of S. Leo the Great, of the same matter.

Last of al, a notable Sermon of S. Cyprian, of Almes dedes.

*Al newly translated into English.*

by Thomas Copley esquier.

*Tobiæ. 12.*

*Bona est Oratio cum Ieiunio, & Eleemosyna, magis quàm Thesauros auri recondere. Quoniam Eleemosyna à morte liberat, & ipsa est quæ purgat peccata, & facit inuenire vitam æternam.*

Prayer is good with Fasting, and Almes, better then to hide vppe treasures of golde. For Almes deliuereth from death, and shee it is which purgeth sinnes, and maketh to finde life euerlasting.

LOVANII,
Apud Ioannem Foulerum. Anno. 1569.
CVM PRIVILEGIO.

# The Translatour to the Reader.

THE loue that naturally men beare to
peace and quiet is so great,that there can
fall no controuersie emong such as be of
the better sorte, but they seeke meanes
euer to compounde and pacifie it.Either
they referre the decision of it to the
Iudge ordinarie of the lawe, or if they mistruste th'execution thereof, either bicause the iudge doth not fullie
vnderstande the matter, or els for that they thinke him
partiall of either side, they seeke the arbitrement and
sentence of some good man, whome they thinke bothe
to vnderstande perfitely right and iustice,and take him to
be affectionate of neither parte.In which doing they flee
not from the lawe, but seeke the true and right vnderstanding thereof without affection at his handes. I considering this order (Christian Reader) and moued with 2.Cor.5.
the Charitie that should binde vs all, waying with my
selfe the great controuersie that hath benne in this age
about sundrie pointes of Religion, namely in the article
of our Iustification: seing also that the matter tendeth
not to the losse of patrimonie or landes,but to the plaine
disherison of life euerlasting,and that emong vs, who all
professe to be the children of peace: I haue bene desirouse to propounde some meane of Pacification. And
bicause I see the trauaile that sundrie men haue taken as
it were pleading in this cause, hath not ended the controuersie, either bicause the doers were thoughte to be

parties of the one side, and thereby affectionat: either bicause being borne in this age, and liuing in the time of the controuersie, they had not the autoritie and credite of Iudges: I haue thought good to moue all such as finde in them selues either controuersie or doubt concerning that matter, to putte their owne opinion in arbitrement and compromisse. Not calling them hereby from the holy Scriptures, which as a Soueraine lawe the diuine wisedome hath lefte vnto vs, but leading them to the true vnderstanding of the holy Scriptures, vttered by such *as*
Ephe. 4. *God hath placed in his Churche, to be Pastorus and teachers*
Danie. 12. *to instructe manie to rightuousnes.*

I offer for Arbitrators, not men of this age such as may be thought any waie partiall or suspected, but such as in all mens iudgementes, and for all respectes, be or should be without exception. For the principall pointe of Iustification, I offer S. Augustine, a reuerend and most lerned Bishop in the Catholike Churche, not onely in high estimation in all Christian Regions, emong all estates and degrees during his life, but also for his excellent vertue worthely after his death taken for a Saincte, and for his singuler learning and knowledge in holy Scriptures, taken for one of the foure Doctours, and that the principallest of the Latin Churche, as one meete, whome all learned menne should followe as a lanterne and light in decision of matters of greatest weight. Who also in expounding of the holy Scriptures, may be the more safely trusted, for that he had in all his writinges a speciall care,
Lib. Con- not to seeke his priuate and singular opinion in the vn-
fess. 12. derstanding of them, as appereth by his owne woordes,
cap. 25. saying, *that God hath terribly geuen vs warning, that wee*

*should*

*ſhould not drawe his truthe to our owne priuate conſtruction, leſte wee were depriued of it.* And therefore hauing his opinion, thou arte ſure to haue the opinion of that moſte learned age, that he liued in. Againe, bicauſe that time framed vnto it ſelfe no newe doctrine, thou knoweſt alſo by him, what was the opinion of the Church before his time, euen from the Apoſtles vnto his age. And bicauſe he hath not ben contraried in that matter of any godly and learned, before this oure age, yea and in this our age is highly commended of ſuche as haue bene of greateſt credite, euen of the contrary ſide: thou knoweſt by him what hath bene the opinion of the Churche in all times touching the queſtiõ of our Iuſtification. Which he decideth thus farr, to wit, whether faith without good woorkes may ſaue a Chriſtian mán, or no. Whereunto he was moued by a corrupte opinion of ſome menne in his time. For whereas whole countries then, were not yet fully conuerted to Chriſte, and therefore diuers of al ages as they were brought to the faith, came yearly to be chriſtened: ſome were of opinion, that as manie as would beleeue the right faith, though they liued vngodly, yet might be receiued to Baptiſme, and be ſaued through faith and the Sacramentes, without good workes. Againſt whome he wrote this godly and learned Booke entituled: *De Fide & operibus*, of faith and woorkes, prouing therein at large, that faith without good life can ſaue no manne.

*Luther. in Sermone Germa. ad mulieres partus In-felicita. afflictas. Phi. Melanc. in decla. de S. Auguſtino. Caluinus Institut. cap. 18.*

The occaſion of S. Auguſtines Treatie of faith and vvorkes.

And bicauſe the value and eſtimation of good workes hath been, and yet is, called in queſtion, to wit, what accompte God maketh of them, and whether any reward be geuen vnto them eſpecially of life euerlaſting, and whether they be necessarie and able to healpe vs to attaine the same: I haue also chosen certaine Arbitrators touching the especial and chiefe workes commended by Christe, as Praier, Fasting, and Almes dedes. And those suche men, that in their handes thou mayste without daunger put thine opinion and iudgement. For Praier I haue chosen S. Chrysostome: for Fasting S. Basil and S. Leo: for almose deedes S. Cyprian, and S. Leo againe. The first and second Confessors, but so liuing for certaine yeares, that they daily looked to be Martyrs. The third also a Confessor, but such as in his life by a Generall Councell of 630. Bishops was called S. Leo, and since his death hath ben so taken of the Churche, and hath also for his most excellent learning bene surnamed Leo the Greate. The fowrth, a flower of the worlde in his life for vertue and learning, and in his death a moste constante and vndoubted Martyr. S. Cyprian and S. Augustine, liued in Africa: S. Basil in Asia: S. Leo in Europa: S. Chrysostome parte of his life in Asia, parte in Europa. And so by these doo we heare, as it were speaking in them, the voice of the whole Catholike Church, *which is the piller and staie of truthe*: against the whiche no man well aduised will frame him selfe a singular opinion. For vnto the Churche is *the holy Ghost the teacher of al trueth promised*, which promise no priuate man hath. Their Antiquitie is suche, that the latest and lowest of them al liued within 400. yeres after Christe. Peruse and way without affection (gentle Reader) the Treaties of these holy Fathers. I might require thee also to stand to their decision, bicause there is no exception to be taken against them. But that I leaue to Gods gracious working, and

*Concil. Chalcedo. Sess. 3.*

*1. Tim. 3.*

*Ioan. 15. & 16.*

thine

thine owne good will: bicause I take not vppon me to be Iudge of the cause, but a motioner toward peace: Only this muche I saie of them, that whereas Iudges should be voide of hatred, freendshippe, enmitie, and pittie, these men are suche. For as S. Augustine saieth of them and of others like: *Nullas nobiscum, vel vobiscum amicitias attenderunt, vel inimicitias exercuerunt: Neque nobis, neque vobis irati sunt: neque nos, neque vos miserati sunt: Quod in Ecclesia inuenerunt, tenuerunt: Quod didicerunt, docuerunt: quod à patribus acceperunt, hoc filijs tradiderunt:* They neither regarded friendshippe, nor were at enmitie with vs, or you: they were neither angry with vs, nor you: nor tooke compassion of vs, or of you. Looke what they founde in the Church, that they held: suche as they learned, they taught: what they receiued of their Fathers, that deliuered they to their children. Salust. de bel. Catil. Aug. contra. Iulia. Lib. 2.

Take therefore Christen Reader, if thou be a childe of the Churche, these thy Fathers lessons. *Aske thy Fathers,* saieth the holy Scripture, *and they will shew thee: enquire of thy Elders, and they will tell thee.* These be thy Fathers, these be thy Elders. These are suche, of whom Christe saied, *he that heareth you, heareth me, he that dispiseth you, dispiseth me.* These are the high Pastours of Christes Church, of whom Christ saied, *he that heareth not the Churche, let him be to thee, as an Heathen and Publicane.* These are the lightes of the Church, of whom Christe saied: *You are the light of the worlde:* whose predecessours saied also of them selues, that *they were placed to be a light to Nations, to woorke saluation euen to the vttermost of the earth.* Of whome also an other saied: *He that knoweth God, harkeneth vnto vs. He that is not of God,* Deut. 32. Luca. 10. Matth. 18. Matth. 5. Acto. 13. 1. Ioan. 4.

*of God, harkeneth not vnto vs. In this we trie the Spirite of Truthe, and the Sprite of Errour.* If thou wilt then be lead by Truthe, and not ſeduced by Errour, harken to theſe holy and learned Fathers, all Biſhoppes and chiefe Paſtours in the Churche of Chriſte, in that time and age, whiche the Aduerſaries them ſelues accompte for the pureſt. Let theſe hardely be thy Arbitrers in deciſion of theſe preſent controuerſies. They lacked no learning to know the Truthe. They wanted no vprightneſſe to write as they knewe. They can not be partiall: They knewe neither parties. They liued, taught and flouriſhed in the time of Truth by the Aduerſaries owne Confeſsion. To ſpeake farder in the commendation of theſe most holy and learned Fathers, it were but a vanitie. There nedeth no candle, when the day light ſhineth. Where good wine is, there nedeth no garland to hange out. Theſe Fathers commende them ſelues. All the Chriſtian worlde reuerenceth them, and crediteth them, as holy Fathers, as moſt learned Doctours, as ſingular lightes of the Churche of Chriſte, bothe Greke and Latin. To whom this publike teſtimony of all Chriſtendome ſuffiſeth not, to him nothing will ſuffiſe.

Reade therefore, Chriſtian Reader. Vſe, and peruſe. And reading theſe, remember that thou readeſt not any writer of late yeares, any priuate learned man, any particular Iudgement or doctrine. But that thou readeſt in theſe the doctrine of the primitiue Churche, Auncient and generally approued Fathers, briefely the publike Teſtimony and common voice of all Chriſtendom. And that not certaine of their ſayinges, culled out from the whole, but their whole and full Treaties, word for word

as they

as they wrote them, laied before thee. Last of all, not any suche writinges, as they wrote by waie of controuersy as against an Aduersary, but partly a settled and deliberated doctrine, such as S. Augustines Treatie is, partly Homelies and sermons made and pronounced to the whole people (suche as all the rest are) in whiche kinde of exercise the Pastour of Goddes people, will be most aduised what he speaketh, and muche more what he writeth. To make an ende: Thou hast hitherto hearde learned men prouing and debating matters now in controuersy, by certaine of the Fathers sayinges, gathered together, with their owne deuise and industry. Nowe thou hearest the Fathers them selues to tell their owne tales. Thou seest the maner of their writing. Thou learnest by their owne talke, what their faith was. Onely I haue made them to speake in English, as faithefully, as truly, and as familiarly, as I coulde possibly doo, not swaruing one iote from their wordes and meaning. Accepte my poore labour in good parte, which I haue taken to edifie many, to offend none. And our Lorde of his mercy geue bothe to thee (gentle Reader) and to me, of his holy Grace, that we may folow and practise in woorkes, that which these holy Fathers do teache vs in woordes. That as sinne hath bene the cause of this horrible schisme and manifolde heresies that nowe raigne, so amendement of life maie be a meane to stay the raging course thereof, and to call vs home to vnite againe, to the honour of God, and peace of his Church.

Amen.

# A TREATISE MADE BY *THAT BLESSED AVNCIENT* FATHER, S. AVGVSTINE, BIS- *ſhoppe of Hippo in Afrike in the yeare of* our Lord, 380. Which he intituled: *Of Faith and Woorkes.*

Againſt them that did admitte all men to Bap- tiſme without any difference.

## *THE FIRST CHAPTER.*

SOME be of opinion, that all perſons, without any difference, ſhould be admitted to the fonte of regeneration, which is in our Lorde Ieſu Chriſte, although they haue no will to chaunge, their lewde, and filthie life being infamouſe with notoriouſe crimes: yea and though by open proteſtation they profeſſe, that they meane to continewe therein. As for example: If a man kepe a harlot, he ſhould not be commaunded firſt to departe from her, and then to come vnto Baptiſme, but that euen remaining with her, and meaning ſtil ſo to doe, he ſhould (notwithſtanding that his preſumption) be admitted and baptiſed, and ſhould not be ſtaied from being a member of Chriſt, though he continew the member of an harlot: but ſhould afterward be taught how euil a thing that is, and ſo being baptiſed, ſhould be inſtructed to amende his manners. For theſe men thinke it a peruerſe and prepoſterouſe thinge, *An olde errour.*

first to teache them howe a Christian shoulde liue, and after to baptise them. But in their iudgement the Sacrament of Baptisme should rather goe before, that the doctrine of life and manners may after folowe. Which if the baptised wil kepe and obserue, he shal doe it with profit: If not, but retaining the Christian faith (without the which he shuld perish euerlastingly) he perseuer in al wicked and sinneful liuing, yet shall he be saued, as by fier: euen as he whiche
1.Cor.3. vpon the foundation (which is Christe) *buildeth not golde, siluer, or pretiouse stones, but wood, haie, and stooble*, that is to saie, not iust and chaste conuersation, but wicked and vncleane. The cause of this their imagination and opinion is, that that they see such are not admitted to baptisme, who being menne, and putting awaie their wiues, marrie others. Or being wemen, and forsaking their husbandes, marrie others. And that bicause our Lord Christ doth testifie these to be, without al doubt, adulteries, and not mar-
Matt.5. riages. For these men, when they could not denie that to be adulterie, which the truth it selfe doth without al question pronounce, and confirme to be adultery, and yet had a desire to helpe them to the receiuing of baptisme whom they sawe so intangled in that snare, that if they were not admitted to Baptisme, thei had rather liue, yea and die to, without any Sacrament at al then to be deliuered of that snare, with breaking their bond of adulterie: they were moued with a certaine humaine pittie and compassion, so to consider of their cause, that they thought meete to admitte vnto baptisme, not them onely, but also all maner of lewde and shameful liuers: though they were neyther rebuked with any prohibition, nor corrected with instruction, nor amended by any penaunce: as thinking except

that were done, they ſhould periſh euerlaſtingly, but if it were done, though they ſtil continewed in thoſe euils, yet ſhould they be ſaued through fier.

That the Church indureth the Commixtion of euil perſons togeather with the good, and yet doth not omitte the seueritie of diſcipline.

## THE SECOND CHAPTER.

TO whiche ſorte of men for anſwere: firſt this I ſay. Let no man ſo take thoſe teſtimonies of Scriptures, which either declare a commixtion of bothe good and euill in the Church preſently, or foretell it to come aſſuredly: let no manne, I ſaie, being (not taught by thoſe Scriptures, but) deceiued by his owne opinion, ſo take them, as to thinke therefore, either ſeueritie of diſcipline, or diligence in noting and puniſhing of vice is to be omitted or taken awaie. For al be it Moyſes the ſeruaunt of God moſt paciently ſuffered that commixtion in the firſt people: yet ſo was it that he puniſhed alſo diuers with the ſworde: And Phinees the Prieſt did with the reuenging ſworde thruſt through both the adulterers being found together. Which thing verely was ſignified ſhould be alſo done by degradations and excommunications in this time when in the diſcipline of the Churche the viſible ſworde ſhould ceaſe. Neither the bleſſed Apoſtle, albeit he moſte paciently lamented emongeſt falſe brethren, yea and ſuffered ſome being driuen forwarde with diueliſh prickes

*Num.23.* Degradations. *2.Cor.11.* *Ad Phil.1* *1.Cor.1.*

of enuie to preache Christe, did yet thinke meete to spare him which toke his Fathers wife: whome he commaunded (the Churche being assembled) *to be geauen ouer to*
1. Tim. 1. *the Diuell, into the destruction of his bodie, that his sowle might be saued in the daie of our Lorde Iesu Christe*: or did
1. Cor. 5. him selfe therefore lette to *deliuer vppe others to Sathan, that they should learne not to blaspheme*. Neither did he in vaine saie: *I haue written to you in mine Epistle, that you shoulde not keepe companie with fornicators: I meane not with fornicators of this worlde, or couetouse persons, or extorcioners, or suche as serue Idolles, for then you should haue gone out of this worlde: but nowe I haue written to you, not to keepe companie with any suche of your brethren as is knowen, and named, to be a fornicator, a seruer of idolles, a couetouse man, a slaunderour, a dronkerd, or an extorcioner, no not so muche as to take meate with suche: for as of them which be without, howe can I iudge? But of them whiche be within, doe not your selues iudge? Of them whiche be without, God shall iudge. Take awaie the euill from emong your selues.*

Whiche wordes [*from emong your selues*] some doe vnderstande, that eche man should take awaie, and remoue the euil out of him selfe, that is to saie, that he him selfe should be good. But how so euer it be vnderstanded, eyther that lewd persons should by seueritie of the Church be rebuked, and throwen out by excommunications, or els that euery man by taking vp and correcting him selfe, should remoue the euil out of him selfe: yet that which is afore saied, hath no doubt, or ambiguitie, where he forbiddeth vs not to accompanie those brethren, which are noted of any of those vices afore named: That is to saie,

be infa-

be infamouse, and notoriouse offenders in any of them.

Howe and after what manner sinners are to be rebuked and corrected.

## THE III. CHAPTER.

BVT with what minde and with what charitie, this merciful seueritie should be vsed, he shewed not only in that place, where he saith: *that his soule may be saued in the day of our Lorde Iesu Christ*, but also very euidently in an other place, where he saieth. *If any doo not harken vnto our worde, note him by your Epistle, and do not companie with him, that he may be ashamed: not yet esteeming him as an enemy, but rebuking him as a brother.* And our Lorde him selfe being a singular example of patience whereby euen emong his twelue Apostles he suffred and endured a Diuel, euen til his pasion, who also saieth, *suffer both to growe vp vnto the haruest, least while you goe about to gather the cockle, yee also roote vp the corne therewith*, and fore shewed, that those nettes drawen in a similitude of the Churche vnto the shore, that is, vnto the ende of the worlde, should haue in them both good and euill fisshes, with suche like, wherein either openly or by similitude he spake of the commixtion, and entermedlie of the good and the euil: did not yet thinke therefore the Discipline of the Churche to be omitted: but rather admonished it should be vsed, where he said, *Take heade to your selues: if thy brother sinne against thee, goe and rebuke him secretly betwene him and thee: if he heare thee, thow haste gained thy brother, but if he heare thee not, then take with thee one or twoo, that in the mouth of two, or*

2. Thess. 3.
Ioan. 6.
Math. 13.
Math. 18.

*three witnesses all your talke may rest, that if he do not heare them, then tel the Church, but if he wil neither harken vnto the Church, then let him be vnto thee as an heathē and publican.* And immediatly he addeth a most greuous terror of
Math. 7. that seueritie, saying in the same place: *what so euer you lose in earth, shalbe losed also in heauen: and what so euer you binde in earth, shalbe bound also in heauen.* He also forbiddeth *that which is holy to be geuen to dogges.* Neither is the Apostle, when he saith: *rebuke the offenders before all,*
1. Tim. 5. *that the rest may be affraid,* cōtrary therfore vnto our lord, where he saieth: *rebuke thy brother betwene him and thee.* For both is to be done, euen as the diuersitie of their weakenes (whome we meane not to destroy, but to correct and amend) doth require: and one is to be cured in one sort, and an other in an other sorte: euen in the same sort, there is a manner and order also of tolerating, and bearing of euil persons in the Churche: And there is againe a like consideration to be had in chastising, and rebuking: in not admitting, or absolute excluding and remouing from the Communion and fellowship of the Church.

Of such as vnderstand the Scriptures amisse.

## THE IIII. CHAPTER.

BVT men do erre in that they keepe not measure, and when they haue begonne easely to be inclined to one syde, they do not regard other testimonies of diuine auctoritie, wherby they might be called backe from that mind, and stay in that truth and moderation which is tempered of both: and that not in this thing alone whereof now the question is, but also in many other thinges. For some

ſome beholding the teſtimonies of the diuine Scriptures, witneſsing vnto vs one God only to be ſerued and worſhipped.haue thought the ſame which is the ſonne,to be alſo the Father,and the holy Ghoſte:Others againe being as it were ſycke of the contrary diſeaſe,while they attended thoſe thinges whereby the Trinitie is declared , and could not conceiue in their braine how there ſhould be but one God , ſith the Father is not the Sonne , nor the ſonne the father:nor yet the holy Ghoſt,either the father or the ſonne:thought hereupon,that diuerſitie alſo of ſubſtances was to be affirmed and mainteyued.Some beholding in the Scriptures the prayſe of holy Virginitie, haue cōdemned mariage.Some againe folowing thoſe teſtimonies wherby chaſt mariages are commended , haue made wedlock equal in worthines with Virginitie.Some when thei did reade. *It is good(my brethern)not to eate fleſh,or to drincke Wine* , haue thought ſome other lyke creatures of God , and ſome meates in their fantaſie to be vncleane. Rom. 4. Other ſome reading that euery creature of God is good and nothing to be caſt awaye,or refuſed, whiche is receiued with thankeſgeuing , haue fallen into glottony and dronckennes:not being able to eſcape one vice , but that they fel on the contrary ſide,to a greater. Euen ſo in this matter which we haue now in hand , ſome hauing an eye to the preceptes of ſeueritie and ſtraightnes,whereby we are admoniſhed *to rebuke the vnquiet : not to geue that is holy vnto dogges,to repute the deſpiſer of the Churche,as an heathen*:to pul away from the knot and vnitie of the body, that mēber which cauſeth ſcanlder or offence:do ſo trowble the peace of theChurch,that thei go about before the time to ſeparat the cockle:and ſo blinded by this error do

rather

rather ſeparate them ſelues from the vni tie of Chriſte. And ſuche is our cauſe againſte the ſchiſme of Donatus. And this not with them that knewe *Cecilianus* (who is charged not with true, but with ſclaunderous crimes) nor with them that ſtande ſtubbornely and impudently in charging him ſtyll: but with them, to whome we ſaye: Put the caſe they were euil men, for whoſe ſakes your ſelues be not in the Churche, yet ought you by bearing with them, whom ye could not amend or put away from you, haue remained notwithſtanding your ſelues in the Churche. But againe ſome perilouſly aduenturing on the other ſyde (when they ſee the mingling of good and euil in the Churche ſhewed or foretolde, and haue learned the preceptes of patience which doo make vs ſo ſtrong, that although there ſeeme to be cockle in the Churche, yet ſhould not our faith or charitie thereby be hindred, or at leſt for that cockle, whiche we ſee in the Churche, we ſhould not therefore our ſelues depart from the Churche) do thinke, that both the Church and Diſcipline is to be newe inſtituted: geeuing vnto the Prelates, and rulers thereof a certayne moſte peruers ſecuritie, as though to them appertayned only to tell vs whereof we ſhould beware: or what we ſhould doo: but not to care what in deede any man doth.

That for euil mens ſake we ſhould not depart from
the Churche, and after what manner the
euil ſhould be either corrected, or
ſuffered in the Churche.

THE

## *THE V. CHAPTER.*

BVT we thinke it to apperteine vnto ſound doctrine, by bothe theſe teſtimonies and allegations of holy Scripture, to take a moderate and middle waye. As thus. That both to keepe peace in the Churche, we ſuffer dogges within the Churche: and yet when the peace of the Churche may otherwiſe be kept, *not to geue that which is holy vnto dogges*. When therefore we find euill perſons in the Churche, either through negligence of the Prelates, or by ſome excuſable neceſsitie, or by cloſe and couert ſurreption crept in, whome we can not correct or brydle by Eccleſiaſtical Diſcipline: then leſt that wicked and daungerouſe preſumption might ariſe in our mindes, whereby we ſhould thinke it needeful to ſeparate our ſelues from ſuch ſinneful perſons (thinking that otherwiſe we ſhould be defiled with their ſinnes, and ſo goe about to drawe after vs a company as it were of cleane and vnſpotted Diſciples, broken of from the knot of vnitie: vnder colour of auoyding euil company) let vs cal to remembrance thoſe parables, thoſe diuine oracles, and moſt euident examples out of the Scriptures, by which it is ſhewed and foreſpoken, that euil perſons ſhal be mingled in the Churche with the good, euen to the ende of the world and day of laſt Iudgement: and yet ſhal not therefore, in the vnitie and participation of the Sacramentes, hurt the good which do not conſent vnto their doinges. But when the Paſtours and Prelates of the Churche are able without the breache of common peace, to exerciſe and execute dewe diſcipline againſt lewde and wicked perſons, then agayne leſt through dulnes and ſlowth

*Math. 7.*

CC we ſal,

we fall a sleepe, we are to be waked and stirred vppe with other spurres of preceptes whiche perteyne to seueritie of correction. That so by bothe manner of testimonies and sayinges of holy Scripture directing our steppes in the waye of our Lorde, he being our guyde and helper, wee neyther waxe dull vnder the name of patience, nor yet cruell vnder the pretence of diligence.

VVhen, and to what personnes
Baptisme is to be
geuen.

## THE VI. CHAPTER.

THIS moderation then according to sound doctrine being kept, let vs looke to that whereof wee nowe intreate. That is: Whether men are so to be receaued to Baptisme, as that no care or regarde be had therein, least that whiche is holy be geeuen vnto dogges: so farre forthe, that not so muche as open committers of adulterie, yea and professing a continuance therein, should seeme meete to be kept from a Sacrament of so great holinesse. Whereunto without doubt they should not be admitted, if during those very dayes in the whiche (after theyr names geeuen, and preparing them selues to receyue that grace) they are with abstinence, fastinge, and Exorcismes, purified and purged, they should professe to lye with theyr true and lawefull wyues, and woulde of this one thinge (being at any

abstinēce, fasting, and exorcismes, preparatories, to receiue baptisme.

at anye other tyme lawefull) for those fewe solemne dayes, denie the forbearing. Whiche being so, howe should an aduouterer refusing amendement, be admitted to those holy thinges, whereunto euen a lawefull married man, refusing but a litle abstinence, is not admitted?

But (saye they) let hym be firste baptised, and afterwarde taught, what apperteyneth to good lyfe, and manners. So is it donne, when it happeneth any man to be nere his end, and at the point of death, when at the pronouncing of those few wordes (wherein yet al other thinges are conteyned) he beleeueth, and so receaueth that Sacrament: to the ende that if he happe to goe out of this life, he maye departe free from gilte of all his sinnes past. But whereas such a man recouering agayne desireth space and tyme to learne those thinges, whiche are to be learned, what other tyme may be founde more conuenient, wherein a man maye learne howe to becomme faithfull, and howe he ought to lyue, then that tyme, wherein with a minde very attentiue, and holden in suspense of very religion, he requireth to haue the Sacrament of saluation? Are we so farre alienated from our senses, that eyther wee remembre not our selues, howe diligent, and howe attent we were to that, whiche was commaunded vnto vs by them whiche first entred, and instructed vs in the faith at what time we required the Sacramentes of that font, and were also therefore called * *Competentes*: or elles that wee marke not others, which euery yeare runne to this font of regeneration, how they behaue them selues for the time of those dayes wherin they be instructed, exorcised and examined,

Obiectiō.

Ansvver.

Catechising.

* *Competentes* are they, that stand to be baptised together, and cause their names to be taken for that purpose.

howe carefully and diligently they come together, with what a desire they burne, and in what greate expectation they depend? If that be not a tyme to learne, what lyfe most agreeth with so worthy a Sacrament, as they then desire to take, what tyme will there be for it? What? when they haue receaued it? remayning yet in so many, and great crimes, and being euen after baptisme not new men, but old offendours? so as with strange preposterousnes, it should be first saied vnto them, *put on the newe man*, and when thei haue put him on, it should then after be said vnto them, *put of the olde*? Not so the Apostel. Who keeping right order of speache: saith, *first put of the olde, and then put on the newe*? Yea our Lorde him selfe crieth, *No man soweth new clothe to an olde garment, ne doth any man put newe wine into olde bottelles*. And what elles I praye you, doo they all that tyme, when they stande in rewe, and beare the names of *Cathecumenes*, but harken what should be the faith, and life of a Christian man? That when they haue *prooued them selues, then they may eate of our Lordes table, and drinke of his cuppe? Bicause he that eateth vnworthely, eateth and drinketh iudgement vnto him selfe*. But that thing whiche is done in all that meane tyme, in the whiche by right good order of the Church, they which come to professe Christes name, do first take the degrees of Cathecumenes: the same is much more diligentely, and more instantly donne in those dayes, wherein they are called *Competentes*, when (I saye) they haue already geuen in their names, to receaue Baptisme.

Colos. 3.

Math. 9.

1. Cor. 11.

The blessed Sacrament ministred together with Baptisme.

That

## That suche as are to receiue Baptisme, must be taught as well the woorkes of Faith, as Faith.

### THE VII. CHAPTER.

WHAT, saie they, if a maide vnwitting, marrie her selfe vnto the husband of an other woman? Forsooth, if shee neuer knowe it, shee shall neuer be thereof an adulteresse. But if shee knowe it, shee shal from thence forth, beginne to be an adulteresse, after that shee shall wittingly lye with an other womans husband. Euen as in the right of landes, so long is a man rightly termed, a lawful possessour without any fraude, as he is ignorante that he possesseth an other mannes lande: but when he shall knowe it to be an other mannes possession, and dothe not then departe from it, then shall he be reputed an vnlawfull possessour, and then is he rightly called a wrong dealer. God forbid therefore, that by compassion not humaine, but vaine, we should so sorrow, when wickednesse is corrected, as though Marriages were broken. Namely, *in our Lorde his Cittie, in his holie hill, that is the Church*, where not onely the bond of Marriage, but the Sacrament thereof is so commended, that it is not lawfull so muche as to the husbande him selfe, to graunt his wife vnto an other man. Which thing yet in the Romain common welth, it is saied, Cato did, not onely without blame, but also commendably.

An obiection.

Answvere.

Matrimonie a Sacrament.

But I neede not dispute any farther in this pointe, sith they them selues, to whome nowe I answeare, dare not affirme that this is no sinne, nor yet deny it to be adultery, lest they should be conuinced manifestly to gainesaie our Lorde him selfe, and his holie Ghospell. But whereas they are of opinion, that such shoulde be first admitted to the Sacramente of Baptisme, and to our Lordes Table, although with open mowth they refuse correction, yea rather that no admonishmente shoulde at all be geuen them of this faulte, but that afterwarde they shoulde be taught, that if they will take vppon them to keepe the commaundementes, and to amende their faulte, they shoulde be accompted emong the good corne, but if they contemne the same, they shoulde be tolerated emong the cockell: in this saying they shewe plainely inough, that they doe neither defende these crimes, neyther yet esteeme them as lighte, or no crimes. For what Christian manne is there of any towardnesse, that will esteme adulterie as a small, or as no crime? Notwithstanding, they perswade them selues, that the manner and order how these faultes and crimes in others, may eyther be corrected, or tolerated, they haue founde out in the holie Scriptures, when they saie: thus did the Apostles: bringing foorth for that purpose out of their writinges, some testimonies, where they finde, that the Apostles firste taught the Doctrine of Faith, and afterwarde deliuered the preceptes of manners.

Wherevpon they gather and inferre, that onely the rule of faith must be shewed, and opened to them, which come to receiue Baptisme: but the preceptes of good lyfe must be geuen after Baptisme: As though they read some of the Apostles Epistles, disputing of onely Faith, written to suche as were not yet baptised, and some other Epistles disputing of good lyfe, written to suche as were

alreadie

alreadie baptised. But nowe whereas it is well knowen, that the Apostles wrote their Epistles onely to Christians already baptised, why yet doe their Epistles then conteine bothe these preceptes? I meane, preceptes towching faith, and preceptes towching good lyfe? But wherefore shoulde they not so doe? Thinke these men (trowe wee) that to suche as come to be baptised, we ought not to geaue bothe, and to suche as are baptised we must geaue bothe? Whiche if they thinke absurdly spoken, then lette them confesse, that the Apostles in their Epistles gaue their doctrine perfecte, of bothe those pointes: but therefore to haue most commonly begunne with Faith, and then to haue folowed with that whiche apperteineth to good lyfe, bicause that in man him selfe, onlesse faith goe before, good lyfe can not followe. For what so euer man seemeth to doe as well, onelesse it be referred to pietie, which is to God, it must not be called a good woorke.

Nowe if some foolishe and vnskilful personnes would thinke the Epistles of the Apostles to haue benne written to Cathecumenes, and suche as are not yet baptised: truly then must they withall confesse, that preceptes of good manners agreable with faith, are togeather with the rules of faith to be opened and taught vnto suche are as not yet baptised. Onlesse perhappes by this their disputation and reasoning, they will haue vs to saie, that the former partes of the Apostles Epistles, wherein they spake of faith, were to be readde of the Cathecumenes, and the latter partes, wherein preceptes are geauen howe Christians shoulde liue, to be readde of the faithfull. Whiche is to fonde a thinge to be spoken of.

Their

Theyr Doctrine therefore hathe no proufe out of the Apostles Epistles, nor argument to perswade vs to thinke that those which are to be baptised, shoulde be instructed in faith onely, and those that be baptised, instructed in good life, by reason that in the former partes of their Epistles, they commended faith, and after consequently exhorted the faithfull to liue well. For although, that be in the first place, and this in the later place, yet are bothe, by one vndiuided maner of speache, most often to be taught: bothe to the Cathecumenes: both to the faithfull: bothe to them that are to be baptised, and bothe to them that are alreadie baptised. To the one, that they may learne: to the other, that they forgette not what they haue learned. To the one, that they may professe: to the other, that they may continewe in moste holsesome and sounde doctrine. To the Epistles then of Peter, and of Iohn, out of the whiche they bring certaine testimonies, lette them adde both the Epistles of S. Paule, and of al the other Apostles, and vnderstande them all, so to be written, as that they would haue first faith, and then maners to be ioyntly spoken of. And this to be their meaning, I haue (if I be not deceiued) euidently declared vnto you.

That it behoueth men not onely to knowe, but also to leade a good lyfe, before they come to receiue Baptisme.

## THE VIII. CHAPTER.

An Obiection.

BVT in the Actes of the Apostles (saie they) Peter spake in suche sorte to the three thowsandes, whiche hearing his woorde were in one daie baptised, as that it may it may appeare he preached vnto them onely the faith, whereby they should beleeue in Christ. For when these men had said vnto Peter, What shall we doe? He answered them: *Doe ye penance, and be ye baptised euery one of you, in the name of our Lorde Iesu Christ, into the remission of sinnes, and ye shall receiue the gift of the holy Ghost.* But howe then is it, that they doe not marke these woordes: *Doe ye penance?* For therein is expressed a throwing away of the olde life, that they which be baptised, may put on a newe. But to whome is that penance, whiche is done from dead woorkes fruitful and auaileable, if he perseuer in adulterie, and other wickednesse, wherein the loue of this worlde is wrapped? *Actor.2.* Answere.

But he meant (saie they) that they shoulde onely doe penance for their infidelitie, bicause they beleued not in Christe. A marueilouse presumption (I wil not terme it nowe more grieuousely) that hearing it saied: *Doe ye penance*, they will thinke the onely actes of infidelitie are spoken of, sith that in the Doctrine of the Ghospell it is plainely taught, that the olde lyfe must quite be changed into a newe. In whiche place also, and euen in the same sentence the Apostle saieth: *Let him that did steale, steale no more*, and so foorth: where more at large he prosecuteth the same matter, teaching what it is to put of the olde manne, and to put on the newe. And yet if they woulde haue marked, but these very woordes of S. Peter, whiche they alleage, they might haue had good cause, better to consider of the matter. For when he had said: *Doe ye penance, and be ye baptised euery one of you, in the name of our Lorde Iesu Christe into remission of your sinnes, and ye shall receiue the gifte of the holy Ghoste:* An obiection. Answere. *Ephes.4.* *Ephes.4.* *Actor.2.*

*For to vs is this promise made, and to our children, and to all, as many as it shall please our Lorde God to call, be they neuer so farre of.* He that wrote the booke, immediately added these woordes: *And he testified this in many other woordes, saying: Withdrawe your selues from this wicked worlde. And they moste greedily receiuinge and embracing his woordes, beleeued, and were baptised, and three thowsande sowles gained and wonne in that one daie.*

Nowe who seeth not here, that in those *many other woordes* (whiche the writer of the Actes (S. Luke) for length omitteth) S. Peter earnestly laboured, that they should withdraw them selues, from this wicked worlde? For euen the sentence it selfe is briefly shewed for the inforcing and perswading whereof S. Peter vsed *those many other woordes?* For the summe and effecte of his whole perswasion is plainely sette downe, when it is sayed: *Withdrawe your selues from this wicked worlde.* But howe this thinge shoulde be donne, Peter gaue proofe in *many other woordes*. In whiche woordes (no doubt) was comprised the condemnation of deadde woorkes, which the louers of this worlde wickedly doe committe: and the commendation of good lyfe, whiche they should obserue and followe, *that withdrawe them selues from this wicked worlde.* Nowe therefore, if they thinke good, lette them perswade vs, that he *withdraweth him selfe from this wicked worlde*, whoe beleeueth onely in Christe: yea though he purpose to perseuer in suche vices as he liketh, euen to the very open profession of adulterie. Whiche if it be abhominable to saie, then lette them whiche are to be baptised, not onely heare

what

what they oughte to beleeue, but alſo howe they may *withdrawe them ſelues from the woorkes of this wicked worlde*. For at that time and place muſte they learne, howe they oughte to liue, after they dooe beleeue.

## VVhat it is to preache Chriſte: And of the Baptiſme of the Eunuche.

## THE IX. CHAPTER.

THE Eunuche (ſaie they) whome Philip baptiſed, ſaied nothing els: but *I beleeue that Ieſus Chriſte is the Sonne of God*. And in this profeſsion he was preſently baptiſed. What? Will you therefore that menne ſhoulde onely make that aunſwere, and ſo be baptiſed foorthwith? Is there nothing to be aſked by the inſtructor, or to be profeſſed by the beleeuer, touching the holy Ghoſte? Nothing touching the holy Churche? Nothing touchinge the remiſsion of ſinnes? Nothing touching the reſurrection of the dead? Laſtly, nothing touchinge Iheſus Chriſte him ſelfe, but that he is the Sonne of God? Is there nothing to be learned or profeſſed touching his incarnation of the Virgin? His Paſsion, his death on the Croſſe, his buriall, Reſurrection the thirde daie, or of his Aſcenſion and ſitting on the righte hande of his Father? For if when the Eunuche had anſwered: *I beleeue that Ieſus Chriſte is the Sonne of God*, it ſeemed he had done that whiche was ſufficiente

An Obiection. Act.8. Anſvvere.

The holy Churche profeſſed in the Creede, by the Catecumenes.

to be presently baptised, and so to goe his waie: then why doe we not followe that onely, and let passe those other thinges whiche we must needes expresse, euen when the streightnesse of time dothe vrge present Baptisme, by asking questions, where vnto he that is to be baptised, must in al pointes aunswere: yea though he haue not ben able to knowe them without the booke? But if the Scripture forbare the reporting, and left to our supposing and vnderstanding, those other thinges which Philip did, with the Eunuche then to be baptised, and in that it saith: *Philip baptised the Eunuche*, would vs to vnderstand, that all other thinges requisite therevnto, were firste complete and finished (whiche although for shortnesse sake they be not in the Scripture spoken of, yet by the course of the tradition, we know they were to be fulfilled) then in like sorte also, where it is written, *that Philip preached the Gospell and our Lorde vnto the Eunuche*: We can not doubt, but in that instruction, al was said vnto him, that perteine vnto the life and maners of him that beleueth in our Lord Iesu. For to *preache Christ*, is not onely to tell what is to be beleeued concerning Christ, but also what things are to be obserued of him, who commeth to the vnitie of his mystical body: yea and throughly to open al things which are to be beleued of Christ, not onely whose Sonne he is, of whome he was begotten, as touching his Diuinitie, and of whom as touching his humanitie, what he suffered, and wherefore, what is the vertue of his resurrection, what gift of the holy Ghost he promised and gaue vnto the faithfull, but also what manner of members he seeketh to be head vnto, to teach, to loue, to deliuer, and bring to euerlasting lyfe and glorie. When these thinges are opened

Traditiō, vvher Scripture faileth.

at some-at ſome tyme briefely, and in fewe woordes, at an other tyme largely and amplely, then Christ is preached. And yet not only that which perteineth to faith, but alſo that which concerneth the manners and woorkes of the beleeuers, is declared.

## VVhat it is to knowe Chriſte crucified, and who loueth God and his neighbour.

## THE X. CHAPTER.

IN this ſenſe alſo is that to be taken, which they alleage out of S. Paule, ſaying: *I ſaied among you, I knowe nothing but Ieſu Chriſt and him crucified*. Which wordes they thinke to haue ben ſo ſpoken, as though nothing els had ben taught them, but that they ſhould firſte beleeue, and afterward being baptiſed, ſhould learne al ſuch things as appertayne to lyfe and manners. This (ſay they) did at the ful ſuffiſe the Apoſtle, who ſayed vnto them, that: *although they had many ſchoolemaſters in Chriſte, yet had they not many Fathers, for he had by the Ghoſpell begotten them in Ieſu Chriſte.* An other Obiectiō. 1.Cor.2. 1.Cor. 4.

If then he which begat them thorough the Ghoſpell, allthough he thanked God, *that he had baptiſed none of them but Criſpus, Gaius, and the familie of Stephana*, taught them no more but Chriſte crucified: what if ſome man ſhould alſo ſay they had neuer heard of Chriſte his Reſurrection when they were *begotte thorough the Ghoſpell?* Which if theſe men wil not ſticke to graunte to, then let them remembre, what he ſaied in an other place to the Anſvver. 1.Cor.1.

DD iij very

very ſame his ſcholers. Thus he ſaieth: *I haue firſte opened vnto you that Ieſus died according to the Scriptures, was buried, and roſe againe the thirde daye according to the Scriptures*: Nowe if they will ſay, that this point of Chriſtes Reſurrection is contayned in the Doctrine of of *Chriſte crucified*, then let them alſo knowe, that in *Chriſte crucified*, men doo in deede learne many other

Rom.6. thinges: Namely this alſo, that *our olde man is crucified with Chriſte: that the body of ſinne be brought to naught, and that we be no longer ſlaues vnto ſinne*. And there-

Galat.6. fore thus ſaith he of him ſelfe: *but God forbid I ſhould glory but in the Croſſe of our Lorde Ieſu Chriſte, thorough whome the worlde is crucified vnto me, and I vnto the worlde*.

Hovv vve learne Chriſt crucified.

Let them then marke, and conſider howe Chriſt crucified is taught, and learned: and let them vnderſtande, that this is one pointe of our leſſon, when wee learne Chriſte crucified, that we in his bodie be crucified vnto the worlde. In whiche phraſe is vnderſtanded all manner brideling of our euil concupiſcences. Hereof it foloweth, that to ſuch as haue learned *Chriſte crucified*, open aduouteries can in no wiſe be permitted. For the Apoſtle Peter doth alſo admoniſhe vs of the Myſterie of Chriſtes Croſſe that is, of his Paſsion, that they whiche, are conſecrated therewith, ſhould ceaſe to ſinne: ſaying

1. Pet.4. thus. *Chriſte therefore hauing ſuffered in the fleſhe, arme ye alſo your ſelues with the ſame minde: for hee whiche is deade in the fleſhe, hath ceaſed to ſinne, that he may nowe liue the reſt of his tyme in the fleſhe, not after the luſtes of menne, but after the will of God*, &c. And ſo forthe: Where conſequently he ſheweth, that he truly apperteineth

tayneth to Chriſte crucified, that is to ſaye, hath ſuffered in his fleſhe, who beyng crucified in his bodye to all carnall luſtes, lyueth well according to the Ghoſpell.

But what a thinge is this, that they thinke alſo thoſe twoo commaundementes, whereon oure Lorde ſaieth, *that all the lawe and the Prophetes doo depende*: doo confirme this their opinion, reaſoning thus? God vttered firſte this commaundement: *Thowe ſhalt loue thy Lorde God with all thy harte, with all thy ſowle: and with all thy minde*: And after thys he vttered the ſeconde lyke vnto this: *Thowe ſhalt loue thy neyghbour as thy ſelfe*: Ergo, the firſte perteyneth to hym that is to be baptiſed, where the loue of God is commaunded: and the ſeconde perteineth to them that are already baptiſed, where the order of conuerſation with menne ſeemeth to be taught. For here they forgette cleane that which ys other where written: *If thow looue not thy brother, whome thowe ſeeſte, howe canſte thow looue God, whome thowe ſeeſte not?* And an other ſayinge alſo in the ſame Epiſtle of S.Iohn: *If a man looue the worlde, the loue of the Father is not in him*. For whereunto belongeth all the wickedneſſe of euill life, but vnto the looue of this worlde? Obiection Math.22. Deuter.6. Leuit.19. Anſwere. 1.Ioan.4.

And hereof yt followeth, that the firſte commaundement, whiche they thinke belongeth to them that are to be baptiſed, can by no meanes be obſerued without good woorkes. I will not ſtande any longer herein. For if wee marke well, wee ſhall finde theſe twoo preceptes ſo to depende the one of the other, that neyther the looue of God can be in man, if he if he loue not his neighbour: nor the loue of his neighbour, if he loue not God. But to the matter nowe in hande this whiche we haue said of these twoo preceptes suffiseth.

### VVhat is signified and meant by the comming of the Israelites out of Egypt.

### THE XI. CHAPTER.

An other Obiectiō. Exod. 14. Exod. 20. Ansvver.

BVT the people of Israell (say they) was firste ledde through the red sea wherby baptisme is signified: and afterward receaued the lawe wherein they shoulde learne how to liue. If this example helpeth them, then why do we deliuer so much as the Crede to such as are to be baptised, and make them to rendre it vs againe? For no such thing (you wote) was done to them, when God through the red sea, deliuered them from the Egyptians. But againe, if they wil haue this their opinion to be signified by the Mysteries that went before, as by *the postes sprinckled with the sheeps bloode, and by the sweet breade of sinceritie and truth*, why doo they not also consequently vnderstand, that their departing from the Egyptians signifieth a departure from sinne, which they that are to be baptised do professe? For hereunto agreeth wel that, which was said by S. Peter. *Do ye penance, and be ye baptised euery one of you in the name of our Lord Iesu Christ*: as though he should say: Depart ye from Egypt, and passe through the red sea. And therefore in the Epistle writen to the Hebrues, when mention is made of the firste beginning and

Exod. 12.

Act. 2.

rudi-

rudimentes of them which are baptised, there is plainely expressed repentaunce from dead workes. For thus he saieth: *Wherfore letting passe the beginninges and rudimentes, whereby wee were entred into the knowledge of Christe, let vs looke, and haue regard, to the ende and consummation: not laying againe the foundation of penaunce from dead workes, and of the Faith, whiche wee ought to haue in God, the doctrine of the water of regeneration, of the imposition of handes, of resurrection of the dead, and of the last and eternall Iudgement.* All whiche thinges the Scripture there doth sufficiently, and clerely witnesse to apperteine to the entrie of the nouices in the faithe. Hebr. 6.

But what other thing is *penance from dead woorkes*, then a renouncing of such thinges, whiche must be mortified in vs that wee maie liue? Of whiche kinde if adulteries and fornication be not, what is to be named emong dead woorkes? But yet the profession of renouncing suche workes doth not so suffice, except also al sinnes past, which doo as it were followe and pursue vs, be taken awaie and destroied by the foont of regeneration: no more then it suffised the Israelites to departe from Egypt, except the multitude of ennemies, whiche followed them, had perished in the same waues of the sea, which opened them selues to the passage and deliuerie of Gods people. He therefore that professeth he will not forsake his adulterie, how may he be ledde through the redde see, when he yet refuseth to departe out of Egypte? Againe they doo not marke, that in that Lawe which after the passing of the redde sea was geauen vnto that people, the first commaundement is: *Thou shalt haue none other Goddes but me, thou shalt not make to thy selfe any Idolles, nor the leeknesse* Exod. 20.

EE *of any*

*of any thinges which are in heauen aboue, or in the earth beneth, or in the water, or vnder the earth, thow shalt not adore nor serue them*, with the rest pertaining to that *commaundement*. Let these men then affirme (if it leeke them) against their owne assertion, that euen the woorshipping of one God, and fleeing of Idolatry is not to be preached to them, which are yet to be baptised, but to them which are all ready baptised : and so let them no more saie, that to them whiche are to receiue Baptisme, the faith onely which is to be had in God, is to be preached, and after the receiuing of that Sacrament they are to be instructed of good life, as of a second precepte teaching that, whiche belongeth to the looue of their neighbour. For the lawe whiche the people receiued after the passage of the read sea, as it were after Baptisme, conteineth bothe. Neither was the distribution of the commaundementes so made, that before the pasing of the readde sea, the people was taught to beware of Idolatrie: and after they were passed, were taught, *that their Father and Moother were to be honored, that they should not committe adulterie, not kill*: and suche leeke orders of a good and innocent conuersation emong men.

### That suche as will not change and amende their wicked life, are not to be receiued to Baptisme.

## THE XII. CHAPTER.

IF therefore any man so come to the requiring of holy Baptisme, that he professe, he will not departe from the

the ſacrifices of Idols, except it be perchaunce after when he liſt him ſelfe, and yet doth preſently requier Baptiſme, and earneſtly praie that he maie be made the temple of the liuing God, being not onely an Idolater, but alſo a continuer in moſt wicked ſacrilege: I aſke of thoſe menne, whither they woulde thinke him ſo muche as to be allowed for a Cathecumene? No doubt they will crie, he ought not. For we can not iudge otherwiſe of their meaning. Let them therefore render a reaſon by the teſtimonie of the Scriptures, (whiche they thinke ſo to be vnderſtanded) howe they dare repell any from receiuing Baptiſme, whiche will proteſt, and ſaie thus: I haue learned, and I woorſhippe Chriſte Crucified: I beleeue Ieſu Chriſte to be the Sonne of God: Differre me no longer. Requier no more of me. The Apoſtle woulde not them, whome *Acto.8.* he did begette through the Ghoſpell, to knowe any thing els for that time, but Chriſte Crucified: And Philippe, after that the Eunuche had pronounced, that he beleeued Ieſus Chriſte to be the Sonne of God, did not delaie the baptiſing of him. Why then doo you forbidde me the woorſhipping of Idols? And why refuſe you to admitte me to the Sacrament of Chriſte, except I doo firſt departe from Idols? I haue learned to worſhippe Idols from my childhood. I am rooted in it by a longe cuſtome: I will leaue then when I am able: and when it ſhall be conuenient: but though I doo not, let me not yet ende my life without the Sacrament of Chriſte, leſt perhappes God aſke my ſoule at their handes.

What, thinke we, woulde they anſwere to ſuche a

man. Would they haue him admitted? God forbidde. I doo not beleeue them to be so farre gonne. What then will they answer to him that shall so saie? Yea, and that shal adde farther that nothing ought to be saied vnto him (at the least before baptisme) of forsaking Idolatry, no more then that former people heard thereof, before their passage through the redde sea: bicause the lawe whiche they receiued, after their deliuery out of Egypte, taught them that.

Truly they would saie to that man: Thou shalt become the temple of God, when thou hast receiued Baptisme. But the Apostle saieth, *What hath the temple of God to doo*
2.Cor.6. *with Idolles?* But why then doo they not see, that it is leekewise to be saied: Thou shalt become the member of Christe, when thou hast receiued Baptisme? The members of Christ can not be the members of an harlot. For
1.Cor.6. thus saieth the Apostle also in an other place: *Erre not, for neither fornicators, nor seruers of Idolls,* nor diuers others which he there reckeneth vp, *shall inherite the kingdome of heauen.* How then is it that wee exclude from baptisme Idolaters, and thinke meete to admit fornicators. When both to these, and to other euil liuers, the Apostle saieth: *And truely suche haue you bene, but now you are washed, sanctified, and iustified in the name of our Lord Iesu Christ, and in the spirite of our God?* What is then the cause, that when it appeareth wee haue power to repell both sortes, yet I permit the fornicatour cōming to baptisme to remaine in his lewdnes, and doo not permitte the Idolater? Especially when I heare it spoken both to the one and to the other, *this haue you been, but nowe are you washed.*

But the grounde of these mens errour is, that they thinke

thinke all ſuch which beleue in Chriſte, and haue receiued the Sacrament of Baptiſme, are ſure to be ſaued, but yet through fire, though they be ſo negligent in correcting their manners, that they liue extreme wickedly. Whereof I ſhall by and by ſee by Gods helpe, what is to be thought and iudged according to the Scriptures. The errour, vvhich S. Auguſtin in this vvorke cõfuteth.

VVoorkes of faith ſhould go before Baptiſme.

## THE XIII. CHAPTER.

BVT as yet I will ſtande a while vpon this queſtion, wherein they holde, that ſuch as are baptized ſhould be inſtructed in good life, and ſuche as come to be baptized, onely to be inſtructed in the faith. Which if it were ſo (beſides ſo many thinges which we haue ſaied already) Iohn Baptiſt woulde not haue ſaied to them that came to his baptiſme: *Generation of Vipers, Who ſhewed you to flie from the Wrathe to come? Doo ye therefore Woorthy frute of penaunce &c.* In whiche words he warneth them not of faith, but of good workes. In like manner to the ſouldiars ſaying, *What ſhall We doo?* He ſaid not: beleeue firſt and be baptiſed, and afterward ye ſhal know what you muſt doo: but he foretolde them and forewarned them (that in dede like a forerunner he might prepare and cleanſe their life, againſt our Lordes comming into their harte) ſaying: *Vexe no man, ſclaunder no man, content your ſelues With your Wages.* Likewiſe to the Publicans aſking what they ſhould doo: *exact* (ſaith he) *no more then that Which is appointed to you.* Th'euangeliſt thus briefly reporting theſe thinges (for he needed

Matt. 3.

Luca. 3.

The holy Scripture reporteth not all thinges.

not at large to put in the whole Catechiſmes ) gaue ſufficiently to vnderſtande, that it apperteineth to his dutie, who inſtructeth the perſon to be baptiſed, to teache him and inſtruct him in good life. Now in caſe theſe men had aunſwered Iohn flatly, wee wil not doo worthy frutes of penance, wee will ſlaunder, we will vexe, we will exact thoſe thinges which are not dewe vnto vs, and yet notwithſtanding after this their proteſtation, Iohn had baptiſed them, yet could it not therſore be ſaid in this matter (whereof now our queſtion is) that when a man cometh to be baptiſed, he ſhould not be inſtructed to leade a good life. But to paſſe ouer other thinges, let them remember and marke, what our Lord him ſelfe anſwered when the riche man aſked of him, *What good he might doo to attaine the life euerlaſting: if thou wilt* (ſaith he) *comme vnto life, keepe the commaundementes:* When he had aſked what commaundementes, our Lord rehearſed to him the preceptes of the Lawe: *Thou ſhalt not kill, Thou ſhalt not cōmitte aduoultrie,* and ſo foorth. Whereunto when he had aunſwered, that all theſe thinges he had done from his youth, then did our Lord adde farther the precept alſo of perfection: *that ſelling all that he had, and beſtowing in almes on the poore, he ſhould haue treaſure in heauen, and follow the ſame Lord.* Let them behold therſore and marke that it was not ſaid vnto him, he ſhould beleeue and be baptiſed (by which only helpe theſe men thinke, a man may come to life ) but the preceptes of manners and workes were geuen vnto him: which yet can not be kept or obſerued without faith. Neither bicauſe our Lord ſeemeth here to haue omitted the inſinuacion of faith, do we therſore preſcribe and content our ſelues, that only preceptes of man-

Matt. 19.

of manners should be opened to them that desire to come to life. For both be mutually knit together ( as I said before) bicause neither the loue of God can be in a man that loueth not his neighbour, neither the loue of his neighbour in him which loueth not God. Therfore do we find, that the Scripture doth somtime mention the one without the other, now faith, now workes, eche for a ful and perfite doctrine, to the end we may thereby vnderstand, that one of them can not be without the other. For why? He that beleeueth God, ought to doo that which God commaundeth: and he that therefore doth, bicause God commaundeth, must of necessitie beleue God.

That onely faith doth not suffice to saluation without good workes.

## THE XIII. CHAPTER.

LET vs now therfore looke vnto that point, which is to be beaten forth of all religious hartes, least by a lewde securite they lose their saluatiõ, if they thinke onely faith to suffise to the obteining hereof, and be negligent to liue wel, and to kepe on in the way of God by good workes. For euen in th'Apostles time some not vnderstanding certaine darke sentences of the Apostle Paul, thought him to saie: *Let vs doo euil, that good may come:* because he had saied: *the lawe entred, that offence might abound, but where offence abounded, there was grace the more abundant.* Which saying of S.Paule is true in this sense, that menne receauing the lawe, and most proudly presuming of theire owne strengthe and abilitie, to kepe it: not by right faith calling vpon the grace of God, to ouer-

The principall point of this Treatie, and vvel to be marked.

Rom. 5.

to ouercome their euil concupiſcenſes, and luſtes againſt the lawe, were iuſtely burdened beſide the tranſgreſſing of the lawe, with moe, yea and more greuous offences. And ſo extreme gilt compelling them, they fled to faith. Whereby, *they might deſerue the mercie of pardone, and helpe of our Lorde, which made heauen and earth, that charitie being, thorough the holy Ghoſt powred in their hartes*, they might doo with loue thoſe thinges, which were commanded againſt the concupiſcenſes and luſtes of this worlde, according to that which was foreſaid in the pſalme: *their infirmities were multiplied, and then they made haſt.* Therefore where the Apoſtle ſaith: *He thinketh man to be iuſtified by faith without the workes of the Lawe:* he meaneth not, that after faith receiued, and profeſſed, the workes of iuſtice ſhould be contemned, but that euery man may knowe, that he may be iuſtified by faith, though the workes of the Lawe haue not gonne before. For they doo followe him that is iuſtified, they go not before him, that is to be iuſtified. Of which matter I neede not farther to diſpute in this preſent woorke. Namely ſince I haue vppon this queſtion alreadie ſette forth a large booke which is intituled: *Of the letter and the ſpirit.*

*Pſal.120. Rom.5.*

*Pſal.15. Rom.7.* Hovv S. Paule is to be vnderſtanded.

This is meant of the firſt Iuſtification. See the Treatie before.

Bicauſe therefore this opinion was then euen in the Apoſtles time ſpronge vp, the other Apoſtolical Epiſtles of Peter, Iohn, Iames, and Iuda, doo chiefly direct their intention and purpoſe againſt the ſame opinion: ſo farre that they plainely * affirme, faith without workes to profite nothing: as Paule him ſelfe alſo defineth, not euerie faith whereby a man may beleeue in God, but that to be the healthfull, and Euangelicall faith, whoſe workes procede

Note, hovv olde the hereſy is of only Faithe.

* Therfore Luther thought good vtterly to reiect the

procede of Charitie: *that faith* (ſaith he) *which worketh thorough loue or Charitie.* For which cauſe alſo he ſheweth, the ſame faith, which ſome men thinke to ſuffiſe vnto ſaluation, to be ſo farre from profiting any whit, that he ſaith: *If I haue all faith, ſo as I may remoue mountaines, and yet haue not Charitie, I am nothing.* But where this faithfull Charitie woorketh, there without doubt is good life. For, *the fulnes of the Lawe is Charitie.* Wheruppon to make the matter plaine, Peter in his ſecond epiſtle, where he exorteth vnto holineſſe of life, and woorkes, and foreſhewed, *that this world ſhould paſſe away, but new heauens, and new earth, was to be loked for, which ſhall be geuen to be inhabited of the iuſt*: that they might hereby take good hede how they liued, to become mete and worthy of that habitation, knowing that out of certaine darke ſentences of S. Paull ſome lewde perſonnes, had taken occaſiō, to be careleſſe of wel liuing, as being ſure of their ſaluation which is in faith, ſaid: *that certeine thinges there were in S. Paules Epiſtle moſt hard to be vnderſtanded which men did peruert euē as they did other ſcriptures, to their owne deſtruction*: (whereas yet the ſame Apoſtle Paul thought (no doubt) of the euerlaſting ſaluatiō (which is not geauen but to good liuers, euen in ſuche ſorte, as the other Apoſtles did): Peter, I ſay, knowing, this, ſaieth as foloweth: *All theſe thinges then periſhing, of what ſorte ought ye to be in holy conuerſations, and woorkes of pietie, expecting and haſtening to the preſence of the day of our Lorde, by the which the heauens burning ſhalbe loſed, and the elementes by the heate of fier diſſolued. But we looke for according to his promiſſes, newe heauens, and a newe earth, wherein iuſtice inhabiteth. VVherefore (moſt deerly be-*

Epiſtle of S. Iames, in his vvritinges againſt kinge henry the viij.

*Galat.* 5.

1. *Cor.* 13.

*Rom.* 13.

Note.

2. Pet. 3.

*ly beloued ) sins you looke for these thinges, labour that ye may be found before him sounde, and without spot, in peace: and thinke the patient expecting of our Lorde to be healthful vnto you, euen as our deerest beloued brother Paul wrote, vnto you, according to that wisedome, which was geuen vnto him, speaking of these thinges, in manner in all his Epistles, wherein are some thinges harde to be vnderstanded, which vnlearned, and wauering persons doo peruert, euen as the rest of the Scriptures, to their owne destruction. You therefore (deerly beloued) now foreknowing these thinges, be ye ware lest being seduced into the errours of suche as be false, ye fall from your strength. But increase in grace, and the vnderstanding of our Lorde, and Sauiour Iesu Christ: to him be glory both nowe and for euer.*

*Iames.2.* But Iames is vehemently offended against them which conceiue faith to be of value vnto saluation without woorkes, in so much that he compareth them euen with diuelles, saying: *Thou beleuest that there is one God: Thou doest well, and the diuelles also beleue so, and tremble thereat.* What could be saied more truely, more briefly and *Marc.1.* more vehemently? Verely we reade in the Ghospel, that *Matt.16.* the diuelles said no lesse, confessing *Christ to be the sonne of God*: whiche saying yet in them was rebuked, though in Peter praised and commended. *What shall it profitte* *Iac.2.* *Note.* *you (my brethern)* saith Iames, *if a man say he haue faith, but haue not workes? can faith saue him?* He saith also in the same place: *that faith without workes is dead.* Howe farre then are they deceiued, that by a dead faith, promise vnto them selues euerlasting life?

Faith

Faith and good workes together are required for the attaining of ſaluation.

## *THE XV. CHAPTER.*

WHERFORE we muſt diligently conſider, how that ſentence of the Apoſtle Paul, which in dede is hard to be vnderſtande, ought truely to be taken: where he ſaieth: *for other foundation can no man lay, but that which is laid, which is Chriſt Ieſu. But if a man build vppon the foundation, gold, ſiluer, precious ſtones, blockes, hay and ſtubble, euery mans woorke ſhalbe ſhewed: for the day of our Lord ſhal declare it, bicauſe it ſhalbe reuealed in fier, and the fier ſhall trie what euery mans woorke is. If the woorke that any man hath builded thereon, do tarry, it ſhall receiue rewarde, but if any man his woorkes doo burne, it ſhall receiue hurt, but him ſelfe ſhalbe ſaued, ſo yet as by fier.* 1.Cor.3. Which wordes of the Apoſtle ſome do ſo expounde, that they be ſaid to build vppon this foundation, golde, ſiluer, and precious ſtones, who doo adde good workes vnto the faith, which is in Ieſu Chriſt: and they to builde hay, blockes, and ſtubble, who hauing the ſame faith, doo euill woorkes. Whereupon they thinke, that through certaine paines of fier, theſe later kinde of menne may be purged and made meete to receiue ſaluation, through the merite of the foundation, whereupon they build. If this opinion be true, then we graunt, that theſe men vpon a charitable cōſideration, do labour that al perſons ſhould without difference be admitted to baptiſme: not only men and wemen that be adulterers, pretending falſe mariages, againſt Gods ordinance, but alſo common harlottes perſiſting in their moſt filthy profeſsion: whom

ſurely no Church (how meanely ſo euer it were gouerned) hath vſed to admitte, onleſſe they firſt forſoke that ſhameleſſe proſtitution of them ſelues. But by this their opinion, why they ſhould not abſolutely be admitted, I ſee not. For who had not rather, that ſuche as laying firſt the foundation, though they heape thereon blockes, hay, and ſtubble, ſhould not (though with ſomewhat the longer fire) be purged, then to periſh euerlaſtingly? But then ſhould thoſe textes be falſe, which are cleere, and haue in them ſelues no darcknes, or ambiguitie at all: *If I haue all*
1. Cor. 13. *faith ſo as I may remoue mountaines, and yet haue no charitie, I am nothing. And what ſhall it auaile (my brethern)*
Iac. 2. *if a man ſay he haue faith, and yet haue no workes: can his faith ſaue him?* That alſo ſhal be falſe, where it is ſaid: *Be not deceiued, for neither fornicators, Idolaters, Adulterers,*
1. Cor. 6. *effeminate perſons, offenders againſt kind, nor theues, couetous perſons, Dronckards, ſclaunderers, or extorcioners, ſhal inherite the kingdome of heauen.* Then alſo is that falſe:
Gala. 5. *Manifeſt are the workes of the fleſhe, which are, fornications, vncleanes, lechery, Idolatry, witchcraft, enmite, contentions, emulations, ſtomaking, diſſenſion, hereſie, enuie, dronckennes, glottonie, and ſuche like, which I foretell you, euen as I haue done heretofore, that they which doo ſuche thinges, ſhall not poſſeſſe the kingdome of heauen.* Theſe places, I ſaie, by their opinion ſhalbe all falſe. For if they onely beleeue and be baptiſed, though they perſeuer in ſuche euils, they ſhalbe yet ſaued thorough fier: ſay they. And ſo they that are baptiſed in Chriſt, yea though they doo ſuch thinges, ſhal poſſeſſe the kingdome of heauen which S. Paul denieth. Againe in vaine is it ſaid: *ſuch haue*
1. Cor. 6. *you bene, but you are now whaſſhed*, if they that be waſſhed

and baptized, remaine yet ſuch. In vaine alſo may that ſeeme to be ſpoken by Peter: *Euen ſo in like manner doth baptiſme ſaue you, not the laying down of the filth of the fleſh, but the teſtimony of a good conſcience.* For by them, Baptiſme ſaueth euen thoſe which haue the worſt conſciences, and ful of al wickednes and iniquitie: yea though they be not chaunged by any penaunce, from thoſe euils. For thorough the foundation, which in the ſame Baptiſme is laied, they ſhall be ſaued: (ſaie they) though it be by fier. Neither doo I ſee to what purpoſe Chriſte ſaied: *If thou wilt come to life, keepe the commaundementes*: or why he taught thoſe thinges that pertaine to good woorkes, if without keeping them a man may come to life, by onely Faith, which without woorkes is dead. And how ſhal that be true, that to them which he wil put on his left hand he ſhal ſaie: *Goe ye into euerlaſting fier which is prepared for the diuel and his aungels*, where he blameth them, not bicauſe they did not beleue, but bicauſe they did not good woorkes. For truly leſt any man ſhould promiſe vnto him ſelfe eternal life, by faith, *which without woorkes is dead*, therfore did he ſaie he would cal out and ſeperate all nations, which being mingled together did feed as it were in one and the ſame paſtour, that it maie plainely appeare, thoſe they are, that ſhall ſaie vnto him: *( Lord, when did wee ſee thee ſuffer ſuche and ſuche thinges, and did not miniſter vnto the? )* who beleeuing in him, did not care to woorke good workes: as though by their dead faith, they ſhoulde come to euerlaſting life. But what? Shall they (trowe wee) goe into euerlaſting fier, whiche leaue the woorkes of mercie vndone, and ſhal not they go, which haue taken awaie other mens goodes, and haue ben vn-

*1. Pet. 3.* *Matth. 19* *Nota.* *Iacob. 2.* *Matth. 25* *Nota.*

mercifull againe them ſelues in corrupting within them ſelues the temple of God? as though the workes of mercy did profitte any thing, without Charitie, conſidering that the Apoſtel ſaieth: *If I geue all my good vnto the poore,*
1.Cor.13. *and haue not Charitie, it auaileth mee nothing.* Or may a man loue his neighbour as him ſelſe, whiche doth not
Pſal.10. loue him ſelſe? *For he that loueth iniquitie, hateth his owne ſoule.* Neither can that be ſaied here, which ſome do ſaie, and ſo deceaue them ſelues, that it is termed euerlaſting fier, but not euerlaſting burning. For they thinke, that they to whome for their dead faith, they promiſe ſaluation by fier, ſhould paſſe through a fier that ſhall be of it ſelfe euerlaſting, but that their burning, that is the operation of the fier vppon them, ſhould not be euerlaſting. For this alſo our Lord forſeeing, concluded thus: *So ſhall*
Matt.25. *they goo into euerlaſting burning, but the Iuſt into euerlaſting life.* Their burning therefore ſhall be euerlaſting, euen as the fier is, and the truth it ſelfe ſaieth, that they ſhall go into this fire, *in whom he hath ſhewed not faith*, but good woorkes to haue failed. If therefore all theſe places and others innumerable whiche maie be founde, ſpoken without any ambiguitie, throughout al the Scriptures, ſhalbe falſe: then maie that vnderſtanding be trewe of blocks, hey, and ſtubble, that they ſhalbe ſaued through fier, which holding onely faith in Chriſte haue neglected good workes. But if theſe ſayinges be true, and clere, then without doubt an other vnderſtanding muſt be ſearched out, in that ſentence of the Apoſtle, which maie iuſtly be placed emong thoſe, whiche Peter ſaied to be in his writinges harde to be perceiued: which menne muſt not peruert to their owne diſtruction, by aſſuring the wicked, of

ked of ſaluation, againſt theſe moſt manifeſt teſtimonies of the Scriptures, namely where they doo moſt obſtinately continue in their wickednes, and be not tourned by amendement or penaunce.

### VVhat faith it is that ſaueth a man, and what it is to beleeue in Chriſte, alſo the expoſition of the place of S. Paule.

### *THE XVI. CHAPTER.*

HERE perhappes it maie be demaunded of me, what I my ſelfe thinke of this ſaying of S. Paule the Apoſtle, and how I thinke it to be vnderſtanded. I confeſſe, I had rather heare in this pointe menne of more learning, and vnderſtanding, that might ſo expounde and laie foorth the ſame, that all thoſe places of holy Scripture, which I haue before alleaged, might remaine true, certaine and vndoubted: and euen ſo of other textes alſo not by me reherſed, whereby the Scripture dooth moſt euidently witneſſe, that no faith profiteth, but only that whiche the Apoſtle defineth: to wit, that, *Whiche Woorketh through looue and Charitie:* and *Galat.5.* that the ſame faith without woorkes, can ſaue no man, either without fier, or by fier. For if it maie ſaue by fier, then yet it ſaueth: but it is abſolutely, and plainely ſaied: *What auaileth it a man to ſaie, hee hath faith* *Iacob.2.* *and yet Wanteth Woorkes? can his faith ſaue him?* Yet will I ſaye, as breefely as I canne, what I my ſelfe thinke

thinke of this sentence of the Apostle, whiche is hard in dede to be vnderstanded. My former protestatiō alwaies reserued, where I said I had rather heare, and geue place
1.Cor.3. to my betters. Christ is the foundation in the woorke of the wise and circumspect builder. This needeth no exposition. For it is plainly saied: *Other foundation can no man laie, besides that is laide, which is Christ Iesu.* But if Christ be the foundation, then without doubt the faith of Christ
Ephes.3. is the foundation. For, *Christ dwelleth in our hartes by faith*, as the same Apostle saith. Now the faith of Christ is none other, then that which the Apostle defineth, to witte, *that whiche woorketh, through looue and Charitie*. For the faith of the diuels, wherwith they beleeue also, yea and tremble, and confesse Iesu Christ to be the Sonne of God, can not be taken for the foundation. Why so? Bicause that is not a faith which woorketh through looue: but is a faith wrested out by feare. The faith therefore of Christe, the faith of Christian grace, that is to saie, *the faith, which woorketh through charitie*, being laide in the foundation, suffreth no man to perishe. But now what it is, to build vppon this foundation gold, siluer, precious stones, and blockes, hey, and stubble: if I shall labour exactly to expounde, I feare least the verie exposition it selfe will become somewhat harde also to be vnderstanded. Yet will I endeuour, so farre as our Lord shall geeue me grace, bothe breefely, and as plainely as I can, to open that I thinke. Beholde, he that sought to learne of the good Master and teacher, what good he might doo to come to euerlasting life, had this aunswer,
Matth.19. *if he would come vnto life, he should keepe the commaundementes*. And when he asked further, what

com-

commaundementes? It was saied vnto him, *Thou shalt not kill. Thou shalt not committe adulterie: thou shalt not steale. Thou shalt not geeue false witnesse. Honour thy Father and Mother: Looue thy neighbour as thy selfe.* To the ende that doing these thinges, he might holde the faith of Christe: that faith no doubt, whiche worketh through loue. For he could not loue his neighbour as him selfe, excepte he had receyued the loue of God, without the whiche he could not loue him selfe. But if he would further doo that, whiche our Lorde there added, saying: *If thou wilt be perfit, goe and sell all that thou haste, and geaue to the poore, and thou shalt haue treasure in heauen, come and followe mee*: then should he haue builded vppon that foundation, *golde, siluer and pretiouse stones*. For he woulde not then haue thought, but of those onely thinges that pertaine to God: howe he mighte please God: and these thoughtes to please God, are as I thinke, *golde, siluer, and pretiouse stones*. But now if he had yet a certaine carnal affection and loue towarde his richesse, though he gaue great almes thereof, and neither woulde for the increase thereof, attempt any fraude or extortion, or for feare of diminishing or loosing them, fall into any lewde or wicked doing (for by so doing he shoulde quite leese the foundation it selfe) but if (for the carnall affection, which as I saied before, he bare to those goodes) he could not without griefe and sorrow lacke them, then shoulde this man builde vpon that foundation, *heie, blockes, and stubble*. Especially, if he had also a wyfe, and vsed her in suche sorte, that he would for her sake thinke the more earnestly of those thinges which appertaine to the worlde, and howe he might please her.

Exod.20.

1.Cor.7.

Take hede Reader, least thou leese the foundation, by louing to muche vvorldly thinges.

Seing then, that these goodes loued with a carnal affection, are not loste without sorrowe, for that cause they whiche so haue and possesse them, as long as they keepe in the foundation that faith, whiche worketh thorough Charitie, and doo not by any meanes, or couetousnes preferre those worldly pleasures before the looue of God, doo by susteyning hinderaunce in the losse of them, attayne yet by a certayne fyer of sorrowe vnto saluation. From whiche sorrowe and losse a man is so muche the more safe, and sure, by howe muche the lesse he hath looued those thinges, and enioyed them in suche sorte, as though he had not had them. But he that eyther for the keeping, or for the getting of wordely riches committeth murther, adulterie, fornication, Idololatrie, and suche lyke, shall not bycause of the foundation, be saued through fyer, but loosing quyte the foundation, shalbe tormented with euerlasting fyer.

Wherefore that also whiche they alleage out of the Apostle (thinking to proue thereby that only faith profitteth) where he saieth: *If the infidell partye departe, let him, or her, departe: for a broother, or a sister, is not in suche thinges subiect vnto bondage*: that is to say, that for the fayth of Christe, euen the very wife coupled in lawfull Matrimonie, should without fault be forsaken, yf she will not tarry with a Christian man, onely for this cause bicause he is a Christian: they marke not withal, that by the same saying of the Apostle shee may very wel, and lawfully be dismissed and put away, yf shee say vnto her husband, I will not be thy wyfe, onlesse thou heape riches vnto me by theft, or except thou (nowe thou art a Christian man) vse thy accustomed robberies, where-

1. Cor. 7.

The duty to God is to be preferred before the bonde of wedlocke wherewith thou diddest furnish our house: or any other kinde of lewdnesse or wickednesse, that her husband before had vsed wherewith shee being delighted did either satisfie her lust, or get her liuing easely, or goe the more gaily apparelled. For then he to whom his wyfe shal thus saye, if he haue truely done penaunce from deade workes at his comming vnto Baptisme, and haue in his foundation faithe, *Whiche woorketh through looue*, without doubt he shal haue more regard to the looue of the grace of God, then to the voluptuousnes of the fleshe, and will *Gal.5.* strongly cut awaye the member that doth offende him: and what soeuer sorrowe of his harte he doo by carnall affection to his wyfe, indure, by suche separation, that lo is all the hurt that he shall suffer, that sorrowe is the fyer, by the whiche his heie being burned, he shall be saued. But yf he so enioyed his wife, as that he kepte her not for concupiscence, but for charitie and pitie, to see yf perhaps in time he might winne her to the faith, yelding rather, then requyring, the duty of wedlocke, truly he shal not be carnally sorry, when he is separated from such mariage. For why? he did not, though married, purpose any other thing, then godly, and howe he might *1.Cor.7.* please God. And by this meanes looke howe muche the more he buylded by such godly purposes, gold, siluer, and *Math.5.* pretious stones, so much the lesse losse should he susteyne: and so muche the lesse coulde his buylding, whiche was not nowe of heie, but of substantiall golde and siluer, be burned with any fyer. And thus whether men do suffer such thinges in this lyfe only, or that after this lyfe, some such Iudgementes do followe, the saying of S. Paule thus expounded, doth not (I trowe) vary from reason, or truth.

How be it, if there be any other good expoſition thereof, that my happe is not to choſe or to light on, yet ſo long as we holde this, we are not forced abſurdely to ſaie vnto
1.Tim.1. vniuſt perſonnes, rebelles, traitours, the lewde and defiled killers of their fathers or mothers, murtherers, fornicatours, offenders againſte kinde, theeues, bribers, lyers, periured perſonnes, or ſuche like, whiche are contrary to the ſownde doctrine, whiche is according to the Goſpel of the glory of the bleſſed God: if ye do no more but beleue in Chriſt, and take the Sacrament of his Baptiſme, though ye doe not forſake your moſte wicked lyfe, yet ſhall ye be ſaued.

Neither can herein the woman of Chananee preſcribe againſt vs, becauſe our Lorde gaue her at the firſte, that ſhee aſked, when he had ſaied before: *It is not good to take*
Mat.15. *the breade of children, and geaue it vnto dogges.* For he being the ſearcher of the heart, ſawe her chaunged within, whome he praiſed by worde of mouthe. And therefore he ſaide not: O dogge, great is thy faith, but *O woman, great is thy faith.* He chaunged his terme, bycauſe
Mat.15. he ſawe the affection chaunged in her, and knewe that of ſuche his rebuking of her, was growen good fruite. But it were in deede to be maruailed at, if he had praiſed in
Iac.2. her, *faith without good workes*, that is to ſaie, *a dead faith, and not ſuche a faith as might woorke through loue*: which S. Iames was not afraied to call a faith not of Chriſtians, but of Diuelles. Finally, if they will not vnderſtande this woman of Chananee to haue chaunged in her heart, her wicked woorkes, and manners, when Chriſte by contempt and reproche rebuked her: then, whome ſo euer they ſhall finde onely to beleeue, and yet not onely not to
hide

hide their wicked life, but freely to professe it, and neuer meane to chaunge it: let them on Gods name heale their children if they can, as the daughter of that woman of Chananee was healed, but let them not make them members of Christ, which wil not forbeare to be the members of an harlotte. In dede they doe not amisse vnderstande, that he doth sinne against the holy Ghost, and is without pardon, giltie of eternall sinne, whiche till the very ende of his life wil not beleue in Christe. But this were true, if they rightly vnderstoode what it were to beleeue in Christe. For it is not, to haue the faith of Diuelles, which is rightly called *a deadfaith: but to haue that faith which worketh through loue and charitie*.

Suche as obstinately continue in lewde and vngodly life, should be put backe from Baptisme, and what it is to hide our Lord his money.

## THE XVII. CHAPTER.

WHICH thinges being so, when we dooe not admitte suche vnto Baptisme, we goe not about to pul vppe the cockle before the time, but we are lothe to goe farther and sowe cockle as the Diuell dothe. Neither doe we lette or kepe of him that is willing to come vnto Christe: but by their owne profession we conuince them, that they haue no will to come vnto Christ. Neither doe we forbid them to beleue in Christ, but we plainely shewe, that they will not beleue Christe, who doe either saie that it is not adulterie, which he saith

is adulterie, or els doe beleeue that adulterers may be his members, who (as he teacheth vs by his Apostle) shall not inherite the kingdome of heauen: but *are enemies to*
Gallat.5. *the sownde doctrine, which is according to the Gospell of the*
1.Tim.1. *glory of the holy God*. And therefore these men are not to be accompted emong them, which came vnto the mar-
Luc.14. riage feast, but emong them that woulde not come. For when they dare moste openly gainesaie the very Doctrine of Christe, and contrary the holy Gospel: they are not repelled when they come, but them selues refuse to come.

But as for them who renounce the worlde, at the the least in woordes, though not in deedes: they come and are sowen emong the wheate, they are heaped vppe in the flower. They are numbred emong the sheepe, they are entred within the compasse of the nettes, and mingled emonge the Gheastes. But whether they be hidden and vnknowen, or whether they appeare and be seene, so they be within: then shal there be a reason to beare with them, when there is no meane or abilitie to amende them, and when wee may not presume to seperate them. But God forbidde wee shoulde so vnder-
Mat. 13. stande, that whiche is written: *They whome they founde, were broughte in to the marriage feaste: bothe good and euill*, that it shoulde be thoughte, they brought in suche as professed they woulde stil continew euill. For then the very seruauntes of the Maister of the howse, didde sowe cockle. And so shoulde it be false whiche is written: *but the enemie whiche soweth the same, is the Diuell.* But bycause this can not be false, therefore that the seruauntes broughte in bothe good and badde, is to be

ment

ment that thei brought in ſuch as were either ſecrete and vnknowen naught, or elles after they were brought and lette in, appeared to be naught. Theſe woordes, *good and badde*, may alſo be meant to haue ben ſpoken in reſpecte of common conuerſation of mannes life: in which reſpecte ſuche as haue not yet beleeued, are ſometime eyther praiſed, or diſpraiſed. And in this conſideration our Lorde admoniſhed his Diſciples, whome hee firſte ſent foorthe to preache his Ghoſpel: *that into what Cittie ſo euer they came, they ſhoulde enquire, who was there woorthy, that they mighte dwell with him, till they departed thence*. For who ſhall be that woorthy, but he that by the eſtimation of his owne neighbours ſhall be counted good? And who vnwoorthy, but he that is knowen emong them for euill? Of bothe theſe kindes there come vnto the faith of Chriſte. And ſo there are broughte in bothe good and badde, when thoſe that be euill doe not refuſe penance from their deade woorkes. But if they refuſe, then are they not repelled, being deſirouſe to come in: but they them ſelues doe by open denyall, departe from entring in. Mat.10.

Neyther ſhall that ſeruaunte be blamed or condemned emong the ſlowthfull that woulde not beſtowe his Maiſters talente vppon ſuche as theſe are. For vppon theſe he woulde haue employed it: but they woulde not receiue it. For this parable was propownded for them whiche will not take on them the office to be Gods Miniſter or Stewarde in his Churche, pretending a ſlowthfull excuſe, that they will not make an accompte for other mennes ſinnes, whiche heare, and dooe not, that is to ſaie, whiche receiue, and render not. Mat.25.

Of them that hide Gods talent.

But

But when a faithfull and diligente stewarde readie in laying foorthe, and moste desirouse of his maisters gaine, saieth to the Adulterer, bee no more an Adulterer: if thou wilte be baptised, beleeue Christe whiche saieth, that this, whiche thou doest, is adulterie: if thow wilte be baptised, be not the member of an harlotte, if thou wilte be the member of Christe: and if he aunswere I will not obey, I will not so doe, this manne will not take our Lordes true money, but rather will bring in to our Lordes treasure, his owne forged and counterfaite coyne. But if he would professe and promise to doe it, and did it not, nor woulde be afterwarde by any meane corrected, there woulde be founde, what to be done with him, least he be vnprofitable to others, which coulde not be profitable to him selfe: to the intent that if there were an yll fissh within the good nettes of our Lord, yet should it not entangle our Lordes fisshes in his naughtie nettes: that is to saie, though he leade in the Churche an euill life, yet shoulde he not there institute an euill doctrine. For when suche personnes doe defende suche their euill deedes, or openly professing, that they will continewe therein, are admitted to Baptisme, they seeme to teache plainely, that fornicatours and adulterers, yea though they continew in their wickednesse to their liues ende, shall possesse the kingdome of God, and that they shall come to
Iac.2. lyfe and eternal saluation, by merite of faith, which *without Woorkes is deade.* These are the naughtie nettes, which the fisshers ought chiefely to beware of, if at the leaste, by that parable of the Gospell, Bisshops and other inferior rulers of the Churche, are meant by the woorde
Mat.4. *fisshers*, bicause it was said: *Come yee, and I Will make yee fisshers*

*fisshers of menne.* For in good nettes may bothe good and yll fisshes be taken: but in euill nettes good fisshes can not be taken. For in good doctrine, bothe he may be good, that heareth and followeth, and he euil, which heareth and followeth not. But in euill doctrine, bothe he that taketh it for true, although he doe not obey and folowe it, is euill: and he that obeyeth and foloweth it, is woorse.

See the fruite of euil doctrine.

It is no newe Doctrine, that suche shoulde be kept from Baptisme, who openly saie, that they wil continew in their lewde liuing.

## *THE XVIII. CHAPTER.*

THIS truely is to be maruailed at, that our brethren whiche are otherwise minded, then we nowe defende, whereas they ought to departe from this so perillouse an opinion, be it new or olde, doe yet say, that this is a new doctrine, whereby wicked men openly professing without shame, that they will perseuere in their wicked deedes, are not admitted vnto Baptisme. As though they were wandering in some straunge countrie, I knowe not where, and sawe not, that harlottes, plaiers, and other suche like professours of publike filthinesse, are not suffered to come to the Sacramentes of Christe, till those their bondes be first losed, and broken. Yet should suche kinde of people by these mennes opinion be all admitted. But it is wel, that the holy Churche hath kept

The auncient custome of the church

and continewed this auncient and firme custome descending of that most cleare truth, whereby it is assured, that *those which doe such thinges, shall not possesse the kingdome of heauen.* Hence it is, that they which refuse to doe penance from those dead workes, are not suffered to come vnto Baptisme. And if any haue crept in, vnlesse they afterwarde being amended doe penaunce, they can not be saued. But if drunkerds, couetouse personnes, and sclaunderers, or committers of the like damnable vices, can not by their open deedes be conuinced or reprooued, yet are they sharpely corrected, with preceptes, instructions, and Catechismes. And then all such changing their willes into a better purpose, are seene to come vnto Baptisme. But if they haue perhaps seene and noted some negligently, in some places to haue vsually admitted adul-

Exod. 20. terers, whome not mans lawe, but Gods lawe condemneth, that is to saie, which kepe other mens wiues as their owne, or women, whiche companie likewise with the husbandes of other women, they oughte by those good vsages of the Churche indeuour to refourme suche euill doinges, that is to saie, prouide that neither these offendours be admitted, and not by these euil doinges to depraue the good and right order: by thinking it not meete or necessary so muche as to instructe suche, as desier Baptisme, of the correction and amendemente of their maners: and so consequently to admitte al the professours euen of those publike villanies, that is, harlottes, Baudes, swoorde players for lyfe and deathe, and suche like, yea though they continewe in their euilles. For concerning all those vices whiche the Apostle numbreth vppe,

Galat. 5. concludinge *that suche as doe those thinges, shall not*

*possesse*

*possesse the kingdome of God*, they whiche haue dewe and earnest care of their charge, dooe (as is seemely and meete) blame and sharpely rebuke suche thinges when they bee opened vnto them: and suche as doe resiste, and professe to continew therein, they doe not admitte at all to the receiuinge of Baptisme.

## Of the false opinion of them, that saie three onely vices are to be punnished by excommunication, and all other to be recompenced by almes deedes.

## THE XIX. CHAPTER.

BVT some there be, that thinke that all other sinnes are easily recompensed by almes: and onely three to be deadly, and to be punnished by excommunication, vntil by a more seuere penaunce they be healed: to wit, vnchaste life, idolatry, and murther.

It is not nowe needefull to dispute what opinion this is, and whether it be to be corrected, or allowed, least we drawe this worke whiche we haue nowe taken in hande, to muche in length by reason of this question, whiche to the finishing of our woorke in hande, is not nowe necessarie. It suffiseth also, that if all vices dooe exclude from being admitted to the Sacramente of Baptisme, emong those, al adulterie is comprised. And if there be but three onely to be excepted, then is yet of those three, adulterie one: whereof this our disputation was firste mooued. But for so muche as the manners of euill

Chriſtians, which haue bene before time very euil, ſeeme yet not to haue proceded ſo farre as to this vice, that men woulde marry other mennes wiues, or women the huſbandes of other women, it is like that hereby this negligence hath crept into ſome Churches, that in the Catecheſing or inſtruction of ſuch, as required Baptiſme, theſe vices were neither required of, nor reproued. And thereof came to paſſe that men beganne euen to defende them, whiche yet are rare and ſeldome ſeene emong them that are chriſtened, if by remiſſe negligence we make them not defenſable. For ſuche negligence in ſome, wante of experience in others, and in others ignorance we may probably iudge, that our Lord ſignified by the ſleape in man,
*Mat.* 13. where he ſaieth: *But when menne ſlept, the enemies came and ouerſowed cockle*. And it is an argumente to thinke, that thoſe vices haue but now of late appeared in the maners of the woorſt Christian men: bycauſe that S. Cypri-
S. Cyprians ſermō *De lapſis*. an in his Sermon made of ſuche as were fallen in time of perſecution, when lamenting and reprouing vice, he had remembred many thinges vnto them, whereby he ſayed the indignation of God was iuſtly moued, to ſuffer his Churche to be ſcourged with intolerable perſecution: he dothe not at all mention there, any of theſe vices forenamed. And yet dothe he not paſſe ouer in ſilence, but earneſtly auouche, that it was a pointe of euill manners, for Chriſtians to ioyne in marriage with Infidelles: which ſaieth he (in that place) *is naught elles, but with ſhame to proſtitute the members of Chriſte to the Gentilles*. Yet now in theſe our daies, this is ſcant thought to be a ſinne, bicauſe there is nothing in dede cōmaunded therof in the new Teſtament. And therfore haue ſome other thought

it lawful

it lawefull, or elles leaft it as it were in doubt. A And euen so, is that doubteful, whether Herode maryed the wyfe of his broother lyuing, or elles after he was deade. And therefore is it not very playne, what it was that Iohn saied, was vnlawefull for him to doo. Lykewise there maye be some doubte, whether a Concubine professinge that shee will neuer knowe other manne yf shee be put away from him to whome shee is subiecte, should not be allowed to the receyuing of baptisme. B And farther it may seeme, that he whiche putteth awaye his wyfe taken in adulterie and marrieth another should not be wayed in equall ballaunce with them, that put awaye their wiues without cause of adulterie and marry others. C And that poynte seemeth so darke in the diuine Scriptures, whether he who may without doubt, for adulterie put awaye his wife, should be yet accompted an adulterer, if he marry an other, as that (I thinke) to be deceaued in the vnderstanding of that poynte, were a veniall sinne. Wherefore suche as are manifest crimes of shamelesse vnchastitie, are vtterly to be reiected from Baptisme, onlesse the partyes by chaunging their mindes, and by penaunce be amended. But for suche as are doubtefull, it is to be laboured, and foreseene by all meanes, that suche coniunctions be not made. For what neede is it for a man to put his heade vnder so great daunger of doubt, and ambiguitie? D But yf any suche matches or coniunctions fortune to be made, I can not certainly say whether suche persons as make them, should by like reason be thought vnmeete to be admitted to Baptisme.

A. See the Notes folovving after this Chapter.

B.

C.

D.

## *Necessary annotations for the better vnderstanding of this xix$^{th}$. Chapter, in some doubtefull places which by misvnderstanding may perhappes minister some cause of Error or scruple to the Reader.*

A. [Euen so is that doubtful.] The doubt which S. Augustine findeth heere in the worde of S. Iohn the Baptiste vnto Herode concerning his mariage, is by him selfe resolued, after the writing of this Booke, in a Sermon that he preached to the people, vpon the. 140. Psalme, where he hath these wordes. *Occiditur ab Herode, qui dicebat ei: non licet tibi habere vxorem fratris tui: Neque enim frater eius sine posteritate decesserat.* He is slaine of Herode, which said vnto him: It is not lawful for thee to haue thy brothers wife. For his brother died not without issew. He saith it was not lawful for him to marry his broothers wife, and addeth the cause, for that his broother had issue of the same wife.

*In Psalm. 140.*

B. [And farther may seme] How that case is to be weighed he resolueth plainly and directly determining in the Bookes, whiche he wrote long after vnto *Pollentius* of vnlawfull mariages, saying: *Maius adulterium quis esse negat, vxore non fornicante dimissa, alteram ducere, quàm si fornicantem quis dimiserit, & tunc alteram duxerit, non quia & hoc adulteriũ non est, sed quia minus est, vbi fornicante dimissa, altera ducitur:* who denieth it to be a greater adultery, for a man hauing put away his wife not fall in fornication by her cõmitted, to marry an other, then if putting her away for fornication, he then marry an other? not bicause this is not also adultery, but for that it is the lesse, then the firste, where the wife being put away for fornication, an other is married. And in the same Chapter he farther saith: *Ambos enim, licet alterũ altero grauius, mœchos tamen esse cognoscimus.* VVe know both of them to be adulterers, though the one more greuous then the other. And so we see that though not in equal and euen ballance, yet are they both weyed in one balance of adulterie.

*Tom. 6. li. 1. cap. 9.*

And

[And that point semeth to darke.] In the bookes before alleged which he wrote to *Pollentius*, it was vnto him a matter so euident and plaine, that being out of al doubt thereof, he doubted not to say: That whether a man put away his wife that hath cōmitted no adultery, or her that hath ben taken in adultery, if he mary an other, he cōmitteth not a smal or venial offence, but manifest adultery, which is a mortal, and dedly sinne, saying: *vtrosq; mœchos esse minimè dubitamus*. VVe nothing doubt but that they be both adulterers. And in an other place of the same worke speaking of them, who for vnchast life put their wiues out of their cōpany, he saith: *Non alia quærant coniugia, quia non erunt coniugia, sed adulteria*. Let them not seeke other mariages: for they shalbe no marriages, but adulteries. To the same effect in an other worke, whiche he wrote also, after this booke, he saith, that who so euer, in that case marrieth againe: *Lege Euangelij, reus erit adulterij*: By the law of the Ghospel, he shalbe guilty of adulterie. C. *To. 6. li. 1. ad Pollēt. cap. 9.* *To. 6. li. 2. ad Pollēt. cap. 19.* *To. 7. de Nupt. & Concupis. lib. 1. c. 10*

[But if any such matches fortune to be made I can not certainly say.] Touching this point also, he saith in an other place, in the person of his aduersary, yet as a truth in both sides graunted. *Quòd videlicet qui dimittit, & viuere permittit adulteram, si alterā duxerit, quamdiu prior illa viuit, perpetuus adulter est, nec agit pœnitētiam fructuosam à flagitio non recedens. Nec si Catechumenus est: ad baptismū admittitur, quoniā ab eo quod impedit non mutatur.* That he which putteth away his wife for adultery, and suffereth her to liue, if he marry an other, as long as that former wife liueth, he is a continual adulterer: neither doth he any fruteful penance, as long as he cōtinueth in that wicked acte. Neither if he be a Catechumen, can be admitted to Baptisme, bicause he leaueth not that, which letteth him from baptisme. D. *Tom. 6. de Adulterinis Coniugijs ad Pollent. li. 2. ca. 16.*

Thus much haue I thought good to say here (good Reader) to the end that neither thou shouldest misconstrue S. Augustine, neither doubt of his mind and opinion in these pointes, which albeit he doth not resolue here, yet as thou seest, he doth in other and later Bookes, by him written, clearly define, and plainly teache.

VVhat

VVhat they ought to doo that are to be baptised, and what benefit they take in baptisme.

## *THE XX. CHAPTER.*

THerefore to shewe nowe what is the sownd and true doctrine, lest a daungerous securitie be geeuen to any deadly sinne, or elles a more daungerous authoritie graunted : this is the order of the cure and remedy thereof: That they whiche are to be baptised, do beleeue in God the Father, the Sonne, and the holy Ghost, in such order and sorte as the Creede is deliuered, that they do penaunce from thier deade workes, and doubte not but that they shall receyue in Baptisme a ful and perfect remission of all their sinnes paste. Not yet so, that it shall be nowe lawfull for them to sinne. But that it shall be no more hurtful to them, that they haue before sinned. And that it is a remission of al that is past, not a permission to do the like any more. Then may it truly be said euen
*Ioan.5.* spiritually, *behold thou art made whole: nowe sinne no more*: which our Lorde therefore saied, of the bodyly health, bicause he knewe, that to him whome he healed, that paine and disease in the fleshe was happened, by the desert of his sinnes. But to him that entreth an adulterer to be baptised, and being baptised, goeth forth an adulterer, I maruaile howe these menne can thinke it may be saied, *behold thow art made whole*. For what can be a greuous and deadly disease, if adulterie shalbe accompted healthe?

It is

## It is not to be thought, that the Apostles admitted to Baptisme suche as liued in great and heinous sinne.

## THE XXI. CHAPTER.

BVT in the three thousandes (saie they) whom the Apostles Baptised in one daie, and in so many thousandes of beleeuers, emong whome the Apostle preached, and filled with the Gospell the whole countreis between Hierusalem and Slauonie, it is leeke there were some menne cowpled with other mens wiues, and some weemen with other wiues husbandes, wheruvpon the Apostles shoulde haue made a certaine rule, which should from thence foorth, haue been kepte in the Churches, whither suche should not be admitted to Baptisme, except they had first forsaken and corrected their adulterous liues. As though it might not leekewise be saied against them, that they finde not any one mencioned, who being suche, was admitted. Or as though the Scripture could conueniently, haue made mention of the particular crimes of euery man. Which truly would haue growen to an infinit matter, and nothing needfull: sith that generall rule is sufficient at the full, where Peter at large protesteth to suche, as were to be baptised, saying, *Withdrawe your selues from this wicked worlde.* For who doubteth adultery to appertaine to the wickednes of this worlde, and those especially which choose to continue in that iniquitie? But in like manner maie it be saied of common harlotes, (which no Church admitteth to Baptisme, till they be deliuered from that filthy life)

Obiectiō. Acto.2. Rom.15. Answer. Acto.2.

that emong ſo many thouſandes then of beleeuers, emong ſo many nations, ſome ſuch might be found, and that the Apoſtles ſhould haue geuen for the rules of their receauing, or of their repelling. But by ſome ſmaller matters, wee maie well gather coniecture, of the greater. For if the Publicans comming to the Baptiſme of Iohn, were forbidden, *to exact any more, then was appointed and taxed vnto them*, I maruaile if adultery could be permitted to ſuche as came to the Baptiſme of Chriſte.

Luce. 2.

Obiectiō. They ſaie alſo, that the Iſraelites committed many and greuous offences: and ſhedde muche blood of Prophetes: and yet not to haue deſerued, by thoſe factes, to be vtterly rooted vppe, but for their onely infidelitie, that they would not beleeue in Chriſte. But here they marke not, that their ſinne was not onely in that they would not beleeue in Chriſte, but alſo in that they killed Chriſt: of which two crimes, the one grew of infidelitie, the other of crueltie. As that therefore is contrary to right faith, ſo this is repugnant to good life. But he is voide of both theſe faults, which hath faith in Chriſt: *not a dead faith without woorkes* (which is alſo found in the diuels) but the faith of Grace, *whiche woorketh through loue*.

Iacob. 2. Galat. 5. Luca. 17.

This is the faith, whereof it is ſaid: *The kingdome of heauen is within you*. For this do they breake into, which doe violence by beleuing, and obtaining by praier the Spirit of Charite, in the which the fulnes of the law conſiſteth: and without the which, the law in the letter, made them gilty, euen of the tranſgreſsiō and breach thereof. It is not therfore to be thought, that for this cauſe it was ſaied: *the kingdome of the heauens ſuffreth violence, and they which do the violence, breake in to it*. for that euen lewde parſons onely by be-

Rom. 13. Math. 11.

by beleeuing,and yet lyuing wickedly, do come into the kingdome of heauen :but bycause that the same gilte of transgression (whiche the onely lawe , that is, the letter, without the spirit,made by commanding) is by beleeuing loosed:and by force of faith the holy Ghost is obtained,by whome *Charity being powred into our hartes*,the law is fulfilled , not for feare of paine, but for loue of Iustice. *Rom.5.*

VVhat it is to know God and that it is not sufficient for saluation to haue faith onely, without good workes.

## *THE XXII. CHAPTER.*

LET not therefore a rechelesse mind be deceiued in thinking it selfe to knowe God , if he with a dead faith , that is without good woorkes, doo after the manner of diuels confesse God. Let no man thinke him selfe vpon only faith in Christ assured to come vnto euerlasting life, bicause our lord saieth : *thus is life euerlasting, that they may know the one true God,and Iesu Christ, whom thou hast sent.* For he must also call to remembrance, that it is writen : *In this we knowe him , if wee keepe his commaundementes: who saith that he knoweth him,and keepeth not his cōmaundēmentes, he is a lier and truth is not in him.* And least any man should thinke,that Gods commaundementes appertained to onely faith (allthough yet no man hath presumed so to saie)cheefly bicause him selfe named commaundementes,in the plural number,and lest by that number men should imagine and thinke of many mo, he comprehended them all in two , saying : *In those two dependeth the whole lawe, and the Prophetes :* and although it might in soome sense rightly be saied , the commaun- *Iohn.21.* *1.Iohn.2.* *Math.22.*

Galat.5. dementes of God are included in only faith, if not a dead faith be vnderstanded, but a quicke, *Whiche woorketh*
1.Iohn.3. *thorough looue*, yet S. Iohn him selfe afterwarde opened his whole meaning, when he saieth: *This is his commaundement, that we beleue in the name of his Sonne Iesu Christ, and looue one an other.* This therfore profiteth, to beleeue in God, with a right faith, to honour God, to know God: to thentent that both wee maie haue helpe from him, to liue wel: and if wee sinne, wee maie deserue of him, in-
Psal.40. dulgence and pardon: not continuing recklesse in euill woorkes which he hateth, but departing from them, and saying vnto him: *I haue saied Lord haue mercy on me, heale my sowle, bicause I haue sinned against thee:* which they can not saie vnto him, that doo not beleeue him: and in vaine doo suche saie it, who being so farre from him, are vtterly straungers to the grace of the mediatour.

Hereof also be those woordes in the booke of wise-
Sapien.15. doome, whiche I knowe not how these mens pernicious securitie doth interpret. *And if we sinne, yet be we thine.* For how is this true? Forsothe bicause wee haue, a good and a great God, whiche will and can heale the sinnes of the penitent, but not suche a one, as feareth to destroie them that remaine in their wickednes. Therefore the same Writer when he had saied, *wee be thine*, he added, *knowing thy power*. verely suche a power as, the sinner can neither withdraw nor hide him selfe from. And therfore following, he addeth further: *but wee haue not sinned knowing that wee be deputed to be thine.* For who worthely thinking of the habitation, that is with God (wherin by predestination all be deputed, whiche are called according to his purpose) will not labour so to liue, as

maie

maie be aunſwerable, and ſitting, to ſuche an habitation? That therefore which S. Iohn ſaith: *Theſe thinges haue I written vnto you, to the end ye ſinne not, and if any haue ſinned, we haue an aduocate with the father Iheſu Chriſte the righteous, and he is the interceſsion for our ſinnes*: He ſaith not to the end wee ſhould ſinne, with ſecuritie and careleſneſſe, but that deparing from ſuche ſinne as we haue committed, we ſhould not diſpaire of pardon, hauing that aduocate which the Inſidels haue not.

## That by this word, *Iudgement*, in the holy ſcripture, is meant eternall damnation, not any eaſier paine or punniſhment.

## *THE XXIII. CHAPTER.*

THERE is not therefore any ſuch fauorable condition promiſed by theſe places alleaged, that men beleeuing in God, may remaine therefore in their euill workes. And much leſſe of thoſe wordes, where the Apoſtle ſaith: *they which haue ſinned without lawe, ſhall periſh without lawe, but they which ſinned in the law, ſhall be iudged by the lawe*: as though in this place there were ſome difference, betwene periſhing, and being Iudged. For here by diuerſe wordes, one and the ſelfe ſame thing is ſignified. For the ſcriptures vſe to putte *Iudgement* euen for eternall damnation, as in the Ghoſpell our Lorde ſaith: *The houre ſhall come, wherein all they which are in their graues, ſhall heare his voice, and they which haue donne well, ſhall come forth to the reſurrection of life, but they which haue donne euill, to the reſurrection of Iudgment.*

*Rom. 2.*

*Iob. 5.*

*ment.* And marke that it is not ſaied there: this for them which haue beleeued, and that for them, which haue not beleued: but this, ſhal they haue, which haue donne wel: and that, they which haue donne euill. For good life can
Gal.5. not be parted from faith, *which worketh thorough loue.* Nay rather that faith is good life it ſelfe. We ſee therefore that oure Lorde vſed this woorde, *reſurrection of Iudgement*, for reſurrection of eternal damnation. For of all them that were to riſe againe, in which number no doubt were alſo thoſe which beleeue not at all (for they alſo were in their graues) he made but two partes, wherof the one he declared ſhould ariſe *into reſurrection of life*, and the other, *into reſurrection of Iudgement.*

Now if they will ſay that thoſe are not meant there which beleeue not at al, but thoſe which ſhal be ſaued by fier, bicauſe they beleeued, although they liued ill, thinking thereby, that by the name of *Iudgement*, their tranſitory paine is ſignified (although this ſhould be moſt impudently ſaid, ſeing that all, who without exception ſhal riſe againe, among whome, no doubt, the vnfaithfull ſhall alſo be, our Lord hath diuided onely into two partes, to wit, *life and Iudgement*, meaning thereby that the Iudgement ſhould be vnderſtanded eternal, as wel as the life, though he did not there adde that woorde: for neither ſaith he there, into reſurrection of eternall life, though he would not haue it any otherwiſe vnderſtāded): yet let them then conſider, what they will aunſwer to that, where he ſaith:
Iohan.3. *But he which beleueth not, is already iudged.* For here (no doubt) they muſt either vnderſtand, *Iudgement*, for eternall paine, or els preſume to ſay, that infidels ſhall alſo be ſaued thorough fier. For, ſaith Chriſt: *He which beleeueth*

*neth not, is allready iudged*, that is to ſay, is allready deſtined and appointed to Iudgement. And then where is that, which they promiſe for a ſingular benefite, to ſuch as beleeue, and yet liue wickedly, ſith that they alſo which beleeue not, ſhall not be damned, but iudged? Which if they dare not to affirme, then lette them not preſume to promiſe ſo fauourably vnto them, of whom it is ſaid, *they ſhalbe iudged by the Lawe*. For now it appeareth, that eternall damnation, is alſo termed *Iudgement*.

But nowe as touching thoſe that wittingely ſinne, what if we finde them not onely not to be in more eaſie, but to be in much woorſe and harder caſe? Verely theſe be they chiefly, whiche haue receiued the lawe. For (as it is written): *Where there is no lawe, there is no tranſgreſsion*. And to this ende alſo is it ſaied: *I had not knowen concupiſcenſe, except the lawe had ſaid, thou ſhalt not luſt. Sinne therefore, taking occaſion of the lawe, hath wrought in me all concupiſcence*: with many other ſuch like whiche the ſame Apoſtle ſpeaketh of this matter. But from this moſt greeuous gilt doth the grace of the Holy Ghoſt, deliuer vs through Ieſu Chriſt oure Lord, which Grace, Charitie being powred into oure hartes, doth make vs to delight in iuſtice, by the which immoderate concupiſcence is ouercommed. Hereby therefore is it proued, not onely no eaſier, but much more greuous paine to be maent to them, of whom it is ſaid, *they which ſinne in the lawe, ſhalbe iudged by the lawe*, then to them, which *ſinning without the lawe, ſhall periſh without the law*. It is proued alſo hereby, that Iudgement in this place is not ment, for tra̅ſitory paine, but for that eternal paine, whereby

Rom. 4. Rom. 7. Rom. 5. Rom. 2.

whereby infideles ſhalbe alſo iudged. For they that vſe this ſentence, to geue hope of ſaluation by fier, to them whiche euen beleeuing, doo liue moſte lewdely, ſaying to them, *they whiche haue ſinned without the Lawe ſhall periſh without the law, but they which haue ſinned in the lawe, ſhalbe iudged by the lawe*: as though it were ſaid, they ſhall not periſh, but be ſaued thorough fier: coulde not ſee, that the Apoſtle ſpake this bothe of them which ſinned without the law, and of them which ſinned in the law. For th'Apoſtle there in dede treated both of the gentiles and of the Iewes: ſhewing that the grace of Chriſte whereby they might be deliuered, was not only neceſſary to the Gentils, but to the Iewes alſo. All which, that very epiſtle to the Romains doth euidently ſhew. Therfore let them now (if it like them) promiſe euē to the Iewes alſo, ſinning in the law ſaluatiō through fier, though the grace of Chriſt deliuer them not. For of them alſo it was ſaid, *By the lawe, they ſhall be iudged*. Which if they do not, then ſpeake they againſt them ſelues who confeſſe, that they are tied, with the band of the moſt greuous, and heauie crime of infidelitie. Why do they then applie to Infidels, and to the faithful a like (in a thing appertaining to the faith of Chriſt) that which was ſpoken of them, that ſinne without the lawe, and of them which ſinne in the lawe ſithe, all this was ſpoken (not of the faithfull, but) of the Iewes and the Gentiles, inuiting them bothe to come to the faith of Chriſte?

Of the libertie of a Chriſtian man, and what Chriſtian libertie is, if it be rightly vnderſtanded.

For

## THE XXIIII. CHAPTER.

FOR it was not ſaied, they which haue ſinned without faith, ſhall periſh without faith: and they which haue ſinned in faith, ſhall be iudged by faith: but the wordes are: *Without the law, and in the lawe*, that it might plainely appeare, that matter was touched, which was in hand betwene the Gentiles, and the Iewes, not betwene good and euill Chriſtians. And yet if in that place they will needes by the word, *Lawe*, vnderſtand faith (which were to vnreaſonable and to abſurd) yet may they reade the ſentence of the Apoſtle Peter, which is in this matter moſt open and plaine: ſpeaking of them, who tooke to maintaine their fleſhlines, and to couer their nawghtines, that, which is written: *We which appertaine to the newe Teſtament, be not the ſonnes of the handmaide, but of the free woman, by that libertie whereby Chriſt hath made vs free*: thinking that hereby was ment they might liue freely, take all thinges as lawful, whatſoeuer liked them, being now put in ſecuritie by ſo great a redemption: not marking withall that which was ſaid: *Brethern, ye are called into libertie: only make not that libertie an occaſion of carnalitie*. Whereupon S. Peter him ſelfe alſo ſaieth: *Free, not as hauing libertie, for a cloke or couer of naughtines*. Of the which ſorte alſo he ſpeaketh in his ſecond Epiſtle: *Theſe are drie ſpringes, and clowdes driuen with an hurlewind, to whome a miſte of darcknes is reſerued: for ſpeaking proude thinges of vanitie, they allure in concupiſcences vnto vnclennes of the fleſh, thoſe which were eſcaped a litle, being conuerſant in errour, promiſing vnto them libertie, when them ſelues were the bondmen of corruption. For of what*

Rom. 2. Gala. 4. Gala. 5. 1. Pet. 2. 2. Pet. 2.

*soeuer a man is ouercome, to the same is he become bond. For if fleyng backe from the filthines of the worlde into the knowledge of our Lord and common Sauiour Ihesu Christ, they being againe wrapped, and intangled in them, be ouercome, the latter are become to them, woorse then the first: for it had bene better for them not to knowe the way of Iustice, then knowing it, to returne backe from the holy commaundement once geeuen vnto them: for in them is the prouerbe truly verefied, The dogge retourned to his vomite, and the sowe being wasshed, to wallowing in the mier.* Why then is ther yet promised against this most manifest truth, a better state vnto them, which haue knowen the way of Iustice, that is, our Lord Christe, and liue naughtely, as though they had not knowen him at all, when it is most cleerely saied: *It had bene better for them not to haue knowen the way of Iustice, then knowing it, to returne backe from the holy commaundement deliuered vnto them?*

It is more daungerous for a man, that hath receaued the faith, to liue vngodly therein, then though he had neuer come to the knowledge of it.

## THE XXV. CHAPTER.

FOR *the holy Commaundement* in this place is not to be vnderstanded that cōmaundement whereby wee are commaunded to beleeue in God, though in that all be conteined, if wee meane that faith of beleuers, Gal. 5. *which woorketh through loue?* But he openly expresseth there, what he called *the holy Commaundement*. For sith that, whereby we are commaunded, that departing from the

the vncleannes of this world, wee ſhould liue in chaſte conuerſation. For thus he ſaith: *If hauing gone from the filthines of this World, into the knowledge of our Lord Ieſu Chriſte the Sauiour of vs all, they being againe Wrapped, and entangled therein be ouercomed, the latter are become to them, Worſe then the firſte.* He ſaieth not, departing from the ignorance of God, or departing from the infidelitie of the worlde, or ſuche lyke, but, *from the filthines of the Worlde*, wherein verely is compriſed all vncleannes of filthy vices. For of theſe ſpeaking afore, he ſayeth, *Banqueting togeather With you, and hauing theyr eyes full of adultery, and of continuall ſinne.* Therefore alſo doth hee calle them, *Drie ſpringes*, that is to ſaye: *ſpringes*, bycauſe they had receaued knowe-ledge of oure Lorde Chriſte: but: *Drie*, bicauſe they liued not accordingely. Iudas the Apoſtle, ſpeaking alſo of ſuche, ſaith: *These be they Whiche doo Without feare banquet together With you, feeding them ſelues, beeing ſpotted, in your Charitable almoeſe Feaſtes: clowdes Without Water &c.* For thoſe whome Peter nameth, *Banqueters together With you, hauing their eies full of adultery*: thoſe doth Iudas call *ſpotted perſons, Without feare, banqueting With you, and feeding them ſelues in your Charitable almoeſe Feaſtes*: For they are mingled with the good in the banquetes of the Sacramentes, and in the almoeſe geeuen to the poore. And that whiche Peter calleth *a drie ſpring*, that doth Iudas name *clowdes Without Water*, and *that* dothe Iames terme, *a deadde faieth*. The tranſitorie paine of fyer therefore, is not promiſed to ſuche as leeue filthilie and wickedly, bycauſe they haue knowen

2.Pet.2.
*Iudæ.*
2.Pet.2.
*Iudæ.*
*Iac.* 2.

the way of Iustice. For the infallible scripture witnesseth: *It had bene better for them not to haue knowen it.*
Matt.12. Luk.11. For oure Lorde also speaking of such, saith: *And the last of that man, shall be woorse then the first*, bycause that not receauing the holy Ghost, which should haue dwelt in the house of his cleansed soule, *he made the vncleane spirit returne thereinto with more company.* Except perhaps these of whom we now treat, be to be accompted better, bycause they did not returne to the vnclennes of adultereis, from the which they neuer departed, neither being purged, did againe defile them selues, but refused to be purged at all. For neither doo they vouchsafe (that they may enter into Baptisme with a lightned conscience) so much as to cast out by vomit, their old vnclennes, which after the manner of dogges, they may take vppe againe: but stubbornly contend to keepe their vndisgested wickednes, in their rawe stommake, euen amidde the holines of the funte of Baptisme. Neither doo they with so much as a feined promise hide the same, but belk it forth by impudent profession and auowing thereof. Neither doo they goinge foorth of Sodome, looke backe againe like Lothes wife, but vtterly disdaine once to go forth of Sodome, nay they labour with the iniquities of Sodome, to enter into Christ. Paule the Apostle saith: *I which was before a blasphemer, a persecutor and an iniurious personne: but I haue gotten mercie, bicause in incredulitie and vnbeleefe, I did it ignorantly.* But to these it is * now saied, then chiefly shall ye get mercy, if being euen in the faith, yee doo wittingly liue ill. It is to longe, and almost an infinite matter, to gather al the testimonies of scriptures, wherby it appereth that their case, which leade wittingly a

Gene.19.

1.Tim.1.

* Euen so is it likewise tought in these our daies bie Luther

ly a

ly a lewde and wicked life, is not onely not more easy or likely to finde pardon, then they which doo it ignorantly, but also euen for that cause, much more perilous and greeuous. Therefore let these suffice. Caluin, and the rest of the nevve Religion.

The life of a Christian man ought to be aunswerable vnto his Baptisme, and standeth not onely in saying, but also in doing.

## THE XXVI. CHAPTER.

LET vs therfore diligently take hede with the helpe of our Lorde God, that wee make not men lewdly carelesse, or secure, saying vnto them, that if they be baptised in Christ, how so euer they liue in the faith, they shall come vnto eternal saluation. Neither let vs so make Christians, as the Iewes made Proselites, to whom our Lord saieth: *Woe be vnto you scribes and Pharaseis, for ye goe about sea and land, to make one proselite, and when ye haue made one, ye make him double more the child of hel, then your selues are.* Matth.23 But let vs rather holde in both, the sounde Doctrine of God our Master, and let a Christian mans life be consonant to the holy Baptisme: neither let eternal life be promised to any man, if either of both want. For he that saied: *Except a man be borne againe of water and the holy Ghost, he shall not enter into the kingdom of heauen,* John.3. he saied also: *Except your righteousnesse doo abound abooue that of the scribes and Pharisees, ye shall not enter into the kingdom of heauen.* Matt.5. For of them he saieth: *Scribes and Pharisees sit in the chaire of Moises: doo as they saie, but not as they doo. For they saie, and doo not.* Matt.23. Their righteousnesse

See, vvhether, men become not novve Protestāts as by the Pharisees they became proselites.

therefore, is to saie, and not to doo: and by thys saying he woulde haue our righteousnesse to be aboove theirs: that is, both to saie, and to doo. Which if it be not, there is no entry for vs into the kingdom of heauen. Not that any man ought so to extoll him selfe, I will not saie, in boasting him selfe to others, but not so muche as with him selfe to presume to thinke, that he is in this life without sinne. Verely if there were not euen among Christians some vices so greeuous, that they were to be pounished euen with Excommunication, the Apostle would not haue saied: *Assembling your selues together, and my Spirite with you, geeue suche a man vppe to the Diuel into the destruction of his flesh, that his soule maie be safe in the daie of our Lorde Iesu.* Wheruppon he also saieth: *I feare least I shal be driuen to lament, when I come, and to mourne for many of those whiche haue sinned before, and not done penaunce for their vncleannes, and fornication whiche they haue committed.* Againe, if there were not certaine sinnes, whiche need not to be healed by suche humilitie of penaunce, as is geeuen in the Church to them which are properly called Penitentes, but by some other medicines of rebuking by woordes, our Lorde woulde not saie: *Tell him his fault betwene him and thee alone: if he harken to the, then thou hast wonne thy broother.* Finally, if there were not some faultes without the whiche this life is not lead, he woulde not haue geuen vs a daily remedy, in the praier which him selfe taught, wherin he willed vs to saie, *forgeue vs our trespasses, as we forgeue them that trespase against vs.*

The difference betvvene a Pharisee and a good Christian man in his life.

Notorious and infamous Crimes.

1.Cor.5.

2.Cor.12.

Crimes mortal, but not infamous.

Matt.18.

Venial sinnes.

Matt.6.

The Conclusion, with a learned recitall of all that hath beene saied before.

THE

## THE XXVII. CHAPTER.

NOW haue I sufficiently laide foorthe (I suppose) what I thinke of that whole opiniõ, wherein three questions haue risen. One of the mingling in the church of good and euil, as of wheat, and cockle. Wherein wee must take heede, that wee thinke not these parables and similitudes propounded to that ende (whether it be that of the vncleane beastes within the Arke, or what so euer suche lyke which signifie the same) that Ecclesiasticall discipline should therefore sleepe (whereof it was saied in the figure of that wooman, *Seuere are the conuersations of her house*) but that vnaduised, and rash temeritie, rather then diligent seueritie, should not so farre proceed, that it presume as it were, to seperate the good from the euil, by wicked schismes. For neither by these similitudes, parables, and foreshewinges, is there geuen to the good, any counsel of slouth or slacknes, wherby they should neglect that, which they ought to forbid: but of pacience, wherby (preseruing alwaie the doctrine of truth) they may suffer and beare that, whiche they can not amende. Nor yet bicause it is written, that there entred also vncleane beastes into the Arke to Noe, therfore the Prelates shoulde not forbid, and stay, if any most lewde and vncleane persons will presume to enter to Baptisme, as light dawncers, which were verely lesse yll, then filthy adulterers: But by this figure of a thing done, it was foreshewed, that vncleane persons should be in the church, by meane of toleration, not by corruption of doctrine, or dissolute breaking of discipline and good order. For the vncleane beastes came not in, where, and of whiche side them listed, the fast frame of the Arke being in any part broken

*Prouer.* 2.
*Genes.* 7.

broken,or ſundered:but the ſame being whole and ſound they entred all at one onely doore,which the woorkman had made.

An other queſtion is vppon that it ſeemed good vnto them, that only faith ſhoulde be preached to them that were to be Baptiſed,and that after Baptiſme, they ſhould be taught,of woorkes and manners. But if I be not deceiued, it hath beene ſufficiently ſhewed, that it dooth then chiefly appertaine to the care and dewty of the ouerſeer, when all they whiche deſire together the Sacrament of the faithfull , doo moſt intentiuely and carefully harken, to all that is ſaied then , expreſſely and plainely to open the paine, which our Lord threateneth to them that liue yll: leaſt they become gilty of moſt greuous crimes,euen in the Baptiſme it ſelfe,whervnto they come to haue the gilt of all their former ſinnes remitted.

The third queſtion is the moſt daungerous of al.Of the whiche ( being ſlenderly conſidered , and not handled according to the woorde of God ) is ryſen (as to me ſeemeth)all that other foule opinion,wherin there is promiſed to ſuche as lyue moſt lewdely, and ſhamefully, yea though they continue in ſuche liuing , if they onely beleeue in Chriſte , and receaue his Sacramentes, that they ſhall come to eternall life and ſaluation. Whiche doctrine is againſt the moſt manifeſt ſaying of our Lorde,
Matt,19. who to him that deſired eternall life , aunſwered : *If thou wilt come vnto life,keepe the cõmaundementes:*and ſhewed farder,what commaundementes:ſuch truly,wherin thoſe ſinnes are forbidden, wherevnto eternall life is nowe ( I
Iacob.2. know not howe ) promiſed thorough faith : *Which without woorkes , is dead .* Of theſe three queſtions I haue

(as I

(as I thinke) ſufficiently diſputed, and haue ſhewed that the euill are ſo to be tolerated in the Churche, that Ecclesiaſticall Diſcipline be not neglected. That they whiche deſire Baptiſme are ſo to be inſtructed, that they may not onely heare, and take vppon them what they ſhould beleeue, but alſo howe they ſhoulde lyue. That eternall lyfe, is ſo promiſed to the faithfull, that no man may thinke he may come thereunto through a deade faith, *whiche without woorkes can not ſaue*. But by that faith of grace, *whiche woorketh thorough loue*. Let not therefore faithfull Stuardes be blamed. Let not theyr negligence or slougthe, be reprooued, but rather the froward ſtuberneſſe of ſome, whiche refuſe to take our Lordes mony, and whiche compell the ſeruantes of our Lorde, to beſtowe and diſtribute their owne counterfait coyne, while thei wil not at the leaſt be of that ſort of euil men, as S. Cyprian ſpeaketh of: *renouncing the world onely in wordes and not in workes*. For theſe men wil not ſo muche as in wordes, renounce the woorkes of the diuel, but with open mouth wil profeſſe, that thei wil continue in ther adultery. If there be any thing els that they do affirme, which I perhaps haue not here touched in this my diſputation, I ſuppoſe it to be ſuch, as whereunto my anſwere was not neceſſary: either bicauſe it apperteined not to the matter now in hande, or els for that it was ſuche a triſel, as might of euery man eaſely be confuted, and reproued.

Note the Concluſion.
*Gal. 5.*
*In Ser. de lapſis.*

*Thus endeth the learned Treatie of that auncient and Bleſſed Father, S. Auguſtine, Of faith and Woorkes.*

# A SERMON MADE BY S. CHRYSOSTOME PATRIARKE OF CONSTANTINOPLE, IN THE *yere of our Lorde. 400. Of praying vnto God: Extant in the fifth Tome of his Woorkes.*

THE ſeruantes of God are for two cauſes woorthy, not onely to be extolled with high prayſes, but alſo to be regarded, and looked vppon with admiration.

Firſte, for that they did ſet the hope of theyr ſaluation in deuoute and holie prayers: and next for that they ſuffered not to grow out of memorye, thoſe laudes, and other ſeruice, whiche with ioy and trembling they vſed to offer vnto God: but haue ben content, that being committed to writing, they ſhould remaine. Whereby thei might powre foorth their treaſure vppon vs, as it were by ſucceſsion of inheritaunce, and by that meane prouoke and ſtirre the whole poſteritie, to a deſyre, of following and of labouring, to be lyke vnto them. For it is well ſytting and conuenient; that bothe the manners of the teachers doo flowe and deſcende, to ſuche as vſe theyr companye, and that the ſcholers of ſuche Maiſters be ſeene alſo to followe and expreſſe in lyfe, the vertue of theyr Maiſters. But this ſhall wee beſt bring to paſſe, if we lyue as menne vertuouſly addicted to continuall prayer, to the ſeruice of God, and to carefull looue of pietie and vertue: thinking

king

king and esteeming, that, to offer our prayers with a pure and sincere harte vnto God, is the only life, the only health, the only riches, and the onely scope, and effect of all that good is. For as the sonne geeueth light vnto the bodye, so dothe prayer illumine and geeue light vnto the sowle. If therefore it be a greate lacke and misse to a blinde man not to behold the sonne: howe muche greater losse is it to a Christian man, yf by continuall prayer, he doo not receyue into his mynde, the light, and cleere bright beames of Christe the Sonne of God?

But nowe who is there, that is not astonned, and doth not wonder at so bounteous courtesy, and singular kindnes as God doth herein extende and shewe to mankinde, in affording to mortall men so great honour, as to admit vs for woorthy to talke with him selfe, and to laye downe our prayers and desiers before him. For of trouth, wee do euen truly talke with God, so often as we applye our selues to prayer. By prayer also, we seuer our selues as it were from that societie, which otherwise wee had with brute beastes: and be in deede cowpled thereby with Angelles. For prayer is the woorke of Angelles. Yea and it passeth in some respecte their dignitie, if to haue present talke with God hym selfe, be a thing aboue the dignitie of Angelles. And that so it is, yea and a muche hygher preeminence, they them selues doo teache vs, offering truely theyr prayers, with muche tremblinge: and geeuing thereby example vnto vs, to knowe and learne, that who so euer presenteth him selfe before God, must doo it with muche ioye, and yet with great trembling. With trembling, while wee

Prayer a familiar talke vvith God

Hovv and after vvhat manner vve shold praye.

 feare

feare leaſte wee may ſeeme vnwoorthy by our prayers to haue ſpeache vnto God. With Ioye, when we thinke of the greatneſſe of the honour, whiche God of his ſo greate care ouer vs, hath vouchesafed to beſtowe on creatures of mortall kinde, that it may be lawfull for vs, continually to haue the Ioye and fruition, of ſpeaking with his Diuine Maieſtie.

The fruit of praier.

By whiche meanes wee obtayne alſo this, that wee being mortal, and hauing continuance but for a tyme, ceaſe ſo to be. For though by nature we be mortal, yet by this ſpeache and familiar life whiche we leade with God, we paſſe ouer to an immortall life. For of neceſsitie it followeth, that he whiche hath familiaritie with God, getteth to be ouer death, and ouer all ſuche thinges as are ſubiect to corruption. And as it can not be, that he which enioyeth the light of the ſonne beames, ſhould be in darkeneſſe: ſo neither can it be by any meanes, that he which vſeth to company with God, ſhould ſtill remayne mortal. For the very heigth and excellency of this dignitie, doth transfer vs to immortallity. For if they that haue free ſpeach with th'emperour, and be cõuerſant familiarly with him, can not lightly be poore after that honour gotten at his hand: much leſſe may it be, that they which by prayer, dayly, and familiarly ſpeake with God, ſhould haue ſoules ſubiect to death. For the death of the ſoule is impietie, and a lyfe which is lead contrary to the lawe of God. Wherof it foloweth, that the life of the ſoule, is the ſeruice of God, and a life worthy of that ſeruice. But a vertuouſe life, and worthy of Gods ſeruice, doth prayer wonderfully winne and procure vnto vs: and being wonne, doth increaſe and laie it vp as a great treaſure in our mindes.

VVhat the death of the ſoule is.

For

For whether a man be possessed with the loue of virginity, or be it, that he hath inclination to embrace the honorable chastitie of wedlocke, or if he study to bridle and restraine anger, and with mildenes to become familier: or haue he desire to be pure and voide from the infection of enuy: Finally, if a man couet and labour to do ought elles that tendeth or appertaineth to wel liuing, he shall by the guide of prayer preparing the waie to suche life, finde a cōmodiouse and easie way to al vertue and goodnes. For it can not be: it can not be (I say) that they which aske of God, chastitie, iustice, mildenesse, and gentlenesse, should not obteine that they aske. For our Lord him selfe saith: *Aske, and it shall be geauen vnto you: seeke, and yee shall finde: knocke, and it shall be opened vnto you. For who so euer asketh, receiueth: and he that seeketh, findeth: and to him that knocketh, there shall be opened.* And againe in an other place *Who is there emong you* (saith he) *of whome if his sonne aske breade, he will geue him a stone? Or if he aske fisshe, he will geaue him a serpent? If you then being euil, can geue good giftes to your children, howe much more will your heauenly Father geaue his holy spirite to suche as sue to him therfore.* With suche sayinges and with suche hope, hath the Lord of al thinges stirred and inuited vs to prayer.

The vertue and force of prayer.

Chastitie, iustice, & other vertues, are obteined by prayer.

Mat. 7.

Luc. 11.

It behoueth vs therefore being obedient vnto God, continually to passe our whole life in prayer, and in praising of God: and to haue muche more care of the seruice of God then of our owne lyfe. For so will it come to passe, that wee shall leade a lyfe suche as is meete for a manne. For who so euer dothe not praie vnto God, nor hath desier to enioye the delight of daily talking with God, that man is deade, wanting life, and of a sicke and deseased minde.

For éuen this is a moste euidente argumente of a franticke and fonde minde, not to vnderstande the great excellencie of this honour: not to loue and delight in prayer: and not to knowe, that then the sowle is dead, when it is not with all looue and humilitie, laied prostrate before the feete of God. For euen as this our bodie, if the sowle and lyfe be awaie, is truely dead and stinking: euen so the sowle except she raise and stirre her selfe vppe to prayer, is dead, wretched, and of very euill and vnpleasant sauour. And to the ende we may truely conceiue this, and thinke it in dede a more heauy and sorowful thing then any death, to be depraued of the benefitte of prayer, that Prophet Daniel dothe wel teache vs. Who did chose rather to suffer death, then onely by the space of three daies to be kept from praying: for the King of Persians Darius, did not require of him to committe any wicked acte: onely this he obserued, if any manne within three daies shoulde be taken with asking owght of any God or man, saue of him selfe onely. But the Prophet indured not to forbeare prayer so muche as for that little space. For why? He knewe that if God be not intreated and made fauourable vnto vs, no good thing can enter into our sowles. But God beeing intreated and made fauourable vnto vs, our labours are furdered, our doynges doe prosper, and merueilousely goe forewarde. But then is God intreated, when he seeth wee loue to praie, and continually to sue vnto him, feruently expecting all good thynges at his handes, and of his goodnesse.

A notable example.

*Daniel.6.*

Therefore

Therefore for mine owne parte, when so euer I see a man that dothe not loue prayer, or delight therein, or that is not as it were possessed with a vehement desire and feruent mindefulnesse thereof: by and by it is a manifeste token vnto mee, that suche a manne possesseth no greate good gifte of grace in his minde. Againe, when I see any man vnsaciably cleauing and fixing him selfe to the seruice of God, and to accompt it one of his greatest losses, if he doe not continually praie: then doe I probably coniecture suche a one to be stedfastly geauen to thinke of all vertue, and to be a very true temple of God. Note vvel

For if a mannes apparraile, if his gate and manners of going, if his gyrning or fond countenance shew what a man is (as the wise Salomon hath saied) muche more is praier, and the seruice of God, a signe and cleare token of all righteousenesse: For prayer is a spirituall and Diuine ornament, procuring vnto our mindes a singular bewtie and comelinesse. It frameth a mannes life, and suffereth not any filthie or absurde thing to haue dominion in the heart. It perswadeth vs to feare God, and to yelde vnto him the honour whiche we owe vnto him. It teacheth vs to repell all the sleigtes and deceites of the wicked spirit, driuing awaie all vile and vnseemely thoughtes. *Eccles.19* Hovv prayer bevvtifieth the minde.

Finally, it confirmeth a mannes minde in the contempte of all vaine voluptuouse pleasure. For this kinde of pride onely becommeth them whiche serue and honour Christe, to disdaine in any sorte to be thrall and bonde to any filthines, and to kepe their mindes free in liberty and vprightnesse of life. And thus I thinke it is A Christian pride.

manifest

manifest to all men, that it is impossible for a man simply without the helpe of prayer to passe his tyme, and to leade out his lyfe in vertue. For howe may it be, that a manne may exercise vertue, excepte he doe continually repaire vnto, and humbly fall downe at the feete of him, who supplieth and geueth all vertue vnto menne? Againe howe maye it be, that any man can desier to be temperat, iuste, and vertuouse, excepte he willingly talke and company dayly with him, who requireth at our handes these and many other such thinges?

Prayer cleanseth from sin.

Yet thus much in fewe, wil I further open vnto you, that al be it prayer doe finde vs euen stuffed with sinnes, yet doth the same lightly purge and make vs cleane therof. What thing then, more high, more excellent, or Diuine, may be applied vnto vs then praier, sith we finde and plainely knowe the same to be a presente medicine to our sicke and diseased mindes? First therefore let vs consyder the Niniuites, whome it is manifest by the meane of prayer to haue obteined remission of their manifolde sinnes, and muche wickednesse, wherewith they had prouoked against them the wrath of God. For so sone as they were entred into the loue and zeale of praying, the same did sone drawe them vnto righteousenesse and vertue: presently amending, and as it were transfourming that Citie which before exercised it selfe in all wantonnesse and lewdnesse, and which (to be short) lead altogeather a lawelesse and moste abhominable life. For prayer being mightier, and of more force then was their long and inueterat custome of sinne, filled that Citie of theirs, with heauenly lawes, and drew also with her into the same Citie, temperance, gentlenesse, mildenesse, and

The example of the Niniuites

care

care of the poore. For prayer dothe not indure without these vertues to dwell or companie emongest vs poore mortall men: but in whose heartes so euer shee chooseth vnto her selfe a seate, those dothe shee fill with al righteousnes, teaching and excercising them to all vertue, and driuing forth al malice and inclination to euill. If therefore a man, who before had well knowen that Citie of the Niniuites, had then entred therevnto, truly he would not haue knowen it. So suddeinly was the same tourned from moste filthy life to pietie and vertue. For euen as a man seeing a beggarly woman whiche was woont to be clothed in vile, and ragged, and filthie clowtes, suddenly decked vppe in garmentes of golde, could not lightly knowe that woman: So if a man had before knowen that Citie, being poore and beggarly, that is to saie, voide of al treasure of vertue and godly behauiour, sure he would not haue knowen what citie that had ben, seeing it then so altered and changed by the mightie force of prayer, from lewde and dissolute, to sober and vertuouse. But nowe let vs further cast our eyes to that woman, who hauing ledde her whole life in wantonnesse and vnchastitie, so sone yet as shee had throwen her selfe downe at Christes feete, obteined health and saluation. Marie Magdalene.

Yet is not this onely the vertue of prayer to purge from sinne, but shee repelleth also and driueth away exceding great daungers and imminent perilles. For Dauid that King and wonderfull Prophet, did by the helpe and force of prayer, put to flight many and mighty fierce enemies: not trenching or fortifiyng his Host with any other weaponnes or municions, then Prayer: and yet by the meane thereof, deliuered vnto his soldiers an vnbloudy Prayer preserueth frō dangers and troubles.

victorie. And some other Kinges haue vsed to repose the hope of their safety in the skill of their soldiars, in the arte of warre, in Archers, in menne of armes, and in light horsemenne, so that great King Dauid, in steede of a wal and rampier, trenched and backed his Host, with holy and deuout prayers: not making accompte of the fiercenesse of his Chiefetaines, Marshalles, Centurions, or other Capitaines, nor gathering masses of money, nor prouiding armure or weapons, but by prayer obteining and bringing downe from heauen the armour of God. For a heauenly armour in deede is Prayer plentiousely powred foorth before God. And that alone is a sure holde and a safe defence, to them whiche haue with assured confidence committed them selues to God. For as for the strength and skill of menne at armes, experience of Archers, and sleight in betraiyng the enemie, many times those are deluded and proue to nothing euen by a countenance onely and shewe of the contrary battaile, stoutnesse of the enemies, or by many other accidentes and occasions that fall out. But Prayer is an inuincible armour, and a most sure defence that neuer deceiueth: ouerthrowing as easely innumerable thowsands of enemies, as it doth one poore soldier. For by prayer, not by weapons and armour, did that Dauid of whome we
1. Reg. 7. spake before (a manne woorthily to be wondered at) ouerthrowe that huge Goliath, when like a terrible diuell he furiousely sette vppon him. Suche a strong and a puissaunte armoure is Prayer, eauen to Kinges againste their enemies in battaile. Yea and an armour of lyke strength is it to vs against diuelles.

3. Reg. 19. By this meane also Ezechias the King hadde the better

better hande in that battaile, whiche was made vppon him by the Persians, at what tyme he armed not his Hoste, but onely fronted the greate multitude of his enemies with prayer. He also escaped death, when with suche reuerence and religion as became him, he didde prostrate hym selfe before God. Where also onely prayer obteined for the Kinge that he might recouer. *3. Reg. 2.*

But nowe that Prayer dothe also readily purifie and cleanse the sowle being indaungered to sinne, that Publican dothe plainely teache vs, who besowght of God remission of his sinnes, and presently obteyned it. The leper also clearely sheweth vs, who so soone as he fell downe at the feete of God, was made cleane. Nowe if God did so lightly heale the bodie infected and corrupted with sicknesse, muche more readily and kindely will hee heale the sowle whiche is diseased. For looke howe muche more pretiouse is the sowle then the bodie, so muche the more deere is it likely to be vnto God. Innumerable are the examples that might be recited bothe olde and newe, if a man were disposed, to reporte all them that haue ben preserued and saued by the benefitte of prayer. *Luc. 18.* *Matt. 8.*

But some menne perhappes, of the number of those who being geuen ouer to slowth and dulnesse hath him selfe no list earnestly and hartily to praie, will goe about to perswade, that against prayer God spake these wordes: *Not euery one that saith vnto mee Lorde, Lorde, shall enter into the kingdome of heauen, but he who doth the will of my Father which is in heauen.* In dede if I beleued onely Prayer to suffise to our saluation, a manne mighte seeme *Matt 7.*

not without cause, to obiecte that place against me. But nowe when I professe Prayer to be the heade and chiefe of all good thinges, the foundation and roote of a fruitful life, there is no cause why any man should abuse those woordes to the excuse of his sluggishnesse. For neither can temperance alone, bring saluation to a man, if other good thinges be failing, neither care ouer the poore, neither benignitie, nor any other of those thinges which are vertuously done. But it is necessary they doe all concurre togeather in our sowles: Yet Prayer (I saie) as the roote and grownde, is the foundation to them all. For as in a shippe or howse, that whiche is first vnderlaied, doth make the same strong, and holdeth it togeather, that it fal not a sunder, so doth diligence and continuance in prayer holde togeather our life, and make it sownde, firme, and wel defended on euery side: in so muche as without that, there can no good fall vnto vs, or owght that may auaile vs to saluation.

For these causes dothe S Paule so earnestly and so often exhorte vs herevnto, saying: *Be yee instant in prayer,*
Colos.4. *watching therein with thankes geauing.* And in an other place hee commaundeth vs, *that wee praye incessantly,*
1. Thes.4. *without intermission, geauing thankes in all: for this is* (saieth he) *the will of God.* And againe in an other
1. Thes.5. place: *Praie* (saieth he) *at all times, watching therevnto in spirite, with all instance and diligence.* So with many Diuine and heauenly woordes dothe the Prince of the Apostles stirre and prouoke vs to continuall prayer. It becommeth vs therefore being taught by him, to leade the course of our lyfe in prayer, and therewith diligently to moist and water our mindes. For hereof

haue

haue we mortall men, no leſſe neede, then trees haue of the moyſture of water. For neither can they bring foorth frute, except their rootes receyue ſome moyſture, nor yet can we be loden with the excellent and preciouſe frutes of pietie, excepte our mindes be watered, and refreſhed by prayer.

Wherefore we muſt both early forſaking our beddes, preuent with our ſeruing of God the riſing of the ſonne: and euen ſo when we come to our foode, and when wee betake our ſelues to the nightes reſte: nay rather wee ought euery howre to offer vnto God a prayer: that the courſe of our prayer might make euen with the courſe of the daye. But in the winter tyme it becommeth vs alſo to beſtowe the greateſt parte of the night in prayer, and on our knees with muche trembling, to continue inſtantly thereat: thinking our ſelues therein happie, and bleſſed, that wee may beſtowe our tyme in the Seruice of God. the times of Prayer.

Tell me, ( I pray thee ) with what face canſt thou behold the ſonne, if thou doo not firſt adore him, who geeueth vnto thine eyes, that moſt comfortable light? Howe canſt thow feede on that is ſet before thee, excepte thou doo firſte woorſhip him, who doth geue and ſupply ſo many good thinges vnto thee? With what hope canſt thou betake thy ſelfe to the night? With what dreames thinkeſt thou, thou ſhalt be vexed, if thou do not firſt defend thy ſelfe with prayer, but geeueſt thy ſelfe to ſleepe vngarded and without protectiō? Verely thou ſhalt yeeld thy ſelfe as an abiecte, and eaſy to be taken of wicked ſprites, who continually walke about, laying waight for vs, that they may ſuddainly catche vp, whome ſo euer they find vnarmed of the defence of prayer. But if they find vs fensed with prayer, by and by, they be gone: euen as theeues and lewde persons, when they see the souldiars sword shaken, and threatened ouer their heads. And if it happen any man to be naked, voyde, and destitute of this munition of prayer, surely he being pulled out, and as it were torne of, is carried away with diuels, and throwen into many calamities and sundry mischeifes. It behoooueth vs therefore, that fearing al these thinges, thus truly layde before vs, we do continually rampar, and enuironne our selues about with Hymnes and Praiers: that God hauing compassion of vs may make vs worthy of the kingdome of heauen, through his only begotten sonne Iesu Christe, to whom be all glory and rule for euer and euer.

AMEN.

*Thus endeth the Sermon of Prayer, made by S. Chrysostome.*

A SER-

# *A SERMON OF FASTING MADE BY THAT MOST* LEARNED AND HOLY FATHER *S. Baſil, ſurnamed the great: Archebiſshop of Ceſarea in Cappadocia, in the yere of our Lorde, 360.*

Tranſlated into Engliſh, and diligently conferred with the Greeke Original.

BLOWE *out* (ſaith the Prophet) *and ſound with the trumpet in the new mone in the notable day of your mirth, and reioyſing.* This is a commaundement vttered by the Prophet. But to vs doo the leſſons, and readinges out of holy Scripture ſhewe the ſingular ioye and feſtiual ſolemnite of theſe daies more openly and diſtinctly, then any trumpet, and more cleerely then any muſical inſtrument. For we haue learned the grace and benefit of faſting out of the Prophet Eſay, who reiected the Iewiſhe manner of faſting, and gaue to vs a paterne of the true faſt. *Faſt not* ( ſaieth he ) *to contention and variance by ſute of lawe, but loſe the bond of iniquitie*. And our Lorde him ſelfe ſaieth : *Be not of ſad and heauy contenance, but waſh thy face.* Let vs therefore be ſo affected, as we be taught, not making ſhewe of ſorrow in our faces in theſe faſting daies at hand: But let vs be cherfully diſpoſed in them, as becometh the holy. No man is crowned, that is of an abiect mind. No man erecteth a monument of victory with a ſad and a heauy cheere. Be not ſad when thou art cured. It is an abſurd thing to be ſad againſt the alteratiō of meates, and not to reioyce when the ſoule is healed, and ſo to ſeeme

*Leuit.23.* *Pſal.80.* *Eſay.58.* *Math.6.*

to seeme thereby to be more addicted to the voluptuousnes of the beally, then to the cure of the soule. For full feeding pleaseth the belly, but fasting purchaseth gayne vnto the soule. Reioyce, that there is by the Physition geeuen vnto the a medicine that taketh awaye sinne. For euen as wormes breed in the bowels of children, are killed, and auoyded, with strong and sharp medicines, euen so fasting, searching euen to the very soule, dothe kil sinne deeply rooted and dwelling in vs, to the bottom: and therefore is truly most worthy to be tearmed an healing medicine. *Annoynt thy head, and washe thy face.* This speeche dothe call thee to high mysteries. He that hath oynted other, him selfe is anoynted. He that hath wasshed, is clensed. Transferre this precepte to thy inner partes. Washe thy soule from sinnes. Annoynt thy head with holy oyle, that thou maiste be made a partaker of Christ, that is, of the annoynted, and in that manner come to thy faste.

A simili-tude.

*Math.6.*

*Doo not darken thy face, as hypocrites doo.* The face is darkened, when the inward affection is drawen ouer with an outward counterfeit shewe, and couered with a false vayle. He is an Hypocrite, that in a stage, taketh on him an other mans person, as the seruaunt often doth his maisters, and the subiect his Kinges. So in this life as in a stage, or shewe place, of the course of our life, many geue forth a disguised shewe, carrying in their harte one thing, and geeuing foorth to men a superficial shewe of an other. Doo not therefore hide thy face. Appeare suche as thou arte. Transforme not thy selfe to sadnesse, thereby to hunt after glorie, because thou shewest thy selfe abstinent. Finally neither is there anye profit of the almes,

*Ioan. 13.*

The propertie of an Hypocrite.

almes, made knowen by the ſounde of the trumpet, nor any gaine of the faſt, whiche is taken, to the ende it ſhoulde be publiſhed, or openly knowen. For thoſe thinges whiche are done for oſtentation, doo not ſtrech their frute to the worlde to come, but as they reſpecte cheefly the praiſe of menne, ſo doo they ende therein. Runne therefore freſhly and with a ioifull cheere to the gifte of faſting.

Faſting is an olde and auncient gifte, yet not wearing, not growing olde, but euer wexing yonge, and euer floriſhing as it were in the beſte age. Thinke you I drawe the antiquitie thereof from the law? Naie: I ſaie: Faſting, is more auncient, then the lawe it ſelfe. And if thou wilt tarie a while, thou ſhalt finde my ſaying true. Thinke not the daie of propitiation, whiche was commaunded to Iſraell in the ſeuenth moneth and the tenth daie of the moneth, was the beginning of faſting. Goe to then: followe the hiſtorie, and ſearche foorth the antiquitie thereof. For it is no newe or latter inuention. It is the treaſure of the fathers. And what ſoeuer excelleth in antiquitie, is venerable, and to be had in reuerence. Honor the auncient and hore heares of faſting. For faſting is as olde, as mankynde it ſelfe. In Paradyſe was it inſtituted. The firſt commaundement that Adam receiued, was, *ſee that you eate not of the tree of knowledge of good and bad*. This woorde, *Eate not*, is a commaundement of faſting, and abſtinence. If Eue had forborne, and faſted from that tree, wee ſhoulde not nowe, haue needed this faſte. For the ſicke, not the ſounde, haue neede of the Phiſicion. Wee are ſicke and diſeaſed through ſinne. Lette vs then be healed

The antiquite of faſting.

*Leuit*, 23.

Antiquity to be had in Reuerence.

*Gen*. 2.

Matt.9. thorough penaunce. But penaunce without fasting is
Gen.3. vaine. *The cursed earth shall bring thee foorth thornes and brambles.* Thou arte commaunded, to endure paine and sorrowe, not to leade thy life in delicacie. By fasting therefore purge thy selfe to God.

But euen the life it selfe in Paradyse, is an image of fasting. Not only bicause manne being a companion and fellowe dweller with Angelles, did by beeing contente with fewe thinges, attayne to be leeke vnto them: but also bicause what so euer thinges the sharpenes and finenes of mannes witte, did afterwarde finde out, were not yet deuised of them that liued in Paradyse. For neyther the drinking of wyne, nor the kylling of quicke and liuing thinges, nor ought elles that troubleth the mynde of man, were there as yet then practised. Bicause we fasted not, therefore wee fell out out of Paradyse. Lette vs therefore faste, that wee maie retourne agayne therevnto. Doest thou not see
Luca.16. Lazarus, howe by fasting he entred into Paradyse? Followe not the disobedience of Eue. Take not againe the serpent for thy counseller, applying thee with meate to the pamparing and pleasing of the fleshe.

Fasting not hurteful to the body, but healthful.

Clooke not the matter by the Infirmitie and weakenesse of thy bodie. For these pretenses and excuses thou doest not tell to mee, but to him that knoweth the truthe. Els tell me, I praie thee, canst thou not faste, and yet canste thou glutte thy belly with meate, and wearye thy body with the burden of those thinges, thou hast eaten? Verely I haue knowen, that Physicians

cians haue commaunded euen vnto ſicke menne, not varietie of meates, but hunger and abſtinence. How then maie he whiche canne doo theſe thinges, excuſe him ſelfe, that he can not doo the other? Is it not muche eaſier for the belly, with thynneſſe of diete to beare quietly the night, then to lye loden, with ſuperfluitee of meates? Yea and not to lye neither, but rather to be toſſed, and tormoiled all night, panting and groning for payne? Excepte perhappes thou wilt ſaie, the ſhippemaiſter canne better rule his veſſell being ouerfraihgted, and ouerladen, then when it hath his light and iuſt peyſe? For that whiche is oppreſſed with abundance and waight, a litle raging of the water drowneth: But that whiche is moderately frawghted, dooth eaſily gette aboue the waues, whyle nothyng letteth it to riſe a lofte. Euen ſo mennes bodyes being loden with continuall full feeding, are lightly ouerwhelmed with infirmities. But thoſe, whiche vſe a ſpare and thinne diete, doo bothe eſcape that euill, whiche is by ſickneſſe looked for, as it were a tempeſte beginning to riſe, and alſo repulſeth that greeſe whiche is already come, euen as it were the meeting of ſome raging waue in the ſea.

A Similitude.

But it ſeemeth by you, that it is more paynfull to reſte, then to runne: and to bee at good eaſe, then to wreſtle: if you ſaie it be more conuenient for ſicke perſons to fare deliciouſly: then to feede ſparingly. Verely the animall vertue gouerning the life, doth eaſely concocte, and diſgeſte, that which is but ſcarce and ſufficient, and doth well applie, and appropriat it, to that, whiche is to be nourisshed. But when shee is charged and accumbered, with diuersitie of meates curiously dressed, the same not being able to staie it, till being kindly digested, it maie be conueied orderly to the partes, which are to be nourished, bredeth sundry kindes of diseases.

But nowe lette vs goe forwarde with the historie, prosecuting the antiquitie of fasting: and howe all holy menne haue kept the same, as an inheritance receiued of theyr Fathers: the father still deliuering it to the Sonne, as it were from hand to hand. Whereby this possession hath also benne continued, euen to vs by succession. Ther was no wine in Paradyse: there was no killing of quicke thinges: there was not yet any eating of flesh. After the floodde came wyne, after the flood ye fell to eating all thinges, as commonly as before herbes. When perfection was dispeired of, then was fruition of those thinges graunted. A cleere proufe that wine before the flood was not knowen, appeered in Noe, who was vtterly ignorant, of the vse of wine. For it was not yet come to the vse of mans life, nor knowen at all emong menne. When therefore he neither had sene any other drinke it, nor had tried it him
Gen.9. selfe, he was vnwares hurt thereof. *For Noe planted a vine, and dranke of the frute, and was made drunke.* Not that he was a great drinker, or geuen to be drunke, but bicause he was not acquainted with the measure, that was to be taken thereof. So wee see, that the drinking of wine, was a latter inuention, then Paradyse. And so is the Authoritie of fasting of more Antiquitie.

But

But we haue also learned, that by fasting Moyses came vnto the hill: For he durst not haue aduentured (the top of the hil smoking) to haue entred into the darke cloude, if he had not benne firste armed with fasting. By fasting he receiued the Commaundementes written with the finger of God in plates of mettal. So was fasting the cause of the lawe making aboue, but glottony, the cause of falling to madde woorshipping of Idolles beneth. *For the people sate downe to eating and drincking, and rose vp to plaie.* One drunken fit, marred and defeated, the constant Continuance of God his seruant, in fasting and praying, by the space of fortie daies. For the tables written with the finger of God, which fasting had receiued, drunkennes lost: the Prophet thinking it vnsemely, that lawes should be deliuered from God to a drunken people. In one moment of time, that people which was taught from God, and traded by woonderful miracles, was thorough glotony throwen downe into the beastly woorshipping of the Egyptian Idoles. Compare now bothe together: and see how fasting leadeth to God, and howe deliciousnes, loseth saluation. And being now entred into the way, descende forward to later times. What defiled Esau, and made him the seruant of his brother? Was it not one onely eating, for which he lost the prerogatiue, of being the first borne? But did not praier with fasting, gette and geue Samuel to his mother? What made that great Conquerour Samson, to be inuincible? Was it not fasting, wherewith he was conceiued in his mothers wombe. Fasting nourished him, in steed of a nurse. Fasting made him a man. For that was commaunded to his mother by the Angell in these wordes: *What soeuer*

*Exod.19.* The effectes and frutes of fasting. *Exod.32.* *Gene.25.* *1.Sam.1.* *Iud.13.*

*proceedeth out of the vine, let him not eate, ne let him not drinke wyne, or stronge hote drinke:* that is to ſay, any drinke that may make droonke. Faſting bredeth Prophetes, ſtrenghtheneth the mightie, and teacheth wiſedome to lawemakers. It is a good bulwarke to the ſoule, a ſure companion of life to the bodie, a target to them that doo valiantly, an exerciſe to ſuche as ſtriue for the game. This remoueth temptations, this annointeth to pietie. This is the companion of ſobrietie, the woorker of temperance. This teacheth to doo manfully in battaile, and inſtructeth to deale quietly in peace. This ſanctifieth men dedicated vnto God, and maketh perfit the Prieſte. For it may not be, that a man without faſting ſhould preſume to celebrate ſacrifice, not onely nowe in the myſticall and true ſeruice of God, but not ſo muche as in the figuratiue ſacrifice, brought in by the Lawe.

Examples of faſting. This faſting made Elias, with his eies to behold a great miracle. For when hee had by the ſpace of forty daies
3.Reg.17. purged his ſoule by faſting, he was made woorthy in the denne in Choreb to ſee oure Lorde, ſo farre as it was poſsible for man to ſee him. He by faſting reſtored to the widdowe here ſonne, ſhewing him ſelfe by faſting ſtronge and mighty euen againſt death. The voice goinge foorth from his mouth hauing benne longe faſting, did for three yeres, and ſixe moonethes, cloſe the heauen from the people liuing againſt the Lawe. For, to mollifie the vntamed hartes of that ſtiffe necked people, he was contente to condemne him ſelfe alſo to affliction
3.Reg.17. and penurie. *So ſure* (ſaieth hee) *as oure Lorde liueth, there ſhalbe no water in the earth, but by my mouthe.*

And

And thus he forced vppon all the people, a fast thorough famine, to the end he might thereby correct their iniquities growne of their delicate, and dissolute life. But what manner of life did *Eliseus* leade? How did he vse him selfe when he hosted at the Sunamites house? Or howe did he receiue and welcome the Prophetes? Did not wilde herbes of the wood, and a littell meale furnishe his table? At the whiche time also suche as had eaten of the * Coloquintes, were in daunger to haue died thereof, if by the praiers of him being purged, and made acceptable thorough fastinge, the poysone hadde not benne dissolued. In fewe, it is easie to finde that fastinge had leadde, as it were by the hande, all the holy Fathers to a diuine wisedome, and to a heauenly kinde of life.

4. Reg. 4.

* Coloquint, is an herbe, vvhich after some mennes opinion, may be called, a vvilde goorde.

There is a certaine stone, or substance, whiche we Grecians * calle *Amianthon*, of that nature, that it is not with fire to be consumed. For being put in the flame, it semeth to be burnt vnto coles, but being taken out of the fier, it appereth more pure, as doth water being clarified. Such were the bodies of those three children in Babylon, hauing thorough fasting, the vnconsumptible nature of the *Amianthon*. For in the great flame of the fornaice, they, being as of the nature of golde, did ouercome all the force of the fier. Yea they appeared to be of muche more excellencie, then golde. For the fire dyd not mealt them, but preserued them whole. Yea and that, when nothing in the worlde did stay or keepe backe the flame. But contrary, *Naphtha*, a kinde of naturall, and vnquencheable lime, pitche, and small twygges, dyd so nourrishe it, that it was spread the

* *Vide de hoc lapide Dioscoridē lib. 5. cap. 147.*

*Naphtha apud Dioscor. lib. 1. cap. 99.*

the length of xlix.cubites, and ſo feeding rounde about, conſumed many of the Chaldeans. The children then being entred, with bodies purified by faſting, did treade vnder their feete, and ouercomme that deadly fier, breathing a moiſte aire, as it were a ſweet dewe, vpon that vehement fier: whiche yet durſt not touche ſo muche as their heare, bicauſe the ſame had ben bred and nouriſhed by faſting.

*Dani.9.* Daniell alſo the man of God ſpecially beloued, whoo in three weekes neither eate bread, nor drancke water, being put downe into the denne, taught alſo euen the *Dani.6.* lions to faſt. For as though he had ben made euen of ſtone, or braſſe, or ſome other harder ſubſtaunce, the lions could not once enter their teeth into him. So had faſting hardened the body of the man, as ſteeled yron, and made it inuincible to the lions. Nay they coulde not ſo muche as once open theire mouthe againſt that holy man.

Faſting quenched the force of the fier. Faſting ſtopped the mouthes of the lions. Faſting ſendeth praier vp to heauen: being as it were a winge thereunto, to carry it vpward. Faſting is the wealth of the howſe: the mother of health: and the ſchoolemaſter of youth. Faſting is an ornamente to olde menne: a good companion to wayfaring perſons: a ſafe, and truſty conuictour to ſuch as dwell together. The huſband ſuſpecteth not to be deceiued by his wife, when he ſeeth her delight in faſting. The wife fretteth not with ielouſie, when ſhe ſeeth her huſband geeuen to faſting. Who euer ſawe a houſe decaie by faſting? Vewe what thinges are at this daie within thy houſe, and ſurueie them agayne hereafter, and

thou

thou shalt find nothing thereof wanting, through fasting. No beast or other liue thinge lamenteth his death. No bloud is seene in thy house. No heauie sentence of death, geeuen by the vnsatiable belly against the poore beastes. The cookes knife is at rest. The table of the faster is content with such thinges, as voluntarily do rise and growe of the earth. The Sabaoth was geeuen to the Iewes: *That thy beast* (saith God) *and thy seruaunt may be at rest*. Let thy fasting be a rest of continuall labours, vnto thy seruauntes, that serue thee all the yeere. Suffer thy cooke to be quiet. Geue rest vnto thy Sewer. Forbeare the hand of thy cupbearer, and butler. Let him haue some repose, who prepareth thy manyfold Iouncats and banccketting disshes. Let thy house sometime be quiete from those innumerable tumultes, from smoke, fulsom sauour of rost, and from the running vp and doune of them that do nought but minister vnto the bellie, as to a dame, that can neuer be pleased. Euen exacters of tributes do sometime affoord some libertie to the subiectes. Let the belly likewise geue some truce to the mouthe. Let that which is euer crauing, and neuer ceasseth: which receiueth to day, and forgetteth to morrowe, geue vs truce for fiue daies. When it is full, then it disputeth of abstinence. When the meate is a litle passed, then it forgetteth quite all such doctrine. Fasting knoweth not the nature of death. The table of the faster dooth not sauer of vserie. The fathers vseries doo not strangle the litle child of the faster, in his nonage, winding about him like serpentes. And truly besides all this, sometime to faste, is a meane to the increase of pleasure and delight. For as thirst maketh drinke to seeme pleasaunt, and as hunger gone before, dooth make

Exo. 20.

the furnished table the more delightsome,right so dooth fasting encrease the gladsome lyking of meates. For that putting it selfe betwene,and thereby interrupting in part the continual glut of delicacies,shall make the receiuing thereof againe,the more pleasaunt,euen as of a friend retourned from far countries. Wherfore if thou wilt make vnto thy selse thy table pleasaunt,take vnto thee somtime a chaunge by fasting. But thou that art excessiuely possessed with the looue of deliciousnes,doost not perceiue that thou diminishest much of thy delight, by continuall vsage thereof: and for looue of pleasure lesest in dede the chiefest pleasure. For nothing is so pleasaunt,but that by continuall fruition it waxeth fulsome. But of those thinges which are rarely had,the fruition is delightsome.

A Similitude.

Euen in this sort,he which hath made vs,hath deuised: that by chaunge and orderly retourne of thinges in this life,the pleasure of those thinges which he hath graunted vs,might still remaine with delight vnto vs. Doest thou not see how after night,the sonne is more bewtiful? And waking more pleasaunt after sleepe? And health the more desired, and esteemed, after feeling of sicknes and aduersitie? Euen so after fasting,is the table also the better welcome both vnto riche menne, and suche as haue it well furnished, and also to poore folke, which haue but from hand to mouth,that which the earth yeldeth.

Luc.16.

Feare the example of the riche man. Deliciousnes of life brought him to the fier.For he was not broiled in the flame of the furnaice,bicause he was accused of any iniustice,but for his soft and delicate life. We haue therefore nede of water to quenche that fire. And fasting is not only profitable for the time to coome, but also presently very

very healthsome vnto the bodie. For the best health, and state of mannes bodie, being growen vp to the highest, falleth backe, and decaieth of it selfe, very nature failing, and not being hable to beare the burthen of so great strength. Beware least thou which now spittest water, doo not hereafter with the riche man, desire and longe after a drop of water. No man euer surfeted of water. No mans head did euer ake, and was heauy with water. No man pasing his life with drincking of water, had euer any neede of an other mans feete. No mans legges haue bene bound, no mans handes made vnprofitable by drinking of water. For the default about disgestion (which necessarily happeneth to suche as liue delicately) doth bring vnto their bodies vehement diseases. The coulour of the man that fasteth, is reuerent: not flowring vp to an vnshamefast readnes, but adorned with a temperate palenes. His eye is gentle: his gate humble: his face modest: not disgraced by fonde lawghter: his speeche moderate: his hart sincere and pure.

Calle to thy remembrance the Sainctes and holy men that haue been from the beginning: of whome the worlde was not worthy: *They walked in sheepes skinnes* Hebr. 11. *and goates skinnes, they were forsaken, pressed with many vexations, and hardly afflicted.* Followe their life, if thou seeke after their portion. What brought Lazarus to rest in Abraham his bosome? Was it not fasting? The Matt. 3. life of Iohn Baptist what was it, but as it were one continuall faste? He had no bedde, no table, no lande to plowe, no drawing oxe, no corne, no baker of his bread, nor any other of these temporall thinges. And therefore *rose there neuer emong the children of weemen a greater* Matt. 11.

*then Iohn Baptiste*. Fasting allso dyd carrie vppe to heauen S.Paule with others, which he dooth him selfe recite emong the glories that he had ouer his trobles and persecutions. But our Lord, the head of all those before remembred, when by fasting he had prepared and fortified the flesh, whiche for our sakes he tooke vppon him, did then susteine therein the assaultes of the Diuell: to the end he might thereby both teache vs by fasting to arme and exercise our selues to the conflictes of temptations, and also by his famine and pouertie, encourage and geeue occasion to the aduersarie to come vnto him. For he was not to haue beene approched of him by reason of the heigth of his Godhed, if he had not firste by hunger brought him selfe downe to the weakenes of mannes estate. But ascending into heauen, he tooke meate, to shewe and perswade thereby the true nature of his body which was risen.

*2.Cor.6. & 11.*

*Matt.4.*

But thow wretched manne ceasest not to pamper and to fat vp thy bodie, staruing in the meane time thy minde with hunger and famine, not hauing any care of healthsome instructions, whiche geeue life thereto. Knowest thow not, that as in a battaile to be fought, succour comming to the one side, weakeneth the other, and maketh it the more easie to be ouercomme: so he whiche helpeth and encreaseth the fleshe, weakeneth the spirite? And on the other side he that encreaseth the strenghth of the spirite, bryngeth the fleshe into subiection. For these two are opposite, and contrary the one to the other. Wherefore if thow wilte make thy minde strong, tame thy fleshe by fasting. For this is it, whereof the Apostle speaketh, saying:

A very apte Similitude.

*By how*

*By howe muche the outwarde man is decaied, by ſo muche the inward is renewed.* And againe: *When I am weake, then am I mightie.* Wilt thou not then deſpiſe theſe corruptible meates? Wilt thou not hunger after that heauenly table, which faſting in this life doth procure and prepare vnto thee? Dooſt thow not knowe, that by immoderate full feeding, thou doeſt breed vnto thy ſelfe a fat worme to gnawe thee? For who in abundaunce of meate, and continuall delicacie, hath been partakener of the graces and giftes of the Spirit? Moyſes receauing the ſeconde time the tables of the lawe was of neceſsitie driuen to a ſeconde faſt. Yf the brute beaſtes had not alſo faſted with the Niniuites, they had not eſcaped their threatned deſtruction. Whoſe limmes and carcaſes were thoſe that fell in the deſert? Were they not theirs, that ſought after the eating of fleſh? They, ſo long as they were content with Manna, and water out of the rocke, ouercame the Egyptians, made waie thorough the ſea, and there was not one ſicke of all the Tribes. But after they had ones made mention of their fleſhpottes of AEgypt, and luſted to retourne thither agayne, they neuer came to ſee the land of promiſe. Dooſt thow not feare this their example? Dooſt thow not abhorre now inſaciable feeding, leſt it exclude thee alſo from the good thinges, that thow hopeſt for? But neither had Daniell ſeen the viſions, if by faſting he had not illuminated, and made more cleere and bright his ſoule. For of groſſe nurriture, ſmoky vapors mounte vppe: whiche lyke a thicke clowde doo intercepte and ſtoppe the bright beames of grace, that are ſent and deriued from the holy Ghoſte, into our hartes. And ſurely if there be any meate proper vnto Angelles,

2.Cor 4. 2.Cor.12. Exod.34. Iohn.3. Num.11.

Psal.77. it is bread, as saieth the Prophete. *Man hath eaten the bread of Angels:* not flesh, not wyne, not those thinges, which are exquisitly sought out by them that serue their bellie. Fasting is a Target for the warre against diuels. *For some kinde of diuels dooth not goe foorth, but by praier and fasting.* Matt.17.

Loe what a number of commodities grow by fasting. But sacietie, and fulnes in feeding, is the grownd and beginning of all misdemeanour. For with delicates, dronkennes, and many kind of sauces prouoking glottony, presently entreth al kind of brutish and insolent behauiour. Hereof menne are made, as it were, madde and furious horses towarde weemen, by the beastly outrage ingendred in their mindes thorough suche deliciousnes. Yea, drunkardes chaunge nature, and goe against kinde. But fasting dooth make knowen euen the honest measure of wedlock woorke, chastising the vnmodest vsage euen of those thinges whiche are permitted by lawe: That, grawnteth leisure by mutuall agreement to either partie, to attende vnto praier.

Yet maiest thou not limite the goodnes of fasting, to consiste onely within the compasse of abstinence from meates. For the true fast is the forsaking of euils and vitious doinges. Lose all bond of iniustice, remitte to thy neighbour all trouble, forgeue him his det: fast from sutes and contentions. Thou forbearest eating of flesh, but yet eatest thy broother. Thou abstainest from wine, and yet doost not temper thy selfe from doing of wronges. Thou tarriest till night before thou wilt take thy foode, and yet spendest thy daie in the lawe courtes, in sewtes, and contentions. *Woe be to you* (saieth the Prophet) *that be drunke, yet not*

The true fast.

Esaie.29.

*yet not with wine.* For wrath is also a drunckennes of the sowle, bringing the same out of the waie euen as wyne dooth. Heauines lykewise is a dronckennesse, whiche drowneth the minde. So is feare also an other dronckennes, when it is, where it ought not to be. *From the feare of myne enemy* (saieth the Prophet) *deliuer my soule, O Lord.* In fewe, euerie pasion, disordering the minde, is rightly termed by the name of dronckennes. Consider the angry man, how he is dronken in that pasiõ, and is not him selfe master of him selfe. He knoweth not himselfe. He knoweth not them that be present. He stryketh all, as one that fighteth in the night. He offendeth all. He triumpheth ouer all. He speaketh vnaduised thinges. Hardely canne he be tempered. He reuileth, he beateth, he threateneth, he sweareth, he crieth out, and tormenteth him selfe. Flee from this drunckennes. But beware also of that whiche commeth of wine.

*Psal. 16.*

Anger, a kinde of dronkenesse.

Doo not by muche drincking of wine, make thy waie to drincking of water. Let not dronckennes leade thee to the holines of fasting. There is no entry into fasting by dronckennes, nor to iustice by auarice, nor to temperaunce by riot, nor (to conclude in fewe) is there any entrie by vice, vnto vertue. There is an other gate into fasting. Dronkennes maketh waie to insolent behauiour, but conuenient sufficiency vnto fasting. He whiche is to trie for the best game, dooth exercise him selfe before hand: He whiche fasteth, must first exercise and prepare him selfe by abstinence: laie downe glottony fiue daies before, not as one that would thwart the ordinary daies, or deceiue the lawe maker. For fondly doost thou labour, to wery thy body, and yet not to mitigat nor

Against those, that glut in one daie, to fast an other.

to re-to releaſe thy crime and euill appetite. A falſe ſtore-howſe is that bodie. Thow draweſt into a bottomleſſe barrell. For the wine paſſeth, and runneth his naturall waie. But thy ſinne and inſatiable luſte remaineth within thee. The ſeruaunt runneth awaie from his maſter that beateth him: yet thou remaineſt ſtyll with wine, whiche dailie beateth thy head. The beſt meaſure of the vſe of wine, is the neceſsitie, and the lacke that the body maie haue thereof. But if thou exceede thoſe boundes, to morow thou wilt come complaining of the heauines of thy head, yaning, gyddy, and ſmelling yet of the vndigeſted wine. Al thing wil ſeeme to moue, al thing to go rownde with thee. For drunkennes as it maketh men ſleepe, as if they were dead, ſo it maketh men to wake, as if they were in a dreame.

Dooſt thow not conſider whome thou comeſt to receiue by this faſting? Euen him which promiſed to come vnto vs, ſaying: *I and my Father will come, and make our dwelling with him.* Why therefore dooſte thou by drunkennes preuent his comming, and cloſe the entrie againſt our Lord? Why dooſt thou allure and take in thine Enemie, to take poſſeſsiō firſt of thy munitions? Drunkennes doth not receiue our Lorde. Drunkennes driueth away the holy Ghoſte. For as ſmoke driueth awaie bees, ſo dothe ſurfeting and belly cheere put to flight and driue awaie al ſpirituall graces. Faſting is the ornament of the Citie. The ſtrengthning of the place of Iuſtice. The peace of our howſes: and the ſauing and preſeruation of our gooddes and poſſeſsions. Wilt thow ſee the bewtie of faſting? Then compare me the euening of this feſting daie, with the euening of to morrow being faſting daie. Thow

A Similitude.

ſhalt

ſhalt ſee the Citie chaunged from tormoyle and tempeſteous waues of great ſturre, to a ſure calme and quiete tranquillitie.

But I wiſh that both this day may be like vnto to morrowe in holineſſe and modeſt comlineſſe: and that to morrow may want nothing of the mirth, and ioye that is this daye. And further I beſech our Lorde, who hath by the courſe and reuolution of the yeere, brought vs about to this time, that it may pleaſe him to graunt vnto vs being as it were tryers for the maſtery, that by theſe excerciſes, wee may ſhewe foorth the firmeneſſe and ſtrength of our conſtancie: and that we may come to the day appointed for the receyuing of our crownes: Now by dayly recording of that healthfull Paſsion ſuffred for vs, but then in the world to come by receauing retribution and rewarde, according to our life lead here, and that in the iuſt iudgement of Chriſte him ſelfe, to whome be all glory for euer.

AMEN.

*Thus endeth the Sermon of S. Baſil, made of faſting.*

# THE THIRD SERMON, MADE BY S. LEO, SVRNAMED THE GREATE, AND POPE OF

*Rome in the yere of our Lorde .450. Vpon the Fast of the tenth Moneth, and of the almes to be done in the same.*

How Gods fielde is with faith to be fenced, and inclosed, with Fasting to be tilled and tempered, with almes to be sowen, and with prayers to be donged, and made frutefull.

The fast of the tenth moneth, is the imber fastvvhich is kept in the moneth of December.

IN our Lordes field, whose laborers and workemen we be (most deerly beloued) we must prouidently, and diligently exercise the spiritual tillage: to the end that we with continual industrie, foreseing and doing that, which is at euery season, duly and orderly to be done, may ioye in the plentiful increase of our good and vertuous workes. Whiche if thorough sluggish idlenes, or dul lasynes, they be neglected, our ground can bring foorth no worthy spring, no good graine, nor holesom fruite, but being ouergrowne with thornes and brambles, shal bring foorth nothing woorthy to be laied vp, and kept in storehowses, but suche thinges onely as are meete to be burned and consumed with fier. This fielde (deerly beloued) by the sweete dewe of the of the grace of God falling therein, is first inclosed and fenced by faith: tilled, tempered, and seasoned, by fasting: sowed with almes deedes: donged and made fruteful by praiers, to the ende that in our ground thus husbanded, no bitter or vnholsome rote spring therein, nor sap of any noisome stocke rise vp: but that (al seed of vice being killed, and distroyed in vs) the worthy corne of vertue, may ioyfully and plentifully growe vp together.

To whiche diligence, the maister and teacher of pietie, doth in all tymes exhorte vs, but in these dayes, which are more specially appointed to this woorke, wee muste styrre vp in our selues a more cowrage and feruent care hereof, least it be found a wickednesse in vs, to neglect that, being taught and instructed, whiche vertue and pietie would vs to doo, though we were not commaunded. We doo therefore exhorte and admonish you, that this Fast of the tenth moneth, (whereunto wee knowe your charitie with a religious intent and disposition is prepared) wee celebrating with one minde by the helpe of Christ, may euery of vs shine in good works, according to the measure and proportion of the abilitie, which he hath receyued of God. And that the more feruentlie, bicause our enemies, which are greeued and vexed at our sanctification, doo in these dayes, wherin thei know vs disposed to a better attendance of our dewty, are most fearce vpon vs, and with more craft and subtelty, lye in waight for vs: To the end that, by fearing some, with doubt of pouertie which may grow by their liberal geuing of almes, and putting into others a heauines, and repining at the paine of fasting, they may draw many from the vertuous fellowship of this deuotion. Against which temptation (most deerly

The diuel is most busye vvhē men are best disposed.

 belooued)

beloued ) let there be kept waking in vs the zealous intent of a charitable harte. And let these thoughtes of mistrust, be far repelled from Christian mindes. For it is a smal thing, which to a poore man is inough. Neither is his diet, or apparel chargeable. Poore foode is it, that he hungreth after: poore drinke it is, that his thirst wil be quenched with: His nakednes nedeth to be couered, and asketh not to be decked. And yet our Lorde is so kinde a Iudge of our workes, so louing an esteemer thereof, that euen for a cup of colde water, he wil not fayle to geeue reward. And in that he is a Iust beholder of our mindes, he will not onely recompence the charge of our woorke, but also reward the workers affection, thorough Christe our Lorde.

*Math. 20.*

THE

# THE FOVRTH SERMON MADE BY THE SAME S. LEO VPPON THE SAID FAST OF THE *tenth Moneth, and of the Almes to be done in the same.*

Of what valew againſt ſinne faſting is, which in bothe Teſtamentes is obſerued.

WE doe with good cowrage and confidence (moſte deerely beloued) exhorte you to the workes of pietie, bicauſe by experience we perceiue how gladly and willingly you receiue our exhortations. For you knowe, and by the teaching of God him ſelfe be aſſured, that the obſeruing of the Commaundementes of God, dothe auaile you to eternall ioye. In the executing and keeping whereof, bicauſe mannes frailtie dothe often wexe weary, and by her brittle infirmitie, offende in many thinges: our good and mercifull Lorde hath geauen vnto vs remedies and helpes, by the whiche we may obtaine pardon. For who coulde poſsibly eſcape ſo many flattering allurementes of the worlde, ſo many crafty deceites of the Diuell, and finally ſo many perilles growing of his owne mutabilitie and frailtie, vnleſſe the wonderfull clemency of the eternall Kinge, had a wil rather to repaire vs, then to loſe vs? For though

The vvar of Christians is continual
1.Ioan.5.

wee be already redemed, already regenerated and made the children of light, yet ſo long as wee are detained in this worlde (whiche is all ſette in wickedneſſe) ſo long as corruptible and temporall thinges doe flatter the infirmitie of the fleſſh, no man can paſſe this life without tentation. Neither doth there lightly happen to any man ſo vnblouddy a victorie, that emong many enemies, and daily conflictes, though his fortune be ſo good to eſcape death, he be altogeather free from woundes. To cure therefore the harmes whiche they often fall into, that warre with the inuiſible enemie, theſe three remedies are for medicine chiefely to be applyed: Inſtance in prayer, chaſtiſing of our ſelues by faſting, and the bountifull geauing of almes. Whiche three thinges, when they are togeather putte in vre and exerciſed, God is made mercifull vnto vs, the faulte is blotted out, and the Tempter is repulſed. Of theſe helpes truely owght a faithful ſowle alwayes to be prouided and furniſhed: but chiefely and with greateſt care are they nowe to be exerciſed in theſe dayes whiche are moſte properly and peculiarly appointed to thoſe woorkes of pietie. Of whiche kinde and degree is alſo the ſolemne faſt of this tenth Moneth. Whiche is not therefore to be neglected, bicauſe it hath benne taken vnto vs out of the obſeruaunce of the olde Lawe: as though this were one of thoſe thinges which with the diſcerning of pure meates, from vnpure, the differences of waſſhinges, and the Sacrifices of byrdes and beaſtes did in the newe Lawe ende and ceaſe. For thoſe thinges in deede which bare the figures of thinges to come, were ended, when thoſe thinges were accompliſſhed, whiche they ſignified.

But

But the profitte of fasting, the grace of the newe Testamente hath not remooued nor putte awaye. But with good and vertuouse obseruation hath still admitted continence and abstinence: as thinges alwayes profitable bothe to the bodie and the sowle. For euen as there remaine receiued and retained in the heartes of Christians these Commaundementes: *Thou shalt woorshippe thy Lorde God, and serue him alone*: And, *Thou shalt loue thy neighbour as thy selfe*, and suche other like Preceptes: euen so that whiche in those bookes is commaunded of the sanctification and healing by fasting, is not made voide, or frustrate by any interpretation. For in all tymes, and in all ages of this worlde, fasting maketh vs the stronger against sinne. Fasting conquereth concupiscence, repelleth tentations, abaseth pride, allayeth wrath, and all the affections of a good minde and disposition it nurrisheth vppe to ripenesse and perfection of all vertue. Especially, if it be also ioyned with the beneuolence and pietie of charitie, and doe prouidently exercise it selfe in woorkes of mercie. For fasting without almes, is not so much a purging of the sowle, as it is an affliction of the fleshe. And it is rather to be reputed to be donne for couetousenesse, then for continencie, when a manne dothe so absteine from meate, that he also absteineth from pietie and good woorkes. Let therefore our fast (deerely beloued) abownde with fruites of liberalitie, and lette them be plentifull to the poore of Christe, with charitable giftes, and louing rewardes.

Fasting though it vvere obserued in the olde testament is also to be kept in the nevv.

Mat. 4.

Matt. 22.

And lette not the meane and inferioure sorte be stayed from this woorke, bicause it is little that they can

take

take out of their ſmall ſubſtance and abilitie. Our Lorde knoweth euery man his abilitie, and being a iuſt looker on, ſeeth wel out of what meaſure and portion eche man geaueth. For ſubſtances that be in equalitie vnlike, can not geue like almes. But many times is it made equall in merite, whiche is vnequall in charge. For the minde may be like, where the rente and ſtore is vnlike. To the ende therefore, that theſe thinges may by the helpe of God be regarded with pietie and deuotion, let vs faſt the fourth and the ſixth daie of this weeke. But on the Satterdaie let vs celebrate Vigil and watching at S. Peter the Apoſtles Church by whoſe prayers we being helped, may in all thinges merite and deſerue the grace of God.

Wedneſdaie, Fridaie, and Satterday the ymber dayes, aboue a xj. hundred yeres agoe

# THE FIRSTE SERMON MADE BY THE SAME S. LEO VPPON THE FAST OF THE *ſeuenth Moneth.*

Of the praiſe of Abſtinence, and almes deedes.

The faſt of the vij. moneth is the ymber faſt kepte in September.

WE knowe your carefulneſſe (moſt deerely beloued) to be of ſuche deuotion, that you doe not onely till and temper the ſowles with the ordinary faſtinges appointed by the lawe, but alſo with voluntary abſtinence. Yet haue we thought good to adde to this your good diſpoſition, our exhortation and warning.

warning. To the ende, that if there be any of you ſlacke in this vertuouſe exerciſe, they doe obediently ioine them ſelues with the reſt in this publique, and generall faſt appointed in theſe daies. Wherein we muſt more attentiuely celebrate this moſt holy cuſtome, and vertuouſe vſage, that by humilitie of faſting, we may merite the helpe of God againſt all our enemies. For it is a principall woorke whiche both by authoritie we charge you, and of charitie we aduiſe you, that the libertie of eating being for a time reſtrained; we geue our ſelues to the chaſtiſing of our owne bodies, and to the feeding of the poore, whome who ſo euer refreſheth, he feedeth his owne ſowle, and tourneth his temporall meates into eternall delicates. In place therefore of euill and voluptuouſe delightes, let there ſucceede in vs the plentifull increaſe of holy deſires. Let iniquitie ceaſe: but let not righteouſeneſſe be idle. Let ſome man feele him helping, whome no man feeleth oppreſsing. For it is litle, not to take away thoſe thinges which are an other mans, except thou doe alſo geue of thine owne. We be vnder the eies of the iuſt Iudge, who knoweth what abilitie to wel working he hath geuen to eche man. He will not haue his giftes idle or vnbeſtowed: Who ſo diſtributed vnto his ſeruauntes the proportions of the myſticall Talentes, *Mat. 25.* that to him that had liberally imployed that, whiche was *Luc. 19.* committed vnto him, he increaſed: And tooke away from him that had barrenly kept, and vnfruitfully hidden his Talent.

Sins therefore (deerely beloued) we are nowe to celebrate this faſt of the ſeuenth Moneth, we earneſtly aduiſe and admoniſh your deuotion, to faſt with vs on the fourth and ſixth daie of this weeke. But the Satterdaie, let vs watche togeather at the Churche of the bleſſed Apoſtle S. Peter, by the aſsiſtaunce of whoſe merites, we may deſerue to be abſolued and loſed of all our troubles, through Chriſte our Lorde.

Amen.

# THE THIRDE SERMON MADE BY THE SAME S. LEO OF THE FAST OF THE SEUENTH MONETH.

Howe neceſſary faſting is, and of the publique and priuate lawe of faſting, prayer, and almes deedes.

HOWE muche religiouſe faſting dothe auaile (moſte deerely beloued) to the intreating and obteining of Gods mercy and to the repairing of mannes frailtie, it is made knowen vnto vs by the reporte and teachinge of the holy Prophetes, who doe proteſt and geaue witneſſe, that the indignation of Gods iuſtice, whereinto the people of Iſraël did often fall by iuſt deſerte of their iniquitie, coulde neuer be uer be appeaſed but by faſting. Whereof the Prophete Ioël alſo geaueth warning, ſaying: *Thus ſayeth the Lorde your God: Tourne you vnto mee with all your hearte, in faſting, weeping, and mourning: and cutte your heartes, not your garmentes, and be yee tourned vnto the Lorde your God, for he is mercifull, paciente, long ſuffering, and of much mercie.* And againe: *Keepe holie your faſting, proclaime the cure and healing, aſſemble the people, ſanctifie the Churche, &c.* Which exhortation (deerely beloued) is alſo to be embraced in theſe our daies, for that the remedies and meanes of this curing, are now neceſſarily by vs alſo to be taught and openly preached: To the ende that in the obſeruation of the olde ſanctification, that may be gotten by Chriſtian deuotion, whiche was loſte by the Iewiſsh tranſgreſsion. For the reuerence of the Diuine Decrees hath alwayes this priuiledge and preheminence aboue all priuate and voluntarie obſeruaunces: that it is of more holineſſe, whiche by a publique lawe is celebrated, then whiche by priuate obſeruaunce is perfourmed. For the exerciſe of continence, whiche euerie manne dothe of his owne will and good diſpoſition preſcribe vnto him ſelfe, is profitable to one parte and portion. But the faſt whiche the vniuerſall Churche dothe with one conſente celebrate, ſeuereth no manne from the generall purification and cleanſing wroughte thereby. And then is the people of God moſt mighty, when the heartes of the faithful ioyne togeather in the vnitie of holy obedience: and that in the campe of the Chriſtian warfare, there is on euery ſide a like preparation, on euery ſide a like defence. Let the watchefull furie of the blouddy enemie rore and rage, and let him

*Ioel. 2.*

*Ibidem.*

This tranſlation is according to the lxx. Interpreters.

The profit of publique faſting.

on euery side laie his secrete traines: yet no man can he take, no man can he wounde, if he finde no man vnarmed, no man slumbring, no man seuered from this generall woorke of pietie.

To this might and puissaunce therefore of inuincible pietie (most deerely beloued) doth this solemne fast of the seuenth Moneth inuite vs: to the ende we may lifte vppe vnto our Lord, our mindes free from worldly cares, and earthly affaires. And bicause we can not alwayes haue this fixed intention of minde, which were alwayes necessary, and in so muche as we doe oftentimes through humaine frailtie, fall from heauenly to earthly thinges, let vs at the least in these daies which are appointed vnto vs for most helthfull and medicinable remedies, withdraw our selues from worldely occupations, and steale some time to the increase of our heauenly riches, whiche shal neuer decaie. For as it is written: *We doe all offende in many thinges*. And al be it we be by the daily grace of God cleansed from diuerse blottes, yet doe there sticke many tymes within our vnprouidente and vnwarefull mindes, thicker spottes and of a grosser substance, which must be wasshed away with more diligente care, and rooted out with greater charge. But a moste full and perfecte remission of synnes is obteined, when of the whole Churche togeather there is in vnitie, one Prayer, and one confession. For if our Lorde haue promised, that vnto twoo or three holie personnes asking with vertuouse consente, hee will grawnte what so euer they require, what shall be denyed to many thowsandes of people perfourming togeather one generall obseruaunce, and humbly suing in concord with one agreeing

Why prescripte fast is vsed at certaine times.

*Iacob. 3.*

Vnitie of praier.

agreeing ſpirite? For it is (derely beloued) a great thing, and very precious in the ſight of our Lorde, when the whole people of Chriſt doe together by vniforme doing of their duties, inſtantly preſſe vnto him: and when al degrees and al ſortes of perſons of both kindes and ſexes, worke together with one affection, as well in declinyng from euil, as in doing good. When in them all, there is one conſenting mind, when God is glorified in the works of his ſeruauntes, and prayſe is geeuen by the humble yelding of many thankes to him, being the author of all goodneſſe.

The hungry are fed, the naked are clothed, the ſicke are viſited, and no man ſeeketh his owne, but the benefit of an other: while to the releeuing of an other mans miſery, eche man is content with the portion that is competent for him ſelfe. And eaſely it is to finde a glad and willing geeuer, where reaſonable conſideration of the habilitie, doth temper and moderate the meaſure of the woorke. And by this grace of God *which worketh all in all*, the frute of all the faithful is made common, and common is the merite to all. For the minde of them may be like, whoſe ſtore and reuenue is not lyke. And while eche man reioyſeth at the liberalitie of an other, he is made equall in good minde and affection, who could not be equall, in charge and diſtribution. There is nothing inordinate among that people, nothing diuers or varying, where all the members of the whole body agree with them ſelues by mutual conſent, to one couragious practiſe of vertue and piety. Neither is he confounded in his owne meaneſſe, who glorieth in the abundance of others. For the bewtie of the vniuerſal is the excellencie of eche par- 1.Cor. 12.

Rom. 8. This is vvrought through the communion of saintes.

ticular. And when we be al stirred forward by the spirite of God, not onely are those thinges ours whiche our selues doo, but euen those thinges also whereof we reioyce in other mennes doinges. Let vs therefore (most deerly belooued) imbrace the blessed soundnes of moste sacred vnitie, and let vs enter this solemne fast, with an agreyng purpose and consent of wel disposed mindes. Nothing is sowght of any man, which is hard or sharpe: neither is ought commaunded vnto vs, which excedeth our forces, either in chastesing our selues by abstinence, or in large bestowing of almes. Euery man knoweth what he is able, and what he is not able to doo. Let them selues waie their owne abilitie: let them selues taxe them selues, as they thinke reasonable: to the ende that the Sacrifice of mercy be not offered with heauinesse, or accompted among our losses or hinderaunce. Let that be imployed in this charitable woorke, whiche may iustifie the harte, clense the conscience, and which finally may both profit the taker, and geeuer. Happy truly is that minde, and with admiration to be reuerenced, which for the looue of wel doing doth not feare the decaye of his gooddes, and mistrusteth not for his sake to geue, of whome he receyued that which he geueth. But for so muche as this magnanimitie is proper to fewe, and it is also godly, and full of piety, that no man forsake the care of suche as he is charged with, we, (not preiudicating, or meaning to hinder the more perfit) doo by this rule exhort you in generall, that you accomplishe the commaundement of God, euery man according to his portion and habilitie. For it becommeth beneuolence to be chereful, and so to temper it selfe in largesse, that both the refection of the poore may reioyce therin, and the houshold not be greeued for want of sufficiency. *But he that geueth seed to the sower, will also geue bread to eate, and will multiplie and increase the grayne of your righteousnes.* Let vs fast therfore the fourth and sixth daye of this weeke. But on the Satterdaye let vs celebrate the Vigill together at the Monument of the most blessed Apostle S. Peter, by whose merites and prayers we confidently trust the mercy of our God shall be bestowed vppon vs, through Iesus Christe our Lorde, who liueth and raigneth world without ende. 1.Cor.9.

Amen.

*Thus ende the Sermons of S. Leo, Pope of Rome.*

*A SER-*

# *A SERMON OF ALMES DEEDES MADE BY THAT* BLESSED MARTYR S. CYPRIAN

*Biſhop of Carthage, in Afrike, in the yeare of our Lorde. 230.*

GREAT and manifolde (moſt deerly belooued bretherne) are the diuine benefits, whereby the large and abundant clemency of God the father, and Chriſt his Sonne, hath wrought, & yet daily doth worke for our ſaluation. As that the Father for the ſauing and quickening of vs, ſent his ſonne to reſtore vs, and that the ſonne would be ſent, and vouchesafe to become the ſonne of man, to make vs thereby the ſonnes of God. He humbled him ſelfe, to reiſe vp the people, that before laye ouerthrowen. He was wounded to heale our woundes. He became bond, to drawe forth into liberty vs that were bond. He indured to dye, that dyeng, he might geeue to mortall men, immortalitie. Great and manifolde are theſe giftes of Gods diuine mercy.

The benefits vvhich Chriſt hath beſtovved vpon vs.

But yet what a prouidence is that, howe great a clemency of Chriſte, that by healthfull meane, it is foreſeene to our hand and prouided, howe man once redeemed may the more fully be preſerued? For when our Lorde comming, had healed the woundes which Adam had borne, and cured the olde poiſons of the ſerpent, he gaue a law to man being healed, and charged him to ſinne no more, leſt by ſinning of newe, worſe might fal to him thereof. Then were we narrowly beſet, and brought into a

Chriſte a redemer and a lavv maker.

great

great straight, by hauing Innocency prescribed vnto vs. Then knewe not the infirmitie, and weakenes of humane frailtie what to doo, except the goodnes of God, yet once againe helping, had by teaching vs the woorkes of righteousnes and mercy, opened a certaine way to keepe and preserue our health, and saluation (now gotten) by wasshing awaie with almose deedes, all suche what so euer filthe, wee happen afterward to gather, or to brede.

The holly Ghost speaketh in the Scriptures, and saieth: *By almose deedes and faithe, sinnes are purged*. Not those sinnes which were before committed and growen vpon vs. For those are purged with the blood of Christe and * sanctification. Againe he saieth: *As water quencheth fier, so dooth almose quenche sinne*. Heere is it also shewed and proued, that as by the washing in the healthfull water, the fier of hell is quenched, so by almes and iust woorkes, the flame of our offences, is alayde and suppressed. And for that remission of sinnes is once geeuen in Baptisme, diligent and daily well working following, after the manner of Baptisme, doth againe enlarge vnto vs Gods pardon.

*Tobie*.4.

* he meaneth Baptisme.

*Eccles*.3.

This also dooth our Lorde teache in the Gospell: for when his disciples were noted, that they eate, and did not first washe their handes, he aunswered and saied: *He which made that is within, made also that is without, but geue you almose, and beholde all thinges are cleane vnto you*. Teaching and shewing therby, not so much the handes to be washed, as the hart: and the inward filth, rather then the outward to be clensed. For asmuch as he which hath clensed that is within, hath also made cleane that is without: and the mind being purged, beginneth also to be cleane both in skinne and bodie. But teaching and instru-

*Luca*.11.

cting farther by what meane we maie be made pure and cleane, he added, that almose must be don. Him selfe being merciful teacheth and admonisheth that mercy be donne. And bicause he seeketh to keepe whom he hath deerely bought, he teacheth how such as are defiled after the grace of Baptisme, may againe be purged. Let vs therfore (derely belooued bretherne) acknowledge the healthfull gifte of Gods fauour, and to the clensing and purging of our sinnes, let vs (who can not be without some wound of cōscience) cure our woundes with spirituall medicines. Neither let any man so flatter him selfe of his pure and vnspotted hart, that presuming on his innocency, he thinke him selfe not to neede the applying of any medicine to his woundes, considering that it is written: *Who shall glorie that he hath a chast hart, or who shall glorie him selfe to be cleane from sinnes?* And againe when S. Iohn in his Epistle allegeth and saieth: *If wee saie wee haue no sinne, wee deceiue our selues, and there is no truthe in vs. But if wee confesse our sinnes, our Lord is faithfull and iust, who will forgeue vs our sinnes.* Now if no man can be without sinne, and who so euer wil say him self to be blameles, is either prowd, or foolish: how necessary, how gentle and bountiful is the mercy of God, whiche knowing that euen the healed should not yet afterward want their wounds, gaue helthful remedies to the new curing and healing againe of those woundes?

Hovv vvoundes after Baptisme maie be cured.

1. Iohn. 1.

1. Ihon. 1.

Finally (deerely belooued brethern) the worde of God hath neuer ceased, hath neuer bene silent, but in the holy Scriptures, bothe olde and newe, alwaies, and in al places hath stirred Gods people to woorkes of mercy: the holie Ghost still crying out and exhorting vs, that who so euer is instructed to the hope of the Kingdome of heauen, should

ſhould doo almoſe deedes. God willeth and commaunded Eſaie, ſaying: *Crie out ſtrongly, and ſpare not. Lifte vp thy voice as a trumpet, and ſhewe foorthe vnto my people their ſinnes, and to the houſe of Iacob their iniquitees.* And when he had commaunded theyr ſinnes to be vpbrayded vnto them, and when he had vttered their wickednes with full force of indignation, and had ſaied that they could not with praiers or faſtinges ſatisfy for their ſinnes, no nor appeaſe the wrathe of God, though they ſhould be wrapped in aſſhes, and ſhertes of heare, yet in the laſt part ſhewing that God might be appeaſed only by almoſe dedes, he added this, ſaying: *Breake thy bread vnto the hungry, and the nedy wanting harborough, leade into they houſe. If thou ſee one naked, cloth him, and the houſhold of thy kinne doo not deſpiſe. Then ſhall thy light breake foorthe in timely ſeaſon, thy health ſhall ſoone appere, and iuſtice ſhal goe before thee, and the brightneſſe of God, ſhal cōpaſſe the round about. Then ſhalt thou cry out, and God ſhal heare thee, and while thou art yet ſpeaking, ſhall ſaie vnto the: Beholde, I am at hande.* Thus we ſee, that remedies to winne Gods fauour were geeuen by Gods owne woordes. And what ſinners ought to doo, Gods inſtructions haue ſhewed and taught. Eſaie.58. Ibidem.

Againe, that by iuſt woorkes ſatisfaction is made to God, that ſinnes are purged by merites of mercy, wee reade in Salomon alſo: *Cloſe vppe thine almoſe* (ſaith he) *in the boſome of the poore, and he ſhall praie and entreate for thee againſt al ill.* And againe. *He that ſtoppeth his eares not to heare the weake and needy, him ſelfe ſhall call vppon the Lorde, and ſhall not be heard.* For he can not deſerue the mercy of our Lorde, whiche is not him ſelfe mercifull, or obtaine of Gods fauour any thing in Eccleſ.29. Prouer.21

his praier, who is not gentill to the praier of the oorep This also doth the holy Ghoste declare, and proue in the Psalmes, saying: *Blessed is hee that hath regarde to the needy and poore. Our Lorde shall deliuer him in the euill daie.*

*Psal.40.*

*Daniel.4.*

Whiche preceptes Daniell hauing in minde, when the Kinge Nabuchodonosor being feared with a terrible dreame, boiled in great anguishe of minde, he gaue him remedie for the turning awaie, and mitigating of those euils by obtaining God his helpe, saying: Therefore, ô King let my counsel please thee: redeeme thy sinnes with almose deedes, and thy vnrightuousnes with mercy on the poore: and God shall be mercifull ouer thy sinnes. To whome the Kinge not obeying, suffered the terrours and aduersities, whiche he sawe in his dreame: whiche yet he might haue escaped, and auoided, if hee woulde haue redeemed his sinnes by almes deedes. Also Raphael the Angell dooth witnesse the lyke, and exhorteth, that almes be willingly and bountefully geeuen, saying: *Praier is good, with fasting and almes: for almes deliuereth from death, and it purgeth sinnes.* Hee sheweth that our praiers and fasting, be of the lesse force, if they be not helped with almes deedes: and that praiers alone, are of littell efficacie to intreate, vnlesse they be filled vppe, and helped with the adioyning of deedes and woorkes. The Angell dooth reuele, open, and testifie vnto vs, that our praiers are made effectual by almes deedes: that by almes life is redeemed from perill: by almes, soules are deliuered from death.

*Raphael Angelus.*

Praiers vvithout vvoorkes, are of small force.

Neither doo we (derely beloued Brethern) so auouch these thinges, but that wee shall with the very testimony of Truth it selfe confirme that, which the Angel Raphael hath

hath saied. In the actes of the Apostles we haue good proofe hereof, and by a fact done we plainly finde, that soules are by almose deliuered, not onely from the second death (of hell) but also from the first (death of this present life). *Tabitha* being a wooman much geuen and addicted to good woorkes, and dooing of almose, when by sickenes she had departed this life, Peter was sent forth vnto the dead carcas: whoo when readely and gently (as it becomed the mekenesse of an Apostle) he was come thither, there stood about him a sorte of widowes, weeping and intreating him, and shewing vnto him the clokes, coates, and all other the clothing, which they had before receaued of her, making sute for her being dead, not so much by their woordes, as by showe of her owne woorkes. Peter perceiued that the thing in suche sorte sued for, might be obtained, and that the helpe of Christe would not want at the sute of the widowes, since him selfe was also clothed in the widowes. Therefore when kneeling downe vpon his knees he had praied, and as a fitte aduocate, had vttered and sent vp vnto God the praiers, made vnto him by the widdowes, and the poore, turning then to the bodie, which being wasshed lay alreadie vpon a borde, he said: *Tabitha, arise in the name of Ihesu Christ*. Neither did he faile Peter, but straight way gaue helpe, who in the Ghospell had saied, *that what soeuer were asked in his name, should be graunted*. Death therefore was suspended, life retourned, and the reuiued body restored quicke to light, all the company muche maruailing, and being not a little astonnied thereat. Of suche force were the merites of mercy, of suche value and power were good workes.

The good intention helpeth muche praies.

Merites of vvoorkes.

Shee that to the needy widowes had geuen reliefe and ſuccour of life, deſerued at the praiers of the widowes to be reſtored to life.

The teacher therefore of oure life, and the maiſter of our eternall ſaluation, geeuing life to the people beleeuing, and prouiding for euer for them ons brought to life, doth emong his diuine commaundementes, and heauenly preceptes in the Ghoſpell, will and charge nothing more often, then that wee ſhould continue, and perſiſt in geuing almoſe: that wee ſhould not lie and grouell vpon our earthly poſſeſsions, but rather hearde vppe to our ſelues ſome heauenly treaſures. *Sell your goodes* (ſaith hee) *and geue almoſe.* And againe, *Lay not vppe to your*
Luc.12. *ſelues treaſures vppon earth, where mothe and ruſt ſpoileth and decaieth, and where theeues digge vp, and ſteale: but heape vppe vnto your ſelues treaſures in heauen, where neither mothe nor ruſt doth conſume, and where theeues do not breake vp, and ſteale: for where thy treaſure is, there will alſo thy hart bee.* And when he woulde teache one that had obſerued the lawe, howe he ſhould be perfite, he ſaied: *If thou wilt be perfite, goe and ſell all that thou haſt, and geue it to the poore, and thou ſhalt haue treaſure in heauen, and come follow me.* He ſaieth alſo in an other place, that he whiche ſeeketh to purchaſſe the grace of heauen, and to bye euerlaſting ſaluation, muſt with the quantity of his patrimony marchaunt and bie the pretious iewell, that is, eternall life, precious by the bloude of Chriſt. *The kingdome of heauen* (ſaieth he) *is like vnto a*
Matt.13. *marchaunt man ſeeking for good perles and precious ſtones, but when he had found a precious ſtone, he went and ſolde all that he had, and bought it.* He alſo calleth them the

the children of Abraham, whome he seeth to be workemen in the helping and nurrishing of the poore. For when zachee had said: *Beholde, the halfe of my substance I geeue vnto the needie, and if I haue defrauded any man of ought, I render vnto him foure dubble*: Ihesus aunswered, and saied: *This day is saluation made vnto this house, for this man is also a sonne of Abraham.* For if Abraham beleeued God, and it was reputed vnto hym for iustice, verely he that according to God his commaundement, dooth Almose, beleeueth God: and he whiche hath the truthe of faith, keepeth the feare of God. But he whiche keepeth the feare of God, thinketh of God, in shewing mercie to the poore. For therefore dooth he woorke, bicause he beleeueth and knoweth those thinges to be true, whiche are foreshewed by the woordes of God, and that the holy Scripture can not lye, whiche teacheth, That vnfrutefull trees (that is) Barren and fruteleſſe menne, shalbe cutte away, and throwne into the fier: but the mercifull shalbe called vnto the kingdoome. And therefore in an other place also, he calleth the woorkers, and the frutefull by the name of *faithfull personnes*. But as for the vnfrutefull and barren, he saieth they haue no faith, by these woordes: *If in the wicked Mammon, yee haue not been faithfull, whoo will putte you in truste, with that whiche is true and sound? And if in the thing that is not yours, yee haue been vnfaithfull, whoo will geeue you that which is yours?*

Luk. 19.

What it is to beleeue God and to thinke the scriptures true.

Luca. 16.

If thow mystruste, and feare, leaste if thow begynne to woorke bountifully, thy patrimonie beeing consu-

Pouetry is not to be feared, for geuing of almes.

consumed by liberall wo orking, thou maist perhaps be driuen to poouertie, be in that behalfe without feare, stand thou assured and out of care. For that can not be wasted, out of the which, there is disbursed to Christe his vse, and by the which a heauenly woorke is donne. And thus doo I not warrant thee vppon myne owne credite, but vppon the faith and warrant of the holy Scriptures. Vppon the authoritie of God his promise, do I assure it. The holy Ghost speaking by Salomon, saith:
Proue. 28. *He that geeueth to the poore, shal neuer want: but he that turneth his eies from them, shalbe in great penury*: shewing thereby, that the mercifull, and such as worke, can neuer want, but rather that the Niggardes, and fruitlesse doo come in the ende to pouertie. And the holy Apostle Paule also being full of grace of the heauenly inspiration, saieth: *He that sendeth seede to the sower, euen he also*
2. Cor. 9. *shall geeue bread to be eaten: and shall multiplie your sowing, and shall increase the yeeld of your fruitfull Iustice, that you may be made riche in all thing.* And againe: *The administration of this dutie and woorke shall not only supplie in faith the want and neede of the saints, but shall also be plentifull in geeuing, with much thankefulnes towarde God.* For when thankes for our almose and praiers are by the Oraisons of the poore directed vnto God, the substance of the woorker, is by the rewarde of God, heaped and encreased. And our Lord in the Ghospell euen then considering the hartes of such menne, and by his foretelling worde denouncing this vnto the false harted, and vnto suche as would not beleeue, dooth
Matt. 6. protest and say: *Doo yee not take thought, saying, what shall wee eate, or what shall wee drinke, or wherewith*

*shall*

*ſhall wee be appareled? For theſe thinges the Gentiles ſeeke after: but your Father knoweth, that you haue neede of all theſe thinges. Seeke yee firſt the kingdome of heauen: and the righteouſnes thereof, and all theſe thinges ſhall be caſt vnto you.* He ſaieth, all thinges are caſt vnto them, and geuen vnto them which ſeeke the kingdome and iuſtice of God. For our Lorde ſaieth, that thoſe menne ſhall (when the daie of Iudgement commeth) be admitted to receiue the kingdome, whiche haue ben woorkers in his Churche. But thou feareſt, leſt thy patrimonie perhaps will faile thee, if thou beginne of the ſame to yeeld bountifull woorkes. And knoweſt thou not, wretched man, that while thou feareſt the decaie of thy houſhold, thy life and ſaluation bothe doo faile? And while thou arte carefull that nothing be diminiſhed of thy goods, doeſt thou not ſee, that thy ſelfe arte diminiſhed, being a loouer rather of Mammon, then of thyne owne ſoule? Thus while thow feareſt leſt thy patrimonie ſhould periſhe to ſaue thy ſelfe, thy ſelfe doeſt periſhe to ſaue thy patrimonie. And therefore dooth the Apoſtle well crie out, and ſaie: *Nothing brought wee into this world: neyther truely maye wee carrie ought hence, but hauing nourriture, and coouering, let vs be therewith content. For they that will becoome riche, falle into temptation, into ſnares, and into many and hurtefull deſyres, which whelme a man into perdition and deſtruction. For the roote of all euills is couetouſnes, which ſome ſeeking after haue made a wracke of their faith, and haue plunged them ſelues into many ſorowes.*

Ibidem.

1. Tim. 6.

Couetouſnes the roote of al euils.

But doeſt thou feare ſtill, leaſt thy patrimonie may happe to faile, if thou beginne to beſtowe plentifully

Proue.10. thereof? Why? When was it seen, that the iust man could wante reliefe, sithe it is written: *Our Lorde will* 3.Reg.17 *not kill with hunger the iust soule?* Helias was fed in the wildernesse by the ministery and seruise of crowes. And Danie.14. to Daniell being by the kinges commaundement shutte vp in the denne for a praie to the Lions his dinner was from God prouided. And yet fearest thou, leste working and deseruing at Gods handes, thou shouldest wante nourriture? Remembrest thou not, that he him selfe in the Ghospell to the reproche of them which be of doubtfull mindes, and of litle faith, dooth protest, saying? Matt.6. *Beholde the foules of the ayer: for they sowe not, they reape not, they gather not into the barnes, and yet your heauenly father nurrissheth them. Are not yee of more value, then these?* God feedeth the foule, and euen to the sparrowes dailie foode is geeuen: and those thinges which haue no manner sense of thing appertaining to God, lacke neither meate nor drincke. And doest thou thinke, that a Christian man, the seruaunt of God, geeuen to doo good woorkes, and deere vnto his Lord and master, shall want any thing? How may this be? Except thou wilt thinke, that he which feedeth Christe, shall him selfe not be fed by Christe? Or that earthly thinges shall want to them, to whome diuine and heauenly thinges are geeuen? Whence commeth this mistrustfull thought? Whence groweth this wicked and sacrilegious Imagination? What dooth suche a faithlesse hart in the house of faith? Why is he called and named a Christian, whiche dooth not altogether beleeue Christe? The name of a Pharisee is more meeter for thee. For when our Lord in the Ghospell disputed of almose deedes, faithfully, and holesomely forewarning vs, that by prouident woorkyng, wee

should

ſhould of our earthly gaines make vnto our ſelues frendes that might afterward receiue vs vppe into euerlaſting tabernacles, after theſe thinges ſpoken the Scripture addeth theſe wordes: *But the Phariſees (whoo were moſte coouetous menne) hard all theſe thinges, and mocked thereat.* Soome ſuche menne doo wee ſee at this daie in the Churche, whoſe ſtopped eares and blinded hartes doo receiue no light of ſpirituall and holeſome admonitions: At whome wee muſt not marueill, if they contemne a ſeruaunt treating of theſe thinges, when wee ſee that our Lord him ſelfe was of ſuche menne deſpiſed.

He is no Christian, but a phariſee, that vvill geue no almoſe for feare he ſhal lacke.

*Luce 16.*

What doeſt thou pleaſe thy ſelfe with theſe fond and fooliſh thoughtes? As though with feare and carefulnes of thinges to come, thou ſhouldſt be kept backe from doing of good workes? Why doeſt thou pretende ſuch coulours, toies, and deluſions of vaine excuſe? Confeſſe that rather which is true. And bicauſe thou canſt not deceiue them that knowe, lay foorth the ſecret and hidden conceptes of thy mind. No, no. The darcknes of vnfrutefulnes hath benummed thy mind: and (the light of truth being thence departed) the deepe and thicke miſt of couetouſnes hath blinded thy carnall hart. Thou art a ſlaue and bondman to thy monie. Thou art bound with the bondes and cheines of auarice, and thou, whome Chriſte had once loſed, art now againe come in bondes: Thou kepeſt thy money, which being kept, doth not keepe thee. Thou heapeſt thy patrimony, whiche with the waight thereof dooth burden thee. Thou doeſt not remēber what God aunſwered to the riche man, that with fond reioiſing boaſted the great plenty of his abundant ſtore: *Thou foole* (ſaid he) *this night is thy ſoule called for from thee: Therefore*

A vehement exhortation againſt the peuiſh feare of vvorldlinges.

*Luk. 12.*

*whose ſhall thoſe thinges be, which thou haſt gathered?* Why doeſt thou ſtudie and trauaile to gette riches for thy ſelfe alone? Why doeſt thou to thine owne paine increaſe the waight of thy patrimonie, whereby how much the richer thou art to the world, ſo much the poorer thou art made toward God. Diuide thy rentes with thy Lorde God. Parte thy frutes with Chriſt. Make Chriſt a partaker with thee of the reuenue of thy earthly poſſeſsions, that he may alſo make thee with him a ioyntheire of the heauenly kingdoomes.

Thou erreſt, and art deceiued, who ſo euer beleeueſt thy ſelfe to be riche in the world. Heare in the Apocalips the voice of thy Lord, with iuſt rebukes rating ſuche men: *Thou ſaieſt I am riche* (ſaieth he) *I am increaſed in wealth, I want nothing. And thou knoweſt not, that thou art in deede a wretche, miſerable, poore, blinde, and naked. I aduiſe thee to bye of mee, golde tried, and burniſſhed in the fier: that thou maiſt be riche, and maiſt put on the white garment, that the filth of thy nakednes doo not appere in thee. Annoint thine eyes with a medicine that thou maieſt ſee.* Thou therefore that art welthy and riche, bye vnto thy ſelfe of Chriſte gold burniſhed and tried with fier, that (thy filthines being purged as it were with fier) thou maiſt be pure golde, being purged by almoſe deedes, and good woorkes. Bye vnto thy ſelfe a white garment, that thou (whiche by Adam were before naked, quaking, and defourmed) maiſt be clothed with the white garment of Chriſte. And thou whiche art a riche and welthy Gentlewoman, annoint thine eyes, not with the Diuels Alabaſter, but with Chriſtes Medicine: that thou maiſt attaine to ſee God, with good woorkes and iuſt deſert

Apocal. 3.

meriting

meriting well at thy Lordes handes. But thou which art ſuche a one,canſt not woorke in the Churche. For thine eies being ouercaſt with a darke dimneſſe, and blinded as it were in the night, haue not beheld the needy, and the poore. Thou being welthy and riche,beleeueſt that thou celebrateſt our Lord his Temple: yet doeſt thou not one whit behold or regard the treaſure huche thereof. Thou commeſt into the Temple without ſacrifice: yea,thou takeſt part of the ſacrifice, which the poore hath offered. Behold in the Goſpel the widow, who being mindeful of the heauenly preceptes did woorke euen in the middeſt of her owne miſerie,and penurie,putting into the treaſury euen thoſe two mites which onely remained vnto her. Whom when our Lord had marked and ſeene, waying and eſteeming her woorke,not by her liuelyhood, but by her hart and minde,and conſidering not how muche,but out of how muche ſhee had geeuen, he aunſweared and ſaied: *Verely I ſaie vnto you, this widow hath geuen more into Gods treaſure, then all theſe. For all theſe haue geuen vnto God his treaſure, of that whiche abounded vnto them, but this widow euen out of her pouertie,hath put in all ſhee had to liue by.* O very happy and glorious woman, that euen before the daie of iudgement,deſerued to be prayſed by the mouth of the iudge. Let them that be riche be aſhamed of there owne barreinnes and miſerable niggiſhnes. A widow, and a poore widow, dyd deale liberally. And whereas all that is geuen, is beſtowed on the ſuccourleſſe,and widowes,ſhee geueth,who ſhould haue receiued: that wee maie know,what puniſhment remaineth to the vnfrutfull riche man, when by this doctrine, euen the poore them ſelues owght alſo to woorke. And *Lucæ.21.*

that wee maie vnderstand that al suche thinges are geuen to God, and that in doing these thinges, wee deserue and merite at Gods hande, Christe calleth them Gods treasuer, and sheweth that the widowe had put her two mites into Goddes stoare, that it might be made the more manifest vnto vs, that he which hath compassion on the poore, doth lende to God vpon vsurie.

The Care of children ought not to staie from geuing of almose.

Neither lette any Christian man (deerely beloued bretherne) thinke him selfe excused from dooing good woorkes, vppon respecte to doo for his children. For wee ought, in our spirituall expences haue an eye to Christe, who hath professed, that it is he that receiueth our almose. And so, in doing almose to the poore, we preferre not the poore before our children, but we preferre Christe before our children. He him selfe, so teaching and admonishing vs: *Who so loueth* (saith he) *his father or mother, aboue mee, is not woorthy of mee, and who so loueth his Sonne or daughter, aboue mee, is not woorthy of mee.* Also in Deuteronomy, the like thinges are written to the strengthning of our faith, and loue toward God, in these woordes. *They which saie vnto their Father or Mother, I knowe thee not, and haue not knowen their children, these haue obserued thy commaundementes, and haue kept thy testament.* For if wee loue God with all our hart, wee ought not to preferre either parentes or children before God. Which thing S. Iohn also sheweth in his Epistle, saying, that Charitie and the looue of God is not in them; whome we see to haue no regarde to doo good vnto the poore. *Hee that hath* (saith he) *worldly substance, and hath seene his brother want, and hath shut vp his compassion from him, how doth the loue of God dwel in him?*

Matt.10.

Deute.33.

1.Iohn.3.

*him?* For if God geue vſurie for the almes that is geuen to the poore, and that whiche is geuen to the leaſt of them, is geuen to Chriſte, there is no cauſe why a man ſhoulde preferre earthly thinges, before heauenly, or eſteeme man, more then God.

So did that widowe, mentioned in the thirde booke of the Kinges, when after all her goodes conſumed, in the greate drought and famine, ſhe had made her of a litell branne and oyle that was yet lefte, a lofe baked vnder the aſhes, to eate with her children, and ſo to dye, Helias came ſodaynlie vnto her, and deſired ſome parte thereof, to be firſt geuen him to eate, and then ſhee and her children to feede on the reſte. For ſhe neuer ſticked to fulfill his requeſte, neither did ſhee (though ſhe were the naturall mother) any iote preferre her children, in that great hunger and penury, before Helias. But that ſhe did in the ſight of God, which might pleaſe God. Readily and willingly was that offered, whiche was required. Neither of aboundance a porcion, but of a litell the whole was geuen. And an other man was firſt fedde, before her owne hungrie and ſteruing children. Neither did ſhee in that penury and famine, thinke firſte of her meate, and then of the woorkes of mercy: but contrary. To the ende that while in a healthfull woorke the carnall life was contemned, the ſowle might ſpiritually be reſerued and ſaued. Helias therefore bearing the figure of Chriſt, and ſhewing that he rendreth to eche one for mercy beſtowed a retorne of the like, anſwered and ſaid: *This ſaith our Lorde, thy pot of meale ſhall not faile thee, neither ſhall the oile in the cruſe be diminiſshed, vntill the*

*3. Reg. 17*

A notable example.

Helias vvas a figure of Chriſt.

*daie,*

*daie, wherein our Lorde wil sende raine vppon the earthe.* And according to the truthe of Goddes promiſe, the thinges whiche the widowe gaue, were encreaſed, and multiplied vnto her. And for her merites, and good woorkes of mercy, receiuing increaſe and abondance, her veſſels of meale, and oile were filled ful. Neither did the mother (in this caſe) take from her children, that whiche ſhe gaue to Helias, but much more profited her children, by doing ſuche woorke of pitie and mercy. Yet, did not ſhe know Chriſt, neither had ſhe heard his Commaundementes. She was not redemed by his Croſſe, and paſsion, that ſhe might for the ſhedding of his bloud, render him meate, and drinke. Whereby it maie appeare, how much he whiche is of Chriſtes Churche ſinneth, who preferring him ſelfe and his children before Chriſte, doth keepe his riches, and doth not communicate his plentiful patrimony with the pouertie of the needy.

A commõ and daily Obiectiõ ſoluted. But thou wilt ſaie, thou haſt a great many children in thy houſe, and the number of thy children, perhaps doth hold thee backe from plentifull yelding of good workes. Note vvel Verely I ſaie, that for this ſelfe ſame cauſe, thou ſhouldeſt woorke the more bountifully. The moe children thou art the father of, the more haſt thou to entreat for at Gods hande. The ſinnes of many are to be redeemed, the conſciences of many to be praied for, the ſowles of many to be raunſomed. As in this ſecular life, the moe children thou haſt to feede, and to ſuſteyne, the greater is thy coſte and charge, ſo in the ſpirituall and heauenlie life, the more ſtoare of children thou haſt, the more plentifull ought to be thy expence in good An Example. woorkes. So dyd Iob offer many Sacrifices for his children, and according to the number of the children in his howſe, was the number of offeringes whiche he ſacrificed vnto God. And bicauſe there coulde not want ſynne, that dayly offendeth the ſight of God, dayly Sacrifices did not want, whereby ſynnes might be wiped awaye. This doth the Diuine Scripture prooue, ſaying: *Iob a true and a iuste man had ſeuen ſonnes, and three daughters: and he cleanſed them, offering for them Sacrifices vnto God, according to the number of them, and for their ſinnes, one caulfe.* Iob.1. If therefore thou doo truely looue thy children, if thou wilt yeelde vnto them abundant and fatherly ſweetneſſe of looue and charitie, thou oughteſt the more to woorke: to the entent that with thy iuſte and good woorke, thou mayſt commende thy children vnto God. Thinke not hym to be thy chyldrens chiefe Father, who is but weake and feeble and to continue but for a tyme. Winne rather vnto them the fauour of that Father, who is the firme, ſure, and euerlaſting Father of ſpirituall children. Aſsigne vnto hym thy goodes whiche thou keepeſt for thine heyres: Let hym be the Tutor of thy chyldren: Let hym be theyr Craynſire: Let hym by his Diuine Maieſtie be theyr Protector againſt all the iniuries of this woorlde. The patrimonie that is committed to God, neyther dothe the common wealth take awaye, nor confiſcation breake into, nor falſe accuſation or quarrell picte in lawe ouerthrowe. In ſaftie is the inheritance layd vp, whereof God is made the keeper.

We ſhold cōmit our patrimonye to God.

This it is to prouide for our deere children in time to comme. This it is by fatherly pietie to prouide for our heyres, that ſhall be: as the holy Scripture truelye teſtifieth,

Psal.36. fieth, ſaying: *I haue benne yonger, and nowe ame wexen olde: Yet did I neuer ſee the iuſt forſaken, or his ſeed wanting bread. All day is he mercifull and lendeth, and his ſeed ſhal be bleſſed.* And againe: *He whoſe conuerſation is* Prou.20. *without blame, and in righteouſnes, leaueth his ſonnes bleſſed behinde him.*

Hovv Fathers ought to prouide for their children.

Therefore thou art a deceiuer, and a traiterous Father, except thou doo faithfully prouide for thy children, except with true and religious pietie, thou doo in this ſorte forſee to the preſeruation of them. Thou which laboreſt by earthly inheritance rather to betake thy children to the diuell, then by treaſure layed vp in heauen to commend then vnto Chriſte, dooſt twiſe offende, and committeſt a double fault: Both in that thou dooſt not procure vnto thy children the healpe of God the Father, and alſo bicauſe thou teacheſt them more to looue their patrimonie, then Chriſte. Be rather to thy children ſuche a Father, as Tobie was. Geeue vnto thy chyldren profitable, and holeſome preceptes, ſuche as he gaue vnto his ſonne. Geeue in charge vnto thy chyldren, as he charged his ſonne, ſaying: *And nowe* (my Sonne) *I geeue thee in charge: ſerue God in truth, and doo before him that whiche pleaſeth him, and charge thy children, that they doo iuſtice, and geue almes and be mindeful of God, and bleſſe his name at all tymes.* And agayne: *My moſt deerly beloued ſonne, haue God in thy mind all the dayes of thy life, and tranſgreſſe not his Commaundementes. Doo iuſtice all the dayes of thy lyfe, and walke not in the waye of iniquitie. For if thou deale in truth, reſpecte ſhall be had vnto thy woorkes. Of thy ſubſtance doo almes deedes, and turne not awaye thy face from any poore man. So ſhall it come*

An example.

Tob.14.

The preceptes of Toby to his ſonne.

Tob.4.

*come to passe, that the face of God shall not be turned from thee. Geaue Almes (my sonne) according to that thou haste: If thou haue plentye of substance, geeue the more largely thereof, if thou haue scarse and but a litle, yet geeue parte euen of that litle. And feare not when thou geeuest Almes: for thou layest vppe to thy selfe a good rewarde againste the daye of necessitie. For* Tob.12.
*Almes deliuereth from deathe and suffereth not to goe vnto hell. A good woorke, is geeuing of Allmes vnto all them, whiche doo it in the sighte of the Highe God.*

What a pageaunt or game is that (deerly beloued bretheren) the setting foorth whereof, is honoured with the presente behoulding of God him selfe? If at suche largesse and liberalitie, as the Gentilles bestowed vppon shewes, it seemed a greate and a gloriouse matter, to haue presente the Proconsules, or Generalles of Armies, and greate coste and charge was bestowed, by suche menne to please greate personnages: howe muche more noble, and greater is the glorie of our charge, where wee haue God and Christe the behoulder thereof. Howe muche more plentifull ought the preparation heere to be, and howe muche more bowntifull the coste, where all the vertues of heauen assemble, all the Angelles meete to the sight and beholding thereof? Where, to the defrayer of the charge, not a triumphant chariot, or Consulship is asked, but eternall lyfe is geeuen: nor the vayne and temporall fauoure of the common people is sought, but the perpetuall rewarde of the heauenly kingdome is receyued? The frute of Almes deedes.

And that these dull, barren, and pinching peny fathers woorking nothing towardes the frute of their saluation, may be the more ashamed of them selues: that the shame of their reproche, and vilenesse, may stryke the deaper into their filthy consciences, let eche man set before his eyes the diuell with his garde, that is to saye, let him imagine the diuel with his traiterous people, and children of death, to leape foorth in presence, and euen there (Christe him selfe being presente, and iudging) to callenge with prowde comparison Christes people, and to prouoke and require, that an accompte and rekoning of both sortes may be taken, saying in this wise: I, for these that thou seest heere with me, haue neither receyued buffets, nor endured scourging, nor suffered the Crosse, nor shed my bloud, nor redeemed this my familie, with the price of any Crosse and passion: No, neither doo I promise them the kingdome of heauen, or restoring them to immortalitie call them home agayne to Paradyse: and yet see howe sumptuouse games and pageantes, howe great Treasures, what rare thinges long and moste chargeably sought, they prouide for mee? Yea laying to pleadge, ingaging, or selling outright all their goods and possessions to sette foorth to the vttermost these games and pageants? Yea, and if the pageants frame not handsomly to their honesty, they are with wordes of reproch, and hissing often tymes driuen out of the stage, yea and sometime almost stoned to death, with the furie of the people. Nowe Christ let me see, such setters foorth of sightes and shewes of thy side. Shew me these riche men flowing in aboūdance of welth, whether though thy selfe sittest aloft in thy Churche, and lookest on them, they make vnto thee

A liuely Representation.

thee any ſuche chargeable preſentes, by engaging or ſelling their goodes: Naie rather by chaunging for the better, the poſſeſsion of them, tranſlating them into heauenly treaſures. In theſe vaine and worldly ſhewes before men, nobody is fedde, none clothed, none ſuſteined with comforte of meate and drinke. Al the charge betweene the madneſſe of the ſetter foorth, and the foly of the beholder, through a prodigall and fooliſh vanitie of diſceiuing pleaſures, is loſte and commeth to naught. Yet emong thine, thou arte thy ſelfe clothed and fedde in thy poore and needy: and thou promiſeſt eternall lyfe to ſuche as woorke. All this notwithſtanding thy people being thus honoured by thee, with Diuine rewardes and heauenly giftes, are ſcarſe to be compared in number with myne, that haue at my hande for all their coſte, no rewarde, but damnation.

That vvhich S. Cyprian ſpeaketh heere of plaies and pageants, may be applied to banquetinges, exceſſe in apparaıl, and ſuch other riot novv common euerie vvhere.

What ſhall we aunſwere herevnto, deerely beloued brethren? By what meanes may we defende the mindes of the ryche menne ouerwhelmed with ſuche a ſacrilegiouſe barrenneſſe, and as it were palpable darkeneſſe? By what excuſe may we purge our ſelues, whoe are fewer in number, then the Diuelles ſeruauntes, who doe not repaie vnto Chriſt for the price of his Paſsion, and bloude, no not ſo muche as ſmall trifles?

Chriſte hath geauen vnto vs commaundementes: he hath inſtructed his ſeruauntes, what they haue to doe, he promiſeth rewarde to ſuche as woorke, and threatneth punniſhment to the vnfruitfull. He hath vttered his ſentence, and tolde vs before what iudgement he wil geue. What excuſe can there be to the negligent? What defenſe to the barren and nigarde, but that to the ſeruaunt

a revvard to ſuch as vvoorke, and punniſhment to the idle

who doth not that which he is cõmaunded, our Lord wil
Mat.25. do that whiche he threatneth, ſaying: *When the Sonne of man ſhal come in his glory and al his Angels with him, then ſhal he ſit in the throne of his glory, and all Nations ſhall be gathered together before him: and he ſhal diuide them one from an other, as the ſhepheard diuideth the ſhepe from the gotes, and ſhal place the ſheep on his right hand, but the gotes on the left: then ſhal the king ſay vnto them which ſhalbe on his right hand: Come ye bleſſed of my Father, receiue the kingdome which hath ben prepared for you from the beginning of the world: for I haue ben hungry, and you gaue me to eate: I haue ben thirſty, and you gaue me drinke: I haue ben harborles, and you led me in: naked, and you clothed me: ſick, and you viſited me: I haue ben in priſon, and you came vnto me. Then ſhal the iuſt anſwere him, ſaying: Lord whẽ haue we ſene the hungry, and did feed thee? Thirſty, and did geue the drinke? When haue we ſene the harbourles, and did leade the in? Naked, and did cloth the? But when haue we ſene the ſicke and in priſon, and haue come vnto thee? Then the King anſwering ſhal ſay vnto them: Verely I ſay vnto you, ſo long as you haue don it to one of theſe my leaſt brethren, you haue don it vnto me. Then wil he ſay vnto them which ſhal be on his left hãd: Depart from me ye curſed into euerlaſting fier, which my Father hath prepared for the diuel and his angels: for I haue ben hũgry, and you gaue me not to eat, I haue thirſted, and you gaue me not to drinke: I haue ben harbourles, and you toke me not in: naked, and you clothed me not: ſicke and in priſon, and ye viſited me not. Then ſhal they anſwere and ſay, Lorde when haue we ſene thee hungry, or thirſty, or harborles, or naked, or ſick, or in priſon, and haue not miniſtred vnto the, and he ſhal ſay vnto thẽ, verely I ſay vnto you, ſo lõg as ye haue not don it to one of theſe litle ones, ye haue not don it to me. And the vn*

*iuſt ſhal*

*iust shal goe into euerlasting burning: but the iust into euerlasting life.* What could Christ say more vnto vs? How could he more prouoke vs to the woorke of iustice and mercy, then in telling vs that to be don to him selfe, what so euer is don to the nedy and poore? And in shewing him self to be offended if we do not geue helpe to the poore and nedy: to th'end that he which is not moued with the respect of his brother, a felow mẽber of the Church, should yet be moued with the contemplation of Christ: and he which cõsidereth not his felow seruant, being in nede and pouerty, might yet be moued to consider our Lord and Master, present in him whom he despiseth. And therefore (most derely beloued) let vs that feare God, let vs that (despising and treading the worlde vnder our feet) haue our mindes lift vp to diuine and heauenly things, let vs (I say) with ful faith, deuout mindes, and continual good working, bestow our seruice to winne our Lord and Masters fauour. Let vs geue to Christ earthly garmentes, that we may receiue of him heauenly clothing. Let vs geue our worldly meat and drinke, that with Abraham, Isaac, and Iacob, we may be receiued to the heauenly feast. Let vs sow much, least we reap litle. Let vs while we haue time, prouide for our safty and eternal saluation. For so Paul th'Apostle admonisheth vs, saying: *Therfore while we haue time, let vs do good to al, and namely vnto such as are of the houshold of faith. But let vs not faint in doing good: for at due time we shal reape the fruit.* Let vs consider (deerely beloued brethren) how the faithful people did in th'Apostles time, when in the beginning the mind florished with greater vertues, when the faith of the beleuers was yet feruent with the new heate of faith. Then did they sell their howses and landes, and willingly

We muste prouide for our saluation.

*Galat. 6.*

willingly, and largely offered vnto the Apoſtles their goodes to be diſtributed vnto the poore, transferring their poſſeſsion (after their earthly patrimonie, ſo ſolde and diſtributed) vnto that place where they ſhoulde receiue the fruite of eternall inheritance: prouiding for them ſelues manſions there, where thei ſhould beginne to dwell for euer. Suche was their plentifulneſſe in good woorkes, as was their vnifourme conſente in loue and charitie, as we reade in the Actes of the Apoſtles in theſe

Act. 4.

woordes: *But the multitude of them whiche beleeued, wrought with one minde and with one harte, neither was there emong them any diuerſitie, neither did they iudge owght as their owne, of the goodes whiche they had: but all thinges were to them common.* This is by ſpiritual byrth, truely to be made the Sonnes of God. This is by the heauenly lawe to imitate the goodneſſe of God the Father. For what ſo euer is Gods, is common for our vſe. Neyther is any man repelled from the vſe of the benefittes and giftes of God, but that all mankinde may equally enioye the goodneſſe and bountifulneſſe thereof. So doth the daie geue light, the ſonne brightneſſe, the raine moyſture, and the winde blowe to all alike. So is ſleepe alike and common to all them that take reaſt: the ſhining of the ſtarres and Moone is alike and common to them all.

Al things vvere by charitie and mutual loue, as it vvere common emōg the Apoſtles.

By whiche example of equalitie, he that being a poſſeſsioner in earth diuideth his rentes and reuenewes with his brethren in Chriſte, while by voluntary liberty, he being iuſt, maketh his goodes common, is a follower of God the Father. What a glory ſhall there be (moſte deerely beloued brethren) to them that woorke?

Thinges are not common, but by voluntary liberalitie.

Howe

Howe great and exceding ſhalbe the ioye, when our Lorde ſhall beginne to take vewe of his people, and ſhall render for our merites, and good woorkes the promiſed rewardes: for earthly thinges, heauenly: for temporall, euerlaſting? When for ſmall, he ſhall geeue great, when he offereth vs vp vnto his Father, to whome by his ſanctification, he hath reſtored vs? When he ſhall geue vnto vs the eternitie and immortalitie whereunto he hath reuiued vs, by the quickning of his blood? When he ſhall leade vs againe into Paradyſe, and by the faith and ſurety of his promiſe, open vnto vs the kingdoome of heauen?

Let theſe thinges (bretherne) cleaue and ſticke firmely in our vnderſtanding. Let them be conceiued with a full faith. Let them be looued with our whole harte. Lette them be bought with the couragious perſeuerance of inceſſant well doing. A beutifull and heauenly thing (deerly beloued bretherne) is well doing: a great comfort to ſuche as beleeue: a ſtrong ſauegarde of a quiet conſcience, a fortification of hope, a defence and ſhilde of faith, and a remedy againſt ſinne. It is a thing ſette in the power of him that dooth it. It is a great thing, and yet eaſie. A Crowne of peace without perill of perſecution. It is the true gifte, yea the greateſt gifte of God, neceſſarie to the weake, and glorious to the ſtrong. With this a Chriſtian being furniſhed, he ſheweth foorth ſpirituall grace, he deſerueth well of Chriſte the Iudge, and he maketh God his debter.

An exhortation

The frutes of good vvorkes.

To this price of healthfull woorkes lette vs willingly, and cheerfully contende. Lette vs all runne in the courſe and race of iuſtice: God and Chriſte looking on: And lette vs that haue now begonne to get aboue the worlde, and these transitory thinges, not staie now our course by any couetousnes, or lyking of them, or of the worlde. If the daie either of our departing, or of persecution shall finde vs light, and free without burthen, running in this race of good woorkes, our Lorde will neuer faile to rewarde our merites. He will geeue to suche as ouercome for their woorkes in peace a white and pure Crowne: and to suche as gette the victory in persecution, he wil geeue a dubble Crowne of purple colour for their pacience and suffering.

Amen.

*Thus endeth the Sermon of that blessed Martyr and Bishop, S. Cyprian: Of Almes dedes.*

*Opus istud de Iustificatione cum alijs in linguam Anglicam versis lectum et approbatum est ab insignibus viris, sacræ Theologiæ & Anglici idiomatis peritissimis, quibus ideo tutò credendum esse existimo.*

*Cunerus Petri, Pastor S. Petri, Louanij indignus. 15. Ianuarij. An. 1569.*

## Faultes escaped in the printing, of the Translations.

| Leafe. | Side. | Line. | Faulte. | Correction. |
|---|---|---|---|---|
| 43. | 2. | 14. | depraued | depriued |
| 45. | 2. | 1. | And | And as |
| 66. | 2. | 1. | oorep. | poore |
| 67. | 1. | 4. | (death | death ( |
| 67. | 2. | 11. | bearde | horde |
| 76. | 2. | 28. | liberty | liberalitie |

# RICHARD BROUGHTON

*The First Part of the*
*Resolution of Religion*
[*1603*]

# THE FIRST PART OF THE RESOLVTION OF RELIGION,

DIVIDED INTO TWO BOOKES, CONTEYNING *A DEMONSTRATION OF THE* NECESSITIE OF A DIVINE AND SVPERNATVRALL WORSHIPPE.

(* * *)

---

IN THE FIRST, AGAINST ALL ATHEISTS, and Epicures: In the seconde, that Christian Catholicke Religion is the same in particuler, and more certaine in euery article thereof, *then any humane or experimented knowledge, against Iewes, Mahumetans, Pagans, and other external enemies of Christ.*

*MANIFESTLY CONVINCING AL THEIR SECTS* and professions, of intollerable errors, and irreligious abuses.

NEVVLY PRINTED AND AMENDED.

---

PRINTED AT ANTWERPE BY RICHARD VE-
*STEGAN.* *M. DI. III.*

# THE EPISTLE OF THE AVTHOR
## *TO THE READER.*

*AS among all duties, and offices of man, (deare Reader) there is none by infinite inequalitie, either so excellent or deserued, as that reuerence and homage he oweth to God, his most soueraigne and omnipotent Prince, in whome all preeminencies and dignities are conteined, and from whom, all benefits and created prerogatiues are deriued: So among all other sciences and knowledges of this worlde, none can be in any degree so certaine and vndoubted, as that worship, taught, and reuealed of the same infinite wisdome and goodnesse, which can neither be deceaued in himselfe, or bring others into error. Yet the corrupt malice and ingratitude of man hath growne great, that at this present our meanest Function and obligation is not more neglected, and the very base, and contemptible things of this life preferred before that Supreame Honour, to which wee are bounde by so manie Titles. And the wilfull blindnes of prophane people reiecting the infallible Rule of Religious causes, and measuring secret and supernaturall misteries by their owne shallow and depraued Iudgments, doe esteeme that moste certaine and vnchaungeable veritie of diuine Adoration, more doubtfull and vncertaine then recanted conceits of humane affaires. Thus hath Man by negligence and malice shewed vndutifull disobedience to his Creator, and abused his owne vnderstanding, and will, so excellent powers of his intellectuall and immortall Soule, feeding the first with errors, and making vnlawfull appetites the obiect of the other: in such order that no sentence is so certayne, but one or other hath called it into question, no paradoxe so incredulous, but some embrace it, nothing so good, but it hath beene refused nothing so leawde & impious but some men haue approued it. The manyfold euen hundreds of false Religions, that haue inuaded, and now beare dominion in the world, and the irreuerent and irreligious liues of men and practise of al offences, Atheisme, and Epicurisme them selues wil beare me witnes. Some wauering and staggering in fayth, others by this number of errors vncertayne what to beleeue, and those which make aduantage of such times, to procure excuse to their own impieties either in opinion the dutie of Religion, or in desire wishe there were none at all, no God, no Heauen, no Hell, no Immortallitie after death, no pleasure but in filthinesse. Wherefore fullie to satisfie all English Subiects, I haue made demonstration, not onlye of the necessitie of a supernaturall Religion in generall, against all Atheists and Epicures: but by diuers Arguments by which true Reuerence may be prooued, or error impugned and confuted, and farre both greater in number and more forcible then can be alleadged, to establish anie error: that onlie Catholike Christian worshippe is the same in particuler, against all enemies as well Iewes, Mahumetanes, Pagans, and other externall aduersaries, which I will performe with so much more breuitye, by howe much I may hope there is lesse need thereof in a Christian Nation: as also against all Heretickes and internall enemies more at large, by aboue an hundred vnanswerable Reasons (as the present occasion more requireth, in which the former Infidels will likewise bee more plainly confuted) manifestly conuincing all theyr Sects and Professions of intollerable errors and vn-*

*sufferable abuses, euen by the light of Nature, and without all shew or apparaunce of true Reuerence, hauing no grounde, either naturall, or aboue nature of such doctrines, beeing only resolued into the lying, and manifest deceitfull and false inuentions of the Diuell, and licentious deceauers: and contrariwise euery Article of that worship I defend, by Arguments diuine and humane, supernaturall and by nature, Testimonies of God and creatures, Attributes, Properties, Offices, Prerogatiues, Endes, Effects, Name, Nature, and signes of true Relygion, and priuiledges of truth, to be the moste certayne knowledge in* Aug. lib. 7. confes. c. 10. *the worlde, as certaine (to vse S.* Augustines *example) or more vndoubted then that a man liuing is a liue, or any other manyfest veritie in nature, and resolued vnto the most faithfull and vndeceaueable trueth of God, whereupon not onlie the whole substance, but euery priuate question thereof is bulded. For which cause amongst others I haue named it a* Resolution of Religion, *because it is resolued into that first and vnfallible veritie, which by no possibilitie can be deceaued. By which proportion in naturall Sciences, Philosophers affyrme those conclusions and arguments to be moste true, which can be resolued to the first principles which cannot be false. And as in practicall and compounded thinges, that composition and potion of Phisicke (to giue example) which as it is composed of diuers simples in it selfe, is not perfectlie to be discerned, what vertue and operation it hath, but if it be resolued to those particuler things of which it is made, and their natures and effects declared, the operation of the whole confection is euydentlie prooued: euen so it is in that great and noble Composition of spirituall preseruatyues in Religious causes, as I haue declared. So that no particle or least question of diuine worshippe, though neuer so secrette in it selfe, can haue the least suspition of doubt, beeing resolued into that infinite wisedome. And as all errors, that can be deuised concernyng Religion, are defended by one of these three kindes of people, Atheists, Epicures and Nullifidyans, which denie all worshippe: or by externall Infidelles, Iewes Pagans, and Mahumetanes, which although they professe a worshippe, yet they both disalow the true Reuerence, and* Christ *the author thereof; or by internall enemyes and heretickes, which though they acknowledge* Christ *for a true* Messias, *(which lykewise Mahumetes did) and that he deliuered true Religion; yet they doe erre in the manner of worshippinge in particuler: So will I prooue these three conclusions: that there is a Religion to be vsed, against the first; that the Religion which* Christ *deliuered is true, against the second; and to the third, that Christian Catholike Religion is the same. In proofe of which Propositions not onlie the true worshippe shall bee inuincible prooued, but all doubtes, difficulties and obiections of these misbeleeuers solued and resolued: For which cause also I haue intituled this worke a* Resolution. *And so I end humblie desirynge all Readers of these books, which by them shall eyther be confirmed in truth, or reclaymed from error, sometimes to vouthsafe to remember in theyr deuoutest prayers, the poore Author hereof.*

Their Catholicke Countrieman. *R. B.*

# THE FIRST BOOKE OF THE FIRST PART OF THE RESOLVTION OF RELIGION:

## *PROOVING THE NECESSITY OF A SVPERNATVRAL VVORSHIP.*

(* ⋆ *)

### Chap. 1. *Of the Name and Nature of Religion.*

RELIGION, among other names is so tearmed of the Latines, either *a Relegendo*, of often reading, repeating, and ruminating things appertayning to diuine Reuerence: or *a Religendo*, of chusing to please God againe by submission, whome by want therof we had forsaken; or lastly, of *Religando*, in that we are bound vnto him by many Obligations, both in respect of excellencies conteyned in himselfe, as benefits bestowed vpon vs: And after the same proportion is tearmed of the Greekes *Threschia*, or *Eusebia*, a pleasing of God, pietie, and dutie vnto him. And was charactred of the hieroglyphicall Egiptians in the same sence, and of the true religious Hebrewes, named *Zebach*, a Sacrifice, which is the supreame worshippe of God, or *Chucath holam*, an eternall and euerduring statute, or *Chucath hatorah*, a statute of the lawe, ordeyned by the lawe of God, and euer due to him. And by generall consent and conceit of all men, of whatsoeuer profession and estate, Infidels, or true beleeuers, Heretickes, or Catholickes, vnlearned, or Philosophers, alwaies vsed for that honour and reuerence we owe to God, our maker and preseruer.

Isodo. l. 10. Etimol. c. 17 Cic. de Inu. lib. 2. 4. 8. Aug. l. ver. Relig. 10. c. 4. & l. 10. ciuit. 2. c. 4.

Iacob. c. 1. Actor. c. 26. Leuit. c. 16. 7. ver. 36. Exod. c. 29. ver. 9. Num. c. 29.

### Chap. 2. *Of the absolute necessity of God, and a first cause most exceellnt, and deseruing Worshippe and Religion.*

VVHEREFORE vsing this worde *Religion*, in the same sence and acceptance, there neuer was (or can be) any nation, people, or particuler person, so impious, ingratefull, or irreligious, but if they acknowledged, or confessed a God, supreame gouernor and cause of things, from whome they had their beeing and preseruation (as both *Lactantius* and other learned Authors witnesse, and experience prooueth al Atheists haue done, when they come to die and see their owne defects) but they

*All people, euen Atheists themselues, in time of misery confessed a God, and Religion &c.*



yeelded

yeelded vnto him one religion or other. For although many, or most by their owne demerits and wickednesse, were ignorant of the true felicity of man, what it was, (humane reason not able to clime so high) yet knowing, which by no possibility they coulde not but knowe themselues to be creatures, and so dependant, must of necessity acknowledge all their perfections, howe many and excellent soeuer, to be communicated and deriued vnto them, from a former and independing cause: so that for gifts and benefits already receaued, thankes and gratuity, for those that should afterwades want, submission, prayer, and obsecration, and in regarde of his exceeding dignity and preeminence, all worship and reuerence were due, and to be rendred. For seing he, from whome all these thinges were imparted vnto man, must needes be the first, originall, greatest, most perfect, and without dependance of any other, and all graces, dignities, and perfections that be, or coulde be produced in all creatures, that are, haue beene, or by possibility coulde bee created (for such also shoulde bee his workes) were to be obtayned of him, in him also they were to be founde, in a far more eminent & excellent degree: for nothing can giue that vnto an other, which it hath not in it selfe, either in the same, or a better manner: which must needes be most true in the first, and principall cause; for if this shoulde want the perfections and excellencies which be, and were to bee made by it, it coulde neither giue them to others, because it selfe should want them; neither obtaine them for it selfe of any other, because it is the first, and can haue no former cause from whome to receaue them. Then seing all those dignities, & prerogatiues of wisdome, bonity, iustice, mercy, knowledge, prouidence, immutability, eternity, and the rest, for which, faith, hope, loue, reuerence, feare, obedience, sacrifice, adoration, or any kinde of honour and worshippe is required, are connected and vnited togither, in that one eternall and vnchangeable essence, and not after that limited and participated manner, as they be in creatures, but in such an infinite and incomprehensible sort, that the least perfection wee can imagine, and conceaue in him, is infinitely greater then all creatures, and their perfections, (for euery thing in God that is but one most simple and vndeuided essence, is also God infinite and vnmeasurable) all true reuerence and religion, must needes bee due and belonging vnto him; though any man, or creature of vnderstanding, could be so mad to thinke himselfe a creature, not to be dependant of that most perfect and infinite diuine nature. For excellency of it selfe is cause worthy of honor, though there be no farther obligation, or bande of reuerence. But let no man thinke, that I intende in this place, to make a formall dispute, to prooue

*The excellency of God, the first cause worthy all Reuerence.*

that

that there is a God, of which my confidence is, no reasonable creature can be doubtfull. For all Arguments will be testimonie, and the meanest of so many millions of creatures as be in the worlde, giue demonstration in this case, and that was euer so vndoubted, and euident to all kingdoms, countries, and particuler persons, in all places, times, and generations from the first creation, that neuer any nation, neuer any priuate man, except mad, or franticke with passions, and beastly pleasures, to excuse his filthinesse, in so many thousands of yeares hitherto, made it a question, & whereof euery Argument of this worke will be a witnesse. But I chieflie contende at this time, to vpbraide the Irreligious people of these daies, how vnnaturall a thing it is for any reasonable creature, (such as euery man by nature is) to neglect this dutie to his soueraigne King and maker, which is not only to proclaime himselfe an irreligious & disobedient traytor, and rebbell vnto his Creator, but by the least deniall thereof, falsely to affirme there were neither Creature, or Creator, God, Man, or any thing else in the worlde. For since nothing can be made; but of some cause, and in causes an infinite number maie not be graunted, either this first cause of thinges, and religious dutie to him must be confessed, or else we must say, that nothing is, or can be made: when we thinke we see the heauens, elementes, & so many glorious creatures in this world, we are deceaued, because no such thing is, or can be framed: that we our selues which conceaue such variety, are not, neither doe we imagine any such thinge at all. For if we take that reuerentiall originall, and absolutely independing cause awaie, nothing either already is, or by posibilitie can be hereafter. For although some haue defended, that the power of creation & producing some thing of nothing, may be communicated of God to a secondarie cause, yet they say, that in such case, this second agent shoulde onely be an instrumentall cause, which euer remaineth a principall worker, and they alwaies suppose such an one to be communicating that property to the other; for where a principall and communicating cause is wanting, an instrumental cause to which such power is deligated, cannot be, neither by any power is immaginable. For euerie receauer, receaueth of some, and there cannot be any thing produced, where there is no power deligate or indeligate, instrumental or principal of such production. Wherefore, seeing there be so many millions of thinges, and kindes of creatures, most certainely produced and existing in the worlde, as all our sences are witnesses, no man can say these thinges were made of them selues, for so the same shoulde be, and not be togither, which is a repugnancie in nature: neither of anye other former dependinge cause, for

*All creatures in the worlde, all authorities and euery argumente for religion in this worke, prooueth a God.*

*The necessity of God, to bee the first efficient cause, and Religion due to him.*

Magist. 4. dist. 5. Duc. 2. Sent. &c.

that likewise must haue an other to prduce it. Therefore, sith nothinge is made of nothinge by nature, which alwaies worketh in a subiecte and something; nothing of it selfe, nothing of any thing that is depending; and yet so many thinges be in the worlde, and the first of those created effects must be of nothinge (otherwise they shoulde haue former, secondary, and created causes) and betweene being, and not being, nothing, and something, nothing, and so many thinges as nowe be, there is infinite difference and improportion, that cause which of nothing created all thinges, of necessity must be infinite, omnipotent, and illimited, conteyning all goodnesse and perfection, and so worthy all reuerence, worship, and whatsoeuer homage may be conceaued belonging to Religion.

*The preseruation of thinges by God, binding to Religion.*

And as so many millions and distincte degrees of thinges, coulde not in the beginning be created, without an infinite, and omnipotent cause, so as well the orderly productions, and generations of all creatures since then, and the daily and howerly preseruation of them, and all those excellencies wherewith they be endued, from falling to corruption, cannot be attributed to any inferior agent. The continuance and duration of essence and perfection, is as much depending of an infinite and illimited agent, as their first production was: and as in the beginning without the worke of that omnipotent cause, they coulde not possibly haue bin made of nothing, as they were, so without the like assistance, they woulde in an instant be annihilate, and come to nothing againe. For though we should graunt to all conceited men that euer were, or woulde be accounted Philosophers, that these inferior things be compounded of elementarie causes, that they be produced by creatures of their owne kindes, men, by mẽ, beasts, by beasts of the same nature, and so of others, that they are assisted of the celestiall bodies, and receaue influence from the heauens, that respiration is from the aire, heate from the fire, & other necessaries frõ other elements, yet neuer any Philosopher or man of iudgment can bee so absurde in reasoning, but confesse that all these thinges themselues both in production of other creatures, as also in their owne being & preseruance, depend of a former infinite cause, and that these as they made nothing in the beginning, but were made and had emanation for themselues of an other, so they cannot either produce others, or themselues continue without like assistaunce. Therefore in euery least action, duration, or preseruance for euery minute of time, we must of necessity appeale to that first and omnipotent Creator. For no proceeding can bee infinitelie without end, either in the production, emanation, or preseruance of things: For so al causality and effecting operations should be taken a way, and no least

effect

effect could be produced. For in ordinate causes the latter dependeth of the former, and al latter causes of some precedent & first cause, but where there is no beginning, there is no first, and so no causality, and consequently no effect, nothing is, nothinge euer was, nothing can be produced or preserued hereafter, all things are already returned to nothing, which is euidētly vntrue, therfore that first cause must needs be most honorable, & deseruing all reuerentiall duty, & submission. Moreouer experience teacheth, that there is an infinit number of things in the world, whose essence and being, is not of necessity, but contingent, so that they may, and may not be: and whether they be or no, no absurdity in nature can be concluded. For who can say that man (to giue example) or any other creature, is absolute and necessary to be, either in respecte of himselfe or any other for their beeing, or not being? If he be absolute necessary for the being of other creatures, of necessity those creatures, both in being and preseruation must depende of him, which is euidently vntrue. For if man were not, other things might be, as the heauens and diuers others were before he was created, and if all men were consumed, yet all other thinges might remaine in safety. In respect of himselfe he cannot be named absolutely, and of necessity to be, for so he should be of himselfe, and without dependance of any other, which is euidently false of euery limited and depending thing, such as man and all creatures are. Therefore aboue all depending thinges, and such as bee not of necessity, wee must at last arriue to one, that is of it selfe absolute and independing, of which the rest must haue dependance, and to whom religion and dutie is belonging, both for that absolute and independing preeminence in himselfe, as also that of necessity we depende of him.

*One absolutely necessarye, and independing essence, which is God, worthy al worship.*

The same reason ioyned with experience, teacheth, there is a subordination in all inferiour things, none of them is altogither for it selfe, nothing without some order to an other. In artes and sciences belonging to the minde and intellectuall powers, there is a subalternation. In corporall and bodily thinges the matter is more apparant, the heauens, their motions & influences are not for themselues, but for others, that take benefite of their motion, and receaue influx for them; the simple and elementary creatures are for compounded things, no compounded thing is for it selfe, but is subordinat: beasts, fowles, fishes, and the rest, are referred to man, man as he is not of himselfe, so much lesse to himself can he be subordinat, and so of euery thing that made not this subordination. Therfore at last we must come to some excellent thing, which as he appointed this subordination, & of himselfe can be subordinat to none, because he is

*The subordinatiō of things by God. &c.*

the first deuiser of this order, so they all must needes be subordinat to him. And when in all orders of thinges, alwaies that which is the end of others, is most perfect, and no reasonable and intellectuall agents, doe thinges by themselues, without instrumentall causes, or worke by instruments, and secondarie helpes, but to some ende and purpose: Then seeing so many intellectuall, eternall, glorious, and admirable things of the world, coulde not possibly be framed, ordered, or disposed of, by any thing inferior, vnreasonable, and not intellectuall: of necessity as the first cause in producing, and ordering so many and meruailous degrees, and estates of creatures, argueth both a firste cause, and infinite and omnipotent power in him, so in ordeyning them to some ende, that ende must be the most perfecte thinge, then seeing none coulde be more greater then he, or equall to himselfe, for his honour and dignity they were created, and he was, and is their end, because his infinitnesse in power, excludeth assistance, his onlie immensity in goodnesse and perfection, debarreth all other last and finall endes, and admitteth no companion in equalitie of perfection. And euerie man and creature, is so much more indebted and religed to him, then to any inferiour agent, parent, Prince, or potentate, to whome we yeelde reuerence for benefits receaued, by howe much his infinite greatnesse and perfection, exceedeth any limited and depending thing, and by howe much euery effect is more beholding to the first, and vniuersall cause, without which absolutely it cannot be, then to any secondarie and particuler worker, without which by the power of the former, absolutely it may be produced. But if sence and experience may not be admitted with these sensuall and beastlie men, if no reason can haue allowance with such vnreasonable mindes, and all naturall arguments & demonstrations, and daily experiments must be condemned with such vnnaturall monsters, if we should grant them all they can demande, with so many impossibilities in ordinary and connaturall things, that inferior causes could worke, without dependance and assistance of the superiour, that no creature is depending either in essence or operation: that there is no first and principall cause, that chaunce and fortune (which can be nothing but the accidentary concourse or effect of inferiour causes) made al thinges, and whatsoeuer impossibility any foolish and franticke braine can imagine, to excuse their wicked and lasciuious liues. Yet thousands of effects which haue beene, and coulde not be by the production of any created cause, must needes condemne them. For all nations and people in the world, *Christians, Iewes, Mahumetans, Pagans*, and all estates of men, haue proued, and must, & do acknowledge that infinit, miraculous, and supernaturall

*God the finall ende of all.*

*Supernaturall miracles, which coulde not be produced by anye creature &c.*

naturall operations haue bin wrought, which no limited power with al the coniunctions, inclinations, aspects, constellations, either of celestiall, elementary, or compounded things, which they can deuise coulde possibly doe, hauing no potentialitie in them, to effect the meanest of those strange and meruailous operations, onely able to be produced by an omnipotent and infinite agent. And further, to shewe an absolute dominion ouer all creatures, to resist and restraine the most vsuall, and naturall habilities of all inferiour causes, as the most mooueable heauens, that they did not mooue, but stande, as it were amazed at so greate a maiesty, that the greatest planets (which coulde be commanded of no inferiour agent) haue changed their course and order. The highest, and ascending Element of fire, hath descended euen to punish the Irreligious: The Aire, hath denied respiration to creatures: The waters, in most huge quantities, haue ascended against their natural propensitie, to drowne both particuler countries, and the whole worlde in the generall inundation: The whole earth hath trembled, and all the firmaments, and foundations of the worlde haue bin mooued at the pleasure of their Creator, which no creature, nor all creatures togither coulde effect: And yet all countries, peoples, and estates, are witnesses to these things. Thus wee see all testimonies crie out there is a God, infinite, omnipotent, and independing, which hath effected these things. This is the euidence of all creatures, all nations, and kingdomes, all estates, and degrees of men, *Patriarkes, Prophets, Priestes, Kings, Rulers, Princes, Philosophers, Christians, Iewes, Mahumetanes, Pagans*, all *Rabbynes, Doctors, Sybils, Flamens, Arch-flamens, Calyphes, Brachmans*, all that can be cited for authority, agree in this, that there is a God. This is the sentence and vniforme consent of them all, that disagree so much about his nature, and religion in particuler. All good men allowe of this, this all impious and wicked haue confessed, except perhaps some fewe priuate men, in so many generations, and times of the worlde, which drowned in all licentious liuing, haue (to excuse their impieties) rather wished it in will, then affirmed in iudgement: and those also, when they came to death and miseries, as I cited before, acknowledged it. And to conclude against barbarous and absurde people with absurdities, if there is no first, omnipotent, and most excellent cause, then no religion, which is onely due to so greate a maiestie is to bee rendred. Then all nations, and people of the world in all generations, and so many thousands of yeares, that euer professed it were fooles: and one *Lucretius*, that liued, and dyed mad, or any particuler and beasty man, that (to tumble in filthynes) woulde wish so vnpossible a thing, is onely wise and holy. If there

*The testimony of all nations and people.*

Lact. supr.

*Absurdities of denying God. &c.*

there is no first, absolute, and independing cause, no operation can be effected, nothing is now done, nothing can be brought to passe hereafter, because depending causes cannot worke without assistance: so there neither is, or can be any change, alteration, generation, or corruption in the worlde, but all thiugs must needes returne to nothing. If there is no God, first, and illimited cause, to haue created the worlde, there is no science, knowledge, or faculty in the worlde, there neither is, was, or can be any creature, or the least effect, because none of these limited and depending thinges, coulde by any possibility be of it selfe, or any other depending cause. And a thousand such impossible absurdities, which follow this most blasphemous, and sacriledgeous assertion, (*there is no God*) if any barbarous and beastly mouth, durst be so impudent to pronounce it. But this will be more manifest in many chapters, and the whole treatise following, to the confusion of all enemies to true Religion. For which cause (as also that I hope no man can bee so vnreasonably blasphemous to make it a doubt) I passe it ouer more briefly in this place.

Chap. 3. *The necessitie of a diuine prouidence towardes man, and other creatures ordeyned for him, and his dutie to render Reuerence and Religion.*

BVT to preuent the prophane, and blasphemous excuses of this impious generation, accusing the infinite wisdome of God of folly and challenging his incomprehensible goodnes of improuidence: If by impossibility things coulde be effected and caused without any cause, which nature generally teacheth, for a most euident contradiction: yet nothing coulde endure, or bee preserued, without the prouidence and protection of an independing cause,. For duration and perseuerance of second causes, is no lesse depending then their first creation. Then how doth that infinite number of thinges, which this worlde possesseth, endure without corruption? Howe can so many and diuers creatures, not onely wanting iudgment, and reason, for their rule and direction, but all sence and life, obtaine their endes, and remaine in order so infalliblye as they doe? When by reason we know, nothing wanting reason can make comparison, conferre, past, present, and future times, and things, iudge and discerne what is daunger, what is not, what euil, and to be auoided, what good, and to be followed: or by any possibilitie either knowe, prosecute, or imbrace that order, and ende, whereunto it is ordained. And yet the certaine, orderly, and indefectiue motions of Heauens, operations of elements, concourse of causes, and workes, of all inseriour & compounded creatures,

*The necessitie of Gods prouidēce, for the dependance of creatures: The vniforme and orderlye course, euen of insensible thinges, that can haue no prouidence in themselues.*

creatures, sensitiue, vegetiue, and such as haue neither reason, sence or vegetation, vtterly vnable to order and direct themseues, giue testimony they are guided dy some most prouident and carefull workeman, cause and director of all thinges, caused and directed by nothing, but alwaies hauing from eternity existence, beeing, and all compleate and possible perfection; to whome consequently, all worshippe and homage, euen by that title, and for that preeminence, is to be yeelded. For, as *Cicero* saith, if it be not possible for a great number of letters, and characters cast togither by chance, without any order or disposition of sillables, wordes, and sentences to make the Annales of *Ennius*, or compounde any history, or worke of learning, if no man shoulde set them in order, how much more is it vnpossible to beleeue this admirable, and wonderfull world, to be made by accidentary concourse and meeting of thinges togither: Yea such absurde and irreligious Atheists must yeelde, that of necessity in either case there is one first originall, and independing, both to frame and compose, as also orderly to digest both the one and other. For neither coulde those characters be made or ordered of themselues, or those causes which by chance shoulde constitute the worlde, be, or haue concurrence without a Creator, and former cause of such agreement. For although some Philosophers with many absurdities defended the eternity of the worlde; and an infinite number in successiue thinges: yet they all euer graunted, both a dependance, and emanation of them from GOD and that it was impossible, an infinite progresse and proceeding, coulde be in essentiall and subordinate causes, such as the superiour and inferiour, first, and secondary causes are: for where no beginning of causes coulde be found, there no operation could either be effected, or begun. And if that coulde by any man be imagined; yet of necessity, euen in that infinite number of causes one of whome the others shoulde depende, must haue that supreame prerogatiue wee assigne to the first and principall cause of things, without which, nothing coulde be either gouerned or created. Wherefore, as *Eusebius* teacheth, as in artificiall things, (to giue example) an house cunningly & curiously builded, & adorned with al kind of furniture, is an vnfallible argument, that there was a builder & disposer thereof; much more doth the meruailous excellencie, number, order, and beawty of all naturall things, in the great, and glorious habitation, and house of the world, giue euidence, that a chiefe Prince and artificer hath made, digested, & still ruleth and gouerneth them. For, (which I prooued before) as to make, is an act of power, and to make & create, where there is infinite improportiō, is an euident argument, of an

Cic. lib. 3. 2. Nat. Deor.

Arist. 2. Met. c. 2. text. 5. 8 Met. cap. 5. text. 41. Auth. l. caus. c. 1. & c.

*Prouidence ouer creatures as much belōging to god as their creation.*

Euseb. lib. 3. Præp. Euāg.

infinitely able and omnipotent workeman; so to see so many millions, and innumerable multitudes of things, not able to rule, order, digest, and prouide for themselues, yet so vniformely without error, so generallye without exceptiō, so many thousands of yeares, as since the worlds creation (and from eternity, if it shoulde not bee created in time) without intermission, to be ordered, ruled, digested, continued, preserued, and prouided for, is a manifest demonstration, that they are thus maintayned and gouerned, by some most prudent, good, and indefectible cause, which performing that prouidence for the vse of man, man a reasonable creature cannot be so vnreasonable and forgetfull of duty, but yeelde vnto him that honour and Religion, which so long & infinite a benefit deserueth. That an infinite number of things besides man are, and haue euer in all ages, places, and degrees of things, bin ordered, ruled, and most certainely prouided for, no Epicure can denie; euery creature and euery sence he hath, will bring euidence it is so. That to rule, gouerne, order, direct, and prouide for thinges, and to bring them to their end is an act and onely operation of reason & vnderstanding, no man can contradict: man is the only reasonable and vnderstanding creature of this inferiour world, he doth not, neyther can he, or any limited vnderstanding so certainly, and infallibly order, rule, and haue prouidence ouer so many millions, infinite, and innumerable thinges: none of them hath reason to order themselues, and most doe want both sence and life, therfore seeing there is neither act, power, or potentiality in them, to order and rule them selues, and nothing else can be assigned to exercise that vniuersall prouidence, of necessity it must bee done by the chiefe and vniuersall cause, their first maker, for nothing else can performe it, and their gouernment most properly belongeth to him. No Prince that hath wonne, instituted, or otherwise obtained a kingdome, will neglect to rule it, no Soueraigne may be carelesse of his subiects, no parent regardelesse of his children he hath begotten, no Artificer, workeman, or cause indued with reason, can be without prouidence of the thinges and effectes he hath produced, although their care and charge require laboure, newe and dayly costes in the agent. Then that God & workeman, whose infinite wisdome cannot alter and repent any worke he hath effected, mislike no ende he hath entended, wose goodnesse cannot be vnprouident or change to thinges he loued, whose power is omnipotent, whose act is but one & eternal with whom it is no greater businesse to gouerne a thousand worlds, then one and the meanest creature, whose vnderstanding is so illymited that nothing can possibly be concealed from him, will not, but take prouidence of

*No creature hath, or can haue the generall prouidence of thinges.*

*No maker of thinges endued with reason, is vnprouident of his workes.*

*The infinite wisdome and goodnesse of God, cannot but haue prouidence of thinges.*

of man, and all creatures he hath created. And as the first creation of all things from nothing, could not possibly be effected, but by an infinit and illimited agent, so both the duration and beeing of the same creatures, which is as it were, one continued productiō, cannot be maintained without the concourse of equall vertue, neyther their actions and operations (which likewise be creatures and dependant) possibly be effected, without the same creator. Neyther can any man imagin, how an inferior & depending cause can beginne, continue, or perfecte any operation, without this prouidence, and assistance of the superior and vnniuersall Actor. And although the heauens and celestiall bodies, hauing a generall influence to inferior thinges, in that respect, are tearmed vniuersall and common causes, in regarde of these lower agents, whose influx and actions are more perticuler, yet both they are inanimate, and so vnfit for gouernment, and if they be compared to God, the supreame vniuersal cause, they are priuat agents, & howsoeuer they be considred they are secondary & depending, and can worke nothing without assistance of their Creator, much lesse can the coniunctions, aspects, sights, and, constellations of planets, only accidents, which worke nothing but in vertue of their subiect, be effectuall of such thinges. And the Stoycks themselues commonly excepted from fatalitie, the wills and free actions of men, which is sufficient for this cause of Religion, which is their homage. And concerning meaner effectes of honour, riches, wealth, prosperity, death, sicknesse, and the like, euery day and minute of tyme cryeth out with experience, that like constellations doe not alwayes, or ordinarily produce lyke dispositions and workes: to exemplyfie, was no man in England borne vnder the constellation of our kinges, that none but they enioyed the Crowne? did not all the worlde bring forth one man, when *Clement* the eight, and *Radulphus* were borne, that none other is a Pope or Emperour? And if such Princes before their powers begunne, coulde prohibit others to be borne with them, yet we see that many thousands daily die with them, whether they will or no, as in so manie battailes, wherin hundreds of thowsands of all estates, ages and coditions, differing from those Nobles, haue beene slayne with Kinges. And yet by these mens arte, all those that died with Kings, should be Kings, al of one age, nature, and condition. Thus many thousands to one it is in their procedings, (besides all other inuincible reasons) that they are deceiued, and God hath prouidence not only of humane actions, but all other thinges, because no other cause can rule; then experience, telleth vs these thinges are true, and their deuyses false. And the same experience is a tutour to euery priuate man, that

*Euēts of thinges cannot be imputed to the heauens and constellations.*

Albert. l. 2. Phisic. c. 8. 9. tract.

at all constellations he is of the same liberty of will, to doe, or not to doe; and howe can the heauens and bodies more spirituall substances? are they animated that they haue dominion ouer soules? are they omnipotent that they can bringe violence to our wils and freedome? are they exempted from a chiefe gouernors authority and rule, that they can gouerne al? are they God and the first agent, that they are independing, and all depende of them? these be the absurdities of such people. Besides which, all reason and reasonable creatures, Angels, gloryfied Saints in heauen, & the vnderstandings of all men of equall iudgment, confirme it by their sentence: all sensible things by their indefectiue order approoue it. All insensible creatures simple and compounded, the heauens, elements, and all others by their vnuariable courses and proceedings, euer haue ratified it to be so: the meanest creature by the wonderfull composition of partes by which it is composed, & certaine direction to come to those ends & perfections, which for want of science it cannot knowe, giueth euidence in this cause. This mooued *Galen* that prophane and irrreligious Phisitian, attributing all to nature, and nothing to the cause and ordeyner of nature, at last (as himselfe is witnesse) to acknowledge the prouidence of God ouer these inferiour things, and to make a Canticle in these wordes following, in honour of our Creator. *Heere trulie doe I make a song in praise of our Creator, for that of his owne accorde, it hath pleased him, to adorne and beawtifie his things, better then by any arte possible it coulde be imagined.* Therefore if the prouidence of God is such, to his meane and basest creatures, the common obiectes of Phisitians, most busied in bodies and more contemptible things, what woulde be said if we shoulde goe about to comprehend the least of so many thousand glorious creatures in the world. What particuler supernaturall prouidence and protection GOD hath alwaies vsed to his religious seruants, aswell whole Kingdomes, Countries, and priuate persons, deuoted to him in religious worship, will appeare in the thirteenth Chapter of this booke, to the confusion of all Infidels and misbeleeuers. In the meane time (which I will omitte in that place) let vs take for our example, the city of Hierusalem, so renowned for religious obseruations, vnder the lawe of *Moyses*, and the high Apostolicke See of Rome, so famous for true worshippe since the time of Christ, yet both odious amonge misbeleeuing people, the first to Pagans, the seconde both to them, incredulous Iewes, and apostating Heretickes of all ages. Concerning the first, let vs passe ouer that miraculous prouidence GOD exercised towardes the Israelites his religious seruants, inhabitants thereof, from the time of *Abraham*, to whome he made the promise, to blesse him & his posterity

*All authoritie prooueth the prouidence of God.*

*Example of Gods prouidence to euery meane creature*

Galen. lib. 3. de vsu part. & lib. 5.

*Cap. 13.*

*Examples of Gods supernaturall prouidence. &c.*

*Gods prouidẽce to Ierusalem before the comming of Christ.*

Gen. 12. 15. 17. 18. 3. Reg. 6.

ſteritie,& take eſpecial care of that nation, whereof Chriſt was to deſcend, vntill the time of building the Temple by King *Salomon*, which was aboue 900. yeares. I will not ſpeake what bleſsings were beſtowed vpon *Abraham, Iſaac, Iacob*, and their diſcent, how miraculouſly they were multiplied in Egipt, with what wonders their mightye enemies were confounded, their meruailous deliuerie thence, the drowning of their enemies, their ſtrange preſeruation, their miraculous life and protection in the deſart, the more then wonderfull conqueſts they obteined ouer ſo many and potent enemies, and other ſupernaturall fauours, not onlie recorded in holy Scriptures, but remembred by other writers, and manifeſtly knowne, to many and great Kingdomes. But to paſſe theſe ouer, what coulde be the fame of Hieruſalem a City of Canaan, a little countrie, when it was deuided into ſo many prouinces, as it was before the Iſraelites inhabited it? what man maketh mention of anie honour or grorie it had? but after religion was ſetled there, howe glorious was it to all nations? it was the ſeate of the Kinges, and it was called the Citie of the King of heauen, the high Prieſt, with the greateſt Maieſtie of that lawe, were planted there, Sacrifices were there offered, not only *Iewes*, but *Proſelites*, and conuerted *Gentyles* of all nations, honoured it with their acceſſe and preſence, *Parthians, Medes, Elamites*, inhabitants of *Meſopotamia, Cappadocia, Pontus, Aſia, Phrigia, Pamphilia, Egipt, Lybya, Cyrene, Romanes, Cretenſians, Arabians*, and others. How ſumptuous, & glorious was the temple to all nations, where all things were almoſt made of Golde? howe pretious and miraculous (as many write) were the attyres of the Prieſts? howe honourable was their Oracle and Propitiatorie moſt ſtrangely glorified with the preſence and anſweres of God himſelfe? with what holie Relickes of the *Arke Manna*, and others, was it ſanctified? to what a mighty nation did that people encreaſe? what Prophets had they? howe were their ennemies *Antiochus* and others puniſhed of God? howe gratious were they to the greateſt Princes? howe miraculouſly were they, their holy Citty, and Temple, preſerued a thouſand yeares togither? how were they diliuered from captiuities? how ſtrangely did God mooue the harts of the mightyeſt rulers of the Gentiles to honour their ſacrifices, and Temple? And when the time was come, that theire lawe in the *Meſsias* ſhoulde ceaſe, and they moſt prophanely had denied and put him to death, not onelye as their owne Prophetes, but the *Sybils* and others amonge the Gentyles had foretolde, and they falne to ſuch notorious impieties, as their owne Hiſtorian *Ioſephus* is witneſſe, that neuer any nation had come to that degree of wickednes; yet god ceaſed not his ſpecial prouidẽce to that people,

Gen. 15. Act. 7. Exod. 12. Exod. 5. 6. 7. 8. 9. 10. 11. 12. 13. 14. 15. 16. 17. &c. Porphyr. l. 4. cont. Chriſt. App. lib. 4. cont. Iud. Ioſeph. lib. 4 Antiquit. Ariſt. l. 72. interpret.

3. Reg. 6. Math. c. 5.

Act. 2.

Ioſep. l. anti. Ariſt. l. 72. interpret.

Machab. 1. Eſdr. 1. 2. 3. Ariſt. ſupr. Ioſeph. cont. Appion. 1. Eſdr. 1. 2. 3. 4. 5. 6. 7. &c. Iſ. 53. Hier. Sybil. apud Lact. 1. 2. 3. 4 diu. inſtit. D. Tho. 3. p. Ioſeph. l. 15. 20. 7. bell.

but gaue them many wonderfull signes for their conuersion. Besides those wdich the holy Euangelists report of the miraculous Ecclips, quaking of the earth, rending of the Rocks, & tearing of the vale of the Temple, arising of the dead and others, *Iosephus* giueth euidence, that in their great festiuity (before their desolution) in the night, there appeared such a light about the Alter & Temple halfe an houre togither, that euery man thought it was day. And at the same time, an Oxe ledde to be sacrificed, brought forth a calfe in the middest of the Temple, and the East doore of the inner Temple made of brasse, and so heauy that twenty men coulde scarcely shut it, beeing locked with strong lockes of iron, and barred with deepe barres let downe into a thresholde of stone, opened of it selfe in the night before the setting of the same fierie Chariots and armed battailes, were seene in the Aire about the City: and the Priests did heare a voice, saying: *Migremus hinc, Let vs go, from hence*. And (that which is a moste strange testimonie of Gods continued prouidence towardes them) one *Iesus* son of *Anani*, foure yeares before the warre began, when the Citye was in great prosperity and peace, vpon the soddaine in their festiuall day, began to cry in these wordes. *A voice from the East, a voice from the west, a voice from the foure windes, a voice vpon Hierusalem and the Temple, a voice vpon newe married husbands, & newe married wiues, a voice ouer al this people*. And this day and night going a bout all the streets of the city cryed, and although he was chasticed for this cry, yet he neither spake any thing for himselfe or against them that punished him, but still continued crying the same wordes. And being led to the ruler of the Romanes to bee punished, & his fleshe torne to the bones with blowes, he neither entreated fauor, or once wept, but at euery blowe bending downe, pyttifully vttered this speech: *Woe, woe, to Hierusalem*, and neuer gaue ouer mourning for the miserable city, and still complained in these wordes, *Woe, woe to Hierusalem*. And thus he continued seauen yeares, and fiue monethes, but principally vpon the festiuall daies: vntill at the time of the siedge going about the wall, he cried out with his lowdest voice, *Woe, woe to the City, and Temple, and people, and at last also he added, woe also to my selfe*, and was presentlye killed with a stone, throwne from the ennemies, hitherto bee the wordes of *Iosephus*, liuing amonge them at the same time.

Math. 27. Ioseph. l. 7. bell. cap. 12.

Tacit. hist. lib. 5.

Ioseph. l. 7. bel. cap. 12.

*Gods prouidence to the Apostolicke See of Rome.* Sibill. apud Lact. li. diu. inst.

And coucerning Rome, where the Pope and high priest of Christians is resident, how vnprobable was it in humane iudgement before S. *Peter* a poore fisher came thither, that the prophesie of Sibilla (*the fishers booke shoulde conquer the Romane Empire*) should be fulfilled. Was not Christ his master put to death by that authority? was not he hiselfe crucified by the same, and all his successors vnto S. *Siluester*, thirtie in number, either actually put to death, or most grieuously persecuted? were not Christians at that time without any friend or fauourer? were not the Romane Emperours the most potent of the worlde, and ruled all places? did not the persecuted Popes preach Christ crucified, pennance and great austeritye to the eares of licentious Gentiles? And yet we see that the prophesie of *Sibilla* was performed, and the especiall prouidence which Christ promised to his holy Apostle and his successors, that their faith should not faile, that it should conquere all enemies, that the gates of hell should not preuayle against it, is miraculouslie effected, and still continued to that holy See. I haue shewed in my *Apologicall Epistle*, how all the Pagan Princes of the world, one time or other were opposed against it, but they wer confoũded. How many Infidell & Pagan Emperors persecuted it, but they were punished, and it preuailed: many hereticall Emperors plagued it, but they were confounded, diuers wicked Christian Emperours & Kinges, both in England and other nations afflicted it, yet it conquered them, how often it was sacked and spoyled by *Gothes*, *Vandals*, *Saracens*, *Lumbardes*, and others, yet it florished still: that it hath beene infested with many schismes, and assaulted by aboue 400. sectes of heritickes before *Luther*, and yet condemned them, and yet at this time warreth against almost 300. knowen heresies, and yet it is more glorious and renowned now, after 1500. yeares, then euer it was before, & dilated further by many degrees (daily encreasyng) then euer any other regiment spiritual or temporall was, and not subiecte to the least susspition to be ouerthrowen, hereafter. And no man can make other reasan of these thinges, then the extraordynarie prouidence of God, to that holy place, the enemies it hath, and euer had, bee more, and more mighty, then euer any city fought against. It vseth not temporall armour against them. The souldiours, and Captaines it vsed, were vnarmed with corporall weapons, their conquest ouer their enemies was by suffering themselues to be killed. That which they taught was vnpleasing to potent Princes againste whome they warred, and carnall mindes with whome they fought, That which they laboured to ouerthrowe, and did destroy, was liberty, and things tending to delight, and yet that hath vanquished, and daily is more glorious and triumphant, the other perish, and become more contemptible. Who will not say but these things proceede from God, & his most holy prouidence & protection to that Religious Apostolicke See? And thus I might exemplyfie, in other thinges. I will passe so many thousandes of miraculous operations, whereof the whole world can witnes, & which could not be effected by any

Epist. Apol.

Bern. Luce. Catal. hær. Casp. Vlenb. 22. caus.

Miracles.

limited or created power, I haue spoken of them already, and must in-
Cap. 10. 11. 13. infr. treate them as well in diuers chapters of this booke, as also more largely
hereafter, against internall enemies and whereof euery Argument I shall
Part. 2. Resol. alleadge for true religion to GOD our chiefe gouernour giueth witnesse,
Arg. miracl. therefore it needeth no more euidence in this place. Onely I will conclude, euery creature in the worlde, euery parte, member, organe, quali-
ty, act, or operation it hath, is a demonstration in this case: God himselfe,
ordinarily and superordinarily doth witnesse it, all reasonable, and vnrea-
*The generall and vniforme consent of all countries and people.* sonable things in their sence affirme it. The heauens, all simple, & compounded things, giue inuincible proofe it is so.

This is the sentence of al nations, Cuntries, Schooles, Cities, Townes,
Hist. Ec. Eus. Niceph. Bed. &c. and people, *Catholickes, Heretickes, Iewes, Pagans, Brachmans, Mahumetanes*, all
Christian and Panim Philosophers, late, auncient, of all ages and places
Alcor. Mah. Thalm. Iud. Pet. Maf. hist Indic. &c. agree in this. None but beastly men, (whose opinion is no authority to
excuse their filthynes) deny it, and they rather in voluptuous desire wi-
shing, then in iudgment affirming it. Neither let them alleadge what
*Obiections of Epicures answered.* multitudes of errors about religion in particuler, are, and haue reigned
in the worlde: for as these errors are to be imputed to the wickednesse of
the authors from whome they proceede, so such great contention for that
cause is an euident argument of worshippe, and the dignity of true religion, otherwise euery man woulde not contende and make claime vnto it,
with so great danger to himselfe, and contempt of others. And the causes of their complainte, that errors and sinnes doe reigne, proceede from
their owne and such mens impious demerits, and are no more to bee imputed to GOD, which neither can, nor will deceaue, or because of sin,
then the wilfull ignorance of a peruerse scholer, to a learned and painfull
master, or the disobedience of a wicked childe or subiect to vertuous Pa-
Cap. 2. 3. sup rents and Princes. That God is free from inducing or leading into errors, is euident already by that most excellent goodnes, which I haue shewed to be in him. And that he hath deliuered so certaine and infallible
meanes for euery man to knowe the truth, that (except wilfully) we neede
Lib. 2. & part 2. Resol. not erre, I will demonstrate by inuincible Arguments hereafter, as also
Lib. 2. c. 6. part. 2. Resol Arg. 5. 6. &c prooue in particuler against all *Infidelles, Iewes, Pagans, Mahumetans*, and all
sortes of heretickes, that their errors and proceedings in them are so ma-
nifestly false, that they cannot be excused from wilfull ignorance: And
that the order of catholickes true beleeuers is so certaine, that they cannot
be deceaued. And to ease this irreligious people of al complaints against
the oppressions, tribulations, and persecutions of the godly, and prospe-
Cap. 12. 13. 14. infr. rities of the wicked, I will shewe that such obiections against Religion, are

a manifest conuiction of a diuine reuerence, and howe the temporall Ca. 12. 13. 14. infr.
fauourers, and preferments of the religious, did alwayes exceede the honours of the vngodly. And to giue them that they seeke, I will proue if Cap. vlt. penult. Seq.
by impossibillytie there shoulde be no religion, nor God, no immortalitie after death, yet that the state of the professors of worship euen in this world, is farre more gloryous, honourable, and pleasant, then of Epicures, and irreligious men.

Chap. 4. *The necessitie of Religion, to obtaine the Immortall and supernaturall end, for the immortall Soule of man which can neither haue anie end in this lyfe, or perish possibly with death.*

VVHEREFORE though we shoulde become such great Politicks, and so fully possessed with selfe loue and delight in religious affaires, that we woulde vse no reuerence or worshippe, but for our owne aduantage, yet we cannot but performe this reuerentiall duety, especiallie when we enter into reckoning with our selues, how many and often helpes and succours we want, necessary to that end whereto wee were ordayned, and that which we moste desire, the better and immortall portion of mans *The ende and felicitie of man cannot be in this life.*
soule, not hauing perfection in this worlde, and yet must receaue it from God: For no corporall or corruptible thinge of this life is able to satisfie and giue rest to the greedy vnderstanding, or vnpleaseable appetite of our reasonable and incorruptible parte, neyther was there any Philosopher, Cicero Tuscul. quest. et paradox.
or student of nature able to finde here the end and felicity thereof. For by felicity and happinesse al men alwaies did, and doe, vnderstand such an estate, as is deuoided of all euill, wee would eschewe, and abounding with all good wee woulde wishe; for as *Aristotle* saith, that is *Blessednesse*, which Aristot. lib. 1. ethic. ca. 1.
all men and all thynges doe seeke, and desyre. Which estate and degree neuer anye nan yet, how much soeuer beefrended of this worlde, coulde taste in this life; but whatsoeuer they either founde for themselues, or deuised for others, it was not so durable, pleasaunt, good, or perfect, but it wanted one thinge or other, wee might wishe to haue: or brought with it some thing vnstable, variable, tedyous, troublesome, painefull, or vnpleasant, which a mā in reason might iustly craue to want; as manifestly appeareth not only in the general conditiōs, which the Philosopher by light Arist. sup. cap. 8.
of nature requireth to the blessednesse of man but in honor, riches, knowledge, delight, or other pleasure, which any sect of Philosophers, *Accademicks, Peripateticks, Stoicks*, or *Epicureans* in particuler appoynted for humane felicity. Wherfore seeing such a condion and estate of happines cannot be

found in this life, and euerie thing one time or other enioyeth his end and felicitie, of necessitie this end and happines of man, must be obtained after death, and receaued of God by dutie to him, as also all necessary helpes, and dispositions thereof, all reuerence and religion must needs bee done vnto him by man, in a more high degree then of any other creature, not ordained to such a supernaturall, and eternall end. And this no Epicure, how much soeuer brutishly blinded in delight, or malitiously iniurious to the perfection of humane nature can deny. For if he aleadge no reason for his impyous and irrelgious minde, then no man can be so foolish to beleeue him: If he pretend any shew of reason, how weake or feeble soeuer it is, thereby he ouerthroweth that by his owne reason and vnderstanding, which his licentious and brutish will laboureth to builde. For reason & iudgement beeing operations onely of the intellectuall part of mans soule, as immediate cause, and not depending of the sensible phantasie, or any corporall, or organicall instrument, (for neither a tree, or any vegetatiue thing, or a dogge, or any sensible creature, can reason, argue, or dispute of things) should be a manifest demonstration, that soule which is endued with those habilities, to be independing of the body, spirituall and immortall, liuing for euer, and so to haue felicity after death, for attaining wherof, a Religion and worship is due to God. Therfor euery one knowing himself to be a reasonable creature, no man can posibly cal the other in question, except first he would doubt whether he be a man, whether he hath reason, iudgeth of things past, present, and to come, compareth one thing with an other, argueth, and disputeth of causes and effectes: for, as both reason, & al learned philosophers teach, that soule which hath these indepēding operatiōs, must needs be seperable frō the body & immortal.

*The vnreasonable absurdities of Epicures, and denyers of the Soules immortallitie after death.*

*Denyers of the Soules immortallitie, denie them selues to be men.*

Mercur. Tris. in Aescul. plat. &c. Arist. lib. 1. an. text. 20. lib. 2. an. text. 22. lib. 12. met. text 37. 1. ethic. cap. 11. &c.

Let vs adde the vnsatiablenesse of the same facultie, whome all the science, and knowledge of this world cannot content; and the natural inclination it hath to knowe the causes of such effectes, as it findeth in this life, & cannot: that vnanswerable appetite, & propension of the will, which neuer enioyeth enough of the thinge it loueth, but desireth more: that liberty and freedome it hath, commandinge all sensible powers, and faculties, either to exercise, or suspend their operations, prescribing, doing or not doing of things, and effecting the will, and election of it self, how vrgent soeuer the repugnant sensible appetites and desires bee. Then how can anie man imagyne that power to be depending of the body, which in it chiefest operations is depending thereof, but euydentlie sheweth superiorytie ouer al corporall & sensible passiions, and suggestions, that it can rule & bridle them as it pleaseth, in such sort, thar no foote can go, no eye can

*The powers of the Soule insatiable in this life.*

*The absolute regiment of the reasonable powers, ouer the sensible & inferior.*

can see, no Member, Organe, or sensible Power is able to execute anie function, if the will forbiddeth. Or what Epicure can be so madde to affirme so manie spirituall vertues, as Religion, Faith, Hope, Reuerence, Feare, Iustice, & such others, which all men at one time, or other in some degree finde in themselues, to bee subiected in a corporall or corruptible power? Or is there anie of this schoole of impietie, but theyr conscyence and vnderstandinge telleth them, that sinne is not to be committed, and when they haue sinned, accuseth them as guilty of transgressing the lawe of God, whome they haue offended, and consequentlie whome they are to worshippe, and reuerence. Of which Saint *Paul*, in the light of nature speaketh in these wordes. *When the Gentiles which haue not the lawe* (of Moyses and Christ) *naturally doe those thinges, that are of the lawe, the same not hauinge the lawe, themselues are a lawe to themselues: who shewe the worke of the lawe wrytten in theyr heartes, theyr conscience giuinge testymonie to them, and amonge themselues theyr thoughtes accusinge, or also defending.*

*Vertues and spirituall qualities of man, cannot be subiected in a Corporall & mortall Subiecte. The conscience and internall experience euen of the Epicures.*

Rom. cap. 2. 5. 14. 15.

And although the vnderstanding in diuers first operations, craueth aide from the imagination: yet in many other noble acts thereof, it is independing: as in the iudgment of spirituall thinges, and the vse of free will, which no sence, corporall organe, or facultie was euer able to produce. For betweene euery operation produced, the cause which produceth it, and the obiecte and matter that is considered, there must be a due and correspondent proportion. No vegetatiue power hath sence, no sensitiue facultie can argue, or conceaue immateriall things. And yet we see, that the vnderstanding of man, is so farre from beeing wholie assisted of the body in these operations, or to be hindred by seperation from it, that experience teacheth, when it is vnited to this corruptible body, the actes of the reasonable partes of the soule be more perfect, by how much they are more abstracted, and independing of the body; as is euident in the exercises of all studious and contemplatiue men, and in some aged and decayed bodies, when the soule hath lesse dependance, when the vegetiue, and sensetiue Organs are enfeebled, and not able so well to excercise their naturall operations, when neither generation, augmentation, hearing, seeing, or other such powers remaine: yet often times when these thinges are nearest corruption, or corrupted, the vnderstanding, and immortall powers of the soule are most perfect, expecting a future ende and felicitie.

*The chiefest operations of the soule, independant of the bodie.*

*The principall acts of the soule more perfecte, when most abstracted from the bodie.*

So likewise it appeareth when we consider that excellency of the vnderstanding, aboue all sensitiue creatures: how it is enabled not only to vnderstand all other things, howe eleuated soeuer aboue sence and ima-

*The reflected actes of mans soule.*

gination, but to reflecte and ponder vpon it selfe, and the other powers of the soule, will, and memory, and those also ouer themselues. For not only the vnderstanding vnderstandeth, and knoweth it selfe to knowe, and vnderstand, or that the will doth wish and desire, or the memory remembreth; but the will it selfe, is reflected vpon it selfe, willing it selfe to will, and the memory aboue it selfe, remembring that it did remember; which is impossible for any corporall, or sensible and corruptible power to doe. The hearing heareth not it selfe to heare, the foote cannot set it selfe, and tread vpon it selfe, and so of others.

*The continuall and contrarie combats of the resonable soul and sensible powers.*

The continuall combats and dissagreements, which the reasonable parte maintaineth against the sensible and corporall motions, which is not in brute and sensytiue thinges, (For where all is like, there can be no dislike and contention, which groweth from vnlikenes and contrarietie) those so often and vrgent feares of spirituall domages, belonging to the soule, and to happen after death, and the hope of eternall pleasures then to be enioyed, which euery man proueth to exceede his corporall feares and bodely delightes, giue euidence in this case.

*The immortal powers of the soule, which cannot be in a Mortall Subiect, demonstrat the soule to be Immortal.*

Then those so many and immortal powers of the soule must haue their end: and seeing the natures of things and their powers and properties must agree, and be of the same order, that substance of the soule which hath immortal and euerduring properties and operations must be immortall: for by no posibilitie where the subiect or substance is mortall, the properties and qualities of that substance can be immortal; for properties and accidents, must haue some thing wherin to be subiected and receaued; and those properties, that be immortall, an immortall subiect. For properties and qualities, be euer the properties of some thing to which they are belonging: Therfore as those operations which the soule exerciseth only by dependance of the body, and corporall organes, as to eate, to walke, to grow, to heare, to smell, and such other vigetatiue and sensible workes, are an argument, that soule which only hath these workes, to perish with the body, as the lyues of Plants, Hearbes, Birdes, Beasts, and Fishes doe, because they wholy depend of that bodie, which doth perish: euen so the operations of the soule of man which are independing of the bodily helpe, demonstratiuelie argue, the separabilitie therof, and so duration for euer. For that which is intellectuall, and spirituall, cannot be corrupted of any corporall, or naturall agent: Neyther hath it originall of decay in it selfe, but is altogether without contrariety, and repugnance. And beeing one symple, spirytuall, and incompounded substance, it must needes be immortall after death, and haue an euerlasting felicitie. For the infinite wisdome of GOD, which coulde not constitute the least creature, or doe anie thinge, but to some ende, hath asigned a certaine state, and place, wherein euery creature, findeth center, and rest, where they enioye and preserue their perfection, as the Element of fire aboue the vppermost Region of the Aire, because it is highest, the Aire in his Regions, as the Nature thereof requireth, the heauier thinges, Water, and Eearth, in their lower elementary places, and so of all other creatures: and yet hitherto neuer any man, howe much soeuer beholding vnto nature, coulde finde in earthly things, a center, and place of rest: for the immortal appetites, and faculties of his soule, wherefore by no posibility, his beatitude can be in this world. For although we admitte in other creatures, that all of euery kinde obtaine not their ende; yet to say that none of any sort doe finde it is euidently vutrue. Then to affirme, that among so many millions of men, so excellent creatures, not one shoulde haue his end and hapinesse, were to take all wisdome, goodnesse, and prouidence from God, and argue him of ignorance, and iniustice; especially when we often see wicked men in this worlde, not only to liue vnpunished, but to be exaulted with honour, and passe their time in pleasures; and the most holy and vertuous, to liue in misery, and to be aflicted with all aduersities; which the infinite goodnes of God would not do except after death he had appointed punishment for the one, and a beatificall reward for the other: for of it owne nature vertue is honourable, & sinne deserueth punnishment. For if there be no religion due to GOD, but the soule of man is mortall and dieth with the body, his ende must be asigned in this life, as it is in beastes, and other creatures, and must consist in corporall and temporall delightes. Then cannot humility, sobriety, temperance, abstinence, patience, virginity, chastity, pennance, prayer, contemplation, and other confessed vertues, which be opposite enemies, and a full priuation of bodily and sensuall pleasures, be accounted vertues, leading to a mans felicity, when they directly depriue him of his supreame beatitude? Or how could pride, ambition, oppresion, couetousnes, drunkennes, theft, rapine, adultery, and all vncleane wantonnes of sensuality, and other voluptuous sins be so esteemed, when they shoulde be the only perfection, and felicity of man? which the very heroical conceit (if there were no other argument) of euery one not drowned in beastlines wil affirme. For there is not one, but in reason would scorne to chuse such things for his *Summum bonum* and felicity. And yet that which is true happines, neither is, nor can be contemned of any, but greedily sought & deserued of al, as a most perfect state, where al things to be wished are present,

*Euery kind of creatures except mã hath an end in this life.*

ſent, and all things to be auoided abſent. To which not only all powers, properties, actes, and operations, of the reaſonable ſoules of men, when they were vnited with their bodies, but many and great numbers of ſoules after their ſeperation, haue teſtified and giuen infallible euidence, to thouſands of credible preſent witneſſes, For if the ſoule be not ſeparable, it coulde not remaine, either by it ſelfe after ſeparation, or be vnited again to that body it had firſt enformed: becauſe in the ſeparation it were to be diſſolued and, periſh: neither could any newe ſoule, be produced in thoſe bodies, no diſpoſition or potentialitie being left in them for ſuch production, Take this away, and not only the nature of euery perticuler man is deſtroyed, but all Communities, Kingdomes, Commonwealths, Societies, Townes, Cities, Families, and ciuill eſtates, which euer practiſed reuerence and cannot conſiſt without Religion, are ouerthrowne. All Teſtimonies, and Reuelations of God in holy Scriptures are to be reiected. Thoſe ſacred writings, approued by ſo manie miraculous, and other arguments, as I will alleadge in my next chapter, that by no poſsibillitie they coulde be vntrue, are not to be regarded. Then can any man become ſo trayterous, and diſobedient a Rebell to his Creator, ſo enuios a perſecutor of his owne dignitie, and preferment, ſo malitious an enemie and oppoſer of himſelfe to all creatures, to giue ſo great attendance and homage to ſhorte and brutiſhe pleeaſures, to liue as though there were no God, to whome he ought dutie, and religion, no felicitie after death, no beatitude for man, but as beaſtes enioy? If this opinion be falſe (as infinite teſtimonies proue it to be) then he is ſure to be damned for euer, if it ſhould be true (as God and all creatures and that man himſelfe in iudgment denyeth) yet hee hath gained no more then other brutiſh creatures haue done, and that which a reaſonable man would not accept.

*Seperated ſoules.*

*All ſcriptures.*

## Chap. 5. *The Teſtimonies of all holie Scriptures, for all thinges belonging to religion: and their moſt certaine and infallible Authorytie.*

VVEE will adde to theſe naturall Teſtimonies, of all reaſonable creatures, the Supernaturall witnes of the Creator himſelfe, regiſtred in holy Scriptures, where not only the Infinit & Omnipotent Maieſty of one Immortal, & Incomprehenſible God, his prouidence ouer al creatures, extraordinary protection to his religious ſeruants, the Immortalitie and euerlaſting bleſſedneſſe of the ſoules of men, and their duty, & religion to God in general are ſet downe: but the very particuler manner & meanes of worſhip, & things belonging to adoration are recorded for all

all peoples inſtruction. And let not any prophane Atheiſt or irreligious monſter take exception againſt them, or any one of thoſe moſt holy & ſacred writings: it is not the condẽned ſentence of any idolatrous Gentile, beaſtlie Epicure, *Diagoras*, or Atheiſt, or apoſtating Hereticke, which all Judgments, and generations haue diſalowed, that can call thoſe vndoubted monuments of the will of God into queſtion. Shall the *Simonians, Baſilidians, Bogomites*, or any heretickes that liued thouſands of yeares after they were written, make them doubtfull, becauſe they be contrarie to his corrupted deſires? when they haue ſo many generations of the moſt renowned countries and peoples againſt them? ſhall it bee lawefull for *Diagoras* the firſt Atheiſt, which liued thouſands of yeares after thoſe things which be entreated in them were effected, onlie reiect them becauſe they witnes a God, and worſhip to him, which all the worlde, and all kingdomes before and after him euer beleeued? ſhall any Pagan Idolater bee receaued to diſgrace thoſe ſacred teſtimonies, when their ſuperſtitions are ſo late in reſpect of that worſhip, which they handle? for as *Ioſephus* doth demonſtrate againſt *Appion* the Pagan, and *Lactantius*, and other approoued Authors are euidence: moſt part of the things recounted in the olde Teſtament were done before many of the panime Gods were borne: and the laſt writers of holy Scriptures, *Eſdras, Aggeus, Zachary*, & *Mallachy* were before moſt of the heathen Hiſtorians. *Abraham* as the Gentiles thẽſelues acknowledge, was long before any of their Gods were extant: the eldeſt of their Poets were not before *Salomon*, which was aboue 900. yeares after *Abraham*. And *Moyſes* himſelfe was much more ancient then *Ceres, Vulcan, Mercury, Apollo, Æſculapius, Caſtor, Pollux, Hercules*, & other their feigned gods and both cõcerning thoſe things he recorded before, frõ the firſt creation vnto his time, he proued thẽ with ſo many miracles, that could not be vntrue, that he was taken for God, and accounted a wonder of the worlde. The reaſon why the Pagans receaued not thoſe holy Scriptures, was becauſe they preſcribe a more ſeuere Religion, then their licentious mindes allowed, and ouerthrowe the corporieties, pluralities, & ſuch impoſsible mutations which they allowe in diuinity, which all reaſon knoweth to be ridiculous. And yet beſides the mighty Perſian Emperours, *Cirus*, & *Darius*, King *Ptolomy, Aram*, and others, that honoured the Iſraelites, their holy lawe, and Teſtament, not onlie the *Sibils*, and other for propheſie moſt renowned amonge thoſe Pagans, confirme the thinges that bee intreated in them. But many others of the greateſt account, as well amonge them, as in later ages: as *Melo, Eupolemus, Triſmagiſtus, Leodemus Ariſteus, Artabanus, Numenius, Pithagoras, Alexander Polyhiſtor, Appion, Porphiry, Saconeathan*,

*The vndoubted Authority of holy Scriptures.*

*Antiquity.*

Iren. l. 1. c. 20. 22. 29. Epiph. hær. 66. Euth. part. 2. panopl. tit. 23. cap. 1. Anton. p. 4. tit. 11. c. 7. Berg. hiſt. in Diag. Geneb. Chr. lib. 1.

Ioſeph. l. 1. cont. Appiõ. Lactant. l. 1. 2. 3. 4. diu. inſt. Euſ. in Chro.

Euphemer. meſſ. in geneal. Deor. Cicero. nat. Deor. Lactant. l. 1. 2. diu. inſt.

Actabã. hiſt. Iud. Polyh. hiſt. Eupol. &c.

1. Eſd. 1. 2. 3. 4. 5. 6. 7. &c. Ariſt. lib. 72. interpret. 3. Reg. 5. Sibil. apud Lact. lib. 2. 3. 4. 5. diu. inſtit. D. Tho. 3. p. Gra. de Simb Ioſeph. l. 1. antiq.

Euf.lib. 9. præp. cap. 4. Nicl.l.fraud. Artab. hist. Iud.Polyh. hist. Iud. Arist. lib. de Iob. Thalmud. Alcoran. Arist. l. 72. interpret. Ioseph.l.10. cont App. App. lib. 4. cont. Iud. Porphyr. l. 4. cont. Christ. Ioseph. l. 1. 3. antiq. Orph. in car. Iustin. Mart. Orat. ad Anton. pium. Dion. halic. lib. 4.

*Berosus*, *Caldæus*, *Ieronimus Ægiptius*, *Nicolaus Damascenus*, *Abydenus*, many monuments in the late discouered worlde, *Mahumet*, the whole Sinagogue of the later *Rabbines*, all *Iewes*, and *Turkes* (of Christians there is no doubt) giue testimoniy to those thinges, that be recorded in those holy writings. Of Iewes and Mahumetanes there is no difficulty allowing the bookes of the olde Testament, which is enough for my purpose now to prooue a God, and Religion, so religiously commended in that law. For the Gentile Pagans, I haue cited their moste auncient, and to exemplifie in one of theyr first: *Orpheus* had those sacred bookes, and the misteries recorded in them in highest esteeme, and plainly both affirmed that they were most ancient, and delinered by God himselfe, his wordes (when he had cited many thinges from thence) are these.

*Priscorum hæc nos docuerunt omnia voces,*
*Quas binis tabulis Deus olim tradidit illis.*

*The voices of ancients haue taught vs these things, which GOD deliuered to them in two tables.* Could *Moyses* (if he were aliue againe) to whom they were deliuered, speake more plainelye? And the Testimonye of the *Sibils* were so manifest herein, that it was made death by the Pagan lawes, to reade theyr bookes. And *Attillius* himselfe *Duum vir*, one of the two principall men, to whome their custody was commited, only because he wrote them forth, was sewed into a sacke and cast into the Sea.

*The holines & excellencie of the writers of holy scriptures aboue al other writers.*

If wee make comparison betweene the writers of holie Scriptures and *Diagoras*, and such Atheists as woulde denie them, or the Panin Philosophers, though wee single them forth that were accounted best, there is no semblance of proporrtion. The prophets & writers of holie Scriptures, were moste holye, and a spectacle of Sanctity to all generations, and many of them dyed, for defence of those thinges they committed to writing. Manye of the Philosophers were of such filthie liues, that theyr sinnes are not to be named, and their errors intollerable, and theyr chiefest men (as themselues acknowledg) did not as they did beleeue, beleeuing one God with Scriptures, and seruing Idols, as *Plato* to *Dionisius* giueth plaine witnesse of himselfe.

Heb. 11. &c. Plato ep. 13. ad Dionis.

*Effecacie of the doctrine in holy scriptures.*

If we consider the effycacie of the doctrine of those holy writers, although they intreated of hard, most difficult, & vnpleasing things to sensuall mindes, & the Pagan Philosophers of pleasing & delightful things: yet the austere doctrine of them hath almost conuerted the whole world to liue as they beleeued, and these philosophers could neuer yet alure one kingdome, or Citie, euen to thinke only as they taught. And yet (as I will proue hereafter) they haue attempted it by all meanes they coulde.

If

If wee talke of consent, or disagreement in writers: ( vppon which in matters of Authoritie, Truth or Falsehoode, may easilie be concluded:) No man is ignorant that not onlie all Pagan and prophane Historians disagree among themselues, and all Philosophers of the deuided Sects of *Stoicks*, *Peripateticks*, *Accademicks*, and *Epicures*, but the professors of euerie of these sects were at warre amonge themselues, and yet they entreated onlie of naturall things, proportionate to humane capacitye: contrariewise, not onely the sacred histories of Scriptures agree, but all theyr Writers, Prophets, Priests, Euangelists, and Apostles agree in one, without any leaste difference or variance in doctrine, and yet they all entreate of matters Supernaturall, and aboue the reache of mans reason. Wherefore, I conclude in this Argument, when so many holy writers, as *Moyses David*, *Esdras*, *Ieremy*, *Ezechiell*, *Daniell*, *Zachary*, *Malachy*, *S. Mathew*, *Marke*, *Luke*, *Iohn*, *Peter*, *Paul*, *Iames* and others, were so diuided in time, seperated in place, as Egipt, Ierusalem, Babilon, Rome and others where they wrote, so distinct in natures, and naturall conceits, and iudgments, as all men are, and yet in so many bookes as the Scriptures conteyne: and in so many supernatural mysteries agreed vniformely togither, without the least dissent or cōtradictiō: this Direction must needs proceed of God, who penetrateth all thinges, and cannot leade into error. When I see so myraculous agreement in the 72. that by the appoyntement of King *Ptolomey* of Egipt, translated the olde Testament, recorded by enemies, and like assistance in later handlers of those Sacred works: and farther consider, how in so manie garboiles and troubles of Nations, many writings of the most allowed Pagans haue perished, & yet these haue bin preserued in al the most famous languages of the world. I cannot be induced but they be the euidence of God, and preserued by him. Further, when I perceaue the greatest humane authority that can be cited for any monument, vsed for the crediting of these religious testaments, as for the books of the first testament all Christians, Iews, Mahumetās, & many Gentils consenting that they be holy, & for euery book of the new testament besides the authorities of all schooles, vniuersities, & thousands of prouinciall Sinods, the whole christian world in their most learned doctors & fathers assembled 20. times in general councels, and confirming them al by their sentence: and neuer so anie ten persons togither iudicially agreeing to approue any Pagan writer in al things: I cannot be of opinyon but these books were penned by holie instinct from God. Moreouer when the light and law of nature & reason make me secure, and al Philosophers, Christians, Pagans, & the learned of the whole worlde euer agreed togither in this, (and giue it for a distin-

*The wonderful consent in all things of all writers of holy Scriptures.*

*The myraculous translation, & preseruation of scriptures.*

Arist. li. 72. interpret.

*The great authorization of Scriptures, in humane proceedinges.*

Thalm. Alcoazoar. I. I. tom. I. 2. Concil. Bel. Chron. Genebr. Chron.

*Certayne foretelling, of future contingēs thynges:*

ction betweene a limmited and infinite power, ) that future things which haue no certaintie in their causes, cannot certainely be knowne and foretolde, but by an infinite knowledge, penetrating things, more perfectlie then they be in their causes, and whosoeuer certainly prophesieth of such thinges, must needs receaue that faculty from God, which can be ignorant of no effect: But the whole sacred Scripture is euidence, that manie things within their causes be moste vncertaine, as depending of the freedome of mans will and election, & others more secret only te be produced at the moste secret will and pleasure, and by the omnipotent power of god himself, haue beene as certainly and plainly foretolde, with their manner and circumstances, many yeares before they came to passe, as if they had beene present witnesses of those things, as so many *Predictions of Abraham, Iacob, Moises, Dauid, Daniel, Esay, Ieremy, Zachary, Christ, his Apostles,* and others in holie Scriptures of the regiment of Iuda, the diuision of the land of Canaan, the perpetual desolation of Ierico, of the birth and acts of *Iosias,* 300. yeares before he was borne, the destruction of Babilon by king *Cirus,* & his name foretolde 200. yeres before he came. And two witnesses named of it, *Vrias* and *Zacharias* which were not borne manie yeares after this was prophesied. The captyuitie of the Israelites in Babilon, the time of that continuance and theyr deliuery againe in the time of *Esdras.* The destruction of *Balsazar* king of Babilon, and the very night of his desolation. The time of the comming of the *Messias,* his life, death, resurrection, ascention, and other misteries, as they were effected in Christ, the miracles which happened then, the reprobation of the Iewish people, conuersion of the Gentiles, destruction of Ierusalem, the pittifull miseries it did endure, and the like which were vncertaine things, aud yet were as certainly foretolde, as they were certaine when they were performed: therfore seing these things be so vndoubtedly come to passe, we cannot make question of anie other to bee effected in his time hereafter, the one beinge as difficult to be foreseene as the other, and conseqently much more all other matters reuealed in those holy writings which be of more easie subiect, are vnfallible true, and so to be beleeued.

Lastly to put all out of doubt, that euen from the first time of committing those misteries to writing, by the holy pen men of sacred Scriptures, euery man might be secure they were spoken and reuealed of God, which could neither be deceaued in himself, or bring others into error: So many miraculous workes and operations, which none but a diuine power, and such as had aurhority frō him could effect, were giuen vnto those chosen Scribes of his holie lawe, and wrought by them to confirme the truth of those

Gen. 12.13. 15. 17. Exod. 12. Gen. 49. Numer. 34. 35. 36. Ios. 15. 16. 17. Deut. 31. 32. Ios. 6. 3. Reg. 12. 4. Reg. 23. 4. Reg. 20. Is. 5. 15. 24. 25. 13. 8. Heirem. 26. Zachar. 1. Hier. 37. 29. 38. 39. 25. 4. Reg. 24. 25. 1. Esd. 1. 2. Esd. 2. Dan. 9. 5. Is. 53. Dan. 10. 9. Is. 42. 40. 50 Malach. 3. Is. 1. Zach. 9. Psal. 80. Os. 2. 3. 6. Dan. 2. Agg. 2. Zachar. 11. Malach. 1. Is. 1. 2. 3. 5. 6. &c. Math. 24. Marc. 13. Luc. 21. 19. &c.

*Miracls to proone the scriptures, that by impossibilitie, they cannot be vntrue.*

those misteries they committed to those holy bookes, that the whole world hath wondred at those miracles: And al Philosophers euer confessed, that such things hauing no cause or power of their production in nature, could not be poduced but by the assistance of an infinit and illimited Agent: & not by him to confirme any falshood or thing vntue. The number of these signes be too many to be remembred, & not only the Scriptures be full of those strange & meruailous workes, but they be reported by heathen writers, and wrought often times in open spectacles and places of viewe before whole multitudes of people, that coulde not be deceaued: of which I shal haue oportunity of speech hereafter, & therfore pas them ouer in this place. Wherefore I may saie in this pointe as that learned Schoole man said in the like: *Domine si decepti sumus, a te decepti sumus. O lord if wee bee deceaued, wee are deceaued by thee.* For no other power coulde effect these things; and not to giue credit to any mistery so confirmed, is the greatest obstinacie aud incredulity can be assigned. Therefore the holy scriptures by no possibility can be vntrue: and if there were no other Argument, either for relgiō in general, or that in particuler which I wil defend; it were most peruerse and obdurate infidelity to deny it, without farther proofe.

Part. 3. Ref. Aug. mirael. & c. 10. 11. seq. &c. Rich. de S. vict.

## Chap. 6. *The example and euidence of all Nations, states of people, and particuler persons.*

THvs wee see, how that diuine maiesty which claimeth reuerence at our handes, is infinite, and euerlastinge, our lord, creator, omnipotent to reward, if we render worshippe, iust and powerable to punish, if we denie it: We are his creatures, seruants, and depending of him in all we are, we haue, or can expect, whether we liue or dye, we are, and must be in his subiection, all reasons dyuine, and humane, tell vs we must render religion to him, no excuse can be found in iudgement, no reason will defende the contrarie cause: Then let vs trie if we can finde anie hope of comfort in company for this irreligious people. For although no man may followe multytudes into error, neyther the testymonie of anie man, or number of menne (if all the worlde woulde bee so wicked to beecome patrons of irreligion) can giue answere to that which is aleadged against it: yet to men that be reprobate in theyr owne proceedings, and dare not defend theyr condemned impietyes, it is some comfort to haue fellowes in damnation; and these people voide of all truth and piety, will not be ashamed to glory in any practizers of this opiniō, though neuer so wicked and vnreasonable. Then let vs moue this question of worship to all kingdomes, Countries, Cities, Communities, and to al persons of what estate, degree, or condition, that euer were in any authoritie, credit, or reputation, or worthy to be imitated in any time, or age of the world, from the first creation to these dayes, and proue what companions we can finde, for these prophane aud beastly schollers of Irreligion, if any such be at this present, which I rather feare then affirme. If we apeale to the Patriarches, that ruled in the lawe of Nature, from *Adam* to *Moyses*, or to Priestes, Iudges, Prophetes, and Kinges, that ruled in Israell and Iurie, from him to Christ, in all that lawe rhere is no controuersy in that generation: for they did not only professe a Religion, but that in particuler which was the true and lawfull worship of God. If we exhibite this complaint vnto all Rulers, Kinges, Emperours, Priestes, Flamens, Arrheflamens, Oracles, or the Gods them selues of the Gentiles, their very names, and all Histories, will tell vs, although they erred in particuler what this dutie was, yet they all agreed to vse Religion, and euer in their Lawes, Practise, Sacrifyces, & so manyfolde Rites defended it. Let vs enquire of such as were most learned amongest them, their Poets, Philosophers, Prophettes, and they giue consent: so *Lynus Thebius*, that lyued 1430. yeares before Christ, speaketh euen of those things, whereof *Moyses* entreated, *Amphion, Mercurius, Liricus, Orpheus Museus, Homer*, and *Æsiodus*, are not vnlyke, and all the later professe Religion. And dyuers of their most learned, auncient, and approoued Philosophers confirmed christian worship (so far they were from denying pietie) but of this hereafter. And from the first to the last, they all with mutuall agreement teach Religion is to be vsed. So *Phegous*, that liued so neare to the deluge, so *Mercurus Trismagistus, Cadmus, Esculapius, Thales, Milesius, Chilon, Pithacus, Bias, Periander, Pheresides, Pithagoras, Anacharsis, Alcmeon, Epinenides, Zenophanes, Democritus, Heraclitus, Themistocles, Aristides, Anaxagoras, Empedocles, Permenides, Milesius, Hipocrates, Zeno, Socrates, Alcibiades, Isocrates, Zenophon, Achita, Plato, Antisthenes, Spensippus, Ermias, Demosthenes, Aristotle, Dion, Carmeides, Eschines. Xenophilus, Phedron, Xenocrates, Hermegitius, Apuleius, Plotinus, Dema, Chalisthenes, Zenon, Chrisippus, Polemon Crates*, and *Crates Licon, Tymon, Diogines* and *Diogines, Onesicitus, Aristobilus, Archimedes, Panetius, Poßidonius, Cathon, Cato*, and the rest generallie giue vs answere, taught in learning, and practised in life, that Relygion is to be vsed, and had in highest estimation. If wee consult with the renowned *Sibils*, so famous in all chiefest Nations of the world, Italie, Greece, Persia, Siria, Egipt, as *Sibilla, Persica, Libica, Delphica, Cumæa, Erithræa, Samia, Cumena, Hellespontica, Phrisia*, and *Tiburta*, or *Tiburtina*, they tell vs in particuler of christian worship, so doe others which liued after, which wil be more euident in

*Patriarches, Priestes, prophets, &c.* Gen. c. 3. 4. Exod. Num. Leuit. Iudic. cap. 2. Phil. Iud. hist Ioseph. lib. antiq. bell. Arist. lib. 72 interpret. Cic l. de Nat Deor. l. diu. Lact. l. 1. 2. 3. 4. &c. diu. instit. Bed. hist. ang *All Kinges, Rulers, priests, Oracles, Arch flamens, &c. of the Gētiles.* Hermod. l. 1. disciplin. Phil. Berg. histor. Euseb. hist. Virg. Bucol. Iust. in Apol Lac. sup. &c. *Poets. Phylosophers.* Iust. tract. 2. Argument. 1 S. Aug. apud Berg. hist.

*Sybilles.* Euri. in prol. Iam. Chrisip. l. diu Neu. lib. bel. Punic. Aristot. in annal. Lactant. lib. diu. instit. Cic. l. Nat. Deor. l. diu. Berg. hist. in Sibil. &c. Lact. in Sibil

in my Arguments for Christians, against externall Infidels. If we wil debate this cause with those, who for their wisdome were called, and euer named the sage and most prudent in the worlde, *Thales*, and his companions; they haue spoken and practised the same, and their religious wittes were the greatest cause of their so excellent cognomination. If wee will propounde this question to the most ancient Legists, and Law-makers, Rulers, States, and kingdomes of the worlde, they will witnesse it was so, from their first foundation. Before the deluge, there is none or little memory kept, but in holy Scriptures, which teach the true Religion. After the deluge, *Noe* that holy and religious Patriarke was Prince in the world, of him and his children, proceeded all later generations. Howe religious he was, it needeth no recitation, he liued after the Fludde 350. yeares, and, as *Philo* is witnesse, did see 14000. of men that were descended from him, by which offspring all Nations of the worlde, were after inhabited, and of his children, *Sem, Cham*, and *Iaphet*, which were borne before the Fludde, were founded 72. Nations, all the founders of these Nations, were the grandchildrē of that holy religious *Noe*, liuing in his time, instructed of him, and coulde not eyther be vtterly irreligions in themselues, or institute nations without Religion: especially when Idolatry & false worships were not knowne in the worlde, some hundred years after these things. And their first God *Lisania* surnamed *Iupiter*, liued in Archadia a country obscure, and inhabited of a barbarous and sauage people, which neither by themselues, nor by any Rulers they had coulde perswade other nations, to their so vilde example. And this superstitious impietie of Idolatrie, was so contemptible to ciuill Nations, that when *Orpheus* which was so pleasing eloquent, that he coulde moue all affections, went aboute to perswade the worshippe of *Bacchus* to the Grecians, hee was so odyous to that Nation, that the woemen themselues killed him with spades, and threw his bodie into the riuer Heber. And when Idolatry was setled in the world, there neuer was any kingedome, nation, state, prouince or cytie, but it euer professed a Religyon: and if anie pryuate man beecame so impyous and ouerwhelmed in sinne, that to excuse his wickednesse, he wished, or protested there was no worshippe to bee vsed, hee was presentlye exploded forthe of all places, and exyled for a monster in nature. So *Dyagoras* which is supposed to be the firste author of this inyquitie, was noted for a *Prodygium*, syrnamed *Atheos*, a denyer of GOD, or Gods, and banished from mens socyetie, liued and dyed myserablie, although wee maie suppose that he onelie denyed the Pagan Gods, and worshippe to them, as his wordes cited in the plurall number doe signifie, as also we

S. Anton. 1. part. hist. Insr. tract. 2. Argu. 1. &c.
*Sages & wise men.*
Phil. Berg. histor. Cic. Eus. &c.
*Legists and Law-makers.*
Genes. Gen. cap. 9.
Phil. Iud. in hist. Berg. l. 2. hist. f. 4. Ioseph. l. 1. antiquit.
Lact. fir. lib. diu. instit. Bergom. in hist. supr. Cicer. lib. de Nat. Deor. instit Apol. Diodor. Sic. lib. 5. hist. Plin. lib. hist. nat. Bergom. lib. 3. hist.
Eus. in Chro. Cicer. l. 3. de Nat. Deor. Berg. lib. 5. hist. fol. 61.

Bergō. hist. sup. li 5. fol. 62.

may construe that saying of *Protagoras, De Dijs non posse statuere an sint, vel non sint,* That he coulde not determine of the Gods, whether there were anie such or no. And yet for that saying he was exciled Athens, driuen into the Ilands, and his bookes consumed with fyre. And as *Lactantius* witnesseth, these men at their deathes, recanted their impious opinion, and exercising Religion, called for helpe of a superior power. After rhese, *Epicurius,* that Master and Doctor of beastialitie, was so bewitched with pleasures, that he denyed the prouidence of GOD to man, and framing a God like to himselse, affyrmed, that he which is *purus actus,* only acte, was idle, and to make himselfe a beast, teaching that only pleasure in this lyfe was mans felicytie, doubted not to affirme the soule to be mortall, and perishe with the hodie, and gaue this document, *Surge, ede, bibe, lude, post mortem nulla voluptas.* Ryse, eate, drinke, and play, there is no pleasure after death. But he became so odious to all people, that his very name is a cognomination to all beastly, and carnall men, from him, to these dayes: and yet Saint *Hierome* sayth, that he was a man vtterly vnlearned, and could not reade, others, as *Cicero,* excuse him from those errors. But howsoeuer it be, the testimonie of a beast, and voluptuous man, is no credite to their cause, but a condemnation, *Lucretius* also, drowned in the like wickednesse of lyfe, defended the same irreligious opinions, was so besotted in lust and lasciuiousnes, that he was madde with verie lecherous passions, and killed himselfe with his owne handes. Or if (as some suppose) any companie of the vnnaturall and more then beastlie *Anthropophages* of Brasilea liued without any law or religion at the time of the comming of the Christian Portugals thither, (which is vncertaine of this, and neuer suspected of any other people) yet the example of such which committed those most fylthy synnes of daylie practised and studied murthers, which as their name is witnesse; those which write of that Nation recount, and experience prooueth, eate, deuoure those they murder, and keepe men and women of fayrest complection, to bring children, which they only reserue for slaughter, and eate, euen their nearest friendes, and committe other offences not to be named; is not to be imitated, but detested for more then brutish, and vnreasonable. These be the authors, and patrons of this impietie, which the whole worlde in so manye thousande yeares, hath noted for beastes, madde men, fylthie monsters, and excrements of the people, such as all practisers and well wishers to that blasphemie, be in these our daies, theues, pirats, murderers, adulterers, drunkards, and men so inexcusable in all wickednes, that they haue taken their harbour in the mouth of hell, beginning to be damned in this lyfe. These

Lact. supr.

August. lib. 18. ciuit.

Hier. de Epi. & apud Berg sup. lib. 5. fol. 64.

Cic. l. 3. de fin. & l. 1. & 2

Lodouic. Molin. in 1. part.

D. Thom. q. 2. art. 1.

Petr. Maff. hist. ind.

Osor. hist. ind.

Epist. Indic.

Monster. in Cosmog.

be

be the fruites of diuision in Religion: the manifolde superstitions of the Gentiles, and the wickednes which they practised, was the fall of *Diagoras*, *Protagoras*, *Epicurus*, and *Lucretius*: the heresies, and pluralities of religions amongste Protestantes, and their impieties, haue brooded vp this beastly generation, as all hereticall ages haue done, at which time this schoole hath most flourished: so that in so many generations, as haue bin, there neuer was so much as any priuat man, which in iudgment affirmed this blasphemous and rebellious wickednes, but euer when they were free from passions, or in times of want, as sicknes, death, and other calamities, professed a religion, and called for helpe, and neuer denied it, but when they were, either vtterly spoyled of their wittes and reason, as *Lucretius*, or their opinion so vncertaine, that either they neuer thought any such absurditie, or else it was so soone exploded, that it coulde not be remembred, as that of *Epicurus*, which, as some suppose, wrote more then any of the Philosophers, & yet in the time of *Cicero*, which liued within 300 years, it was so doubtfull what opinion *Epicurus* taught, that the same *Cicero* affirmeth, he was a man of great sobrietie, and temperance, teaching religion, the prouidence of God, the immortality of the soule, constituting the felicitie of man, in spirituall, and soule pleasure: and *Plutarch* affirmeth that he sacrificed, and practised religion. So that it is manifest, if euer any man defended that most filthy errour, he was condemned of God, and all people for that offence, and of himselfe when he was of better iudgment, and more to be beleeued. In so much that there is not the authoritie of one man, speaking in iudgment, as a man and reasonable creature, that euer gaue conutenance to this blasphemous sentence, but the whole worlde in all times, and places, haue explauded it, for the most impious, sacriledgious, damnable, and vnnaturall sinne. Then to conclude this reason of humane authoritie: the worlde from the first creation, hath now endured by the Hebrewe account, aboue 5500. yeares, by the other computation, 6700. yeares, which if it be compared to any age, or generation, there is no proportion. The globe of the earth, according to the least account, conteyneth in circuite, 19080. miles; as *Fernelius* measureth, 24514. miles; by the sentence of *Alphraganus*, *Almæon*, *Thebitius*, and others, 20400. by *Ptolomæus*, 22500. by *Eratosthenes*, 31500. by *Hipparcus*, 34625. by that opinion which *Aristotle* reciteth, fiftie thousand, and if wee will followe the measure which was taken by the moste learned Geometricians in thirtie yeares labour, by the appointment, and charges of *Iulius Cesar* the Emperour, when the most exact a measurement was vsed, the habitable earth at that time, was founde to bee in circuite,

Berg. hist. supr.

Laer. de Epic. Aug. lib. 18. ciu.

Plut. l. non Poss. &c.

Isod. lib. 3. Etymol.
Aug. l. 5. ciu. cap. 20.
Christ. Cl. in Sph. fol. 229
Fernel. Ambian Cosmother.
Erast. apud Macrob. lib. 1. in Som. Scip.
Arist. lib. 2. de Cæl.
Priscian in sua Cosmog.
Phil. Berg. hist. in Iul. Cæs. fol 96. lib. 7.
Ortel. in Cos
Marst, in Cos
Pet. Maf. hist
Osor. hist.

 31500.

31500. miles, what vaste Regions, and populous Nations haue beene discried since then, no man can be ignorant: the number of the kingdomes, countries, cities, townes, and prouinces, is innumerable: there were before the comming of Christ, infinite idolatries in the world, since his Incarnation; besides sects amongst the Iewes, and Mahumetans not to bee numbred among Christians (if we ioine these present heresies which now raigne, almost 300.) to those 400. & more which haue bin in former ages, there haue bin 700. false professions in christianity, & the impiety of men hath bin such, especially in times of errors, that there was neuer almost any truth so euident, but by one citie, towne, countrie, company of people or other, it hath beene denied: only this verity of Religion, and obligation of worship to God, hath beene so manifest, that in so many thousands of yeares, in no one age, yeare, or day, in so many vaste and populous nations, no little kingdome, prouince, citie, towne, village, or priuate person, but in such sence as I haue declared, and to their owne confusion, called it into question.

Orig. in Exod. Lact. firm. li. 1. 2. 3. &c. Diu. instit. Iustin. Apol. Cicero. lib. de Nat. Deor Casp. Vlenb. li. 22. Caus. Rain. Calu. Epyphan. li. hæres. August. lib. hær. Ber. Lutzenb. Catal. hæret.

## Chap. 7. *Testimony of all intellectuall Creatures.*

OR if the testimony of all inferiour things, the witnesse of the whole worlde, and all reasonable men from the first foundation, till nowe so learned and wise, euery particuler mans practise, and experience by all sences and powers of knowledge, all reasons that can bee alleadged, all proofe in reason that can be vsed, the vniforme & euer agreeing consent, and example of al creatures wil not serue to dispute this question, against the blinde, senceles, and vnreasonablie deluded, and wantonly bewitched appetites of some one, or a fewe beastly and franticke men: let vs seeke for a triall, to intellectuall and spirituall creatures, which as by their perfection of nature, they are of higher, and more infallible iudgment, so in respect they are freed, and exempted of corporall and bodily composition, from whence this blindnes of sensuality proceedeth, are like to giue the truest sentence: such be the heauenly spirits, seperated soules, & the diuels themselues, though depriued of grace, yet perfect in naturall vnderstanding. All testimonies are recorde, all Historians, thousands & millions of men, that haue beene present witnesses, and euery particuler person, euen of this impious schoole it selfe, hath prooued by one experimentall argument, or other, that there be such perfect intellectuall creatures. The rare, & wonderfull effects, which be daily wrought by such meanes, the apparitions of Angelles, illusions of Diuels, their workes, tempests, plagues,

Script. Gen. Tob. Iudih. Dan. Thalm. Iud. Alcor. Mahum. Ioseph. Phil. Arist. Plat. Merc. Tris. Dion. &c. Euseb. l. hist Eccl. Niceph hist. Bed. li. 1.2.3.4.&c. hist. Angl. Gregor. lib. Dialog. Ioseph. lib. antiq. Cris. Arist. l. de cæl. &c.

plagues, and other miseries they haue procured their possessing bodies both of men, and woemen, and beasts, where their effectes are manifest, the appearing of soules deuided, and seperated from their bodies, and still enduring after death, some miraculously vnited againe, and telling what they endured in their seperation, others not restored, reporting either the ioyes they found, if they were trulie religious, or the paines they endured, if they were prophane and wicked, haue testified these thinges. The infinite miracles, and supernaturall effects, which the Angels, and holie religious soules haue wrought in their apparitions, haue euidentlie confirmed their sentence to be true. The vnspekeable torments of the wicked irreligious soules, damned for impietie and irreuerence, prooued by vndeniable arguments, and the deuils, potent and wise, conquered and cast out by pore religious men by nature their inferiors, & these things seene, prooued, witnessed, & written by millions of men of greatest iudgment, Emperors, Kings, Princes, Philosophers, Magicians, & of al condions, not onlie priuate men & in secret, but greatest assemblies in publicke places, are sufficient argument in this cause. But in respect these testimonies haue chieflie beene vsed to prooue true religion in particuler, and not the necessitie of reuerence in general, which for the euidence thereof needeth no such probation, I will passe it ouer to the proper place, againste externall infidels and heretickes, where it shall be handled to the manifest confusion of all misbeleeuers, not onelie Atheists, Epicures, and deniers of worshippe, but all enemies of christian catholike doctrine.

Gen. Tob. Iudith. Greg. l. Dial. Bed. hist. Euseb l. hist. eccles. &c.

Tract. 2. inf. & 2. part. Resol. Ar. 58. 59. 60. 61. 62.

## Chap. 8. *Of the miraculous and most certayne testimony of God.*

I Will passe ouer in this place, the testimony of the Creator, and so manie thousandes of miraculous, and most certaine supernaturall Arguments of God, which can neither be deceaued in himselfe, or be cause of erring vnto others, both in regarde they are needeles in this matter neuer called so farre into question, that it craueth such extraordinary defence, as also that they haue principally beene vsed, to propose true worshippe in particuler to misbeleeuing Nations, of which, neuer any denied a religion in generall. Therefore I am to make demonstration by that Argument hereafter, against all professors of false worships, which in some manner wil also appeare in my Chapters following, of the extraordinary punishment God hath afflicted vpon the irreligious, and the miraculous fauours wherewith he hath honoured his holy, and true worshippers: in this place onely I affirme since the first miraculous creation of man in

Tract. 2. inf. Arg. 1. 2, 6. Part. 2. Reso. Arg. 65. 66. Cap. 10. 11. seq.

Gen, 1. 2. 3.

the beginning, and the supernaturall prouidence of God ouer him, while he continued in obedience, and strange punishing of him, for his neglect of dutie therin, he euer obserued the same order in al estates & conditiōs. The punishment of *Adam*, drowning of the world, confusion of the Tower of Babell, destruction of the Egiptians, abolishing of Idols, desolation of the Iewes, and a thousand strange and miraculous punishments, imposed vpon the irreligious, and contrariewise as strange and wouderfull fauours towardes the godly, exceeding all limits of nature, witnessed by millions of present witnesses, Princes, and whole countries and registred by most credible writers, both Pagan, Mahumetan, Iewish, & true beleeuers are euidence.

Sibil. apud Lact. l diu inst. apud Varr. Ioseph &c. Gen. 6. 7. 8. 11. Exod. 6. 7. 8. 9. 10. 11. 12. 13. Ioseph. l ant. Suet. in Oct. cap. 95. Mahum. in Alcoran Rabb. lib. gener Chr. Calcid. lib. 2. in tin. Sibil. li. 8. oracl. Plin. l. 2. hist. nat. c. 31. Su. in tiber. cap. 48. Dio. l. 57. Plutarch. lib. defect oracul. Dion. l. 37.

## Chap. 9. *Testimonie and Example of all creatures euen insensible.*

AND this religious worshippe is so vniuersally due, and to be performed, that if the very sensible and insensible thinges that are not capable of vnderstanding, were able to vtter that by wordes, which they vniformely practise in their operations, or supernaturallie declare (as often times they haue to the admiration of all, and confusion of such men) that naturall instinct and desire, which is imparted to them all, to do homage and reuerence to their Creator, they would assemble themselues in generall councell against this impious people, and condemne them to be the most vnnaturall and sencelesse monsters of the worlde. For the vnuiolable decree of nature is, that euery effect must yeelde a certaine honor and reuerence to the cause by which it is produced, and exalted: so in creatures of vnderstanding, the childe honoreth the parents by which he was begotten, brought vp, and nourished, the scholer his master, by whome he was instructed, the subiect his soueraigne, the seruant his master by whome they are ruled, and euery depending thing, that more excellent Regent of whome it hath dependance. And all insensible things with one consent doe answere by their acts and deedes, that they owe religion vnto God, are bounde to worship him, and in their kinde performe it: for the heauens and celestiall spheres, so all elements and inferiour creatures, as well liuing, as wanting life, all remayning in that order, in which they were created, and effecting those offices to which they were ordeyned, and neuer varying from that dutie, which is the greatest homage and religion such things can shewe, and that, which the Prophets *Dauid*, and *Daniell*, call the worship and reuerence of God, because in this dutiful obedience, their dependancie is witnessed, and the glory and honour

Psal. 102. Dan. 3. Psal. 18.

nour of God, proposed to be remembred and reuerenced of intellectuall, and reasonable men. And *Daniel*, making a recapitulation of the duty of all creatures to their Creator, expresing that, to which they are obliged by nature, after he had recounted the celestiall, and intellectuall spirits, and the dutie of Israell the chosen of God, his Priests, seruants, spirits, & soules of the iust, religious men, and particuler persons deuoted to him, how they must worship, and reuerence their Creator; he inciteth all inferiour creatures to the same, or rather man so perfect and excellent a worke of God, by the exemplar obedience of inferior things. Where he numbreth the heauens, sunne, moone, stars, and all celestiall bodies, *benedicere, laudare, & superexaltare eum in secula*, *to blesse, praise, and exalte him for euer.* And not only those celestiall and more perfect bodies, but inferiour creatures, as the elements, fire, aire, water, earth, mountaines, hils, seas, riuers, fishes foules, beasts, and other meane and meteorologicall thinges, raine, dewe, frosts, yse, snowe, lightnings, thunders, clowdes, day, night, light, heate, colde, and that which is nothing but only a priuation, as darknes, and the like, which blesse, praise, and exalte him, without intermision, rendring reuerence and honor vnto him, as euery mā daily experienceth they doe, and shoulde be as violent, and portentious a thing for the meanest of them not to performe, as the sunne to lose his light, the earth to be vnstable, or any other deformity that can be in nature. Then how much more rebellious and trayterous is the neglect of doing that dutie in man, by so many titles more endebted to his Creator, then any of those creatures, which were all prouided for his vse and necesity, to shewe this religious obedience to his God? especially if he shoulde not only neglect to doe it, but deny it to be done, as Atheists and impious Nullifidians doe.

## Chap. 10. *The extraordinary and strange punnishments inflicted vpon the Irreligious, and rebellion of all creatures against them for that cause.*

YEA the irreligion and dutilesse behauiour of man is so vnnaturallie, that all those creatures which were ordeyned to be his seruants, & so vnuariable reuerence their maker, that it were a prodigious thing for thē not to do it, yet to shew the greatnes of mans obligation more then theirs: how often haue they forsaken their naturall institutiō at the disobedience of irreligious men, to testify the greatnes of their iniquities, & vngratfulnes to their Creator: proouing thereby, it is more monstrous for man to deny worship & religion vnto God, then for the earth not to support vs, the aire to refresh vs, the fire to comfort vs, & all other creatures to deny their natural operations. So in the first creation, for the Irrelion of *Adam* our progenitor, the earth and all creatures, ouer which God had giuen him ful dominiõ in his state of obedience, rebelled against him. In the daies of *Noe*, when the irreligious world would not be obedient vnto God, the Element of water miraculously, ascended ouer the whole globe of the earth, 15. cubits higher then the highest mountaine, least any thing should be preserued from destruction: and only the religious familie of *Noe* and such creatures as he had gathered togither were miraculously preserued, witnessed not only in holy Scriptures, but in diuers Pagan and other authors, *Hieronimus Ægiptius*, *Mnaseas Damascenus*, *Iosephus*, *Alexander Polihistor*, *Melon*, *Eupolemus*, and others, and prooued by diuers effectes, which could proceede of no other cause. How strangly did God punish the irreligious builders of the tower of *Babel*, and consounded them so that no man vnderstood what was spoken by others, which besides the holy Scriptures, *Iosephus*, *Sibils*, and other witnesse, and the diuersities of tongues to this day, otherwise without originall, are euidence. At which time, and in punishment of which irreligious offence, so many monsters in humane nature were produced, a great scandal to this Epicurish scoole, when it is manifest they were brought forth to be a memoriall, and euerduring penance to mankind, for the same iniquitie and irreligion they defende; this was the beginning of the *Monoclistes*, *Hermophrodites*, *Acephalistes*, *Pigmes*, *Giants*, *Sciopedes*, *Cinocephalists*, and others whose shapes punishments of Irreligion, are rather to be concealed thẽ vttered: only hereby is euident how monstrous Irreligion is, which is repaied with so monstrous penalties. How did God in the time of *Abraham*, miraculously cause the fire, against the naturall propensitie to descend, and destroy all the Irreligious people of Sodome, and those Cities, preseruing the house and familie of religious *Loth*, as both Scriptures, other writers, the piller of Salt into which the incredulous wife of *Loth* was turned, (which *Iosephus* had seene) and other monumentes are record. In the daies of *Moyses* when *Pharao* and his irreligious Egiptians would not permitte the Israelites to worship God, and exercise religion, the same water which miraculously before had giuen passage to the Religious people, drowned King *Pharao*, and his huge armie of prophane Infidels. The base and meane creatures of Frogs, Ciniphes, Flies, Locustes, and such as are ingendred of vile corruption, and the very Metiors them selues that haue no life, as Hayle, Thunder, and Lightnings, yea Darkenes which of it selfe is nothing, and only a priuation of an accident and qualitie of light, so fought against him, that hee and all Egypt were enforced to yeelde, and acknowledge their

Gen. 1. 3. 1. 2.
Gen. cap. 6. 7. 8.
Hier. ægyp. l. anti. Phænic Mnas. Damas lib. 96.
Ioseph. lib. 1 antiq. cap. 3.
Alex. Polyh. &c.
Gen, cap. 11.
Ioseph. lib. antiq.
Sybil. apud Ioseph. & Berg, lib. 2. hist. fol. 6.
1. Orac. Syb.
Aug. lib, 16. ciuit. c. 8.
Plin. l. 7. nat. hist. Solim.
Gen, cap. 19.
Ioseph. lib. antiq.
Ioseph. lib. 3. antiq.
Exod. cap. 8, 10, 9.

their irreligion and disobedience. In the schismaticall and irreligious rebellion, of *Chore*, *Dathan*, and *Abiron*, and their confederates, the earth, the most firme and stable element prouided of God for mans supportation, was opened, and deuoured them S. *Augustine* and *Orosius* are witnesses, that in the irreligious times of the idolatrous Italians, about 70. yeares before Christ, the very domesticall and tamest creaturs, vsed for the seruice of men, rebelled against them, and affirme that their very dogges, horses, oxsen, asses, and other creatures most at the commande of man, sodainly became wilde, ran from their owners, wandring vp and downe with such fiercenesse and contempt to their former masters, and all men, that no man durst, or coulde approach them without daunger. Such prodigious euents appeared against e irreligious people at other times. What supernaturall ecclipse of The Sunne, trembling of the Earth, and renting of most harde and solide Rockes, cryed out against the inhumane and barbarous irreligion of the Iewes, and Gentils at the death of Christ? The earth quaked at such extraordinarie motion, that as the Pagan wrighters affirme, in Asia, so farre distant, twelue Citties were ouerthrowne in such order, that *Tiberius* the Emperour, released their tribute towardes their building againe. The Rockes were torne in peeces, not only about Hierusalem, as the Euangelistes recorde, and Golgatha did witnesse, as S. *Cirill* Bishoppe of Hierusalem reporteth, but in diuerse other farre more remote places, as the mountaine of Auernia in Hetruria, the promontarie of Cayeta, and an hill in Wales, and other Countries. About two hundred yeares agoe, at Sefeelde in Germany, a Village betweene Ausburge, and Iusburge, the harde marble stones of the pauement of the Church, gaue glace, and the grounde opened to swallowe vp the Lorde *Oswalde*, a Noble man of that Countrie, irreligiouslie behauing himselfe, in receauing the blessed Sacrament of the body of Christ, and catching holde of the Altar of the Church made of harde stone, by which he kneeled to communicate, his hande sunke into it, as though it had beene soft clay, the print still remayning so deepe as any man may lay his whole hande therein, as I haue seene, and done: and the blessed Sacrament is reserued, and remayneth in the proper *species* and forme, after so many yeares with watery drops of bloude, in such places as vvere bruised with the teeth of Baron *Oswalde*. All this chauncing in a moste famous assemblie in the festiuitie of Easter, before so many witnesses, and are still to bee seene in the same place, as thousandes can witnesse. How haue the very elements of which our bodies are composed and nourished, persecuted vs for this disobedience? Howe manye irreligious

Num. 16. 26.

Aug. l. 3. ciu. cap. 13. Oros. lib. 5. cap. 12.

Bergom. lib. 12. hist.

Euang. Matt. &c. Dionis. Areopag. ep &c. Phleg. apud Orig. & Eus. Plin. natural. hist. lib. 2. c. 84. Sueton. in Tiber. c. 48 Dio. l. 57. Ciril. Hier. Catec. 13. &c. Euang. Nat. Hieron, ep. 150. q. 8. Regist. eccl. Sefeeld in Ger. sup. hist Ger. &c.

cities, haue beene sunke vp by the earth, whereon they were founded, by
Aug. l. 18. ciuit. the shaking and opening therof: *Bura, Helier*, in Acaia, and in the time
Pantal. chronol. fol. 9. of *Traian* foure Cities in Asia, three in Greece, two in Galatia, How many
drowned by water in the inundation of *Ogigius*, ouerflowing almost all A-
Oros. lib. 7. hist. c. 1. chaia, and the floode of Deucalion in Thessaly? Howe manie infections
Diod. lib. 2. in the ayre, an Element for the comfort and preseruing of life: in the
Consulshippe of *Lucius Cecillius Metellus*, and *Q. Fabius, Maximus Seuerinus*, all
Oros. lib. 4. hist. cap. 4. the irreligious inhabitants of Rome dyed of the pestelence not one remai-
ning: so likewise in the Consulship of *L. Genneus*, and *Q. Serulius*. Howe
hath the Sunne, the very Prince of Planets, and nurse of life, wrought
Oros. l. 3. hist. c. 4. the destruction of thinges, set them so strangely on fire and cosuming
Plat. in Tim. them that some haue affirmed the Elementes and almost the whole world
Oros. lib. 1. hist. c. 11 to haue beene inflamed, and in the Iland of Lippara as it were the mouth
of hell flaming and breaking out in such outrage, that the stony rockes
were set on fire, the Sea boyled, the fishes were killed, and the inha-
bitants suffocated. About such tyme as the regiment of the Irreligious
Turkes began, the Sunne was darkned 17. dayes togither, and gaue no
light. And before in the yeare of Christ 676. about which time, Irreligious
Blond. l. 9. Eut. l. 18. and prophane *Mahumet* entred to delude the worlde, fire fell from heauen,
Fox. t. 1. Mõ. a wonderful rainbowe appeared, & such dreadful signes were seene, that
Pan. Pol. et al in Mahu. men withered away with feare, so excessiue thunder, lightnings, and pe-
stilence reigned, that men thought the end of the worlde to haue beene
come, and *Foxe* himselfe affirmeth, that about the irreligious reuolt of *Luther*, there appeared in Germanie vpon the garments of the Clergy and o-
thers, men and women, bloudie Crosses, and signes and tokens of the
Fox. tom. 2. nailes, spunge, speare, coate, and other things belonging to the passion of
Mon. f. 969. Christ. But of all other nations this matter is most manifest in the Iewish
Io. Car. Fr. Miranb. people, which whẽ it was religious vnto God, was honorable through the
world, and miraculously preserued, but since they fell to their irreligious
forsaking of Christ the *Messias*, all creatures, both reasonable, & vnreaso-
nable, haue sounded alarumme, and proclaimed warres against them.
And to conclude this matter with an example of our own countrey, in the
Tit. Liu. in Bren. time of Paganisme, 300. yeares before Christ; there neuer was any Prince
Pol. Graft. of the British line, so potent & victorious as King *Brennus*, brother to king
hist. fol. 59. *Beline* was, who subdued the *Gaules, Germans, Italians, Grecians*, & many migh-
Stowe. hist. sup. &c. ty Princes, yet when in the top of his pride, he began to make a iest of Religion, & blasphemously to vtter as though none were to be vsed, present-
ly (not to approoue any false religion of the Pagans) but to reprooue the
impietie of *Brennus*, and to manifest the iustice of God vpon such as denie

nie him worship, the earth, as quaking to heare such blasphemous speech trimbled, parte of the Hil *Pernassus* fell vpon his souldiours, and slew them, after haile stones most strange for number and greatnesse destoyed an other parte of his army, wherein he gloried so much, and so wounded that irreligious *Brennus*, that he fell into dispaire and slewe himselfe with his owne sworde. The like punishments (although not alwaies in so prodigious manner) haue fallen vpon all English Kinges, that haue beene Irreligious to the See of Rome: that either they haue beene strangly punished by GOD in their liues, or come to miserable deathes. So likewise all the auncient Pagans, and irreligious Emperours and Princes that were enemies to the Religion of Christ were rewarded.

Epist. Apol.

Euseb. Socr. Soz. Theol. &c. *in those Emp.*

## Chap. 11. *The miraculous obedience and submission of all creatures to the Religious.*

CONTRARIVVISE to those that haue beene most reuerent and religious to God, the same creatures of his haue not only performed and done their ordinary seruice and dutie, but shewed extraordinary obedience, so all sensible thinges as Birdes, Beastes, Fishes, and vnsensible haue done homage not onlye to *Adam* in his religious estate of innocencie, and after to *Noe*, *Helizeus*, *Daniell*, *Ionas*, *Tobias*, and others in the Lawe of *Moyses*, but in the Primatiue Church of Christ to thousandes of martyres and holy Sainctes, as not only approoued ecclesiasticall writers but manie thousandes of Heathen, that were present, haue witnessed. Manie of them chansing in most publique assemblies before Princes and Emperors at the verie Theater of Rome, the most famouse place of spectacles and meetings in the worlde. So the Lion that was appoynted to deuoure S. *Prisca*, a Christian virgine, religious and vowed to Christ, fell downe at her feete before hir persecutors, and manie thousands. So the two Lions did to the two Christian religious brethren *Primus* and *Felicianus*, in the presence of 1200. Pagan witnesses, so that 500. with their families were conuerted. The very seate of *Valence* the Arian Emperor refused to beare his maister, when he would haue sate to giue sentence against S. *Basill* that religious Catholique Bishop, or monkish man as *Luther* calleth him; three pennes one after another refused to giue incke to write the Edict of his exilement, the very cruell Dragons honored and defended *Aman* the Abbot against his enemies. The venimous spiders shrowded and concealed with their webbes S. *Felix* from his Irreligious persecutors. A Rauen a rauening and deuouering birde brought victualles threescore yeares togither, to feede S. *Paule* the

Gen. c. 2. Gen. c. 7. Reg. Dan. Ioh. 2. Tob. &c.

Ex Gest. & Priscill.

Ex Gest. Pri & Felician.

S. Amphil. & al in vita S.Basil.

Luther.

Pal hist. in S Am.Abb. Ex paullin. Natal.

S. Hier. to. I. & in vita Paul. Eremit. S. Athan. in vita S. Antō. Eremite, in the desart while he liued, and when he was dead, the lions digged a graue where this bodie was entombed, Angels, Patriarks, and Prophets accompaning the soule to heauen, as S. *Anthony* the great did see & witnesse: whose sanctitie and religion likewise were such, that the verie diuels thēselues trembled at his verie name. What visions of Angels, lights frō heauen, & miraculous apparitions recorded in irreproueable authors, chancing in the sight of whole townes, and countries, haue approoued the religion & pietie of S. *Benedict* the Abbot, *Geruasius*, *Protasius*, S. *Dominicke*, & thousands in forreigne cuntries, S. *Cuthbert*, S. *Dunston*, S. *Oswalde*, S. *Suitbert*, *Edithe*, *Etheldred*, and others in England? The religion of S. *Leo*, Pope of Rome, violented *Attila*, that outragious infidel, sirnamed the whip of god in his greatest furie to recall his armie from inuading Italy, to the wonder, of al his souldiours. A vessell of boyling Leade, Rosin, and Pitch, woulde not hurt the bodies of S. *Vitus*. *Modestus*, and *Crescentia*, and the Lion prepared to consume them, fell downe and licked their feete: wherupon *Diocletian* the Emperor, causing them to be torne in peeces, the very insensible creatures wrought reuengement, for thundrings, lightnings, and earthquakes, oppressed their enemies, and ouerthrew their idolotrous temples. At the comming of Christ, besides those homages and offices of al creatures, both in heauen and earth, done vnto him, and recorded by the holy Euangelists, the Pagans themselues, and other writers are witnesses, that a miraculous circle compassed the sun in the viewe of al the Romans: and after the same appeared in 3. circles, one being enuironed with a fiery Garland. Three Suns were seene to shine at one time, in the firmament, and to vnite themselues together in one. The high and great trees as he trauailed from place to place, miraculouslie bended themselues to the grounde, and reuerenced him. And at Rome a spring flowed with oyle a whole day togither, when Christ our annoynted was borne. And infinite more miracles of the submission and obedience of his creatures vnto him, are recorded both in ecclesiasticall, and prophane Authors, where we may reade the like alleageance and duty performed to his holie Saints, and religious seruants: but these are sufficient for this purpose, and able to giue answere to the carnal imagination of any irreligious Politicke, or Epicure, which like beasts, only mooued with corporall and sensible delights, are often scandalized to see the impious and wicked, sometimes exalted to honour, and religious innocents, oppressed with miseries. For that honourable testimony, which God hath so often aud strangely giuen for the glory of his Saints and religious friends, at such times as they were most oppressed, and in reproofe and condemnation of the

Greg. lib. 2. Dial. cap. 5. Ambr. de inuent. SS Ger & Protas. Bed. hist. An. l 2. 3. 4. &c. Sur. in vit. Sanct. Lippil & al. &c. Ex Pontific. & vit. S. Leō. Ex Gest. S. vit Modest. & Cresc.

Suet. in Oct. cap. 95. Senec. lib. 1. nat. q. c. 2. Plin. nat hist l. 2. c. 28. Dio histor. Rom. l. 45. Plin. nat. hist l. 2. cap. 31. Eus. in Chrō. Oros. hist. l. 6. cap. 19. cap. 18. Sibil. apud Lact. fir. lib. diu. inst.

the impious their persecutors, so much exalteth the glory and honour of the religious oppressed, aboue the deceitfull happinesse of the other, by howe much the testimonie and glory which is giuen of God, is greater then the witnesse which is brought, & honour that is desired of a carnall and beastly man. And although this extraordinary glory and honour is not sensiblie bestowed vpon euery religious Saint, and oppressed seruant of his in this life; (for so he should be only serued for houour and temporall rewardes) yet in that he hath giuen it to so many, and for the same cause for which the others be oppressed, no man can call in to question, but honour is due and belongeth vnto all, and to be rendred vnto them, either in this life, or after death, as experience sheweth all such religious innocents are glorious and honorable euen with men when they are dead, and their persecutors either forgotten, or remembred with dishonour. And yet of all temporall dignities, glory is the greatest, and that which euery man most desireth.

Chap. 12. *The afflictions and aduersities of the Religious and godlie, for which the Epicures denie Religion, are a manifest proofe therof.*

AND to preuent the carnall obiections of this sensuall people, if aduersities, tribulations, and crosses, had not chanced to the most renowmed, and temporally honoured Princes, *Alexanders, Cesars, Hanibals, Scipioes*, and others, their honour had neuer beene so great: for what hath nobled them so much in glory, as their patience, fortitude, constãcie, & magnanimitie in suffering distresses, and performing difficulte, and heroicall attempts? And if their sufferinges, & valiant enterprises in temporal causes when they were probable to be brought to passe, haue made them noble with men, what shal inuincible fortitude & vnconquerable minds of holy Saints, in causes appertaining to God, and his greatest honor, and in performance wherof they were assured to loose both life and other temporal dignities, deserue? If this be not the merit of honour, nothing can be named honourable, or called glorious. And if these suffringes should be vtterly taken away from the friendes of God in this worlde, the greatest honour that is due to vertue should be wanting. For take this away, and the vertues of patience, fortitude, magnanimitie, and others which be the deseruing causes of glory, cannot be excused, because they principally consist, in vndergoeing aduersities, and effecting difficult thinges. And the excellencie of this vertue of Fortitude, in patiently enduring aduersities, and vndergoeing harde and vneasie businesse, is so greate, that in auncient times among Philosophers, it was euer accounted one of the foure cardinall vertues. And it is conuenient for true Religion, not

to want this tryall and state of aduersitie euen in the greatest and most perfect men. So that the most religious men and such as haue bin in the greatest honour and account both with God and man for that cause, haue
Iob. tasted of both estates, *Iob* sometimes most vnfortunate, sometimes in highest aduancements of prosperitie, S. *Paul* that was rapt into heauen, often depressed to the greatest miseries, & so of others: and not only priuat men, but religious commonweales, Kingdomes, and Empiers: the examples are manifest in histories. And yet no Epicure or Machauel can say, that this is an obiection against Religion or disgrace to the religious friendes of God, which be so visited with affliction; but the contrary, because those vertues be then exercised which otherwise wold not: And that which is the chiefe act of Religion, God reuerenced and honored by them in such sorte, as they perhaps being in prosperitity would not so wel haue performed. And if honour and glorie be the greate dignities of this life, the religious sufferers of affliction are so farre from miserie by enduring calamities, or afflictions, that they are rather made thereby more honourable and glorious.

## Chap. 13. *The temporall honours and delightes of the Religious, were often greater, and their miseries lesse then of the Irreligious.*

BVT to satisfie the carnall and sensuall appetites, and conceiptes of Irreligious and voluptuous men, to whome nothing is good but *Bonum delectabile*, that which is delightfull vnto sense, let vs passe ouer all demonstrations before aleaged, and for this time esteeme nothing of so many vnspeakeable ioyes, which chaunce to the religious euen at those times, when these men adiudge them most vnfortunate in their state of affliction, the endlesse and vnrecitable cares, solicitudes, and miseries the Irreligious vndergoe in procuring pleasures, what labours and dangers in preseruing them? what torments and anguishes in forsaking them? what diseases, sicknesse, violence, and vnhappines to those senses of theirs, in which they would place their pleasures? what immature, sodaine, and vntimely deaths, the ful priuation of all their ioyes and felicities they incurre, in exercising and possesing those banquets, feastings, luxuries, honours, riches, and other pleasures. Let vs forget the honour and glory of the godlie by their sufferrings, and the ignominie and dishonour of the others, when they come to aduersity, the comforts of the religious through their hope in God, whome they worshippe, and the desperation of the irreligious, spoyled of all comsolation. Let the euerliuing vertues, and reputation of the religious after death, and the alwaies during infamie of the irreligious be omitted. Let it not be remembred that religion being a speciall moral vertue is to be repaied with corporal pleasures, such as this world cã giue,

giue, but with eternall, supernaturall, and spirituall rewardes, to obtayning which terrestiall ioyes are often a let and hinderance, by wedding vs to this world, and the pressures of the godly by weaning vs from earthly delights, the safest meanes to winne them. Let me make no argument that the aduersities of the iust in this life, are the causes of their greater glory after death, and that both the pleasures & aduersities of the impious not regarding either the blessings or corrections of GOD, are the cause of their deeper damnation in hell. We will account it no felicitie or comfort for this time that the vertuous in their greatest distresses are lamented of all, and pitied with compassion; often breeding greater ioye, then their miseries bring affliction, and by how much their suffering is greater, by so much bewailed and honoured more, as the miseries and deaths of millions of Martyrs and afflicted Saints are witnesses, honoured both of GOD and all creatures: and the afflictions, distresses, and vnfortunate ends of the wicked neglected and contemned both by GOD and man, all things reioycing in their destruction, and vnhappines. Lastlie to please the appetites of this people although we did grant them their owne absurditie, and that which they seeke to finde, that the cheife and supreme felicitie of man, is to be expected and possessed in this life, and that there is no pleasure or punishment after death, that the bodie is better then the soule, the externall goods which they reckon honour, riches, pleasure prosperitie, and the like, with health, and long life to inioye them, are most to be estemed, and want debasement, pouertie, aduersitie, affliction, and other their infelicities most to be auoyded, although as these being often the cause of our chiefest good, so the others are often the occasion of vnhappinesse. Yet if we should yeeld vnto thē these vnreasonable requests, and argue with carnall men, by carnal Arguments, whatsoeuer thy shal appoint to be the greatest pleasure and happines in this worlde, & to continue and perseuer longest (for such thinges as be priuations of pleasures, and corruptions of life and health, wherin they are to be enioyed, they will not esteeme for pleasures) as honour, riches, health, prosperitie, dignities, and such others, which is asmuch as any Epicure can demand, or a beaste would aske, if it had language and leaue to vtter the internall appetite. Yet notwistanding all this, it will appeare that the prosperous estate, and happie condition of the vertuous, and professors of religion, hath often beene greater, and their miseries and afflictions lesse in this life, then of the impious and irreligious, which onlye seeke for this preferment. And to iustifie my assertion, many Philosophers, nations, and Countries, haue estemed these temporal felicities to be a temporal rewarde of Religiō.

It was not lawfull for any amongst the auncient Egiptians to be a King, except he were a Priest, and religious to the Gods: and *Mercurius*, sirnamed *Trismegistus*, thrice greatest was so called, because he was a Kinge, a Phylosopher, and a Priest. The olde and wise Romanes, had the like custome and obseruation, and all their Sacrifices, Rites, and Ceremonies, some were as thankes for benefits receaued, others to auoide afflictions, to ease aduersities inflicted, to cease plagues and pestilences, to prosper attempts, heale diseases, encrease substance: and the like not only vsed of the Idolaters, and false worshippers, but of the true Israelites, and instituted of God himselfe doe witnesse. They esteemed no happinesse of this worlde, to be without the true worship of God, and many aduersities to come for irreligion. This was the common sentence of the Caldeans, Assirians, Grecians, Persians, English, and all Nations: and to encourage all in this opinion by the generall and receaued decrees of all worshippers, those that were in the greatest degree of professing and exercising of this worshippe, were euer had, and esteemed in greatest honour: so were the Patriarkes, which were Priests in the lawe of nature, *Noe*, *Abraham*, and other the high Priests vnder the law of *Moyses* among the Israelites, the Flamens, and Arch-flamens among the Gentiles, Brachmans, with the Indians, Caliphes, in the lawe of *Mahumet*, and amonge Christians, Popes, aud spirituall Prelates, are reuerenced with the greatest dignities. And not onlie such estates whose calling was dedicated to worshippe, but other conditions amongst all nations, which were most religious, were reputed most honourable and glorious: and not only amonge men, but with God himselfe, for by how much any people or countrie came nearer to true Religion, they flourished more, and they which truly followed it in the daies of their so doings, were most happie and honourable, and such as were most alienated from true reuerence of God, and enemies thereof, were most infortunate and miserable, as many persecutors of the religious haue beene. To giue example, in the ancient religious Iewes, so long as they continued their obedience, God promised vnto them for that cause, all prosperities and benedictions, both spirituall, and temporall. How did he honor them with visions and apparitions of Angels from heauen? what a propitiatory and oracle did he ordaine to answere to their doubts, and releeue their wants? what patriarkes, prophets, priests, kings, captaines, and iudges did he giue vnto them? how miraculously did he multiply their number and nation among their enemies? how strangly did he punish the Egiptians, & deliuered them? howe did he aduance them aboue mighty & potent princes? how many did he depriue

Dio. hist. Rom. Clem. Alex. Cicer. l. de Repub. Arusp Lact. fir. l. de diu. Inst.

Leuit. c. 1. 2. 3. 4. 5. 6. 7. &c. Cic. l. Nat. Deor. Lact. fir. l. 1. 2. 3. diu. inst. Bed. l. 3. hist. Arist. lib. 10. Ethic. c. li 7. cap. 8. 9. 10. Gen c. 6. &c. Exod. 19. 20 Numer. &c. Bed. hist. ang. Fox. t. 1. mo. Pet. Maff. hist Indic. lib. 1. fol. 24. &c. Alcho. Mah.

Plat. in Mē. Ari. l. 10. eth. cap. 9. lib. 7. cap. 8. 9. 10. Hippoc. init. oper. Merc. Trism. Dial. 9. Strab. l. 5. Gen. cap. 12. 13. 14. 15. 18. 22. 28. 32. 35. 49. Exod. c. 1. 2. 5. 6. 7. 8. 9. 11. 13. 14. 16. 17. 19. 33. 40. Leuit. c. 1. &c Num. &c. 33. 34. Deut. c. 2. &c

depriue of their ancient possessions, and made them rulers therof? how miraculously did he protect them in their iornies, feed them in their wants, defend them in their wars? how often, how manie, & miraculous victories did he giue them? how did he inrich them with all temporal blessings, riches, gold, treasure, & abundance of all things which can be desired? how oftē did he promise to continue his care and prouidence, if they remained in duty & Religion? how wel did he performe it, vntill they became irreligious and disobedient? and at such times that they might know (as he had oftē admonished them before) that their Religion was cause of their prosperitie, & irreligion would bring the contrary and vnfortunate miseries, how was that people punished? how often conquered, and subdued, spoiled of wealth, Countrie, Wiues, Children, Temple, Aulter, Kinges, Prophets and all comforts? howe often led captiues, and kept vassailes, and since they fell to their last irreligious apostasie from Christ, how long time, in how many Countries, to how manie Nations haue they beene, and at this time are the most miserable people in the worlde? so that if a man would be so incredulous that he would not beleue the Scriptures, & promises and threates of God contained in them towardes that people, for those causes, yet when the whole world doth witnesse these thinges haue beene so effected in so many generations, no man can bee so impious to denie it. And this he performed, not only to that people in generall, but euen to the verie particuler men of that Nation, as their Priests, Kinges, and other priuate persons. Who was so highly honoured and exalted of God, as *Moyses* their Priest and Captaine? was he not borne of meane parentage of the tribe of Leuie? what patrimonie had he left him? what title had he to be so great a man? was he not condemned to death before he was borne? was he not committed to the waters to be drowned? was he not enforced to forsake his friendes and renounce his countrie, to get his liuing among strangers by keping sheepe? And yet how was he aduanced honoured and exalted of God? what miraculous and wonderfull priuiledges did he grant vnto him? how did he appoint him Captaine and conductor of his people? what victories and conquestes did he giue him ouer *Pharao* & his Egiptians? how did he ordaine him, not only superior to depriue him of his riches, life, and people, but (to vse the wordes of God) *Constituted him the God of* Pharo, *constitui te Deum Pharaonis*, what misteries and secrets did he reueale vnto him? howe did he chuse and elect him alone among so many hundred thowsands to conduct his people to the lande of promise? And yet notwith standing all this, when he shewed but one acte of irreligion and want of dutie at the waters of contradiction, he was for the

Deut. cap. 7. et. 26. &c.

Exod. c. 2. c. 6. 2. Par. c. 23. Exod. 2.

Exod. c. 3. 4. 5. 7. 8. 9. 10. 11.

Exod. 7.

Exod. Num. &c. Exod. c. 11. et 17. &c. Num. c. 20. cap. 27. Deut. c. 33.

the same preuented by death, and neuer entred in, and *Iosue* was chosen to be their guide. So it hapned to *Noe*, to *Abraham, Loth, Iacob, Iosue, Gedeon, Sampson*, and the rest: religion was their exaltation and honour. Thus it was, and chaunced both to rulers and subiects of that people, as to exemplifie in their Kings, whose prosperities, and harde fortunes, and the causes of them were most knowne and famous. What comparison was there betweene the felicities of the religious and irreligious Kinges of Iuda? how honourable and prosperous were the raignes and regements of their religious Kinges, *Dauid, Asa, Iosaphat, Osias, Ionathan, Ezechias*, and *Iosias*, if they bee compared to the lamentable dishonours and miseries of their irreligious Princes, *Saul, Roboam, Abias, Ochozias, Amasias, Ozias*, and the rest that were impious? Howe shorte and impotent were these mens regiments and kingdomes? howe little was their glorie? howe greate their ignomy and dishonour? when contrarie, howe longe and ample were the Empires? howe noble and glorious was the honour of those religious Princes? Such like were the successes, and aduentures of the irreligious Kinges of Israell, that falling from GOD and true religion, fell to schisme and idolatry; they were but eighteene in number, and tenne of them were miserably slaine, *Nabath, Ela, Zamri, Achab, Ioram, Zacharias, Sellim, Phacee, Osee*, and the Scepter and Regiment was nine times translated from the families of the Kings: No family of them continuing the kingome aboue the fourth generation, that the curse and malediction of the irreligious might be imposed vpon them; and there was but one onlie familie of all those, which enioyed it so long, and that was of *Iehu*; which drewe nearest to true Religion, for he ouerthrewe the Altars, Idols, and idolatrous places of the Idoll *Baal*, and put his Priests to death. And although the Kinges of Israell descended of the same linage of *Abraham*, as the Kinges of Iuda did, and were for number of people farre aboue them, being tenne tribes, and the kingdome of Iuda onely two; yet howe were the irreligious Kinges of Israell tossed, turmoyled, and led captiues more then the other? howe were they alwaies inferior and their kingdome of lesse continuance? The enemies of Religion, *Balthasar, Aman*, and others, came to vnnaturall ends, and were lamentablie depriued of all dignities, and life it selfe. So in the time of the Machabees, it came to passe with the fauourers of Religion, and contrary with the irreligious enemies and persecutors thereof. Such relation may be made of the proceedings of other children of *Abraham*, descending of *Cetura*, and from his sonne *Ismaell*; those which were vertuous and religious, flourished as the others did, and their persecutors were dishonourable. And that

Gen. cap. 7. Iudic. cap 8. cap. 6. 13. 1. Reg. c. 7. Ios. 24.

Gen. 17. 22. 28. 35. 43. Exod. 1 2. 3. &c. 7. 8. 9. 14. Psal. 98. Ios. 7. 9. 14. Malach. c. 2. 1. Reg. 5. 17. 8. 3 Reg. 11. 14 2. Reg. 15 2. Paral. 16. 17. 21. 22. 36. 4. Reg. 1. 15. vlt. 17 Ierem. c. vlt. Iud. 1. Ierem. 1. 18. 19. 20. 27. &c.

Gen. c. 15. Exod. 20. 4. Reg. 9.

3. Reg. c. 11. &c.

1. Mach. &c. Ioseph. l. 1 antiq. c. 27. Diodor. Sicu. lib. 3. Plin. l. 6. c. 28. Strab. l. 16. &c. Plin. l. c. 38. Fazel. dec. prior. l. 8.

that it might be euident to all posterities, that the promise of God is true, that he rewardeth the religious, and debaseth the impious, the most holy and religious Patriarke *Abraham*, when there were many more potent & mighty then he, yet because he was so religious aboue the rest, God promised for that cause, *to make him the father of many nations*; and we see how many Kings and mighty Princes haue descended from him. For not the ancient Kinges of Iury and Israell, but of Arabia, Ethiopia, Idumea, Egipt, Colchians, that most potent christian Prince *Pret Ianne* of Iude, and all Christian Kings are either his spirituall or temporall posterity. And as a memory of their discent from *Abraham*, and not for any religious ceremony, the inhabitants of the Christian Empire of *Pret Ianne* are circumcysed, as also diuers other people as aproued writers are witnes. And who doubteth but many potent infidell and irreligious princes, as Turkes, and Arabians, although for themselues, and their owne iniquities and irreligion they neither deserue either temporall or spirituall blessings of God; Yet because they were (as some suppose) the carnall children of *Ismaell* and *Esau* the offspring of *Abraham* and *Isaac*, although in holy scriptures they are depriued of some spirituall fauours, graces, and preeminences, & commanded to be cast out, and haue no inheritance, yet that they possesse and enioy their temporall felicities & possessions, from the temporall benedictions of their religious ancestors *Abraham* and *Isaac*, and the promise of God vnto them; for concerning *Ismael*, God said vnto *Abraham*, *Sed & filium ancillæ &c. But also I will make* Ismael *the sonne of thy handmaid a great people:* which the Angel after promised to his mother *Agar* in the same wordes; such was the benedictiõ of the religious *Isaac*, to his irreligious childe *Esau* in temporall thinges, when he was depriued of some spirituall graces, and inheritance. And this may be a title of such Infidels to their worldly prosperitie, by the religion of their ancestors, for their owne impiety neither meriteth spirituall or temporall fauour.

2. Paral. 8. 1. Mach. 2. Dion. l. 1. Gen. c. 25. Calu. t. l. 2. cap. 9. Geneb. Cro. l. 1. Pag. 56 Ortel. in Theatr. &c. Francis. Alumedin. 1. 2. q. 10. 3. artic. 4. Postel. in cõ. Cosmograp. Maff. hist. lib. 3. Gen. c. 21. Gal. c. 4. Rom. 9. Gen. 26. 27. Gen. c. 21. cap. 25.

## Chap. 14. *The temporall honour and dignitie of Religious Catholicke Christians most commonly greatest, and their afflictions least.*

AND touching true beleeuing, and Religious Catholicke Christians, how much they are blessed of God, both in heauenly and earthly benedictions: as allso, to let the glory of our Religion alone, which only shineth in all the worlde, how miraculouslie haue we from the beginning bin raysed, maintayned, and aduaunced, mauger the might and malice of al enemies and persecutors, though neuer so manie, malicious & mightie: how haue they beene conquered and their pride and puissance depressed: how haue we preuailed, how longe, how large, how great and wonderfull haue our honours, titles, prosperities, and preeminencies raigned and ruled in the worlde? What Empire of the Asirians, Persians, Gretians, Pagans, Romans, Turkes, Tartars, or any other, hath so endured? which of them all was to be compared vnto it in power? And to omit no time, although GOD hath afflicted Christians in these later daies for their want of dutie in Religion; yet when Infidell, and Irreligious Princes at this day are so mighty and potent, as that great Christian of Iude, Emperour ouer threescore and twelue kingdomes. And the Georgians, so called of S. *George* their patrone in warres, a people so potent that they are a terror to the Turkish Empire, and admitted to performe their pilgrimage to the holy Sepulchre in Hierusalem, in the dition of the Mahumetans, with their baners displaied and free from tribute. Or who will compare with the Catholicke and Religious King of Spaine, whose regall reuenewes, much exceede all the vniust and tiranicall Taxes, Tributes, and Impositions of the Turkesh Emperour? his Counties, and Kingdoms are greater, and exceeding the others, his subiectes more honourable, his proceedings more noble. What high Priest euer either among the Iewes, Gentiles, Mahumetans, or any professors of Religion, so reuerenced, renouned, honored, & potent, as our Catholicke Christian Popes of Rome so many hundred yeares exalted aboue the Emperour them selues, and exercising Iurisdiction & authority further then euer any other Prince spiritual or temporal did, euen ouer al Countries in the worlde? How miraculously haue all enemies, that in any time or place opposed themselues against that sacred Iurisdiction of Rome, bin ouerthrowne? The Iewes so pitifully dispersed, the Pagan Emperours, all that persecuted it, liuing and dying in miseries and dishonors, as the histories of all to *Constantine* are witnes. How did those insolent and proude conquerours of the worlde, that killed and conquered whome they would, geue place to the poore Religious Successors of Saint *Peeter* a Fisher, as their Prophetesse *Sibilla* had foretolde? Howe were they that were conquerours of the mightyest, vanquished of the meanest? How haue all aduersaries and persecutors spirituall or corporall, internall, or externall, that euer opposed them selues against it beene subdued and ouerthrowne? as I haue cited before, almost an hundred true or reputed Emperours before *Constantine*. What hereticall Emperours of the Arrians, Eutichians, Iconnoclaustes, or Image-breakers, Monotholits, Manichees, Armenians, as *Constantius*, *Valens*, *Zeno*, *Anastatius*, *Heraclius*, *Constance*, *Iustinian*, 2, *Philipicus*, *Dardanes*, *Leo*, *Isauricus*, *Constantinus*, *Cropronimus*, *Leo Cropronimus*, *Leo Armenius*, *Michael*, *Dalbus*, *Theophilus*? Howe haue the Gothes, Vise-gothes, Ostrogothes, Vandals,

Septē. Castr. l. de morib. & Relig. turc. cap. 21.

Euseb. Ruff. Socrat. & c. in hist.

Sibil. apud. Lact. firm. de diu. inst.

Epist. Apol.

Euseb. hist. Ruff. hist. Socrat. & c. Fox. t. 1. Mō. Cæsar. Bar. t. 2. 3. 4. & c. Plat. vit. Pōt. S. Anth. hist.

Vandals, Frankes, Angles, Mahumetans, Turkes, Tartars, inuaded and perſecuted it? Howe many Irreligious Chriſtian Ringes, ſuch as I haue recounted in Englande and other places? howe many Arch-heretickes ſeauen hundred in number as I recited in the ſame place, and yet as I haue ſhewed before, notwithſtanding all theſe enemies & afflictious, the catholicke temporall Princes thereof, are the mightieſt and moſt honourable in the world & the Popes ſpirituall iuriſdiction three times greater, more noble and ample, then euer any was, either among heretickes, Infidels, or the Iewes themſelues when they obſerued true Religion: Cōtrariewiſe, let any man peruſe the ſtate and conditions of thoſe cuntries of chriſtēdome, that are fallen ro Herefie, and become irreligious, and hee ſhall perceaue them to be in moſt diſhonourable tearmes, both for temporall, & ſpirituall rule; the iuriſdiction of none knowne or acknowledged out of one litle country or Prouince, and thoſe which be the greateſt aduerſaries of our religion, to be in the moſt pitifull, poore, and vncertaine caſe of the reſt. And leaſt any Atheiſt, Epicure, or wicked Politicke ſhould ſay, that although the ſtate of the religious is ſuch, and ſohononrable as I haue deſcibed in the time of peace and proſperitie, yet in the winter ſtormes of aduerſitie, and perſecution, when thoſe Popes that be nowe ſo glorious were ſo often and many in number put to death, when the whole Clergie was perſecuted, when euery Religious Chriſtian was odious, when ſo many thouſands of Martyrs were put to torments, when we were depriued of honours, riches, liberties, liues, and all preferments, as wee haue beene both by Iewes, Pagans, and Heretickes, our glory was nothing at all, but we were wholly oppreſſed with miſeries; I haue alreadie ſhewed, that euen in ſuch times, the honour and glory of the Religious, which were perſecuted, was farre greater, then of their perſecutors, and that euer in the ende, the victorie and triumph was ours. And to giue examples in this caſe; neuer any thing among the enemies of Chriſt, was ſo famous and renowned in the worlde, as the Empire of Rome, aud their Emperours before *Conſtantine* the Chriſtian Emperour. Yet let vs but compare the moſt perſecuted Religious people, which were the Popes of Rome, with the gallant flowers of fortune, and my ſentence will be true. The Popes of Rome were then eſteemed of impious Pollitickes, to be the moſt vnfortunate and depreſſed people, no friend, no humane force to defend them, the laws againſt them, their enemies and perſecutors (with whoſe felicitie I compare them) were the abſolute commaunders of the worlde, and contended with all force, policie and tirannie they coulde, to abandon the name of CHRIST, and his Religion, and all profeſſors thereof, principallie the Popes of

Phil. Berg. hiſt.
Epiſt. apol. ſup. &c.
Pantal. Crō.
Epiſt. Apo.
Ber. Lutzeus
Catal. hær.
Geneb. Crō. lid. 4.
Hoſ. Lind.
Prateol.
Pant. ſiuct.
Lauat. Lypſ.
Caluint. l. 3.
Caſp. vl. l. 22, cauſ.

*obiection anſwered.*

Rome, and put them to death; And yet doe what they could, the true glorie of the Romane Popes at that time, was greater then the glorie of those Romane Emperors, all histories, martirologies, calenders, and records will beare perpetuall witnes, their liues & honor were thrise as long, and yet they were olde before their election, & consecration, and though the life of them al was sought, and most of them died actually in martirdome, yet the number of their enmies & persecuting Emperors that died misera blie, and with reproache in the same time, did three to one exceede them: for from S. *Peter* to S. *Siluester* honored by *Constantine*, there were 31. Popes, and those aged men, and yet of them not aboue 25. or 26. actuallie put to death. And of the Emperours the lustie gallants of the worlde either trulie chosen, pretended or reputed, there reigned in the same space almoste an hundred Roman Emperors, and all they, excepting eleauen or twelue at the moste, were slain, and miserably put to death, and the others which escaped those violent endes, died in greater wrechednesse then those religious Popes they persecuted. And the names of the Popes are honourable, both in heauen and earth, and the names of the others either dishonourablie or not remembred at all. And leaste any should be so vaine to suppose that the miseries were onlie priuate to the Romane Emperours, he shall see how they were common calamities to al our enemies: of the Iews all the world is a witnes to this day, & I will declare hereafter. The Senators of Rome were next in degree to the Emperors thereof, and second in honor and reputation to them, and those which persecuted religion moste in that time; And yet how often were they themselues moste vilie vexed and persecuted of their Emperors fourteene times at the leaste in the same space, by generall persecutions against them, wherein they were violentlie entreated and put to deathe by *Tiberius*, *Caius*, *Nero*, *Domitian*, *Hadrian*, *Commodus*, *Septimus*, *Caracalla*, *Marinus*, *Heliogabalus*, and other Emperours, that in one day at Rome were pittifullie put to death by *Claudius* their own Emperor, fiue and thirtie Senators, & three hundred Knights. So likewise the inferior aduersaries of our religion, how manie thousands of them executed by moste cruell and vnwonted deathes, by their owne idolatrous and irreligeous Emperours? some drowned, some buried aliue, some mured vp in walles, others hauinge theyr eies pulled out, others pulled and and cut in peeces, others cast to beastes in spectacles, and manie hundred thousands violently consumed and destroied in the same space.

And to speake of those moste infensiue enemies of all religious christians in these latter yeares, *Mahumet* and the successors of his impious gouernment, although worldlie happines, and carnall pleasure is the felicity they

Bella. Chronol. Pant. Chrō. Col. pontif. Ruff. hist. Euseb. hist. Fox. tom. 1. Mon. Plat. de vit. Pont. Catal. Pontif. nup. edit. Hieron. in cap. 4. Zachar. Chrisost. lib. 2. contra. Gentil. &c.

Tract. 2. inf.

Cæs. Bar. Annal. to 1. 2. 3. Euseb. hist. Ruff. histor. Bez. ruin. Gen. l. 6. &c. Oros. lib. 7. Dion histor. Rom. li. 58. Baron. tom. 1. annal.

Tertul. li ad Scapul. & in apol. Suetō. c. 61. Mahumet. in Alcor. c. 54. et c. 65. 66. &c. 43. &c.

they expect either in this, or in any other life, yet how strangely they haue bin punished and afflicted, especially at such times as they raged most against vs? what a filthy & beastlie life did their first author *Mahumet* leade, euen by his owne confession? with what vnnaturall diseases was hee tormented? how beastlie & shamefull was his death? how ignominious and odious was he euen to his own friends and followers long after his death? how horrible, odious, & vnnaturall were the liues & deaths of al his next and immediate successors, *Alis, Eubocora, Homar, Osmenus, Mahumetes,* the seconde *Alis, Muauias,* and others, the first ordained of *Mahumet* himselfe, violentlie oppressed and deposed, *Eubocora* poisoned to death, *Homar* murthered of his seruant, *Osmenus* killed himselfe, *Mahumetes* violently and vnnaturallie slayne, *Alis* traiterouslie murthered, *Muauias* so afflicted with schismes and sectes in that profession, that hundreds of Camels were not able to carrie the writings of such as rebelled against him. With what dishonourable and vnseemelie conditions was their most potent Prince, and our greateste enemie *Amuathus* enforced to conclude a truce with *Iustinian* the seconde? how miserablye were two hundred thousande of them soone after killed in Sria? how shameful was the retire of *Zuleman* from the Thracians, and Bulgarians, about the same time? were not three hundred seauentye fiue thousande of theyr souldiers slayne at once by the Spaniards and French in one batatyle? what straunge conquestes and victories did inferionr religious christian captaines, *Ogerus* duke of Denmarke, *Godfryde* of Lorrayne, and others, obtaine against their most puissant and mighty Princes? howe did other base and contemptible men afflict them? was not *Baiazethes* the first their great Emperour subdued by *Tamberleyne* that barbarous & rogish Scythian, lost two hundred thousand souldiers, was taken prisoner, closed vp in a cage of Iron, led vp and downe in chaines; and made a footestoole for a theefe to treade vpon his backe, when he went to horse? was not his wife abused before his eies, her clothes cut off from hir backe, and her whole body left naked from the nauill to the foote, and did not he kil himselfe in open spectacle? was not their Emperour *Orchanes* murthered by his owne Vncle? their Emperour *Moyses* violently killed of his naturall Nephewe *Mahumetes*? and *Baiazethes* the seconde poysoned of *Selimus* his owne sonne, and *Mustapha* the onlie lawefull and true heire of *Solyman*, moste vniustlie, and vnnaturallie murthered by his Father, and in his presence? and so of others, besides the ordinarye and vsuall murthering of brothers after the fathers death, as *Orchanes* that killed his three brethren, *Amurathes* put his onlie brother to death, *Baiazethes* killed his seauen brethren, and so of others,

Blond. l. 9. Plat. Pomp. Læt. Eutrop. l. 18. Sab. & c hist. turric.

Blond. l. 10. dec. 1. Sab. En. 5. l. 7 Sigeb. hist. Aemil. lib. 2. Sabel. Tyr. l. 1. cap. 17. Krants. l. 5. cap. 14.

Egnat. hist. Sabel. Pane. in Chron.

Matin. fum. hist. hungar. lib. 7.

others, and all these of late, since, & in which times, they haue persecuted our religion moste. And if we peruse al histories, and antiquities, we shall euidentlie perceaue, that whensoeuer those irreligious infidels haue preuailed against vs, it was either in time of irreligious heresie, or some such negligence, and disobedience in religion, for which wee were iustlie afflicted, *Heraclius* the Emperour became a Monothelite hereticke, and *Mahumet* with his Sarracens inuaded Hierusalem, Damascus, Egipt, parte of Affricke, Rhodes, and the Iles adioyning. *Vitiza* king of Spaine was a licentious, and irreligious Prince, and permitted concubines, & other impious abuses, & at the same time, the same Sarracen infidels inuaded that kingdome, and possessed that many hundred yeares. The Emperors of the East irreligiously behaued themselues to the See of Rome, and Emperour *Nicephorus* became tributorie to the Sarracens, and his successor *Theophilus* was twice conquered, Hierusalem, Candy, and part of Asia was subdued. The Grecians fell to schisme, and deuided themselues from the Romane iurisdiction, and *Mahumetes* the Turkish Emperor inuadeth those cuntries, subdueth 12. kingdomes, 200. cities, and violently taketh Constantinople in their great festiuity of Pentecost, and comming of the holy ghost, about whose procession they are in error, miserably killed *Constantine* their Emperor, and possesse their Empire. *Martin Luther* beginneth his vnhappy heresies, and presently vpon that irreligious reuolt, *Solymanus* Emperour of Turkey inuadeth those countries, taketh Rhodes, and Belgrade, those two propugnacles of Christendome, inuadeth Hungary, slewe *Lodowicke* King thereof, possessed Buda chiefe citie of the kingdome, besiedged Vienna with 250000. men, and since that irreligious apostacy and by meanes of it, hath often and pittifully afflicted Christians. So that the afflictions we haue receaued from those infidels, proceeded from impiety, and irreligion, & whensoeuer we were religious vnto God, we preuailed against them, which is manifest in the state of christians euen in this time; for as we see those countries and kingdomes for their irreligious heresies and schismes are become vassals and in subiection, as I recounted before in the religion of the Iewes before Christ; so contrariwise, those Kinges, Princes, and countries of Christendome, which haue remayned free from those irreligious defectes, neuer flourished more. And to exemplifie in the Catholicke King of Spaine, in all these times his subiects and countries (excepting the miserable fleemish) haue beene free from these vnhappie and irreligious dealings, and when was the condition thereof so honourable? in what age were the Spaniards accounted such conquerours, and souldiers in the worlde? when was their fame and honour so great?

Blond. l. 4. Dec. 2. Tyr. l. 8. c. 18. l. 9. c. 2. et 5. S. Brand. in Hierosf. Phil. Bergõ. hist. S. Anto. hist. Pant. in Cro Sab. Eutrop. lib. 15. Blond. l. 6. Dec. 1. Tyr. l. 1. c. 2. Sigeb. Pant. Chron. Sab. Eu. 8. l. 8. Phrig. in Cr. Plat. Blond. lib. 10. S. Brand. hist Phil. Bergõ. Chron. Pantal. in Chron. Egnat. 3. S. Brand. hist Bergõ. hist. Pant. in chr Paul. 10u. hist. Manster in Chron. Fox. to. 2. Mon. Graff. in hist in Henr. 8. Stow. hist. in Henr. 8.

great? are not his dominions and Kingdomes greater, richer, more ample, and honourable, then the possessions of any Infidell in the worlde? hath he not in these very times when the irreligious partes of Christendome haue lost and beene infested so much, wonne, and lawfully vnited vnto him, more mightier, richer, greater, and more glorious nations, then any Infidell is owner of, or any irreligious prince or state of Christians enioyeth, as the kingdomes of Castill, legion Tollet, Hispalis, Murcia, and Luzia, and the prouinces adioyning, Burgundy, and the 15. prouinces, the Canary Ilands, Sardinia, Sycilie, Naples, the Dukedome of Millane, Portugall, the Philippine Ilands, so many vaste and rich countries of America, the East and West Indians, obteyned and wonne by the three last Catholicke and religious Kings of Spaine, *Philip* 1, *Charles* 5, *Philip* 2, & in that time when the irreligious places of christians haue lost so much, & yet what other christian wars haue bin, which they haue not defended.

And if it were lawfull to make free comparisons of these latter daies of Protestants, and compare the estate of the countries, where the Protestants haue persecuted, and Catholickes haue beene afflicted, it woulde be no difficultie to prooue, that the glory, honour, and temporall felicity of the persecuted religious Catholicks, haue far exceeded the pompe & prosperity of their persecutors. But so much as I neede to craue leaue to doe for England, it appeareth already in my Epistle. And I am assured Epist. Apol. there is no Protestant in our nation, but (setting the loue of his Abbie-liuings aside) woulde wishe the estate of his countrie for honour, riches, strength, order, friendship of forreigne nations, loue and vnitie of nobility and others, and all other honours and blessings of of a christian kingdome were no worse now, then it was in the 22. yeare of K. *Henry* the eight when he reuolted. If he either consider clergie or laietie, nobility or commonaltie, or let vs viewe the number of religious and Catholicke Priests, which aboue 100. in her Maiesties time haue suffered death for this quarrell; Looke into the liues and deaths of ministers, & for that 100. of martyrs, you shall finde 1000. and more ministers dying infamous, miserable, and beggerly deaths, for most wicked and vnnaturall offences. Looke into those ministers that haue bin best of life, and in greatest fauour with Prince and subiects, and we shall finde, that our banished religious Catholickes doe surmount them, we haue by foraigne princes rewarded with honours of Cardinall, Bishop, and all inferiour dignities, wee haue had more publike professors of diuinity in other vniuersities, then al England hath had at home, our Priests, religious men, and namely the fathers of the societie of Iesus, most odious in England, haue beene in higher reputation,

tation, with the greatest Princes of the worlde in strange countries; then the highest Arche-bishop of protestantes in England, hath beene with his natural Soueraigne. And such is the ordinarie and common ignominie & dishonour to be reputed a Minister in the English Church, that I suppose verie few, or no Catholike Priestes of that Nation would change their honour euen in England, with so base and infamous a generation. What the wealth, riches, and other blessinges be, which the Protestants haue, that wee want, for all this time of persecution, and empouerishing religious Catholickes, I think no man perceaueth so manifest a distinctiou, and yet the charges, taxes, and impositions, which haue been imposed vpon vs, are 20. times greater, then those which Protestantes haue tasted. And if the estate of Catholickes in Englande where they are persecuted is such, howe glorious is it in Catholicke Nations, where they are honoured, if the times of persecution and irreligion, haue done vs no more dishonour? what glorie will Catholicke and Religious times afforde vs? If our owne countrie Protestant Historians can so litle disgrace vs, as the historie of *Stowe* and others will witnesse, what commendation and credit will Catholicks and Religious Cronicles both at home and abroade, yelde vnto vs? so that we see, what honour, glorie, dignitie, or excellencie so euer it is, which a man may or can desire to haue, either spirituall, or temporall, in this, or in the life to come, if it is a pleasure, or preferment to a reasonable creature, such as may be wished or inioyed without sinne, Religion is the mother of all.

Chap. 15. *Though there should be no rewarde for Religion after death, yet the state of the Religious is to be preferred before the Irreligious.*

YEA if we shoulde yeelde so much to this franticke and brutish humor of Irreligious Epicures, to say this Question of Religion is doubtfull (as there is nothing more certaine, then that man oweth Religion vnto God) yet we shall perceaue the Religious state euen in worldly and temporall happines, farre to exceede the condition of the Irreligious, and that these are drowned and plunged in greater & deeper miseries, then the others. For what vnhappines or infelicity can be imputed to professors of religion, if they shoulde be in error? all the pleasures and delightes which can be conceaued to belong to man, consisting of a soule and body, must of necessity be spirituall belonging to the first, or temporall proportionat to the second. The spirituall delights, must nedes be the vertues and perfections of the soule, which only the Religious enioy, and wherof the others are depriued; thus the greatest happines is had of such as approoue Religions, and the enemies thereof haue loste it, as for thinges of delighte appertaining to the bodie, if they be intangled with sinne, they cannot be be accounted pleaſure as before, but rather a double torment to the guiltie conſcience of thoſe which for the repoſe and reſt of delight, offer a violence vnto nature, and yet this is onelie that, wherein the irreligious can exceede, and his exceſſe is in his owne affliction: for I haue prooued before, that actually whether there is any religion or no, that all other externall things which may be accounted goods of the body, fortune, or any extrinſicall preferment, as riches, honours, peace, rule, and other prerogatiues of glory, dignity, and ſuch delights, haue euer beene more peculier and proper to the religious, then to the impious. And that this irreligious generation which onlie ſeeke for eaſe and pleaſure, and to be free from miſeries, by many degrees haue euer in this life beene more afflicted then the reſt. If it hath euer chaunced ſo in former times, though we ſhoulde denie the prouidence of God, to doe the like in future ages, yet if all thinges were ruled by fortune, and came by chaunce, fortune is as like to fauour profeſſors of religion hereafter, as heretofore. And naturall reaſon teacheth vs, that of neceſsity it muſt be ſo, for there neuer was any Epicure, or Atheiſt, ſo impious and prophane, but by reaſon he ſhoulde graunt the opinion of all the vvorlde, and profeſſors of a GOD and religion, at leaſt to be a probable ſentence, thus his owne opinion coulde not bee voyde of feare. Then let vs conſtitute a Religious, and irreligious man, in the ſame eſtate of health, ſickneſſe, riches, pouertie, honour, diſgrace, pleaſure, miſerie, and the like: he that profeſſeth there is a God, by whoſe prouidence all thinges bee ordered, which is infinite in power, vnmeaſurable in goodneſſe, and cannot committe iniuſtice: If he be in health, riches, honour, pleaſure, and ſtate of reſt, his comfort, and delight is encreaſed, and doubled, to conſider that as he infalliblie ſuppoſeth, his God whome hee ſerueth, can, and will preſerue him in that eſtate; ſo likewiſe deliuer him if hee bee in the aduerſe calling of ſickneſſe, diſgrace, pouertie, perſecution, and other miſeries, and if not, yet for his patience hee will rewarde him. Thus his pleaſure is enlarged with iuſtlie conceaued truſt of continuance; in miſery his affliction healed with hope of deliuerie, or retribution for perſeuerance. Theſe comforts and delights cannot bee graunted to the irreligious, hauinge no hope eyther of continuinge and encreaſinge his pleaſures, or abbreuiatinge his afflictions; but hee is vexed vvith the contrarye infelicitie, alwayes in feare and daunger to bee depriued of his good, and perſeuere in his aduerſitye, vvhich experiment althoughe it bee veryfied in the vvhole age of men, yet more appeareth in the decayinge time, vvhen the Religious perswadeth himselfe the ende of all his miseries is at hand, and his greatest ioye is to begin, when contrariewise the other, is inuaded with a double infelicitie, one to lose his delightes, and the other to enter into greater torments: which in the whole circuite of the religious life bringeth a doubled consolation; and that in respect of the hoped happines after, so much greater then all pleasures and delightes which any Epicure can haue, by howe much the infinite goodnes of God, to be possessed of an immortall Soule for euer, exceedeth the short and temporall vncertaine pleasure of the sensible man. For although these ioyes in themselues should not be obtayned, yet seeing the delight and pleasure of the will is framed more or lesse, according to the apprehension and iudgement of the vnderstanding, by which it is mooued and taketh delight, the ioye of an vncertaine felicitie and happinesse conceaued as certain, and so proposed to the will, engendreth as greate a delectation, as that which is certaine doth: for externall obiectes moue not the internall powers of the soule, wherein delights are engendred as they are in themselues, but as they are conceaued and apprehended of those faculties, and so of griefe & affliction, because being extrinsecall, and not in the vnderstanding and will of them selues, but by apprehension and iudgement, they moue not but after the same manner, by which they are receaued and made present. Therfore seeing there is no proportion betweene the delightes of the one and the other, either in respect of the things themselues whereof the delight must arise, or the proportion of man, which doth, and must enioy them, or the time of their duration, whether there is any God and Religion or no, yet the condition of him that professeth Religion, euen in that respect, for which the other doth denie it, (which is only to liue in delight and deuoided of affliction) is to be preferred. And to this the experimented practise of so manie Kings, Princes, & Potentates, both of England, and other nations, which haue voluntarily forsaken their certaine and greatest temporall honours, prefermentes, and delightes, to enioy the consolations of the Religious, and so manie thousands which haue forsaken the corporall pleasures which such Epicures desire, and liued in desarts where they could not be possessed, but only spirituall comfortes must be their hope, haue yelded euidence, where the comfort of gaining heauen, and auoiding hell, haue tourned their troubles into ioyes. As contriwise the beastlie and Epicureous life of prophane and irreligious men, ioyned alwayes (as it can neuer be free from doubt) with cōtinual feare of so great a losse as heauen, and such dread of damnation as is in hell, cannot be accounted a pleasant, state, though euery one should be as potent to procure, and as wanton to possesse

Euseb. hist. Ruff. Sar. &c. Theodor. hi. Bed. hi. Ang lib. 3. 4. 5. Fox. tom. 1. Mon. Hieron. in vit. Greg. l. dial Suru. in vit. Sanct. Lippol. &c.

possesse himselfe of pleasures as euer any *Heliogobalus* was. For danger of the greater paine expelleth the lesser pleasure, and feare of eternall torment, woulde frustrate a momentarie delight. So that howsoeuer the euent shoulde prooue, the professor of Religion hath made the better and more pleasant choise; and in no state delighte can chance to man, if worship vnto God be not regarded. And whosoeuer desireth to liue at rest and haue delight, either in this or the life to come, must not be forget full of that dutie: Whereupon *Plutarch* the Philosopher not only was of this opinion, but wrote a booke intituled, *That no man coulde liue a pleasant life in the opinion of* Epicurus: and these are sufficient for this purpose. For although I doubt not but in these licentious daies, many voluptuous and carnall men forgetfull of the dignitie of humane nature, both in respecte of feare of punishment due for their iniquities, as also that they might more freelie without restrainte wallow themselues wholy in delights, wish in will and affection, there neither were religion due to God, or reuenge to the irreligion of man, yet I cannot be perswaded, that any vnderstanding can be so sottish in iudgement to denie it. Plutarch.

The 16. and last Capter and Conclusion. *Of the absurdities, which the Irreligious must graunt.*

FOR (to come to conclusion against this godlesse generation) what Iudgement or vnderstanding, of any priuate or particuler voluptuous man (for no others euer were Agents in this cause) can dare to enter in to that sentence which all learned and reasonable men in the worlde, in all ages, and places haue condemned for most impious and vnreasonable, all schooles, vniuersities, societies and companies professing knowledge, haue exploded for the greatest detestable wickednesse? which all Patriarkes, Prophets, Priestes, Iudges, Sibils, Rabbins, Legists, Flamens, Archeflamens, Caliphes, Brachmans, all sortes of people, Christians, Iewes, Pagans, Mahumetans, Catholickes, Heretickes, Philosophers, Poets, Magicians, Angels, seperated Soules, Deuils, and all creatures, euen insensible things, by one means or other haue reproued for the most barbarous and vnnaturall disobedience, which can be inuented. That which in so many thousands of yeares, in such diuersities of opinions and errors, in so many vaste and populous nations, in which all other impieties haue bene professed. Neuer any Kingdome, Countrie, State, Prouince, Citie, Towne, or Village practised: and by probable coniectures, neuer one particuler person, except franticke with pleasures, and distracted in minde defended, but only a fewe ignorant, barbarous and beastlie men, made of sinne, and guiltie of their owne hel, wishing for auoiding punishment. For what reason and vnderstanding can make denyall of that, which if he denieth, all authoritie, experience, sence, and ground of reasoning, and reason it selfe is denied? for whose denyall, not the least apparance of one argument can be alleadged, for whose approbation all testimonies of God, and all creatures are certaine, which if it be grannted, and trulie practized, all truthes, graces, honours, dignities, and priuiledges belonging to man, naturall, and supernaturall, either in this life, or after death, are so certainlie obteyned? if it be denyed, all honours & immenities are lost, all afflictions, temporall and eternall are incurred, all absurdities graunted, all vntruthes affirmed, all verities condemned. Sinne is vertue, vertue is sinne, sinne must be practised, vertue may not be allowed, nothing is sinne, nothing is vertue. Falsehoodes, and contradictions are true, all learning reiected. No Community, Kingdome, Magistracie, Discipline, no Soueraigne, no Subiection, no Lawe must be receaued, no barbarous, tyrannicall, or licentious impiety omitted. Mans soule mortall, man a beast, many beasts better then man. And infinite more such absurdities, which directlie proceede from this blasphemous position (*Religion is not to be vsed*) if anie man shall bee so sencelesse to affirme it.

*THE ENDE OF THE FIRST TREATISE.*

---

# THE FIRST CHAPTER OF THE SECOND TREATISE, BRIEFLIE SHEWING AGAINST *ALL EXTERNALL INFIDELS, HOW* *onlie that Religion, which Iesus Christ deliuered to the worlde, is the true worshippe of God.*

HAVING ended my first conclusion (*of the necessitie of a Religion*) against the irreligious, I am next in this time of so manifolde errors, to auoide all daunger of professing false reuerence, to prooue what religion among so many is onlie true, which I will performe in so vndeniable manner, that no veritie shall be so certaine, as that reuerence to God which I wil defend. And first against al external enemies of christ. My next proposition shall be (*that Religion which he taught is only true, and al others false*) which to a people of a professed christian nation needeth not long probatiõ, wherefore to be briefe in this dispute, such is the vndoubted

ted

ted certainty of this ſentence, whether we conſider the excelencie & dignity of the doctrine it ſelfe of the *Meſsias*, and Sonne of God which gaue it vnto vs, or the miraculous manner, wherby it was deliuered and embraced; or the baſeneſſe, impietie, and moſt manifeſt errors of all other profeſſions, the wickednes of the inuentors, and diſorders in inuenting & dilating them, that a man which will giue credit to any probable Argument, cannot call it into queſtion. And he ſhall ſee theſe Teſtimonies not only recorded by the holy writers, Prophets, Apoſtles, and Euangeliſtes, immediatlie illuminated of GOD, but of our greateſt profeſſed enemies: emong whome we doe not only finde confirmed in generall the Religion of Chriſt, but almoſte euerie perticuler article and miſterie ther of regiſtred and allowed: as the Trinitie, Incarnation, the two natures of Diuinitie and Humannitie in Chriſt, the promiſe of his comminge, his miraculous conception, natiuitie, lyfe, death, reſurrection, aſcention, comminge of the holy Ghoſt, conuerſion of the worlde, the ende thereof, his comminge to iudgemente, his giuinge ſentence, the finall beatitude and rewarde of the vertuous, worſhipers of him, and eternall puniſhment of the wicked, and his enemies, and other miſteries of our beleefe, teſtified and ratified of all kinde of Infidels, Iewes, Pagans, Mahumetans, Brachmans, alowed by God himſelfe, apparitions, & witneſſe of Angells fom heauen, and all creatures vppon earth, the heauens and celeſtiall bodies reioyceing in his birth, the Sunne. Moone, all elements, and compounded things lamenting his death. The Sunne againſt nature ecclipſed, the Moone violentinge his courſe, the aire darkened, the earth tremblinge, rocks rending, the windes, tempeſts, Seas contrarie to theyr naturall inclinations performing his commaundements, oracles ceaſing, Idolles fallinge, the deuils and creatures both ſenſible and inſenſible acknowledging and obeyinge him. Many miracles to the ſame effect, and wicked ſpirits profeſſed enemies of al piety caſt forth by authority, future contingent thinges moſte certainlie foretolde, incurable diſeaſes healed, blinde reſtored to ſight, lame to going, deafe to hearing, dumbe to ſpeaking, dead to life, when in all humane reaſon and ſcience of Philoſophers, ſuch effects are vnpoſsible to be performed by naturall meanes, or ſupernaturally to be wrought of God, or any ſecondary cauſe by his cooperation, to giue credit and authority to falſehoode. The moſt ſtrange & miraculous alteration in the liues of thoſe embraced him, the wonderfull conuerſion of the world vnto him, the rare and extraordinalie ſtil continuing puniſhments vpon thoſe refuſed him. And theſe, and ſuch witneſſes not giuen in obſcure and baſe places onlie before ſimple and vnlearned men,

Sibil. apud Lact, firm. l. 2, 3. 4 &c. diu. inſtit,
Merc, Triſm. in Dial.
Plat. in tim.
Porphyr, li. de Oracul.
Mah. in Alc.
Rabb. li. de Chriſt.
Suet. in Oct. cap. 95.
Sen l. 1. natur. q. c. 2.
Plin. hiſt. l. 2 c. 31. c. 28.
Calcid in ti.
Plat. de Stel.
Dio. lib. 47.
Plin. nat. hiſt l. 2 cap. 84.
Suet. in Tiber. c. 48.
Dio. l. 57.
Plut. l. defect. Oracul.
Suet. in Oct. cap. 94. & 70. 29.
Sibil. Lact. lib. 1.

Origen. hō. 15. in Iosue Gaz. in ca. 38. Gen. Rab. Ion. l. col. Rab. Abb. in thren. Rabb. Moys. hadars. in c. 1. 41. Gen. Rab. harcad. in c. 9. Is. Rab. Da. Kinh. l. radic. paraphras. cold in c. 4. Is. & Osee. 1. Rab. Is. in c. 47. Gen. Rab. Sim. in c. 10. Gen. & Iob. 19. Procl. l. 2. & 3. in parm. Plat. Mercur in pem. cap. 1. &c. Lact. firm. l. 1. inst. diu. c. 6. l. 4. c. 6. Varr. lib. de reb. dinin. Cicer. l. 2. diuin. Virg. egl. 4. Suid. in Thal Porp. l. orac. Plut. l. orac. Suid. in Aug Adriā. Imp. Epist. Marc. Aurel. epist. Pilat. epist. ad Tiber. Euseb. lib. 2. hist. Plin. 2. epist. ad Traian. Imper. Rabb. lib. de vit. Christ. Porphir. lib. def. orac. Mahū. Alca. Azo 10. 12. 67. 11. 5 &c. Resv. part. 2.

as Seducers vse to deale, but in frequent and publique places, and most famous Cities, before the mightiest and most potent Princes, Kinges, Tetrarches of Iurie, Syria, and other Nations, yea the most wise Philosophers, crafty & subtile Magitians of the worlde. Written and recorded not only by the holy Prophets, Apostles, and Euangelists miraculously prooued to haue beene directed and assisted, and neuer to haue writen vntruth, or the Patriarkes in their testament cited by *Origen*, that liued within one hundred and threescore years of Christ as then extant, and translated forth of hebrew into greeke by *Procopius* eleauen hundred years ago, where euery one of thē prophesieth nost plainly of Iesus Christ the Mesias. And the generall consent of the ancient Rabbins and expositors of holy Scriptures before Christ, but those which euer were in highest account and reputation among the Gentils, themselues, whether for learning and antiquitie, as *Soroastres, Hermes, Trismegistus* their most renouned, or such as God had illuminated with these misteries, and liued as Prophets for the instruction of that people, as so many of the *Sibils* as plainlie foretelling the misteries & procedings of Christ, of his diuinity, humanity, natiuity, life, death, comming to iudgement, and other secrets of Christian doctrine, as if they had beene personally present, and seene those thinges effected. So did the Oracles and answers of their Gods, and were inforced so to doe, as themselues confessed, and not onlie to priuate men, but to the Emperours and cheife Princes. So doe, and did the most authenticke Registers, and imperiall Recordes, Wrightings, and Edicts, of the Gentile Emperours, as *Tiberius, Traiane, Antonius*, and other Princes, as *Pilate* and *Herod* in Iurie, the Senators at Rome, and others. So those which were the most noysome and offensiue enemies of Christ, the Thalmadists, *Porphiry* and *Mahumet*, that great Seducer, which in diuers chapters of his Alcaron confirmeth the Miracles, and Religion of Christ for most true, and holie. Therfore dealing with men of a Christian Countrie, such (as I hope) all inhabitants of Englande desire alwaies to be accounted, I might make an ende of this matter: but because I haue taken in hand to proue Catholicke Religion to be the onlie true worshippe, and reuerence of God, not only against all deuided sectes of heretickes which I am to performe in my disputation against my countrie Protestants, but also against all Infidels and other misbeleeuers, and by most certaine and lamentable experience we know that Iews, Mahumetans, & other Infidels haue liued in England, without any distinction of different signe from Christians, such as they are bound to weare in Catholicke Countries; and further their wicked bookes, as Alcaron of *Mahumet* and such others, haue bene vsed & perused

perused of manie vnfitte readers and examiners of such blasphemies, and diuers Protestantes not onlie in Germanie and other places, but of Englande haue forsaken the faith of Christ and become circumcised miscreants, I will brieflie in fewe reasons prooue the falcehoode and error of all externall infidelles. Such as suppose the probation of so maniefest a veritie to be superfluous, may passe them ouer, and beeginne with my arguments against Protestants and other internall enemies. Casp. Vlenb. lib. 22 caus. Rain. Calu. turcis. &c.

Chap. 2. and 1. Argum. *For Catholike Christian relligion, againste all externall misbeleeuers, grounded vppon the plaine confession, of all our greateste professed enemies, vppon whose authorities all other worships are founded.*

I Suppose al knowne infidels & misbeleeuers, setting hereticks one side, (with whom I must deale in my next reasons) to be comprehended vnder the names and titles either of Iews, Mahumetanes, or idolatrous Pagans: for neither ecclesiasticall writers, historians, or trauailors of countries, make mention of more, neither can I perceaue in reason, how any mā not professing himself a christian, is forgotten & lefte out in that diuision. For seeing the diuersity of misbeliefe towards Christ, or denying him must be taken from the diuersity of the māner of misbeleeuing or denying, then al infidels either vtterly denied Christ, both in figure & verity as generally the gentils did, neither recauing him for the *Messias*, or expecting any other to worship, but yeelding reuerence to idols, & feigned gods, or else they confessed him in figure & expectation before he came, and in veritie and at his comming denyed him, and such are Iewes, or else both confessing before his comming that he was promised to the worlde, and after he is come, doe acknowledge his comming, but not in that manner wherein he was promised, or in such sorte as he came, or him alone, but allowing an other, as *Mahumet* and Mahumetanes doe, confessing Iesus Christ to bee the true Messias and Prophet, promised in the lawe of *Moyses*, but denying his diuinitie, and receauing *Mahumet* a seducer for a Prophet. So that we see, all Infidelles either be Iewes, Mahumetans, or idolatrous Pagans. Nowe to conclude the onlie trueth and veritie of christian faith, and falshoode of all those erronious worships by their owne confession, and testimonie in such sort in one argument, that it shall not bee lawefull for a Iewe by the very grounds of his owne religion, or a Pagan by the rule and ground of Paganisme, or a Mahumetan by the lawe of *Mahumet*, to denie my argument, which is as much, as any of those misbeleeuers can desire, I must suppose that (which euery Iewe, Pagan, and Mahumetan will willingly graunt, and all histories, and monuments of antiquities affirme to be true) that in euery one of those professions, there was a cer- Part. 2. Reso. Lact. firm. li. diu. instit. Thalm. Iud. & Rab. Thal. Mahumet. in Alcoran.

taine knowen Rule, and proposer of Religion, of whom the rest were to be instructed, what to beleeue, and doe, in things appertaining to their Religion. For else euery man might haue bene a square, and measure to himselfe, no common worship or reuerence could haue beene exercised amonge them, in such sorte as experience and sufficient testimonie do proue there was. Therefore to beginne with the Relygion of the Iewes before Christ, when they were the people of God, and serued him in true Religion as both the Iewes that be nowe, and Christians confesse, and *Mahumet* doth not deny. We all consent that the law which was deliuered to *Moyses*, & by *Moyses* to the Israelites, was the true worship and religion of God, giuen and cōmaunded by him by the testimony and signes of many and wonderful miracles, & for the special protection of that people in true reuerence, and dutie to him, vntill by disobedient apostasie they forsooke him; he did not only giue them an high Priest of whom they were to be instructed, if *any difficult or doubtfull thing should happen*: but gaue them holy Prophets, enspired with knowledge to direct them, and further commanded the same *Moyses* to make a propitiatorie, or Oracle of most pure golde, containing two cubits and halfe in length, and a cubit and halfe in breadth, with a golden Cherubine or Angell on either side: out of which place he promised to giue answere and direction to that people; and thither the highe Priestes resorted, to consulte with the Oracle of God, in matters of doubt or distresse. So that they which were thus taught, either by Prophets immediatlie and internallie illuminated of God or the high Priest instructed likewise of him, or of God himselfe giuing answers in that Oracle, coulde by no meanes be deceaued, for the Misteries which were so reuealed vnto them, must needes be true: After this manner, the Pagan Gentils proceeded in the same matter, for the Gods and Idoles they worshipped being Deuills (as the Prophet saith, & their destruction and vtter ruine & other arguments haue proued) which alwaies were enemies to God & imitators of his honour and worship, appointed Flamens, and Archflamens as high Priests to offer sacrifice to them, & teach Idolatry to their worshippers. This al historians witnes, & countries can record, & England it selfe, where so many Archflamens & Flamens were, as in London, Gloster, & other places almost 30. in nūber. Besides which, they appointed certaine Oracles where thēselues would giue responce, which were accoūted for the highest sentence in the Pagan religion, for being the sentence of their gods (as they called thē) whom they did reuerēce, no greater or more infallible iudgment could be expected. Such were the Oracles of *Appollo*, *Iupiter*, & at *Delphos*, *Memphis*, *Hermopolis*, *Rome*, *London*, and almost of euery Citie. But besides

Exod. c. 3. 4. 5. & c. 12. 13 & c. 19. 20. Deut. 5. Leuit. 26

Deut. c. 17.

Exod. c. 25. 26. 37. 40. Leuit. c. 16. 2. Reg. c 21. 3. Reg. 6. 8. 2. Paral. 5.

Psal. 95.

Cab. in Brit. Stowe hist. Graft. hist. Fox. t. 1. Mō.

Plutar. lib. de oracul. Porph. lib. orac.

besides these, because the true worship of God and eternal beatitude concerned al men, and he would haue no man to lie in excuseable ignorance in a matter of so greate moment, he had true Prophets amonge them for their instruction, as *Iob*, *Sibilla*, *Erithæa*, *Cumena*, and the rest, and other Prophets as their own authors beare witnes, alwaies to haue beene in greatest reputation, and their writings most religiously kept and beleeued. Lastly concerning the Mahumetans, their seducer knowing it was euident in the light of nature, that no true supernaturall religion coulde be ordained by man, a naturall creature, feygned himselfe to bee a Prophet, sent from God, and to haue receaued from him that religion, which his Alcaron conteineth, which is the chiefe rule of the Mahumetanes to this day.

Cic. diu. & l. nat. Deor. Bed. hist. ang l. 1. 2. &c. Cic. l. 2. diu. Virg. egl. 4. Lact. firm. l. diu. instit. Cō. in Boet. Suet. tranq. cap. 3. Suid. in August. &c. Alcor. Mah. Andr. de lacan hist. turric. Leonic. Chal cond. &c.

Thus beeing manifest whereupon the religion of Iewes, Pagans and Mahumetans was and is founded. I will now shew how they all demonstratiuely proue against themselues, the onlie truth of christian doctrine, and condemne their owne for most erronious and ridiculous. And to begin with the Pagan Gentiles, but brieflie because it is handled at large in a late english treatise, did not their highest & renonnedst oracle, answere to the Archflamen at Delphos, and disclose the holie misterie of the Trinitie *of the Father, his deare sonne*, & spirit conteining all: as their own writers *Suidas*, *Plutarch*, *Porphiry*, and others giue euidence. And that deare *sonne of God would be their ouerthrow and destruction*. Like answere was made to *Augustus Cæsar* himselfe about the diuinitie of Christ, and how at his comming, the gods of the Oracles shoulde goe to hell, *Porphiry* that aduowed enemie of Christians is a witnesse, that generallie the Gods and Oracles of the Gentiles gaue testimony to his sanctity, and that where men beleeued in him, the oracles were silent and gaue no answers. Such are the testimonies of *Iuuenall*, *Strabo* and others. And it is generallie verified by all infallible experience, by the ceasing of all Oracles, ouerthrowe of Idolatrie, and confessiou of theyr Gods in all countries in the worlde, where christian religion hath bin preached, either in those that haue so long beleeued, or the Indies & those nations that were latelie conuerted: which was propheticallie foretolde manie hundred yeares before by the holie Prophets *Isaias*, *Saphonias*, *Ezechiell*, *Osee*, *zacharias*, and others, that in rhe time of the *Messias* all such oracles should haue an end, Idolatrie be taken awaie, and the name thereof forgotten as we se it is, and presentlie vpon the birth of Christ, began to take effect. For as *Palladius*, *Fuagrius* (which of them soeuer it was that wrote that historie) witnesseth that accordinge to the prophesie of *Isayas*, the idolles of Egipt a most idolatrous nation shoulde then be ouerthrowne, he himselfe had seene a Temple by Hermopolis, in which

*Howe the very ground and foundation of the Pagās worshippe prooue Christian Religion.* Suid. in Thul Porphyr. lib. de orac. Plutar. li. de defect. orac. Suid. in Aug Niceph. li. 1. hist cap. 17. Porph. li. de laud. philos. & l. 1, Chr. apud Euseb. l. 5. præp. euang. Iuuen. Satyr. 6. Laran. Strab. l. 9. georg. Isaias cap. 2. 19. 11. 31. Sophon. c. 2. Ezech. ca. 6. & 30. Osee c. 14. Zarhar. c. 13 Pallad in hi. in Apollon. Euseb. Demonst, l. 20. Athan. l. incarn. verb. Orig. hom. 3. &c.

when Christ with his mother and *Ioseph* in his flying thither in his infancie, entred into the citie, presently the Idols fel downe to the earth, which worke since hath beene brought to passe in the whole christian worlde, some Oracles ceasing with silence, and saying nothing, others protesting they were compelled by Christ to depart, others acknowledging and cōfessing him, and all one waie or other affirming and confirming his religion to be true, and their owne rites and religion wicked and idolatrous, which in morall iudgment is the greatest argument can be giuen, for no man a professed aduersarie to an other, (such as those Pagans and their Oracles were to Christ, and his religion) especially if the quarrell & contention growe for honour and worship, which all couet and desire, will be commanded by his enemy to giue place, except there be a power and superiority in the commander to doe it. And it is a constant tradition, that *Hieremy* the Prophet prophesied in Egipt, and foretolde to their kings that their Idols shoulde be ouerthrowne when a virgine had a childe, and from that time the Priests of Egipt in a secret place of their temple adored the Image of a virgine with a childe in her armes. And *Sibilla Tiburtina* shewed to *Augustus* the Emperour a little before the time of the natiuity of Christ, a most beautifull virgine holding a childe in her armes, and saide vnto him, *this childe is greater then thou art,* worship him. And in the time of his being an infant, in Egipt the very insensible thinges acknowledged him. At Hermopolis a cittie of Thebais where was a tree called Persis, whose fruite, leaues, or barke healed all diseases, and being very great & high, so soone as Christ approched to the gate of the citie, it bowed down to the grounde and adored him. Balsamum miraculouslie grewe in the orcharde, watered with the well wherein his cloathes were washed: the stone whereon they were beaten and dried, was had in great reuerence euen of the Sarracens and Mahumetans to this time. The place of his habitation alwaies hath a burning lamp by the Mahumetans order. Touching true Prophets that liued among them, what is more auncient then the booke of *Iob*, liuing in the primatiue age of the worlde? and yet what more plaine, then his prophesies of Christ, vttered with such vehemensie and desire of eternall continuance for all posterity, that he requested his wordes might be engraued in the most harde and flintie stone, & the places engraued to be filled with plates of leade, that the letters and writing might be durable, and to be reade of all. And his words which he would haue so surely registred are these. *For I knowe that my Redeemer liueth, and in the last day I shall rise againe with my skinne, and in my flesh shall see God: whome I my selfe and in my flesh shall see, and my eies shall beholde &c.* In which words a whole compen-

Sozom. l. 5. hist. cap. 21. Niceph. l. 10 cap. 31. Baron. to. 1. Ann. fol. 80.

Borcard lib. discript. ter. sanct part. 2. cap. 4. Cornel. Iansen. concord euang. c. 11.

Iob. cap. 19.

compedium and breuiate of Chrstian Religion is conteined: First Christ liued then, and so was God, and Is called his Redeemer, & so the Messias, that was expected. Hee should see him when he was compassed with his skinne, and with his fleshe, and his eyes should beholde him, and he must be man, and that in the day of Iudgement when he shall rise againe, therby acknowledging a resurrection of the bodie, a finall Iudgement, and that Christe shall iudge the worlde. And in all his miseries he sustained, this was his hope as he affirmeth. Of what authoritie the prophesie of the *Sibilles* were amonge them, is not vnknowen, as also howe euidentlie they foretolde the whole summe of the misteries of Christ, so particulerly as if they had beene present. As to cite some of their wordes. *Panta. &c.* Doeing all thinges *with his worde, healing all infirmities: the deade shall be raysed, and the lame shal run apace, the deafe shall heare, the blinde shall see. Those which could not speake shall speake. With fiue loaues and two fishes he shall feede fiue thousand men in in the desarte, and taking vp that which is lefte shall fill twelue baskets. For the hope of manie. He shall commande or bridle the windes, he shall goe and tread vpon the raging Sea, with his feete. He shall walke vpon the waues. Resolue the diseases of men, raise those that be dead to life, & driue greefes from many,* hitherto be the wordes of *Sibilla,* their prophetesse. And she recounteth so manie miracles to be performed by Christ that she hir selfe did affirme the Pagans with whom she liued, whose gods could not doe miracles, and shewe such effectes, would mocke hir and say she were madde, hir wordes are these, *Phisousi Sibillen menomenin*, they wil cal me a *mad Prophetesse, or Sibill, & that I am a lier but when all these thinges shall come to passe, they shall remember mee, and then no man will call me a liar anie longer*, but a *Prophetesse of the great God.* And foretelleth further, that at his comming the lawe of *Moyses*, shall cease, in these wordes: *when all these thinges shall be finished which I haue spoken of him, then the Lawe shall bee dissolued. And* Sibilla erithrea speaking of the same Iesus sonne of the virgin (as they called him) how in his eternall generation he was begotten of the Father. and was true God: Saith that *he was geuen to all faithfull people to be worshipped. And an other* Sibill hath these words. *Auton son ginosche I heon Theou huon ionta. Know him to be thy God: which is the son of God:* The same and like speches *Lactantius* citeth out of *Trismegistus* or *Hermes* from the Oracle of *Apollo Esculapius* and others. And touching the passion of Christ, *Sibilla* vttereth these wordes, *he shall fall into the wicked hands of Infidels: & they shall giue blowes vnto God, with incestious handes & with vncleane mouth shall spit venimous spittings. He shall giue his innocent backe to be beaten, and taking blowes, shall holde his peace; for his meat they shall giue him gall, and vinigre for his thirst.* And rebuking the land of Iurie for such vsage of their *Messias*, vseth these speeches. *For when thou folish*

Sibill. apud Lact. firm. l. 4. instit. cap. 16. & c. 15.

Supr. c. 17.

Sibil. erithr. apud Lact. sup. l. 4. c. 6.

Calcid. l. 2. in tim. Plat. Trismeg li. Logos telios Lact. supr. &c 7. & 13.

Lib. 4. supr. cap. 18.

*didst not know thy God*, dissembled to mortal mindes, *thou didst crowne him with a crowne of thornes, and mingledst horrible gall.* And concerning the miracles at his passion, saith, *that the vaile of the Temple shall be torne: and at mid-day there shal be a wonderful nighty darknesse three houres togither. And yet when these thinges were done, for all these celestiall wonders, they woulde not knowe their wicked offence. He shal ende his death with a sleepe of three daies, and then arising from the dead shall come to light, the first that shall shewe a beginning of resurrection to such as be called.* These be the very wordes of the *Sibils*, and Prophets of the Gentiles, which prosecute the comming of Christ to iudgment, the reward for the good, punishment for the wicked, and other misteries of christian religion, as we beleeue, condemning all other worships to be false, and superstitious. And least any man shoulde imagine, that these so manifest prophesies of Christ, should be deuised by any follower of his, after his comming, it is most manifest in the Pagan Authors themselues, *Erastothenes*, *Cicero*, *Crisippus*, *Apollodorus*, *Neuius*, *Euripides*, *Heraclites*, *Virgill*, *Varro*, *Suetonius*, and almost all Historians of the Gentiles before Christ, that they were both extant in the worlde, and famouslie knowne before, and most reuerently regarded and kept in their greatest places, euen of the Cesars and Emperours themselues; what was the reason that the Pagans did not vnderstande these thinges I haue cited out of their owne wordes. And such as those *Sibilles* were, wee cannot doubt to haue beene in other times and places amonge the Gentiles, to be witnesses of these thinges, as is manifest in their most certaine and vndoubced prophesies, registred in irreprooueable Authors, founde and promulged in such sort, as they cannot be denied. There was founde in the tombe of *Plato* that great Philosopher, a plate of golde vpon his breast, with these words engraued. *Credo in Christum nasciturum ex Virgine: passurum pro humano genere: & tertia die resurrecturum. I beleeue in Christ which shall be borne of a Virgine; shall suffer for mankinde; and rise againe the thirde day.* Yet *Plato* was dead and buried 370. yeares before the incarnatiou of Christ. And in his works were conteyned these euangelicall words that followe. *In the beginning was the worde, and the worde was with God, and God was the worde. This was in the beginning with God. Al things were made by him: & without him was made nothing. That which was made in him was life, & the life was the light of men, & the light shineth in darknes.* Which word for word, is the beginning of the Gospell by S. *Iohn.* And in the time of *Constantine* and *Hyrene* there was found in the citie of Cōstantinople, where many Iews inhabited, an ancient tombe, and vpon the body of him that was buried therein, a plate of golde, wherein these words written before the cōming of christ were engraued: *Christus nascetur ex virgine Maria, & ego credo in eum, O sol iterum me videbis, sub* Constantino & Hyrene.

*Christ*

Cap. 19. sup.

Apud Lact. lib. 7. diuin. inst. cap. 13. 16. 18. 19. 20. 23. 24. & lib. opific. cap. 22. 23. Erastoth. in in antiquit. Annal. Cic. l. de diu. Virgil. egl. 4 Suet. in Aug Varr. l. rer. diu. ad Cæs. Crisip. l. diu. Neuius l. bel. punic. &c. Euri. in prol. Iam. &c.

Comment. in Boet. de disc ipl. schol. Philip. Berg. Chron. f. 64. Eus. in hist. Bergom. sup. in Chr. Ang. lib. 10. ciu. cap. 2.

D. Thom. 3. part. sum. theol. Berg. Chron.

*Christ shall be borne of a virgine called* Mary, *and I beleeue in him. O Sunne thou shalte see me againe vnder* Constantine *and* Hyrene, which was aboue 780. yeares after Christ. And in the yeare 1230. a naturall borne Iewe, and professed enemie of Christian Religion, at Tolletum, diging in the grounde, found a stone, wherin there was a booke for time and continuance difficult to be read, in which, among other thinges, these wordes were written. *In tertio mundo filius Dei nacetur ex virgine* Maria, *& pro salute hominum patietur. In the third age of the worlde the Son of God shall be borne of a virgin named* Mary *and shall suffer for the saluation of men:* And moreouer that the booke should be found in that verie time when it was, in the dayes of Feranda *the Virgin of Castyll*. The times, places, the finders, proposers, and all other circumstances of which prophesies were such, that no man canne denie them to be the effectes of a true propheticall spirite. And so I might recounte of others. Wherby it is manifest that euen in the greatest sway of the Pagans Idolatrie, there wanted not true beleeuers in Christe, and such as gaue testimonie to his comming.

Regist. tol. Chron. hisp. Gran. lib. de Symbol.

*The testimonie of Mahumet, his Alcaron, and Mahumetans.*

Concerning Mahumetanes, we heaue harde before, how their Prophet and proposer of their lawe *Mahumet* (as they esteeme him) in his *Alcaron* hath auouched the same, that Christ was the *Messias* and Prophet which in the law was promised to the worlde, borne of the virgine *Mary*, she stil remaining a Virgine, that he was the gratest prophet that euer was, or shall be, greater then Mahumet himselfe, the worde of GOD, Spirit of GOD, taught true Religion, came to supplie the defectes of the lawe of *Moyses*, and the Gospell was the perfection thereof, and perfecte doctrine, Christes myracles were true, and giuen vnto him for confirming his doctrine, and enforce all Iewes which will professe the Religion of *Mahumet*, first to acknowledge and protest in expresse wordes that *Iesus* was the *Messias* of the worlde, they affirme hee was the worde, wisdome, Spirit, and vnderstanding of God, a Prince to the Iewes, and head of all men. Whosoeuer among them blasphemeth either Christ or his Mother, besides, a great forfeiture of monie is beaten with threescore blowes, with a clubbe. Mahumet further affirmeth, that the Religion of Iewes and *Mahumet* shall vtterly perish, and only the Religion of Christ perseuer to the ende. The keepers therof shall be saued. Christ is exalted aboue all creatures in heauen, and shall come to destroy Antechrist, and restore generallie true Religion, and in the day of Iudgement be pronouncer of the sentence & doome of God. That his Mother was the holiest of all women, moste puer, that shee was one of the miracles of the world, saluted and certified of the conception and birth of Christ by the

Alcoran. azoar. 67. azoar. 10. azoar. 11. 12. azoar. 1. 5. &c. Azoar. 67. Azoar. 19. Azoar. 12.

Theuet. lib. 6. cap. 5. Alc. azoar. 2 Azoar. 20. Theuet Cosmog. lib. 8. cap. 2.

Alcor. &c. Bellon. lib. 3 cap. 3. cap 7. Cusan. lib. 1. cri. rat. Alcor. cap. 2 l. 2. c. 14. Alc. axoar. 31. azoar. 5.

Angel *Gabriell*, that among all the children of *Adam*, onlie Christ and shee were vndefiled, shee neuer committed anie sinne; that shee was a virgine, not onlie before and at the time of the natiuitie of Christ, but euer after, that shee brought forth Christ without anie paine or griefe, S. *Iohn Baptist* was a most vertuous man, S. *Iohn* the Euangelist the holiest that was, that he reuiued the dead, and did other miracles, was assumpted aliue to heauen, that his gospell is full of perfect doctrine, which they reuerence, as also that parte of the gospell of S. *Luke* about the Angels salutation with often kisses, and much deuotion, and reuerence al the Euangelists, they honour and pray to S. *George* and other christian saintes, reuerence their Relickes, & with especiall duty the sepulchre & other monuments of Christ. Which is as great a recorde as can be giuen, and such as demonstratiuelie prooueth against them the religion of christians to be true, and *Mahumet* a seducer. For how can that religion bee vnperfecte which performeth all thinges belonging to religion, bringeth men to heauen, and their happie ende? How can that which only remaineth be insufficient? When Iudaisme and Mahumetisme and all others cease, will God be without honour? shal the world giue him no worshippe? or if he be the worde of God, and wisedome of God, as *Mahumet* confesseth, then hee must needes bee God, which is all he denieth vnto him, for that which is either the worde, wisedome, or any other attribute or propertie of God, must needs be God, for in him that is one incompounded substance, no created worde, wisdome, or accidentall thinge can be imagined. Neither coulde a true Prophette such as he confesseth *Iesus*, be esteemed so, if he had not beene the sonne of God, and perfect God, as he taught himselfe to be.

Azoar. 76. Azoar. 2. 9. I. gener. Mah p. 202. Azoar. 39. Azoar. 1. 2. 3. 9. 20. 21. 13. 17. 29. 31. 34.

*Testimonie of the Iewes and the grounds of their religion.*

Lastlie to come to the Iewes of these times, since Christ: I haue shewed before that the chiefe and principall firmament and foundation of their religion, when they were the people of God, was builded vpon the reuelations of such misteries, as were deliuered from God to *Moises*, their high priests, & prophets, neither euer had they title to true religion, or any promise or expectation of a *Messias* & redeemer either come already, or to be hoped hereafter, but by that meanes, & by that they pretende theyr right to this daie. So that whatsoeuer was foretolde in those holie Prophettes, concerninge the *Messias*, and approuinge Iesus Christ to be him, and christian beliefe to be true, cannot be denied of anie of the Iewish profession if he will remaine a Iewe; for so he should deny himself to haue any religion at all. And yet those holy Prophets so plainly, particulerlie, and perfectlie describe Iesus to haue beene the same, that it is vnpossible theyr description and prophesies shoulde be applied to anie other. So that as if a

nie

ny painter should draw an Image with an vpright body, and head round, with face, nose, twoe eies, twoe eares, armes with fingers, twoe legges, and feete with toes, and all other members, lineaments, and proportions of a man, who except vnreasonable or madde could or woulde affirme it to be the similitude and representation of a beaste, a birde, or anie other creature: euen so the properties and qualities whereby those holie Prophets moste cunning painters of supernaturall thinges, describe and purtrature forth the Messias, be so propper onlie to Iesus Christ, tha without obstinate madnesse they cannot be challendged for any others. We haue heard of his picture drawne by *Iob* already, that he is our God, Redeemer, and shall be our Iudge. And to be briefe in so plaine a matter, the rest of the Prophets speaking of the Messias, expresse him by the tetragrãmaton name of god, which is neuer giuen in holy scriptures, as the Iews acknowledge, but to the true & eternall God, they tearme him by al titles belonging vnto god. Calling him *the sonne of god, begotten in eternity before the world was made. The lord of* Dauid. *That this generation is vnspeakable; that he is God, and his throne eternall; a counsailour. Good. Strong. Father of the future world. Prince of peace. God with vs. God seen in earth. God conuersing with men. Iah. God himself that shall come & saue vs. The name which they shal cal him is god, our iust. A captaine whose going forth is from the daies of eternitye. God that shall dwell in the middest of vs. God to whome manie nations shall be conuerted. To whome the Nations and Gentilles shall be giuen for his inheritaunce. That shall open the eies of the blinde. The eares of the deafe, & raise the dead. That all Angelles and Nations must adore mim. God altering the lawe of* Moises, *and his Sacrifices, and institutinge an other Altar, and honoured with other Sacrifices and Oblations. That he is God, Lorde of Hoastes,* and the like. Wherby he is described and lineamented out by al prerogatiues and attributes proper to god, and incommunicable to anie creature, as is moste euident in this description. And touching his humanitie nothing of moment omitted that passed in the life of *Iesus* on earth. That though he be *God yet shall be seene among vs, conuerse among vs, in the midst of vs. Seene with our eies. That hee shall be conceaued after a diuyne manner, borne of a virgine, in Bethlem, and Citie of King* Dauid. *The singinge of the Angelles. The comminge of the Sheepeheardes. The stalle of the Oxe and Asse, where he was borne. The star that appeared. The iourny and worship of the* Magi: *their oblations of golde frankensence and mirh. The consultation of* Herode *with the Priests, where he shoulde be borne. The seeking of his death. The murderinge of so many thousand infants. His presentation in the temple, flying into Egipt, going into Galilie, dwelling in Nazareth, the preaching & austere conuersatiõ & life of his precursfor S.* Iohn *Baptist, & his testimony of Christ. The begining of Christs preaching and doctrine. His wonderful works and operations, giuen by the prophets for a distinctiue signe of the messias, to be*

Iob. c. 19. Psal. 2. Is. 9. Is. cap. 25. H. V. H. I. Pasm. 2. Psal. 109. Is. 53. Psal. 44. Is. cap. 9. Bar. cap. 3. Is. c. 12. & cap. 25. Ierem. c. 23. & 33. Mich. cap. 5. Zachar. c. 2. Psal. 2. Is. cap. 9. 53. 2. 19. Mal. c. 1. Ezech. c. 20. Ierem. c. 3.

Iob c. 19. Bar. cap. 3. Is. cap. 7. Mich. cap. 5. Ierem. c. 31. Is. cap. 1. Num. c. 20. Psal. 71. Ierem. 31. Malach. 3. Is cap. 21. 31. 45. Zach c. 1. Is. 42. 40. Malach. 3. Zachar. 9. Is. 50.

Dan. ca. 10. Is. cap. 1. Psal. 80. Osee. 2. 3. Is cap. 9. Mich. ca. 2. Zachar. 8. Psalm. 2. Gen. ca. 48. Psal. 40. 50. 108. Is. 53. Dan. cap 9. Psal. 21. 68. Zachar. 9. Ps. 106. 15. Osee. 6. Psal. 67. Psal. 119. Gen. ca. 49. Dan. cap. 2. Psalm. 68. & 108. Ioel. cap. 2.

*discerned by his disputing with the Iews. His strange and triumphant riding vpon an asse into Ierusalem, and circumstaunces therof. His teachinge in the temple. innocencie of life and behauiour. the particuler iniuries he susteined of the Iewish uation, their ingratitude, incredulity, and reprobation for not receauinge him; the errors they are since fallen into, their afflictions, and calamities for that offence susteined to this day, their captiuity, bondage, dispersion, want of sacrifice, priesthood, temple, rites, & ceremonies of religion. The election and calling of the Gentils. The general ouerthrow of idolatry. His selling and betraying by his owne disciple. The very price for which he was solde. How it was bestowed. The desperation of* Iudas *the traitor, and miserable end. The death of Christ, and mãner therof, among theeues, and malefactors. The end to redeeme the world. His voluntarie oblation and dying, the giuing of him gall, & vinegre to drinke, deuiding of his apparel casting lots for his coate, his nakednes vpon the crosse, the piercing of his side, the nailing of his handes & feet. His descending as a conqueror into hell, his victorious rising from death, triũphant ascending to heauen, & the very time & place by markes infallible, & other matters that passed either about his natiuity, life, death, or after: as the chusing of* Mathias *to supplie the place of* Iudas, the miraculous comming of the holie ghost in the feast of pentecost, and the rest. How al these and many others foretolde by the Hebrwe Prophets so longe before of their Messias, were verified & fullfilled in Iesus the Sonne of the blessed virgine *Marie*, I neede not to sette downe the new testament where they are recorded by the Euangelists and Apostles, being in the hands of euerie english reader in his own language; and not only written by christians, but remembred by Gentils in their writings, recorded in libraries, and monuments of Pagan Princes, and Emperors. Confirmed by rhe very testimony of *Pilate* himselfe that put him to death. Witnessed of our greatest enemies *Mahumet* in his Alcaron, the Iews in their Thalmud, and by so many historians, both of Iews, Pagans, and Christians, and could not possiblie either be deuised of our friendes, or denied of our enemies, chauncing for the most parte before thousands of witnesses, in or about Hierusalem, a place so famous, where the Presidente was resydente, and whether resorted Proselytes, and others of all knowne Nations in the worlde. Therefore we conclude against the Iewes by their owne Prophets, and foundation of their Religion, agaynste Pagans by their Prophets, and Oracles, and against Mahumetans by their *Mahumet*, and Alcaron, & all Infidels by the chiefe rules and proposers of their Religion, that Iesus Christ is the true Messias and Redeemer of the world' that onlie the religion of Christians is true, hauinge such a peacemaker and Mediator betweene God and vs, as was able to make the attonement being both God and man, as a redeemer must needs be, & such as both his own workes and operations, and the predictions of those holie

Calcic. li. 2. in tim. plat. Ioseph. l. 14. antiq. ca. 4. & lib. 18. cap. 6. 7. Mah. in Alc. cap. 12. 11. 5. 67. Pilat. ep. ad Tiber. imp. apud. Eus. l. 2 histor. Plin. 2. ep. ad Traian. Imper. Adriã. Imp. in ep. Antõ. Imp. ep. &c. Alcor. ca. 1. 4. 13. Thalm. tract añod. Zara misd. Coh. &c.

Prophets fortolde, and described by the attributes and properties of both natures diuine and humane. His diuine nature by his Eternitie, Omnipotencie, Impassibillitie, Infinitnes, power ouer all creatures, and to produce all supernaturall effectes, to alter and establish religion, to saue, to condemne, to bee honored with diuine adoration, and all names and titles due & belonging to God, as appeareth in their desription I haue recited, confirmed and be expounded generallie by the ancient Rabbins before Christ. As likewise his humane nature is deciphered by the same prophets by al properties and qualities of man (sinne excepted.) Therfore seeing by no possibillitie the wisdome of God canne be deceaued, or his bonitie and goodnesse leade others into error, and Infidelitie, and hee had appointed those properties to be the notes, signes, and tokens to know the *Messias* by, and they were performed only in Iesus our Sauiour, and no other, he must nedes be the Redemer of the world, only christian Religion true, and all other Infidelles, Iewes Pagans, and Mahumetans, seduced, and deceaued. For that which is only proper to one, cannot belonge vnto more, for so it shoulde not bee a proper and priuate but a common and vulgar thing.

Rab. Ionath. lib. collect misd. tehel. in Psal. 2. v. 7 & Ps. 20. Rab. Abb. in thren. Rabb. mos. had. in cap. 41. Gen.

Argum. 2. *Howe all externall and most notorious Notes and Signes giuen by God, to knowe the Messias by, were onlie verified of Iesus Christ, and cannot possiblie bee performed in any other.*

BVT besides these prsonall and internall priuiledges and distinctions of the Mesias; before the redemption of mankinde to be effected by him concerned all people, & nations, in that all had ofended; so the infinite mercy and goodnes of God, that no man should be ignorant of that which concerned him so much, as the receiuing of the Redeemer, & working his owne saluation doeth: had appointed manie other most knowne and famous extrincicall thinges to be the signes and tokens of his comming, whereof many were notorious in all the world, and the reste at the least renowned to that nation of the Iews (from whom he was to descend) and other neighbouring countries to the Israelites; all which were euidently verified in Christ Iesus, & cannot be efected in any other. For breuity I wil exemplifie but in few paticulers, the matter being manifest before.

*The first externall token of the Messias that he should come before it was destroyed &c.*

First, the Temple in Hierusalem was not only the most renowned thing in Iury, but famous in all the worlde, by reporte of Prosolites, and such as resorted thither, especially, when Iury was ruled by the Romans, as it was at the comming of Christe: Therefore when God gaue for a distinctiue signe to knowe the *Messias* by, as not onlie the auncient Iewes and Rabbines, but the *Thalmudists* themselues acknowledge, that both in the time of

Agg. 2. Malach. 3. Rab. Ios. ben leui, in Thal. tract. sanch. c. helec.

of his life he should come to that temple (*then shal come the desired of al nations: and I will fill this house (or Temple) with glory saith the Lorde of hostes. And streight after, shall come to his temple, the Lorde or ruler whome you seeke, and the messenger of the testament whome you desire,*) as the Prophets expreslie foretolde, as Iesus often did, as the Iewes and all Infidels acknowledge: And further, that soone after his death, that Temple shoulde be destroyed, and left desolate, neuer to be builded againe as *Daniel* witnessed in these wordes. (*Christ shall be slaine, and a people with their captaine to come, shall destroy the Citie and the Sanctuarie, & the end thereof shall be vastitie. And after the war ended, there shal ensue the appointed desolation.*) And further expresse the verie time when this should be, iust agreeing with the death of Christ. And it is manifest, that no other in those daies, and with those circumstances is honoured for the Messias, either of Christians, Iewes, Pagans, or Mahumetans, but only Iesus Christ, and that the Temple was then destroyed, as is most euident, and not only the temple in Hierusalem, but that in Egipt called *Onion*, as *Iosephus* recordeth, it was he that was to be distinguished by this signe. For no power of God can cause that any pretended Messias to be hereafter was he, that came to that temple before it was destroyed, or that the destruction of that temple compleated aboue 1500. yeares agoe, shoulde be done after the death of him, that is not yet borne. For things to be, and not to be, are vnpossible to be true. Therefore against all Iewes and Infidels, only Iesus Christ was, and no other can be the Messias by that signe.

Dan. c. 9.

Ioseph. bell. iud. lib. 6. Euseb. hist. Ioseph. bell. l. 7. cap. 30.

*2. Externall Note, of the Messias, that he was to discende of the house of Dauid, and bee borne in his citie of Bethelem.*

Secondly, (as the Iewes themselues agree) the holy Prophets giue for a like distructiue signe, that he was to descend of the line of *Iuda* and king *Dauid*, and to be borne in Bethlem his citie. This family was the linage of the kings, and most honourable in Israell. And had endured in honour and gouernment, aboue 1000. yeares without interruption: And the towne of Bethlem was notable in all Iurie, beeing the chiefe cittie of the tribe of Iuda; but the Iewes themselues confesse in their *Thalmud* it selfe, and all the worlde can tell, not only that Christ Iesus discended of King *Dauids* parentage, and was borne in the same citie of Bethlem, but that aboue 1500. yeares agoe, the familie of King *Dauid* by expresse command of *Vespatian*, (that not one shoulde be left aliue that discended of that line) was destroyed, because he knewe the Messias was of that linage; & soone after, the citie of Bethlem was quite desolate and ouerthrowne, in the time of *Adrian* the Emperour. Therefore (as in the former reason) this signe cannot be applied to any false or forged Messias to come: for neither the towne vnknowne, neither the familie either wholie rooted out, or most vncertainlie confounded with the rest, can be a certaine signe of so sure notice,

Ier. 23. 30. Ezech. 34. Osee. 3. 3. Reg. 7. Thalm. tract Sarch. c. mig mar. had. Euseb. hist l. 3. cap. 11.

Oros. lib. 7. cap. 13. Euseb. lib. 4. histor. cap. 5. Dion. Cass. in Adrian.

notice, as the *Messias* was to be discerned by.

Thirdly, the Sacrifices of the Iewes offred in Hierusalem, their Priesthood, sacraments, and ceremonies of their religion there practised, were most honourable in that people, and not vnknowne to the greatest kingdomes of the earth, and as they had beene kept and celebrated there, with so great applause and concourse of so many nations, 1400. yeares togither, so they could not cease and be taken away, but with the knowledge and wonder of many peoples. The cease of these things was a signe of the comming of the *Messias*, as the prophets, *Daniel*, *Ieremy*, *Malachy*, *Ose*, *Esay* & others, and the *Sibills* themselues among the gentils had most plainely described. But soone after the comming of Christ al these did cease, Hierusalem their citie where these Sacrifices were vsed, the Temple and Altar where they were offred, the Priestes which practised these rites and ceremonies were destroied, banished and exiled that nation, as I haue shewed before, and the whole world can witnes. Therefore seing neither *Iew Gentile* nor *Mahumetan* worship any of that time for the *Messias*, and those signes cannot possiblie bee verified in any since, or to come, only *Iesus Christ* in whome they were compleated, must needes be the *Messias*, as not only Christians but *Mahumet* and Mahumetans acknowledge.

*3. Externall signe, the ceasing of Iewes Sacrifice, and lawe &c.* Leuit. Deut. 1. Reg. 2. Reg. 3. Reg, &c. Dan. 9. Hier. 41. Malach, 1. Osee 2. 3. 9. Sybill. apud Lact. lib. 4. diu. instit. cap. 17. Is. 1. 2. 3. 5. & 24. 28. 25. 29. 32. 48. Mah. in Alc.

Fourthlye, the Idolatries and Superstitions of the Gentiles which (only Iurie excepted) possessed the whole habitable and knowne world, & had practised those things almost three thousand yeares without desolation, maintained and aduanced by so many Kinges and Emperours, were so familiar and experienced to all Nations that they could not cease without a wonderfull and strange alteration, therfore God had also asigned this for a distinctiue badge to beginne at the time of the *Messias*, and to be effected by his Religion, and that those Gentiles and Idolaters should be conuerted vnto Christ. There is no other which can pretend to haue bin cause of these chāges, *Mahumet* doth not challēge it, but yeeldeth it to Christ, the Iews haue not done it, and yet deny *Mahumet*, and there be no knowne professors of Religion at this day but Iewes, Mahumetans, Pagans, & Christians, and among all these, only the remnant of Pagans be Idolaters, the Iewes deny the *Messias* to be come, the Pagans neuer expected any: the rest Christians & Mahumetans alow Christ Iesus only to be the *Messias*, there fore he is to be receaued and only his Religion.

*4. Externall signe, the idolatrye of the Gentyls thē to cease, & they should be conuerted to the Messias.* Lactant. l. 1. diu. instit. Osee 1. 2. Agg. 2. Zachar. 2. 8. Psal. 66. Hier. 31. Malach. 1. Psal. 2. 8. 18. Euseb, dem. l. 6. cap. 20. Athā. l. incar Orig. hom. 3 Pallad. hist. Mah. Alc sup Orig hom 3. Pallad. hist. Mah. Alc sup

Fiftly, from the time of *Abrahā*, in whose dayes God tooke so particuler care of his posteritie, the Iewish Nation vntill their vtter destruction, in the time of *Titus* and *Vespatian*, had passed aboue two thowsand yeares: by which space, that Nation was called the peculiar people of GOD and in

*5. Externall signe, the desolution of the Iewish Natiō.* Gen. Exo. &c Ioseph. l. ant.

respect of the priuiledges graunted vnto them, the whole worlde was not
Gen. Exod. 1. 2. 3. 20. &c. Deut. &c. Ios. l. ant. Phil. Mah. Alc. &c. Orph. Car.
to be compared; so many miraculous & vnwonted fauours shewed vnto them aboue all others, recorded not only in the sacred Scriptures, and the Iewishe historians, but Pagan and Mahumetane writers are witnesse. Therefore that the immutable goodnesse of God shoulde so long time and extraordinarily persecute and punishe that people, which he had so honoured before, was not onely an argument of some grieuous sinne in that generation, (of which I will speake hereafter) but it woulde seeme a most strange and wonderfull thing to all persons. Therefore this was giuen for a signe of the comming of the *Messias*, as the Prophets *Osee, Daniell, Hieremy, Malachy*, and others expresse in most plaine sentences, that they shoulde be *Vagi in nationibus, Vagabonds to all nations. Sine Rege, sine Lege, sine Principe, sine Sacrificio, &c. Without King, without Lawe, without Prince, without Sacrifice*, and without *Altar &c.* Which the whole worlde knoweth, and the Iewes proue by bitter experience to be effected in them, since the time of Christ, and from the last captiuity of Hierusalem, now aboue 1500. yeeres, without al hope of receiuing into fauour with God, and to be restored to their former fauours: therefore Iesus is the Messias.

Osee. 9. 3. Hier 31. Dan. 9. Mal. &c.

*6. Externall signe, the translation of the Septer & regiment from the house of Iuda.*

Sixtly, (because I haue made mention of the Kinges and Princes of Iury) as the Scepter and Kingly regiment of the tribe of Iuda, was the most renowned temporall dignity in that Nation, and had continued from Kinge *Dauid* the first Kinge of that tribe, vntill *Herode* the Ascolanite, aboue a thousande yeeres, so it was renowned in most Countries of the worlde, (seldome any one family enioying princely regiment so long) and could not be taken away without a common wonder and note of people, and therefore was Prophetically giuen by *Iacob* for a signe of the comming of the Messias aboue 700. yeeres before any of this tribe enioyed the Scepter, & aboue 1700. yeers before it was taken from it: the words of *Iacob* are these. *The Scepter shall not be taken from Iuda*, and *a Captaine from his line, vntill he commeth which is to be sent, and he shall be the expectation of the Gentiles (or Nations.)* The Hebrewe text readeth thus. *The Scepter shall not goe from* Iuda, *and a Scribe or Lawemaker from the middest of his feet, vntill* Silo, *or the Messias commeth. And shal be the gathering together of peoples.* And in the *Thargũ* the Caldey reading so honored among the *Iewes*, only the *Messias* is named in that Prophecie, and the ancient Rabbines, euer vnderstode that place of the Messias; the Iewes themselues cannot deny it. But this propheticall signe, cannot possibly be expounded of any other then Christ Iesus, in whose time only, & neuer before, the Scepter & Regiment (as al historians witnesse) was taken from the house of Iuda. For although the Iewishe Nation was often

1. Reg. 2. Reg. &c. Ios. l. antiq. Geneb. Cron &c. Gen. c. 49 Tharg 49. Gen.

per-

persecuted, & made captiue by the infidel bordering kings, yet vntil then, the gouernment was neuer quite taken from the house of Iuda. And neuer any stranger chosen king in *Israell*, but all that ruled euen after the Captiuity were of the house of Iuda, vntil *Herod* the Ascolanite in the time of Iesus entred. The Scriptures be witnes hereof vnto *Zorobabell*, and manie his successours. After them also without interruption, the Scepter remained in the same Tribe, by the mothers lyne, by which the *Assamone* that gouerned vntill *Herod*, were descended of the house of Iuda, as the auncient Rabbines are witnesse, otherwise by no other title without spot of tyranny and vsurpation they coulde haue chalenged the kingdome (although as some suppose these also were by the fathers side of the line of *Iuda*, and of *Leuy* by the mother) for as *Philo* writeth, entermarriage between the kingly & priestly tribes was lawful in that people, & *Herod* himselfe claimed first the kingdome by the title of *Marianne* his wife of that linage, and yet besides this highest princely succession, these continued in the line of *Iuda*, the Zanedrin or Senate of the 72. which ruled by the lawes of that people, were of the tribe of *Iuda*, & as the bookes of the *Machabees* themselues (*The people that is at Ierusalem, & the Senate & Iudas, &c.*) had great Regiment in that Nation in those daies, and were neuer extincte vntill the time of *Herode* the stranger, which both by the Father and Mother, was an Alien, and neither of the house of *Iuda*, or any other Tribe of *Israell*. But at the comming of Christ, both the Kingly Scepter was quite translated, both from *Iuda*, & all other tribes of that people, and the Zanedrin it selfe destroied, and no Ruler lefte of that nation. For *Antigonus* the Iew, and King of that Nation beeing crucified by *Antonius*, and *Hircanus* craftely slaine by King *Herode*, not onely this *Herode* the King was a Gentile and straunger, and lefte the kingdome to *Archilaus*, and after to *Herodes Antipas* borne of *Maltha* also a stranger, as *Iosephus* witnesseth, but in the thirtith yeere of his raigne vtterly destroied the Zanedrin of the house of *Iuda*, and constituted a whole Zanedrin of Proselite strangers. And not only the temporall regiment thus destroied out of the line of *Iuda*, but the most honorable function and calling of the high Priest it selfe was abused, and most prophanely translated and merketed vp and downe by *Herod*, for it was vtterly taken away from the *Assemonies*, the right Tytlers vnto it; and giuen to others. And *Hircanus* the High Priest beeing killed of the same *Herod*, *Aristobolus* without all equity and title was placed in that dignity, but he beeing presently slaine, *Anelus* a base companion fetched from Babylon was substituted in his roome, which was appointed enen in the life of *Hircanus* the lawfull high priest, after deposed & yet after chosen againe. And after

Cyril. l. 8. cont. Iulian. Hierou. in Soph. cap. 1. & in Ezech. cap. 21.
1. Paral. 3.
3 Esder. 5.
Math. 1.
Rabbin. &c.
Cæs. Baron. to. 1. an.

Geneb. Cro. in Machab.

Phil. lib. de Monarch. Ioseph.

Math. 2.

*Ioseph. l. 15.* antip. c. 1.
Dio. hist. Rō. lib. 49.
Iof. lib. 17 antiq c. 1. & Bel. l. 1. c. 18
Phil. l. 2. de tempor.
Iof. lib. 17 antiq. c. 3.
Eus. in Chro.

*Iof. l. 15.* antiq. c. 9. & cap. 3.

him others, without any respecte of the lawe of God, he only regarding
Ioseph.l.20. antiq. cap.8. Euseb. hist. lib.1. cap.6. Hier. in cap. 9. Dan. Ioseph. lib. 18. antiquit. cap. 6. Is. 32. Psal. 71. Dan.2. &c. those that were most potent in bribes, or gratious with him in fauor, as *Iosephus S. Hierome Eusebius* and others are most authentical witnesses. And not content with this, (that he might take all honour and dignitie from all the Tribes of Israell) commanded that the Priestly Stole the most honourable ensigne of the highe Priestly dignitie shoulde bee kept in a most secret and a defended place. Therefore onlie Iesus Christ in whose time these signes were thus effected, is to be conceaued for the *Messias*. Thus I might exemplify in the generall peace vnder *Augustus* the Emperor, and the Romane Empire then begun, giuen for tokens of the comming of the *Messias*, and of other most famous external notes which for breuitie I passe ouer.

Argum. 3. *That the time wherein Iesus Christ was borne, by all accountes and reasons was the time of the comming of the Messias: when the lawe of the Iewes was to cease, and the Idolatrie of the Gentiles, to be ouerthrowne.*

AND if there were no other reason then this, that the high Priesthood, Sacrifice, and Religion of the Iewes was thus left desolate, and their last King *Antigonus* crucified, it was time that a newe Priesthoode should be erected, and that *Iesus of Nazereth King of the Iewes* should be crucified for the Redēption of mankinde, and institute an other law and Sacrifice when the other was thus defectiue; which will be more reasonable to graunt, if with al histories we conceaue the miserable & notorious irreligious errors and abuses the Gentiles were drowned in at that time: no state, cuntry, or condition of people, liuing in dutiful Religion and obedience to God, but growing vnder so great burdens of iniquities, onlie to bee taken away by the comming of the *Messias*. Secondly not only all internall and personall signes of the true Redeemer, the two Natures of God, and Man, vnited togither, his miraculous and wonderful operations, and the whole processe of his Natiuitie, life, death, resurrection, ascention, and the reste as-
Arg. 2. supr. signed for his distinction, and foretold both by the Prophets of the Iewes and Gentiles, as I haue cited before were now compleated and ended, but all memorable externall notes to decipher him from others, proposed in some part in the last Argument were effected and as they were vnpossible not to haue beene, so they could neuer after be vsed for any other to come. But for any such, no note, signe, Argument of distinction can be deuised,
Arg. 1. all being already performed. Thirdly all enemies of christian religion not only (as before) haue in their highest authorities confessed Christ to be the *Messias*, but plainly acknowledged that the time of his comming was in the daies of Iesus. For the Gentils, the *Sibills* set downe the time, and one of them shewed in a vision to *Augustus* then Emperor, both the time and manner

manner of his comming to be effected vnder his regiment. The Oracles and Gods of the Gentiles agreed in the same point, as I haue described. Their Philosophers did write of the miraculous starre, the ceasing of the Oracles, the murthering of the infants by *Herode*, because the Messias was borne, & other wonders chauncing at the comming of CHRIST. *Herode* the Ascalonite a King of their linage knewe and acknowledged that the Messias was come, when to murder him he killed so many infants, destroyed the *Zanedrin* of the house of Iuda, so vsed their high priesthood, killed his owne wife, and sonne by her of the line of *Dauid*, and his sister *Salome* hir husband of the same linage. And their Emperour *Vespatian* hearing that the Messias of the line of king *Dauid* was borne, caused al of that linage which he could finde to be put to death. And it was the constant and common opinion of the Pagans at that time, that the great Messias was come. And *Augustus Cæsar* the Emperour the very day when Christ was borne, commaunded that no man shoulde call him Lorde, hauing perhaps instinct that the great Lorde was borne.

Lact. l. 2. 3. &c. diu. inst.
Arg. 1. supr. Calcid. in ti. Plat. Plut. l. de Oracul. Porphyr. li. Oracul.
Euseb. Chro. Ioseph l. 17. antiq. cap. 3. Euseb. hist. l. 3. cap. 11.
Orof. lib. 7. cap. 22.

Concerning the Iews, the ancient Rabbines before Christ were of that minde, that the Messias was to come at that time, when Christ Iesus was borne, and plainly affirme vpon those propheticall wordes of *Esay*, *a little one is borne to vs*, that six hundred yeares after, the Messias shoulde come, which being accounted, agreeth with the calculation of christians, & falleth out in the daies of Christ. For *Esay* liued in the time of king *Achaz*, about the 3440, yeare of the worlde, and Christ by common supputation, was borne the yeare 4022. so the most part of his life agreeth with that calculation: and as the *Thalmud* it selfe doth witnes, it was an ancient tradition among the Hebrews, that the Messias should be borne about the 4000. yeare of the worlde, which concordeth with the same account. The Iewes that liued in the time of Christ, were of the same opinion, and so enformed both *Herod* their stranger king, & *Vespatian* the Emperor, & thẽselues would haue receaued *S. Iohn Baptist* the precursor of Christ, for their Messias, had he not refused it. And it was so famous among the people that the time of the Messias was come, that many false deceauers tooke that title vpon thẽ and deceaued many, as *Iudas Galileus*, *Iudas Ezechias*, *Thendas*, *Atouges*, & others, in so much that as the *Thalmud* confesseth the *Rabbins* themselues 30. yeares togither receiued *Baronosbam* for the Messias, & so continued, vntil they perceiued hee coulde not deliuer them from the Romans, and so put him to death, wherefore *Herode* intending to make a claime for himselfe, caused his petidegree to be forged frõ the ancient kings of Iuda, as *Iosephus* witnesseth, & called himself the Messias. Whereupon those which flatte-

If. 9. Thalm. in li. Sabbaoth. & tract. Sanch. If. cap. 7. Geneb. Chr. lib. 1. Bened. perer. in Dan. lib. 11. q. 5. Thalm. tract Sanh. c. hel.
Ioh. cap. 1.
Ioseph. l. 17. cap. 8. l. 18. cap. 1. 2. lib. 20. c. 5. 6. Thalm. tract. Sanh. c. hel. Rabb. ben. maim. in sct. Ioseph. l. 14. antiq. c. 2. Matth. c. 22.

Mar. 3. 12. red him in these follies, are called *Herodians* in the Euangelists. What the Thalm. tract. Auodazara. Rab. Moys. bē Maim. ep. ad iud. Afric consciences of the later and present Iews esteme of this matter may be gathered of that I haue spoken of the *Thalmundists* opinion herein, and in that worke they further acknowledge, that it seemed to thē in those daies that diuers hundred yeares had passed since by the scriptures the *Messias* should appeare. And *Rabbi Moises* son of *Maimon* whom the Iews hold in exceding great reuerence, caling him the D. of Iustice, which liued about the yeare Rab. Iosf. ben. leui in thal. tract. Sanh. c. hel. of Christ, 1140. supposeth that the *Messias* should haue bin borne aboue 1000 yeares before that time. And *Rabbi Iosue* affirmeth, that the *Messias* was to be borne before the destruction of the second Temple. So that by all computations of Christians, Iewes, Pagans, and Mahumetans, the time of the comming of the *Messias* was when Christ Iesus was borne, and now beeing past 1600. years, cannot posiblie be verified of anie other. Therefore he and his Religion are only to be receaued. Which also the Prophet *Daniell* had most exactlie by propheticall calculation set downe diuers hun-

*The prophesie of Daniels weekes must needes be fore told of Christ.* dreds of yeares before. Against whose sentence no tergiuersation of anie incredulous person can bee made. First, the signes which the Angell giueth to *Daniell* are most famous, the Edict of the Persian Emperour for the building of Ierusalem, & deliuerie of the Israelites from captiuity wherin they had liued 70. years, & the time of building the city & the Iews returne thither after so many yeares. Therfore the notes are manifest, the Persian Emperour then being the greatest Monarch of the worlde, and the buil-

Dan. cap. 9. ding of that City destroied, so notorious, the wordes are as manifest, which be these, *Knowe and marke from the goeing forth of the worde (or edict) that Hierusalem shall be builded againe vnto Christ* (or Messias) *the Captaine there shall be seauen wecks, and threescore and two weekes: and the streete & walles shall be builded againe in a litle time. And after threescore aud two weekes the* Messias (*or Christ*) *shall be slaine, and it shall not be his people, that will denie him.* This prophesie all agree to be a prediction and token of the time of comming of thē *Messias* and the words are manifest. Then thus I demonstrate against Iews and all misbeleeuers, that it cannot be verified of any, but Christ Iesus. First, the holie Scrip-

Leuit. c. 23. tures make mention but of two kindes of *Hebdomades* or weekes. First, for a weeke of daies or seauen daies, as the Greeke worde doth signifie as in the numbring of weekes from Easter to Pentecost was appointed in the law. This kind of weeke cānot posiblie be vnderstood of the Prophet, the whole summe of his *Hebdomades* of wecks being by that reckoning ended in one yeare and halfe and one weeke of daies, in which time no man chalenged to be the *Messias*, and no man, Christian, Iewe, Pagan, or Mahumetan, receaueth any for the *Messias* that came then, or diuers hundred yeares after. Secōdly, in holy Scriptures an *Hebdamade* or weeke is taken for a weeke of years, or seauen yeares. So in Leuiticus the obseruation of the yeare of Iubily is commanded and set down in these wordes. *Thou shalt number seauen Hebdomades, or weekes of yeares which make 49. years* and the fifteth yeare imediatly following is appointed for the yeare of Iubily. Then of necessitie the prophesy must be performed in this meaning, which is manifestly true in Iesus Christ. For it is euident that *Daniell* was a captaine in Babilon in the time of *Ioakim*, and that the weekes of *Daniell* thus expounded doe expire and ende in Christ, being the number of 483. yeares. And *Daniell* the Prophet himselfe to giue a plaine distinction, that there were meant weeks of years, as I haue expounded it, in the next chapter immediatly following, within two verses of the former prophesie, twice togither speaking of weekes in an other sence, calleth them weekes of daies. Which had beene superfluous, twice to be added in one place, except he would giue vs to vnderstand that in the former he meant extraordinarie weeks of yeares. For otherwise this worde (weeke) without any addition doth vsually signify 7. days & no other time. And this is the expositiō which is giuen in the fourth booke of *Esdras* where it is said, that the *Messias* shalbe reuealed & borne after 400. years, to which if we adde 33. years of the life of Christ, & 50. yeares that *Esdras* was after *Daniel*, they make the same number of 483. years which being begun to be numbred from the first edict of building Ierusalem againe (as the circumstāces) best agree which was in the first yeare of *Cirus*, when (as the 1 chap. of *Esdras* doth witnes) he did not only publish an edict in writing, but made proclamation through al his kingdoms, for building of Ierusalem, & the temple therof, without any difference at al they agree both with the birth and death of Christ as I haue accounted. And howsoeuer we reckon, and begin the accompt from any of the edicts of *Cirus* or *Darius* to build Hierusalem, either in the first yeare of *Cirus* when he first determined the Iews reduction, or the second yeare of *Darius*, when he confirmed the same & put it in execution, or from the 20. yeare of *Darius* whē he made a new edict in fauour of *Nehemias*, & sent him into Iury (al which are manifest in the books of of *Esdras*) they wil end in the raigne of *Herod* vnder whome Christ was borne, or of *Tiberius* vnder whome he was put to death. And cannot posibly be expounded of any other person, or by any other computation. For first if we should imagine any other kind of *Hebdomade* or weeke, then I haue alledged, either of weekes moneths or otherwise, it both taketh away al certainty frō this holy prophesy, of the *Messias*, which being set down in scripture, must by al rules be expounded by such cōputatiōs, as we find in scriptures, otherwise if any mā at plesure might imagin

Leuit. c. 25.

Dan. c. 10. vers. 2. 3.

4. Esdr. 9.

Ioseph. l. 6. & 7. antique. Geneb. Cron

1. Esd. 1. ver. 2. 3. 4. Geneb. cron.

1. Esd. 1. 2. 3. 4. 5. 6. 7. 8. 2. Esd. 2. 3. 4

other strãge accounts, neither heard of before, al things wolud be vncertaine. And yet if we should allow that wantō liberty to any brainsicke man this prophesie could neuer be applyed or verified of any other, which will be euident if any idle person will frame to himselfe a weeke of weekes, or a weeke of moneths, which were twelue times sooner expired, & hundreds of yeares before Christ was borne, when none claimed to be the *Messias.* Therefore where some Iewes are so ridiculous to make conceites of yeares of decaddes, or centures of yeares, that is euerie weeke to consiste of 70. weekes or 700. weekes as some are not ashamed to doe, they make themselues a mockerie to all the worlde. For first, the scripture speaketh of such weekes. Secondlye, it ouerthroweth all certainety in this case of so great importance. Thirdly, it is one impossibillity, in their owne religion. For in their Thalmud, which whosoeuer with them denieth (as they say denieth God himselfe.) It is recorded not only that the Messias shoulde rule 2000. yeares, but that the worlde was only to continue for sixe thousande yeares, 2000. before the lawe of *Moyses*, 2000. vnder the same lawe, and 2000. after that, vnder the Messias. By which account, not only Christ is the true Messias, comming about that time, but these weekes of the Iewes by their decads and centures, cannot be compleated in thousands of yeares after (by their Thalmud) the worlde is ended, such be the fooleries of this people. Therefore by all reckonings and accounts, only Iesus Christ is the Messias, and Redeemer of the worlde, and all other Religions false and erronious.

Med. prol. de fide.

Thal. tract. Sanh. ca. hel.

Argum. 4. *Howe all particuler articles of Christian Catholicke Religion, for which Iewes, Mahumetans, and Pagans denie it, are demonstrated to bee true by their owne groundes and professions.*

BVT because no Infidell shall denie any one point of Catholicke Religion, but by their owne groundes confesse euery article thereof, to be most true and holie. Therefore as I haue prooued before by the highest authority of their owne professions, that in generall, Christian Catholike Religion is onlie true: so in this present reason, I will demonstrate out of the chiefest grounds of those misbeleeuers, all particuler articles of catholicke christianity, namely the misterie of the B. Trinitie, the incarnation & death of Christ the Messias, for the redemption of the worlde, the continuall and daily sacrifice of the Masse, Christs reall presence therein, transubstantiation, and changing of the former elements of bread and wine, into his most holy body and bloud, and the rest, for which these Infidels denie our faith, and which many heretickes in these, and more auncient times, haue disallowed. The sacred misteries of the incarnation, & death

of

of Iesus our Sauiour, his diuine and humane nature, and the distinction of persons in diuinitie are proued alreadie by the true Prophets of God, which the Iewes receaue, by the confession of the *Siblils*, so reuerenced of the Gentiles and (expecting the death of Christ, which *Mahumet* for honor vnto him denieth) by the lawe maker of the Mahumetans, as is conuinced in the 1. Argument, and therefore needlesse probation in this chapter. But to make euidente to all people that these most sacred doctrines are not the onlie collections of christians out of those vndouted & aproued scriptures in the law of *Moyses*, but the same exposition which the holy Rabbins that liued before Christ and which the Iewes receaue with honour, and which the *Sybils* and most auncient Philosophers among the Gentiles for manie thinges approue, I will onlie vse their owne wordes for witnesse in this cause.

And to begin with that most vnscrutable secret of the Nature of God, and Trinitie of Persons in him which we defend against all those blasphemous Infidels, which with one cōsent in impietie, make him an vnperfect, mutable, changeable, corporious, & defectiue thing to which no honor or Religion can be belonging, it is manifest that the holie Prophets, *Isayas*, *Hieremias*, *Zacharias*, *Baruch*, *Michias*, *Dauid*, and others doe asigne a distinction and Trinitie of Persons, giuing all attributes and properties, belonging vnto God to euery one, to be omnipotent, God by Essence infinite, illimited, without beginning or ende, cause of all thinges, equall one with an other, and the like, in which manner as Christian Catholickes expound those sacred writinges and beleeue of that vnspeakeable misterie at this day. So they were euer interpreted of the auncient and learned Rabbines before Christ, *Rabbi Ibba*, *Rabbi Abb*, *Rabbi Haccadas*, *Rabbi Ionathas*, *Abinuziell* and others, which euer agreed with our Catholicke Doctrine. *Rabbi Ibba* (as *Rabbi Simeon* writeth) vpon these words of Deuteronomy, God our Lord is one God, vseth this speech. *By the first worde God or his first Tetragramaton name in this sentence (our Lord)* is signified God the Sonne, that is fountaine of all sciences, and by the second Tetragramaton Name of God, is signified God the holy Ghost, proceeding of them both, to all which there is added the worde (one) to signifie that these three are indiuisible. And *Rabbi Simeon* him selfe vppon these wordes of *Esaye* (*holy holy, holy, Lorde God of Sabbaoth*) writeth thus. *Esay by repeating three times holy, doth as much as he had saide, holy Father, holy Sonne, and holy Spirit, which three holies doe make but one only Lorde of Sabbaoth*. The wordes *Rabbi Abinuziell*. Author of the Caldey Paraphrase knowen in the world before Christ and highlie honored among the Iewes, vpon this prophesie of *Dauid* in his second Psalme

*The mistery of the holy Tyinitie prooued by the rules of all Infidelles.*

Is. cap. 34. 52. 48. 6. Hier. 23. Zachar. 2. Mich. 5. Baruch. 3. Ps. 138. 32. Deutron. 6.

Rabb. Ibb. in cap. 6. Deut. Rabb. Abb. in thrē. Rabb. hacch in cap. 9. Is. Paraph. col. in 45. Is. Thar. in Ps. 2. Rabb. Sim. in Zohar. Deut. 6.

Thar. in Ps. 2.

where God the Fathet speaketh thus to christ(*Thou art my Sonne, to day I haue begotten thee*) are these. *Thes Etohim* (the diuine persons expressed in the plural number)*the Father and the Son are three in one third person the holy Ghost and these three are one, I say one substance, one essence, and one God.* And as the same Rabbine in that place is further witnesse, when he was writing this sentence, a voice spake vnto him from heauē, saying *who is this that dareth to reueale my secrets to the Gentiles?* to which *Rabbi Ionathas* answered, *O Lorde, it is I which for the reuerence and glory of thy name haue presumed to doe it.* For in al Religions there were some thinges concealed for secretes, and therby called misteries, of which the auncient Rabbines ackowledge this misterie of misteries to be chiefest, and that it should be plainly reuealed at the comming of the *Messias*, as now it is, and not before, as *Rabbi Simeon* is witnes, not being lawful for the Iewish people before Christ, to pronounce that Tetragramaton name of God for the Maiestie and greatnesse of him that was ineffable, as that name only compounded of quiescent and insonant letters(as Hebritians call them)do witnes. And yet this secret was not so concealed of the auncient Rabbins, but from them it was come to the Gentils themselues, not only the propheticall *Sibilles*, who tould most plainly of this distinction of Persons in God, but to others, especially the Egiptians, and such as liued in the confined and bordering countries to the Israelites. For breuity I will only produce the wordes of the Oracle of *Serapis* to *Thulis* King of the Egiptians, and *Plotinus* an heathen Philosopher. The sentence of the first is this, *In the beginning God is, then his worde, and to these the spirite is added, these are equall and tending into one.* The wordes of the second in his booke of *the three principall Hypostasies, or persons*, (for so Christian like it is entituled) are these. *Before the worde, not by priority of nature, or time, but only by priority of origination, is the fountaine, and beginning of all diuinitie of this Father, the worde is begotten; further, euery thing which begetteth, loueth and desireth that which is begotten: but that moste chieflie, when the begetter and the begotten are all one.* Against Mahumet I haue prooued a distinction of persons in GOD before out of his owne *Alcaron* and sentence.

Orig. Hilar. Petr. gallat. l. 2. arcan. Rab. Sim. &c. Sibbill. apud Lactant. l. 4. diu. instit. cap. 6. Mercur. Tris. Dial. pim. &c. plato. epim. & lib. 6. Rap. viu. l. 10 ciuit. ca. 10. Plotin. l. de trib princip. hipos.

This being the greatest & chiefest Mistery I haue staied longer therin, & wil passe ouer the rest with more breuitie. The same *Mahumet* affirmeth, that as Iesus was the word of God, so he was the most holy man, that Prophet & *Messias* which was promised in the law of *Moyses*, & was sent to supplie the defects therof. The *Sibills* as I haue proued before, haue sette downe, the whole lyfe of Christ, and all the actions of his humanitie, and tell how he should die for the world, and rise againe. Other Prophesies among the Gentils which I haue aleadged before, affirme that *Filius dei nascetur*

*The Incarnation & death of Christ the Messias proued by the groundes of Infidels.* Alcor. azoar 67. 10. 12. 1. 5. Argū. 3. sup.

*cetur ex virgine Maria et pro salute hominum patietur. That the Sonne of God should be borne of a Virgin called Mary, and shoulde suffer for Mankinde.* The doctrine of the *Rabbins* before Christ so authentical among the Iewes is most comfortable to this sentence. *Rabbi Haccados*, called for his learning & sanctity our holy Master, affirmeth in his booke, intituled a reuealer of secretes, where he expoundeth that the prophetical place of *Esay* touching the *Messias* (*Emanuell, God, strong, Prince of peace*) speaketh thus. *Because the Messias shall be God & man, his name is called Emanuell, God with vs, surely in our bodie and in our fleshe, as Iob doth witnesse; in my fleshe I shall see God. For he did deuise a maruelous consaile of deliuering soules from the diuell, which were damned for the sinne of* Adam, *neither coulde by any meanes be saued, except the king* Messias *should vnder goe most bitter death, & many torments, and for that cause he is called a man. And because he hath all strength, he is called God strong. And because he is eternall, he is named the eternall Father. Also because in his daies peace shall be multiplied, he is called the Prince of peace. And because he shall make hast to take away the spoiles of soules, he is called a swifte spoiler, and taker of preyes. And because he shal saue them & bring them to paradise, he is called Iesus, that is a Sauiour.* Hitherto be the wordes of that most holy and learned *Rabbine.* Rab Haccad. lib. gal. raz. Rabb. Ionat. lib. collect. Misdr. teh. in Psalm. 2. Rabb. Hacc. in 41. Gen. li. gal. raz.

*Rabbi Ionathã*, who died before Christ was borne, applieth the long narration of *Esay* the prophet in his 53. Chapter, to the murther of the *Messias* by the Iewes, and soone after him *Rabbi Simion*, breaketh out into these wordes. *Woe be to the men of Israell, for that they shall kill the Messias. God shall sende his Sonne in mans fleshe to washe them, and they shal murther him.* Rabbi Hadarson vpon the prophecie of *Daniell* concerning the time of the comming and preaching of Christ, vseth this speech. *Three yeeres and a halfe shall the presence of God in fleshe cry and preach vpon the mount Oliuet, and then shall he be slaine.* Which the Iewes ordinary comentary vpon the Psalmes interpreteth of Christes preaching, three yeeres & a halfe before his passion. And the *Thalmundists* themselues haue set downe, that the *Messias* shal be put to death. Concerning our most holy sacrifice of the Body & Blood of Christ, as it is euident before by the testimony of the true prophets of God. The *Sibils* and *Mahumet* himselfe, that in respect of the Lawe of Christ, all their Religions & Sacrifices were vnperfecte & foretolde to cease in him & his oblation. So that the Sacrifice which should be offered in his Lawe, was to be his blessed Body & Blood vnder the formes of Bread & Wine (as Catholike christians beleeue) is most plainly tolde out of those Holy Scriptures, by the auncient and approued *Rabbins* before Christ. The wordes of *Rabbi Iudas* speaking of the Sacrifice of the Law of the *Messias* are these. *The Bread which is offered vpon the Altar, is changed from the nature of Bread, & made the Bodie & substance of the* Messias. *But this Body is inuisible with our eies, and free from all violence,* Rab. Ionathã 53. If. Rabb. Sim. Ben. Iohn. lib. de spe. Rab. Hadars. in 9. Dan. Misdr. teh. Thalm. tract Sãhed. c. hel. *The sacrifice of masse, the reall presence of Christes bodie & blood there and other misteries proued by the same authoritie.* Rabb. Iud. In 25. Exod.

Rabb'. Sim. l. inuest. secret. *and not to be touched. Rabbi Simeon* in his booke of searching secrets, hath the same discourse, speaking euidently of transubstantiating *Bread & Wine,* into that most sacred Body and Bloude, and affirmeth it to be the *Sacrifice, which shall be vsed in the kingdome and Religion of the Messias.* Rabbi Cahana vpon those words of Genesis, (*he shall washe his stole in wine, and his cloake in the bloude of the grape:*) vttereth this speech. *This Sacrifice which daily shall be offered of wine, shall not only be changed into the substance of the Bloud of the* Messias, *but into the substance of his Body, Bread shall be changed, although externally there only appeare the colour of white.* Rabbi Hadarsan saith, *That the Bread which the Messias will giue, is his Body, and there shall be a conuersion of Bread into his Body.* Rabbi Barrachias teacheth, that at the comming of the Messias, *Foode shall come from Heauen, like a little Cake.* Like be the sentences of *Rabbi Ionathas*, and *Rabbi Selomo*, teaching that a rounde cake of wheate as broade as the palme of an hande, shall be changed into the Body of the Messias, and vsed for the Sacrifice of his Lawe, and be lifted ouer the heads of his Priestes. All these *Rabbins* liued before Christ, & yet these be their expositions of the holy Scriptures concerning that most holy Sacrifice, which Christian Catholikes vse, & such other mysteries as depend from thence. The *Sibbills* and *Mahumet*, confesse that Christ shoulde and did abrogate the Lawe of *Moyses.* His Gospel was the perfection of that lawe, that those sacrifices should cease in him, yea he shall destroye Antichrist, Paganisme, Iudaisme, and Mahumetisme, and come in glory in the end of the worlde, and be Iudge thereof, and only his religion to endure. Thus I coulde exemplifie in other questions of Christian doctrine, but because these are the greatest, and those which Infidels most dislike in our religion, I haue giuen instance in them, that it may be euident, how manifestly they be confounded euē by their own grounds & authorities, whether we will consider Catholike worship in general, or the particuler mysteries it defendeth against those misbeleuers, which may also be applied against the Protestant sacramentaries of this time in those points which they now maintaine against those most auncient and learned Rabbins. But of this I must intreate hereafter.

Rabb. Cahā. in 45. Gen.

Rab. Hadars. in Psal. 136.

Rab. Baruch. super. ecl.

Rab. Ionath. li. col. in Ps. 72.

Rabb. Selom. in Psal. 72.

Sibil. apud Lactā. lib. 7. diu. instit.

Alcor. AZo. 67. 19. 12.

Argum. 5. *Founded vppon the straunge and extraordinarie punishments, imposed vpon all enemies of Christ and his Religion.*

OR if extraordinary vengeance of God vpon any people, or person for incredulity and sinne is a certaine argument of the errour & sin of that people or person, as all men acknowledge, it is euident by the punishments of al other professions, only Christian religion to be true. And to passe the Mahumetanes, Pagans, & so many hundreds of Arch-heretics, with their cōplices & confederats, punished of God & extinguished

by

by christian Religion, as I haue shewed of heretickes in my Apologicall Epistle, and of the Pagan Emperours, and Mahumetans in my first treatise, and will be more euident hereafter. So that nowe none of all these remaine, but only Mahumetans, and *Mahumet* himselfe confesseth, that they shall vtterly perish and be ouerthrowne. Then to exemplifie in the Iewes, the only enemies vntouched in this point, and those which before their reiecting of Christ were the people of God. If Christ had not beene the Messias but a seducer, they could neither haue sinned, or beene punished as offendors, but deserued well in putting him to death; so far they shoulde haue beene by that worke free from so many punnishments, as haue beene laide vpon them. But nowe who can imagine any other cause coulde be founde in any people, for which that nation which had so longe continued the peculier of God, of whome he had vndertaken so particuler and singuler protection, witnessed by so many fauours and extraordinary prerogatiues graunted vnto them, aboue all other countries, shoulde deserue so great and during punishment and miserie: that they should lose their Temple, Altar, Sacrifice, Prophets, and Priesthood, to haue so many thousands pined with famine, murdered by intestiue sedition, killed of idolatrous enemies, led captiues and solde for slaues. And not only those of that generation which liued in Hierusalem and Iury, but the Iewish inhabitants of Alexandria, Cæsaria, Scythopolis Ptolemays, Tyre, and all places where they liued, as *Iosephus* their owne historian, and others witnes. Then what sinne coulde be so rigorouslie reuenged of God, rather inclined to mercy, then iustice, and by no possibility to doe wrong, then that which in malice excedeth, & is greater then all others their most Irreligious and vnnatural entreating of the Messias, for which iniquitie they are odious to all people, both Christians and Mahumetans to this day. And if any man desireth to see the particuler of their miseries, and in them the anothomie of a wicked persecuted people, and afflicted enemie of God, he may read their owne historians *Iosephus* and *Philo*, and for such as haue not that opportunity brieflie to recapitulat some of their most worthy punishments, *Caiphas* their high priest & enemy to Christ killed himselfe, *Annas* died miserably, *Herod* that deluded him was banished to Lions by the Emperour *Caius*, and spoyled of all hee had, so *Herodiadas* her dauncing daughter had her head cut off with yse: In Alexandria the Iewes by the permission of *Flaccus* President, suffered to be beaten and killed at euerie mans pleasure, as their owne *Philo* reporteth. *Pilat* that put him to death, perpetually exiled to *Vienna* kept close prisoner, and killed himselfe. The Statua of *Caius* by force placed in their Temple, about Seleucia 50000.

Epist. Apol. Trac. 1. p. 1. Par. 2. Arg. 82. 83. & Ar. 108. &c. Mahumet, in Alcaron. ca. 12.

Ioseph. lib. bell. Egisipp. lib. excid. Hierosf. Euseb. &c.

Ioseph. bell. l. 2. c. 19. 20. 21. c. 17. & l. antiq. 20. c. 34. li. 18. c. 12. l. 19. ca. 7. l. 19. c. 7. li. 18. ca. 9. Philo. in. Flacco. &c. Clem. const. lib. 8. ca. 1. Niceph. l. 2. cap. 10. Ioseph. ãtiq. lib. 18. ca. 9. Philo. supr. Ado. Chron. Orof. lib. 7. Ioseph. l. 18. antiquit. ca. 12. act. 12.

Ios.sup.l.19. cap.7. & lib. 20. cap. 34. of their Iewishe men killed. Their king *Herod* consumed with wormes. In the feast of Pentecost no tumult raised, 20000. stifled to death. Forbidden by the Samaritans to goe by them to Hierusalem. *Ananias* their high Priest sent prisoner and bound like a traitor to *Rome*, by *Quadratus* the president. Al *Iury* full of theeues, and sorcerers. *Ionathas* their High Priest murthered. Murthers committed euen in the Temple it selfe, and in the greatest festiuities. The Priests spoile one another. And after vnder *Florus* their President, their nobility torne in peeces and crucified. Their Sinagogue destroied at *Cesaria*. The house of *Ananias* their High Priest, burnt by rebels and he murthered. And at the same instant while these thinges were donne at Hierusalem, the same day and howre, as *Iosephus* witnesseth, aboue 20000. killed at *Cesarea*. And wher soeuer the *Iewes* were dispersed, if the Gentiles were stronger they were put to death, 13000. by the *Sythopolitans*, 2500. by the *Ascalonites*. 2000. at Ptolemais. 5000. at Ioppe. 1000. at Damascus. At Tyre all killed or commited to prison. 50000. at Alexandria, and all these and other murthers procured against them by a President of their own nation. And when their Citty was besieged of *Cestinus* President of Syria, how often might he haue taken it if he woulde and was desired euen by the nobility of Hierusalem, promising to open the gates and refused, but it was differred for the deliuerie of the Christians thence, and greater punishment of the Iewes. And before it was besieged of *Vespatian*, a hundred thousand slaine, and solde almost fortye thousand, and an infinite number killed of themselues. The high priests were slaine and lay naked in the streets, eaten of doggs and beastes. The city diuided into domestical sedition, two armies in the temple, one within, and the other in the Court. Their Granary where prouision of victual for many yeeres was laid vp, burnt & consumed to ashes: & that factious armie that was planted in the Temple al slaine, not one escaping, those that fled the city for famine, were crucified by *Titus*, 500. euery day, that there was no roome to put them to death. A walle of 39. furlongs was made in 3. daies space, to entrench them as Christ had prophesied, and thirteene Castles to keepe them in, that they could not get forth to eate grasse. The dead bodies in the towne stunke so that they annoyed the campe of their enemie & besiedger. 2000. of them in one night were cut in peeces of the Syrian and Arabian souldiers to seeke their golde within their bowels: and thus they were daily vsed vntill their enemy *Titus* forbade it. From the fourteenth of Aprill when the siedge beganne vntill the last daye of Iulye there were carried forth of deade bodies out of one onely gate (the Porter himselfe *Manneus* beeing witnesse vnto *Titus*) an hundred and

Ioseph. Bell. li. 2. ca. 19. 20. 21.

Epiph haeres. 29. et haer. 30 Ioseph. li. 2. bell. cap. 17.

Ioseph. supr.

Ioseph. sup. li. 6. cap. 1. Cap. 12. 8. 9. 7.

Eus. luc. &c.

and fiftie thousands, besides those which were buried. And the noble men that fled to *Titus* affirmed, that there were six hundred thousands of the poorer sort, that were dead, cast forth of the gates, and that the number of the others could not be reckoned; for whē they could not be caried forth, they were throwne togither on heapes. The famine was so greate, that they did eate dung, thongs, girdles of leather, shooes, hay, & other things not to be named, and the nobility themselues abstayned not from killing and eating their owne children. And at the time their city was taken, although *Titus* had giuen expresse commandement by publicke edict, that the Temple shoulde be preserued, and nothing therein spoyled, yet it was set on fire in such outragious manner, that by no possibilitie, *Titus* labouring what he coulde, it coulde be quenched, but was consumed vpon the very same day, the tenth of August, that it was burned before of the King of Babylon. And six thonsand Iewes that were fled thither by the counsaile of a false Prophet, were vtterly consumed. For as the same *Iosephus* witnesseth, there were many seducers then among them, that promised helpe from God, vtterly forbidding them to yeelde. Eleauen hundred thousands deade in those fewe weekes of the siedge, 97. thousande taken prisoners, some condemned for slaues and sent into Egipt. Those that were stronge kept in all countries to fight with wilde beasts in theatres, and publicke spectacles. All woemen and men vnder 17. yeeres of age, solde for slaues at a most vile price, the number of those which were solde being so great. And after, in the time of *Adrian* the Emperour, the finall desolation and exilement of that people forth of that countrie was contriued: *Iulius Seuerus* his Captaine by his commandement destroying Townes, and Villages, leauing not one stone vpon an other, in all that vaste building of Hierusalem, that the prophesie of Christ might be fulfilled. And in one daie put to death 500. and 80000. not one Iewe remayning in all Iurie, and an imperiall edict promulged against them. that they should neuer returne thither any more, and that they should not remember Hierusalem, that they might not looke towardes the place. What other illusions and afflictions haue they had, and still endure in minde, not only concerning horrible and filthy errours against God and nature, of which I will mention in the argument of the errors of our enemies, but what illusions of Diuels and wicked spirits haue they suffered, especiallie about a *Messias* (for refusing CHRIST) perswading them sometimes that he is in the Caspian hilles, sometimes at Rome in Italy, where in our memory they were so illuded, that they fullie beleeued an Harlot of their linage fornicatiouslie begotten, with childe (as was proued) was to bring

Ioseph. li. 7. bell. Iud. ca. 11.

Ioseph. supr. c. 17. c. 20.

Oros. lib. 7. cap. 13.

Argū. 6. inf.

Grā. de simb. Euseb. hist. eccles.

Cæs. Baron. tom. 1. et 3. Annal.

their Messias forth, vntill to the common laughter of all, shee brought forth a wench. Sometimes at Vlisipon in Portugall, sometimes in the wildernesse, sometimes in the Sea, sometimes, and all times no where. Howe sottishely were they seduced by the Diuell, and worthely, and miraculously punished of God, in the time of *Iulian* the Apostata, as Saint *Chrisostome*, *Ruffinus*, & others are witnesses, when they went about to builde their Hierusalem and Temple againe. When they had digged their trenches, and began to lay and forme their foundation, sodenly such an earthquake chanced, that it did not onely throwe downe the stones and buildings which they had began, but other places where the Iewes resorted, & as many as were in them, were slain. And in the morning folowing, those that had escaped assembling togither, to draw away the dead bodies, a terrible fire sodainly issued out, running vp and downe, burning & consuming as many of them as it met, & after the same order oftentimes issuing forth consumed that incredulous people. Whereby those which were left aliue were conuerted to Christ. And that it might be euident, this punishment to haue bin inflicted for him, the next night after, the signe of the Crosse appeared in all their garments, and remained so firme and manifest, that with no arte or cunning it coulde either be hidden, or taken awaye. And in the yeere of Christ 405. a Cretensian Iewe, or rather a Diuell feigned himselfe to be *Moyses*, and sent from Heauen, to bring all the Iewish inhabitants of that country, which were many thousands into *Iury*, through the Sea, as *Moyses* had donne out of Ægypt, whereupon they all presently followed him, leauing all thinges, and comming to a great rocke hanging ouer the Sea, bad them throwe themselues into the waters, and they should swimme thither like fishes, which they which went before, desperately attempted, and were pittifully drowned in the sight of those which followed, and their *Moyses* vanished away appearing no more. And in this manner in all times and places euer since the death of Christ, they haue beene deluded and afflicted. Therefore no man can say that they are the true worshipers of God, except the same blasphemer will affirme that God is vnmercifull, mutable, vniust, and irreligious to punishe sinne (*vltra condignum*) more than it deserueth, or to inflict punishment and vengeance where none is due.

Chrisost. hō. 2. cont. Iud. Ruffin. li. 1. histor. Philipp. Bergom. hist. in Iulian.

Fascic. Tēp. 450. Bergō. histor.

Argum. 6. *Manifesting the Errors of all other Religions, euen against the light of nature, such as by possibility true worship cannot admit.*

AND although I doe not contend to prooue this to be a demonstration in naturall reason, yet I doe affirme for euident euen in the light of nature, that all worships and Religions in the worlde, which doe not

ac-

acknowledge the Incarnation of God, and veritie of Christian Religion, either Pagans, Iewes, or Mahumetans, are ignorant of the diuine nature, essence, and attibutes of the diuine maiestie, and fallen into most impious and irreligious errors concerning him, so that by no posibility they can worship him as they should, and are farther drowned in other errours which neither any supernatural light & reuelation of God, or light of reason can alowe, so that where the Incarnation of Cod, is not admitted, all other benefits whether naturall as to the Pagans and all pepole, or supernaturall graces and so manie extraordinary fauours to the Iewes, before the comming of Christ, are forgotten and not of force to procure gratitude in men, and all other effectes of God not able to cause them to knowe and honour him as they should. And this shall be another argument against all Infidels euidently demonstrating them to haue no religion, for supernatural illuminations cannot be contrary to the light of Nature, neither God Author of them both, contrary to himselfe. And to begin with the miserable estate of the Pagan Gentiles, who can indure to heare for only eternall, immortall, immaculate, omnipotent & spiritual God, creatour of all thinges, so many incesteous violent, lecherous, and most wicked men and women to be so worshipped such as were the children of men, as *Sibilla Erithrea* doth scorne them, in these and baser wordes. *A God cannot be made and formed of a man and a woman*, So *Hercules* the bastard of *Alcmena*, that poluted all places with lecherie, incest, rapine, and oppresion, was honored for an immortall and eternall God. So *Esculapius* the bastarde of *Apollo*. So *Iupiter*, *Saturne*, *Mars*, *Apollo*, and the rest. What miserable and most wicked oblations were vsed in that Religion? What innocent men murthered, and offered in sacrifice to *Iupiter* among the Cyprians? The Thaures did offer to *Diana*, the strangers that came vnto them. So did the Freache men to *Esus* and *Thutantes*; and Italians to *Iupiter*, the Romans and Italians, both men and infantes to *Saturne*. So did the Carthaginians: as when they were ouercome of *Agathocles* King of Sicilie, thinking their God *Saturne* to be angrie with them, they offrred vnto him for a Sacrifice to appease his anger, 200. children of noble men. Others cut of their shame and secretes, and offred them in Sacrifice. Among the Rhodians, *Hercules* was honoured with a Sacrifyce of 2. oxen, and cursing and banning, and it was accounted a great iniquitie for one worde of pietie or modestie to be spoken. And this was in memorie of the cursing and banning that a plough-man of that Countrie vsed against *Hercules*, taking two oxen from him by violence and so of others. But to passe ouer those Idolaters and come to the Iewes, which before Christ

*Errors of the Pagans.*

Lactāt. firm. l. 1. diu. inst cap. 8.

Cap. 9 supr. Lucil. Luciā. Tarquit. de vir. illustr. Philipp. Bergom, in hist. &c.

Lactāt. supr. c. 10. c. 11. c. 12. & 21.

Varro. l. diu. in Saturn. Ouid. lib. de fast. Postēn. fest. lib. histor.

Lactāt. firm. supr. ca. 21.

*Errors of the Iewes cōtrary*

were the chosen people of God, and had the true Religion, theyr errors conteyned in theyr owne Thalmud and highest iudgement they haue, shall bring witnesse against them. And to omitte theyr blasphemous errors against Christ because they professe themselues enemies to Christians, and speake of those which they maintaine against the most sacred diuine Maiestie, whom they acknowledge for their God, and maker of all thinges, that gaue their lawe to *Moyses*. Thus they write and generallie beleeue of him, that before he made the worlde, leaste he should fall to idlenesse, he exercised himself in framing diuers worldes, which when he had made, he presently destroied and renued them againe, vntil at length he had learned to make this worlde which now we haue. That hee spendeth *the first three howres of the day, in reading the Iewish lawe*. And that *Moyses* ascendinge to heauen, found him writinge accents in the holie Scripture. That on the firste daie of the newe Moone in the moneth of September, he iudgeth the whole worlde, and the nexte tenne daies he applieth himself to write the iust in the booke of life, and the wicked in the booke of death. And manie other like errors they holde, that God hath a place in heauen seperate from all companie, in which at certaine times he bewaileth with manie teares, and afflicteth himself, that he was angrie with the Iewes: ouerthrewe the Temple of Hierusalem, and dispersed this people into Captyuitye. And that daylie hee prayed deuoutelye, and putteth vpon his heade and armes, fillets, or thongs of leather, called Thephalin, and putteth vppon his bodye a linnen coate, named Zezith, and so attyred, falleth downe vppon his knees, and prayeth: that so often as hee remembereth the Calamities which the Iewes suffer of the Gentiles, hee weepeth and letteth twoe teares fall into the Ocean Sea, and for verye griefe knocketh his breaste with both his handes. That for his recreation the three laste howres of the day, hee vsed to play with a huge greate fishe called Leuiathan, that the commaundement of the Sacrifice of the newe Moone was giuen to the Iewes, to purge the sinne which GOD committed when he gaue that light vnto the Sun, which he had vniustly taken from the Moone, and that beeing angrie for a cause vnknowne vvith his plaie-fellovve Leuiathan, hee killed him, and povvdered his fleshe vvith salte, to giue to the soules of his Saintes. That euerye day hee is angrie, and at that time the Combes of Cockes vvaxe pale coloured, and they stande vppon one legge, and if anye man shall curse an other at that moment, hee shall presentlie fall dovvne deade. When certayne Rabbines disputed agaynste *Rabbie Eliezar*, GOD giuing sentence from Heauen for *Rabbie Elyezar*, the other Rabbynes beeinge offended

*to the lawe of nature and repugnant to religion.*

Thalm. ordi. 1. tract. 9. v. 49. ord 4. tract. 4. dist. 5. chart. 17 ord. 4. dist. 2. ord 4. tract. 4. dist 6. ord. 3. tract. 6. Thalm. sup. ord c tract. 4 dist. 3.

Ord. 2. tract. 1. dist. 14.

Ord. 5. tract. 6. dist. 5.

Ord. 2. tract. 8. dist. 5.

Ord. 2. dist. 5 et ord. 1. dist 7.

Ord. 1. tract. 1. dist. 1. ord. 3. tract. 8. dist. 5.

Ord. 1. tra. 1. dist. 9.

Ord. 2. tract. 2. dist. 14.

Ord. 4. tract. 8.

Ord 4. tract. 6. dist. 1.

Ord. 4. tract. 3. dist. 5.

Ord. 1. tract. 8.

Ord. 4. tract. 4. dist. 7.

fended thereat, excommunicated God, whereat he ſmiling ſaid, my children haue ouercome me. That God diſputing with the Rabbines vpon a Ord.4.tract 2.d.ſup.
certaine kinde of leproſie, iudgment betweene them was referred to a very learned Rabbine. And that he hath bin deceaued by ſome Rabbines,
and the like blaſphemies. That the Angell *Gabriell* committed a grieuous Ord.2.tract. 5.diſt.8.
ſinne, for which, God commaunded him to bee ſcourged with a fierie
whippe. That *Dauid* did not ſinne, either in his adulterie, with *Bethſabee*, Ord. 2 tract. 1.diſt. 5.
or murther of her husbande; and whoſoeuer affirmeth he ſinned, is an
Hereticke. That a man may marrie his daughter, or ſiſter; that Rabbine Ord.5 tract. 1.diſt. 2.
which hateth not his enemies to death, and ſeketh not reuenge vpon him,
is not worthy the name of a Rabbine. That they which contradict the Ord 4.tra.4. diſt.10.
wordes of their Scribes, are more grieuouſlie to be puniſhed, then they
which gainſay the law of *Moyſes*, and this man may be better abſolued, but
the other muſt be put to death. If the greater part ſhall condemne a man Ord.4.chart 17.
to death, he muſt die, but if all condemne him, hee muſt be diſmiſſed.
That ſoules doe paſſe from body to body, as *Pythagoras* helde, onlie with Ord.4.tra.2. & ſæpe alib.
this limitation, that if the ſoule ſinneth in the firſt body, it goeth into a ſecond, if it ſinneth in that, it flitteth into a thirde body, in which if it doth
not ceaſe to ſinne, it is throwne into hell. And for example, the ſoule of
*Abell* did goe into *Seth*, and from him to *Moyſes*. That in the reſurrection, Ord.3.tra.2. cap. 3.
the ſoules of the vnlearned ſhall not be vnited to their bodies. Whoſoe- Ord.2.tra.3.
uer ſhall eate thriſe a day vpon the Sabbaoth, ſhal haue euerlaſting life. If diſt 6.
any man ſhall paſſe vnder the bellie of a Camell, or betweene two Ca- Ord.4 tract. 10. diſt. 2.
mels, or betweene two women, he ſhall neuer learne any thing out of the Ziſt.Senen.
Thalmud: wherein there is no end of ſuch blaſphemies, fooliſh, and ri- bibl.Sanctit. Thalmud.
diculous things, he that deſireth more, may peruſe the places cited in the Ord.1. tract. 1.diſt.4.
margine, ſo that we may ſee the iuſt iudgment of God executed vpon that Ord.4. tract.
people, that they which before the comming of Chriſt were the choſen of 8.or 4 tract. 1. diſt. 4.
God, onlie ſeruing him in true Religion, ſince they reiected and refuſed Chart.38.or
him, are fallen into ſo many impious errors, that except they were recor- 4. tract.8. diſt.2. ord.
ded by themſelues, and conteyned in the very rule of their religion, their 4. tract.4.
Thalmud no man would beleeue it, & that euery man may knowe in what diſt.9 ordin: 4.tract 8.
eſtimation the Thalmud wherein theſe, and other errors are conteyned is Ord 2.tract.
with that people, their owne words placed in the preface of that booke are 1.diſt. 5. ch. 11 et 15.or.
theſe, *If any man ſhall denie the bookes of* Thalmud *to be moſt holy, he denieth god him* 2. tract.1. diſt.2. &c.
*ſelfe*. Laſtly, to come to the euiſh and laſciuious *Mahumet* and his Mahu- *Errors of the*
metans, what other thing then ſuch as I haue recited of the Iewes & Pa- *Mahumetanes* Blond. l.9.
gans, can be expected of them, if we either conſider the occaſion of his o- plat.
riginall and beginning, or the wicked and licentious life, either of *Mahumet* Pomp. Eutr. l.8.Sab.

Pantal. Chrō Bergom. hist. in Mahumet. Polid. de inuen lib. 7. c. 8. &c. Gen. ca. 21. Alcorā. azo. 27. 28. 29. 31. 33. 49. 53. Mahūmet in Alcorā. azoar. 1. &c. Blond li. 9. Poly. inuē. l. 7. c. 8. Bern. Lutzenburg. in Catal. heretic. in Mahumet. Graft. hist. & Stowe in Mahum. Mahumet. in Alcorā. l. 2. Azo. 28. 47. 48. 18. 19. Euseb. lib. 6. hist. ca. 28. Cæl. histor. Saracen. l. 2.

the scholler or his Tutors and Counselours, *Ihon* an Hereticke of Antioch, *Sergius* an Arrian and Apostata Monke, & a Iewishe Astronomer or Necromācer. Or the time when he came being borne in the yere of Christ 626 or the place & people where or whence he descended, cōming of the *Ismaelits*, & seed of *Ismaell* accursed in Scripture, by the mouth of God where he is depriued of all spirituall inheritance, & hath no such benediction giuen vnto him, and from the rude, theeuishe, and barbarons *Arabians*, whose manners he exercised in all kinde of iniquity. And touching his errours, with *Sabellius* he denieth the Trinity, with *Aerius* he affirmeth Christ to be a creature. With the *Manichees*, that Christ was not Crucified and put to Death, but another like vnto him, thinking that vnworthy so great a prophet. With the *Anthropomorphites* Iewes and Pagans: that God hath a body, with the *Elchesite*, that religion may be denied in persecution. With the *Originists*, that the diuels shall be saued, that *Lucifer* and the rest of the Angels were condemned because they woulde not worship *Adam*, as though duty were to be donne to the inferiour, & lesse excellent, when excellencie and dignity is the only cause of adoration and reuerence. That men are to be compelled to his religion by warre and force. That God and his Angels pray for *Mahumet*, when God supreame Lorde of all, can praie to none, prayer being a function, of an inferiour, he neuer distinguished the Ciuill and Ecclesiasticall regiment, but confounded them together in his temporall successor, which his owne followers condēned for absurdity & repealed. The originall institution of that deceiuer appointing *Alys* an ignorant and wicked young fellowe for his successour, was not only vnreasonable, but frustrate and without effecte: for contrary to the ordinance of *Mahumet*, his father in-lawe *Eubocora* deposed *Alys*, & within three yeres *Eubocora* himselfe was poysoned. *Homer* his next successour was murdered by his seruant. *Osmenus* which next succeeded killed himselfe, his sonne *Mahumetes*, was violently put to death by *Alys*. *Alys* was traiterously slaine by *Muauias*, in whose daies so many errors were growne in that secte, that two hundred Camels were loaded with books, which were condemned at Damascus. And notwithstanding the capitall Lawe against disputing of the Alcoran they euer were and nowe are diuided into manifold schismes into *Melyos*, *Asaphs*, *Alambels*, *Buanists*, *Babilonists*, *Cayrists*, *Caioranists*, *Marochists*, *Mustysts*, *Almacadists*, and others not to be recounted, and in such odious manner, that they affirme it more meritorions to kill one of those diuisions than 70. Christians. They haue no meanes to compose these controuersies, determine questions, or to choose their Calyphes: but all doubtes are tried by the sworde, and the strongest part of armes is sentenced to holde

Bellefor. Cosm. vniuers. t. 2. l. 6. c. 6. col. 1837. ca. 12. 13. col. 1887 &c. lib. 4. ca. 21. ca. 13. Leuncl in pād ect. turcic. cap. 237. Iou. hist. l. 33 Bellef. cosm. supr. Leuncl. supplem. Annal. turcic. pag. 138.

the

the truest opinion· Neither did *Mahumet* euer ordaine, or that people pra- Supr. arg. 1.
ctise their trial. How doth he extol Christ Iesus to be the *Messias*, wisdome,
spirite, and worde of God, greatest of all Prophets, and institutor of the
most holy law and perfector of the lawe of *Moyses*, which had so long endu- Azoar. 2.
red, and yet most impudently affirme, that presenly after the first prea- Cusã. in cribrat. Alco. l.
ching, it was corrupted euer by the Apostles to whome it was committed, 1. c. 2. l. 2. c.
and whose Gospels himselfe alloweth. How foolish is it for him to denie 14. l. 3. c. 1. azoar. 11.
the death of Christ, witnessed by so many thousandes of present witnesses
of all sortes, Christians, Iewes, and Gentiles, in so publicke place and vniuersall assemblies? how could the Iewes raise this slaunder when so many
Christians, and Pagans were present, and is written in all the Euangelists
which he approued for holy writers? How could those sacred bookes be
vniuersally corroupted of the Iewesh nation, when they were neuer wholy Bibliand. in
in their handes, yea seldome anie one was in their custody? yet these Pa- op. part. 2. in cõfutat.
radoxes he proposeth to be beleued. How is it either probable or possible Alco. pug. 15
that *Mahumet* and an apostata Monke so many hundred yeares after Christ Cuspinia. de Relig turcic.
and *Moyses*, should better know the integritie of their lawes then the Iewes Septemcastr.
and Christians which were euer in possession of those writinges? how con- de relig. tur. cap. 13.
trary is his law of poligamy (where a King hath 600. wiues) the festiuity of Richer. li. 2.
friday for the Sabbaoth, the circumcising children in the seuenth or eight
yeare, and not day, from their natiuity, and other like to the law of *Moyses*?
how different is his corpority in God, beastly paradise, multiplicitie of wiues, errors about Christes diuinity, death, Passion, Sacaments, and other
principal thinges to the doctrine of Christ, which as he teacheth was most
pure, and shall continew for euer? where did euer Christ perswade the
people to worshippe his Mother the blessed Virgine for God, or prophesie of this great prophet *Mahumet*, as this shamlesse seducer affirmeth? or Azoar. 13.
howe coulde Christ which he reuerenceth for the greatest Prophet, and Azo. 74. 71.
truest lawmaker, be Author of such Idolatry? And to be breefe, as he came
in a time of many Heretickes and deceiuers, and to inchaunt his readers
with his beastlie delightes composed his Alcaron in rithmes, and meeters, Cuspin. de
so to allure companie vnto him by expresse decree, he approueth all er- Relig. turc.
rours and infidelities, so that a pluralitie of Gods be not admitted how- Mah. in Alc.
soeuer corporeous, infirme, and corruptible one GOD is beleeued, he Azoar. 37.
neuer reprehendeth but confirmeth. Wherfore to omit the rest and only
exemplifie, in that which most concerneth man which is his eternall beatitude and happie end (which as I proued no Temporall or Corporall Tract. 1. sup.
thing canne be) he assigneth such a Paradise, place, and state of Blessed- cap. 5.
nesse for a reasonable and immortall Soule, as is agreable to the nature &

Auer. lib. 9. Metaph. Arist. lib. 10. eth. Auicenn.

appetite of hogs, & most brutish beastes, in somuch *Auerroes* himselfe some times a Mahumetan, affirmeth that *Aristotle* had deuised a better happinesse for man then Mahumet did; and *Auicenna* a fauourer of that Secte greatly condemned Mahumet in that pointe, and yet these two were the wisest that euer were in his daunger to be seduced. They enforce the eldest sons of Christians contrary to the law of nature to profes Mahumetisme, and be Ienesaries to the Turkish Prince, when no man can be compelled to supernaturall thinges, except he hath first submitted himselfe. He inuadeth and vsurpeth without all title, the landes, territories, and goodes of others, which without manifest iniurie and iniustice cannot be done.

Azoar. 12.

He neuer pretended for title to Religion eyther supernaturall prophesie of thinges to come, any one miraculous operation or argument of reason, but forbad his folower to professe learning or dispute of his lawe, least they shoulde disclose his iniquitie; and pretendeth his claime and interest nothing but the sworde and violence, by which kinde of disputation and reasoning *Iulius Ceasar*, *Alexander*, *Augustus*, and other damned Idolatrous Emperours, should haue had a farre greater title to religion then euer *Mahumet* coulde pretend, being greater conquerours then he or any of his profession. And it is not onlie vnprobable but vnpossible that any accedentary or temporall thing in the power of nature should be an infallible signe & argument of supernatural and most certaine misteries, such as true religion must haue. So that we see Mahumetisme to be nothing else but a fardell of errours, and heresies, iniustice and volouptuousnes, bounde and collected together without any ground or reason, so that had he not begunne his Regiment in those rude and beastly countries where he did, apt and prone to all libertie and filthines, he neuer had preuailed to haue the least shewe of reuerence and Religion. For experience teacheth at this present, how in Greece and other ciuil Nations, which God for their reuoulte and dissobedience to his Church, and See Apostolique, hath deliuered to the turkesh tyranie, although they be infected with the heresies of *Nestorious*, schisme of the Grecians, & other errours, and therby destitute and vnfurnished of grace, rather chuse to become his slaues and vassals, vndergoeing all oppressions then yeelding to such absurdities to be aduanced with honours, as our Apostaties to that Infidelity be.

*Errors of the Brachmans.*

And if we will seperate the present *Brachmans* among the Indians from the olde Idolatrous Gentils, and make their Religion perticuler by it selfe, such is the absurditie of that people, yet professors of learning, that it is vnworthie to be related. But breeflye to giue a note of their superstitions in beleeuing, and Epicurismes in manner of liuing for a certaine time they

Pert. maff. l. 1 histor. lib. 1 histor

they liue at least in externall viewe a sober and penitentiall life, which being expired and ended they are presently exalted to the greatest honours, riches, and dignities, exemted from all lawes, free from all controulment, subiect to no penaltie, punishment, or reprehention, & liue in all delights, sinne, laciuiousnes, and wantonnesse, not to be recited. These be their priestes, and principall professors, so highly esteemed that their Kings are committed vnto them for educatiō, & subiect to their assignements. And their beleefe in worshippe is not vnlike to this practicall profession, for although they reuerence for their principall and most auncient Gods *Parabrammas* and his three sonns, & in memorie of that reuerence alwaies were a triple threade about their neckes, yet for pluralities of other Goddes, which they worshippe with equall diuine adoration, they are not inferior, to the Pagan Romans, but rather exceede them in number of Idolatries, and not content to dedicate Temples and Altars, offering Sacrifice vnto men, but vse and exercise the same diuine reuerence to Apes, Oxen, Elephantes, and the like brute, and vnreasonable creatures.

Indic. fol. 24 351. Cerem. Brachm. in Serm. Lucitan. &c.

Argum. 7. *Further shewing the excellencie of Christian Catholicke Religion aboue all other externall professions, both in speculatiue & practicall doctrine.*

VVHereby it is manifest howe vnpossible it is, that either the worshippes and reuerences vsed by any of those Infidelles, should be true and reuealed of God, which by no power can be author of any error, or (seing of necessitie one true Religion must be graunted) that Christian profession should be false, for all others euidently conuicted of palpable, grosse, and inexcusable errors, and absurdities, by necessarie cōsequence it remaineth not alone & in all things to be approued. And let any Iewe, Mahumetan, or Pagan, suruey the whole sum of Catholicke Religion (for I doe not defende the conuenticles and positions of heretickes) & proue whether he can finde any one such error & inconuenience. And to begin with the nature of God himselfe, which as by his infinit & most excellent preeminences, he is the prime and soueraigne obiect of true reuerence, and to haue this supreame homage and dutie of Religion, so if he be mistaken and any other worshipped for him, it turneth to irreligion and Idolatry by sacriledgious worshipping a falsly pretended God: All those misbeleeuers, Iewes, Mahumetans, Pagans, and Brachmans (as is euidentlie proued before) either constitute pluralities, or moste horrible corruptions, alterations, defectes, and imperfections in diuinitie, which altogether destroy al worship and Religion. For such imperfections and defectes are dishonourable, and not to be reurenced, much lesse with diuine adoration, cotrariwise wee Christians only worshippe one moste simple, in-

increated, vnalterable, infinite, and illimited cauſe, Creator, and conſeruer of all creatures, endued with all poſſible perfections, and ſo worthy of all worſhip. And for the end and happineſſe of man, we doe not aſſigne ſo fooliſh, vncertaine, or ſo corruptible, wanton, and carnall eſtate with defects, and filthines, which cannot poſſiblie content an immortall and reaſonable ſoule, in ſuch ſort as thoſe misbeleeuers do; but ſuch an eſtate either for perfection, continuance, and immutability, that wil, & only can content, & bring felicity to man. And for the meanes to come to ſo great happines and glory, (becauſe there muſt be a proportion betweene the end & ſuch things as bring vnto it.) That external and publicke ſacrifice we vſe, is not any ſuch prophane oblation as the Pagans vſed, no ſuch naked ceremony as the Mahumetans practiſe, and themſelues confeſſe ſhal be taken away, neither any of thoſe of the lawe of *Moyſes*, which already be abrogated, and which of themſelues neuer had validity, but as they had reference to Chriſt, but that moſt pure, and immaculat ſacrifice of the bodie and bloud of the Meſſias, ſo renowned and honoured before the cōming of Chriſt, as I haue prooued, ſo miraculouſlie teſtified of God, as al countries can witnes, & of it ſelfe able to pardon all ofences, euen in rigorous ſatisfaction; which no other religion can ſay. We doe not allowe in our worſhip any thing that may be called ſin, or be interpreted either preiudiciall to the honour of God, or office to man, which religion commandeth, as all theſe Infidels practiſe, in approouing hatred & reuenge vpon others, appointing vniuſt, craftie, and violent vſurping, and taking away of other mens goods and poſſeſſions, as the Pagans did, and their Gods themſelues were honoured for ſuch impieties, and the Mahumetans and Turkiſh proceedings vſe, & the Iews allowe for lawfull (to vſe their owne wordes in their Thalmud) *whether it be by craft, deceite, violence, vſurie, theft, killing, murthering*, or any other meanes. Neither doe we as thoſe misbeleeuers doe, affirme, that ſinne is not committed but by externall acts, when the malice of the ſinne dependeth of the internall conſent, but condemne euen the internall thoughts, and forbid all iniuries both to friends and enemies, commanding nothing to be done to others, which we would not to our ſelues. Omitting nothing that may be named vertue, and allowing nothing can be ſuſpected for vice, and becauſe naturall and morall actions of themſelues cannot merit a ſupernaturall beatitude, all ſuch value we attribute to ſuch effects, dependeth vpon the infinite price and dignity of our Meſſias, which no other profeſsion can make claime vnto. By whoſe merit and oblation, beſides theſe workes of grace, we only haue Sacraments, inſtruments to deriue his benefits, in all neceſſities, to all perſons,

Math. c. 22. Marc. c. 12. Rom. ca. 13. &c.

Argū. 4. ſup.

Lactāt. ſup. l. diu. inſt. in Hercul. &c. Cicer. de nat. Deor.

Alcor. ſupr. Thal. ordin. 1. trac. 4. diſt 3. ord. 2. diſt. 7. ord. 1. trac. 1. diſt 1. & 4. ord. 4. trac. 8 diſt. 2 & trac 4. & 9. &c.

persons, and at all times. When we are first borne, Baptisme to take away originall sinne; extreame vnction to releeue vs when we die, & defend vs against all enemies and agonies of those conflicts. And while we liue, eucharist, & confirmation, to strengthen vs in grace, and pennance to restore vs if we fall. And concerning the particuler estates and conditions both of the clergy and married, order to dignifie the one, and matrimonie to arme and defend the other, so that no state, time, or condition of men, is vnprouided, no sinne left vnpunished, no vertue omitted, but many added which Philosophers did not knowe, as loue to enemies, humility & others. Contempt of the world, & al impediments of felicitie. We exhort perfectiō, conteining a ful abnegatiō of al spiritual lets as riches, plesure, honor, & the like, by professing pouerty, chastity, & obediēce, wherby the great enimies of heauēly things the world, flesh, deuil, are subdued. Do we not purpose for the intellectual & immortal soul of man such a spiritual beatitude, as a greater & more excellēt cānot be deuised, the vision & fruitiō of God himself, conteining al felicity, & voide of al vnhappines? how reuerently do we esteeme of the holy patriarks & saints of the law of *Moises*, of the nature of angels whōe we affirme to be intelectual cretures, in which & other things, how barbarously do those infidels erre.

The 8. and last Arg. *How catholike christian religion hath ouercome al enemies, in all kinds of argument and disputation. And that it is the most certaine knowledge in the world, euen in naturall iudgment, & al arguments vsed against it, euidently false.*

AND to giue a ful & final contentment to al people in this case; when soeuer any matter seemeth doubtfull, or is called into controuersie, by such as pretend title & interest, it must needs be tried and debated with reasons, and arguments, either in writing, or publikely and by speech, by probations naturall & aboue nature, as the cause and question requireth, the first manner of trial hath giuen euident verdict for christians, & manifesty condemned al others of manifold profane & irreligious errors, vnpossible to be in true religion. Now I will shew how by the second kind of trial in conference and places of dispute, only christian catholike religion hath preuailed against al others, & vtterly condemned & conuinced thē for infidels & misbeleuers, both by natural & supernaturall arguments. *Catholike christian religion conquering Mahumetans.*

And to passe ouer Mahumetans, because as is manifest already they acknowledge the religion of Christ to be true, that we shal be saued therby, and it only endure and perseuer, and forbidding the professors of their law to dispute with christians haue giuen vs the victory in this disputation, which also hath bin proued against them by manie supernaturall miracles and most certaine arguments. Let vs come to other infidels against whom *Arg. 1. sup.* *Christians victory ouer all enemies.*

Christ him self most firmely founded & builded his doctrine, both against Iewes and Gentils by vnanswerable arguments, & euidences of truth, by so many humane reasons, so many fulfillings of the Prophets predictions, so manie miracles, so manifest, so publike, so supernaturall. By so manie blinde, deafe, dumbe, leopers, endued with sight, hearing, speaking, cleannes, so manie dead raised, deuils dispossessed, heauens, elements, and all creatures obeying aboue nature in the sight of all, recorded euen by his enemies. And after his death by his Apostles, & their successors, he conquered & subdued the whole world, S. *Steuen* a deacon preuailed so with his miracles and arguments, that neither the sinagogue of the Libertines, of the Cirineans, Alexandrians, or those of Cilicia and Asia which disputed with him, were able to make answere. The Apostles at the feast of pẽtecost amased & confounded Parthians, Medians, Elamites, inhabitants of Mesopotamia, Iewry, Chappadocia, Pontus, Asia, Phrigia, Pamphilia, Egipt, & the parts of Libia, strangers of Rome, Iews, & Proselites, Cretentians, & Arabians at Hierusalem, all those countries bearing witnes. And S. *Peter* at one sermon conuerted 3000. soules, so S. *Paul* first himselfe subdued, confounded them at Damascus, Seleutia, Ciprus, and *Bariehu* the false Iewish Prophet at *Paphos*, and made him blind, and conuerted *Sergius Paulus* the Proconsul. So at Perge, Pamphilia, Antioch, Iconium, Listra, Derbe, and wheresoeuer they were dispersed in his peregrination. So *Gamalcel*, master to S. *Paul* & S. *Steuen*, was cõuerted. So *Egesippus*. And so many in the time, and at the disputation betweene S. *Siluester*, and the Iewes at Rome. So in the great disputation in the yeere of Christ 418, a greate number of them togither with their great Rabbine *Theodorus* were subdued, and miraculously conuerted. So were the Iewes about Bithinia miraculously ouercome, as *Athanasius* witnesseth by the wonderfull bloude that issued forth of a wodden Image of the Crucifix, which one of them had pierced sacriledgeouslie. So about the yeere of Christ 708. in Siria by the like miracle as *Philippus Bergomensis* writeth. So in all places and ages, the most learned amõg thẽ haue bin ouercome. And in the primatiue church of christ, those which were their most learned, & durst not for feare become christiãs, yet did write in cõmendation of christians, as *Philo Iudeus*, *Iosephus*, & others.

Ios. supr. Pilat. ep. ad. Tiber. Mah. in Alcoran. &c. Act. c. 2. 6. Actor. c. 2. Actor. 9. Actor c. 13. Actor. c. 14. Clem. Recog lib. 1. cap. 9. & 10. Zonar. l. annal. to. 1. Metaphr. die 2. Ianuar. Glyc. in ann. Nicephor. li. 7. cap. 36. Cedren. in Camp. Ruff. lib. 1. cap. 38. Socrat. l. 3. cap. 17. Sozom. l. 5. cap. vlt. Athanas. l. post. Imag. Bergom hist. fol. 166.

Thus likewise Christ proued his doctrine against the Pagan Gentils, as appeareth not only in the particuler histories of the Apostles, & others, in the Primatiue Church, but in all ages, & places, as their vtter ouerthrowe and desolation doe testifie. So S. *Augustine* the Benedictine Monke proued catholike religion to the Pagans of the English nation, and subdued thẽ, so catholicke christians (and only catholicks as I will manifest hereafter) haue

*Conquest ouer Pagans.* Bed lib. cap. 25. ca. 26. &c.

haue subdued al Pagan cuntries, & conuerted them to christ. Thus al Sorcerers, Magitians, and Enchanters were vanquished. So *Simon Magus* that had seduced Samaria, and for his strange works of sorcerie named *the power of God*, was subdued and baptized of S. *Philip* a Deacon. And afterwards relapsed to his witchcrafts againe, because he coulde not buy with mony apostolicall authority, was ouercome by S. *Peter* at Rome in open assembly, before that wicked enemy of Christ, *Nero* the Emperor. So *Elymas* by S. *Paul* at Paphos. So *Marcellus* a scholler of *Simon Magus* became a christiã & wrote the combat betweene S. *Peter* and his old master *Simon Magus*. And *Iustinus* the martir & *Origẽ* affirme, that the Magi which trauailed so far to worship Christ in his natiuity, were Magicians, & by the apparition & miraculous conduction of the star, were conuerted. And S. *Ignatius* before them auoucheth the same, adding further, that thẽ al magicke, sorcery, & enchantmẽt began to cease. So S. *Iames* the greater, conuinced *Philetus*, & *Hermogenes*. So *Taurinus*, Bishop of Orleance confoũded *Cambises*, *Zamrim*, & their schollers. *Iustina* subdued *Ciprian* the sorcerer, & made him a christian Martir.

*Conquest ouer Sorcerers and Magitians.*

Actor. c. 8.

Egesip lib. 3. excid Hierosc cap. 2.

Actor. c. 13.

Iustin. Dial. cum Triph.

Origen l 1. contr. Cels.

Ignat. ep. ad Ephes.

Euseb. histor. eccles. lib. 2. cap. 8.

Isodor. l. de patrib. c. 73.

Vincent. in specul. l. 10. cap. 78. 79.

So likewise the most wise & morally vertuous philosophers of the world haue bin conquered, & conuerted in such order, that now neither Stoicke Cynike, Peripatetike, Epicure, or any other sect is to be found, for the light of nature did manifestly instruct thẽ, that their own iudgments & reasons were deceitful, & had often erred and changed, but those supernatural & other arguments of christians only able to be effected by the power of god (as nature taught those Philosophers) by no meanes could be vntrue. So *Dyonisius* the Areopagite & others, euen in that learned & famous vniuersity of Athens were confounded by S. *Paul*. S. *Katherine* a virgin, being but eightene yeres of age, subdued 50. of the wisest Philosophers, which all the credit and command of *Marentius* the Emperour could assemble together. So S. *Iustine*, S. *Basyl*. S. *Augustine*, and others were conuerted. So in the time of *Constantine* the great, a solemne disputation being apointed between the christians and them at Constantinople, they were all confounded and conuerted, by *Alexander* Bishop of of that city. Likewise they were ouercome and put to silence in the generall councell of Nice, (where a great number of them were gathered togither, for the aide of the Arians) by a catholike christian vnlearned, as *Socrates*, *Sozomenus*, and *Ruffinus* witnesse. So in the yeare of Christ 411. *Synesius* and *Euagrias* great Philosophers were conuerted, and S. *Augustine*, affirmeth the same of *Genuadius*. How many of them and how often of their best learned were not able to aunswere S. *Anthonie* the Eremit, a man altogither vnlearned? And all the Philosophers which euer were in the world with al their humaue learning and policie, were ne

*Conquest ouer all Philosophers.*

Actor. c. 17.

Metaphrast. & sur. in S. Katherin.

AmPhiloch. in vit. S. Basil

Euseb. in vit. Constant.

Socrat. l. 1. cap. 5.

Sozom. l. 1. cap. 17.

Ruff. lib. 1. cap. 3.

Sophron. in prat. spirit. cap. 195.

Sines. ep. 79.

Ang, ep. 100

Athanas. in vit. S. Ant.

uer able to conuert one cittye to their opinions, although hauing for their protection, and furtherance, the fauour, countenance, and asistance of the Kings, and Emperours and yet poore fishermen by the dctriue of Christ against the violent resistance of all enemies, haue conquered the whole worlde vnto him. And yet at that very time, when the Apostles & disciples of Christ went about & preached christian doctrine to the world, the Phisosophers as their own writers are witnesses (for the deuil wil imitat God) practised the like in goeing about and perswading their opinions, but preuailed nothing, such were *Apollonius, Dio, Demetrius, Misonius, Damis,* the pithagorean; *Epictetus* the Stoycke, *Lucianus* the epicure *Diogines* the yonger and others. And generally the Platonicks, either became Christians, such as had any consciēce of things, or magitians such as had none at all, and not only the Platonicke Philosophers but all others that were of the greatest learning, & best life among all sorts & sects, were conuerted. And the sect of the Cynicks, Epicures, and Magitians that were the most vile, licentious, and wicked of all the rest, giuen ouer to all liberty and wantonnesse, not only with women, but in such vnnaturall maner as may not be spoken, as both their own opinions & writers do testify, were the greatest enemies we had. And those which were their greatest learned and of most ciuill conuersation such as *Seneca,* and others, & in those times of disgraces & persecutions durst not professe themselues christians, yet were our greatest frinds, and writ most reuerently of our religion. And those Philosophers when they were conuerted, shewed themselues most constant & zelous Christians, and proued the greatest propugnors & defenders of faith, in those turbulent and violent times of persecution, against all tirants, and enemies we had. Such were *Aristides* of Athens, *Apollinaris, Clemens Alexandrinus, Iustinus, Melciades,* & others. And besides al those external Infidels & enemies, so many sorts and sects of heretickes aboue 400. in number before the Apostasie of *Luther,* which in the scoole of Christ haue made ciuill war and rebelion against the catholicke Church & doctrine, haue bin so vtterly confounded, confuted, & vanquished that not somuch as any memory of them is left, except among catholike writers, which haue noted & recorded their heresies. So that what force and validity their witnes was of, they gaue testimony vnto vs, not onlie in the things wherin they discented & were subdued by their ouerthrow, but in those things wherin they agreed with vs, against these present protestants, and are witnesses not only for vs, but against all other enemies from which they discented. So was *Arius* confounded by *Alexander* Bishop of Constantinople, so *Olympus* at *Carthage.* So did S. *Basil* miraculously conquer *Valens* the Arian Emperour. So *Copres* the

Philostr. l. 9. Dio. Rhod. Corinth. Borysth.

Aug. ep. 56. et li. ver. Relig. ca. 4.

Origen. contra Cels.

Senec. ep.

Aristid. in apol. Trithem de script. Apollinar. Clem. Alex. Iustin. apol. Melch. apol. &c.

*Conquest ouer all heretickes & internall enemies.*

Bernard. Luther. l. catalog. hær. Hist. 3. l3. c. 10. Platin in Anastas. 2. Amphil. in S. Basil. Pallad. hist. in Copres.

the Eremit conuinced the Manichees. Thus al other hereticks were ouercome, euen those that had most affinity & kindred with protestants, *Berengarius* the father of the Sacramentaries was confuted & recanted his error in open councel, & acknowledged the Real Presence of *Christ* in the sixt Sacrament. So the Wicklifists in England, in the same point in a most frequent assembly in the church of S. *Paul* in London, were miraculously confounded, & subdued. So were the *Henricians* in France by S. *Bernard*, both in that & other points wherin they agreed with these men? & all opinions now defended by thē one time or other were confounded, & confuted in generall councels, & the most famous & learned assemblies of the world. So that what enemies soeuer they were, Infidels or heretickes, which at any time denied christian Catholike faith, were thus both strangely by miracles, and by argument in reason conuicted & condemned, whether they were Iews trusting to supernatural asistance, or the gentils in the power & pompe of the world, or Magitians in aide of deuils, & damned spirits, Philosophers in their wit, and learning, or any heretické & apostata in what so euer Buckler of defence they vsed. And neuer any of them could hitherto bring either supernatural argument or sufficiēt natural reason against vs. Yea the Iews so famous with miracles before Christ, since they denied him had neuer any miracle among them, except such as Christ and Christians haue wrought to confoūd them, their *Piscina Probatica* that so miraculously healed diseases at the discending of the angel, thē ceasing as their own writers *Iosephus* & others witnes. For their figures ceasing in Christ, God the worker of miracles wold no longer giue testimony vnto thē. So likewise of *Mahumet* and his Mahumetans: and he himselfe so acknowledged, confessing that miracles were granted vnto Christ. What likly-hood there is in finding any such thing among the Pagan Idolaters, whose gods were deuils, as is proued before, which could worke nothing supernaturall, euery man knoweth, and besides the very confession of all these Sects, the thing in it selfe is manifest. For euery one of them defending so manifest errours and blasphemies as I haue proued, it is imposible that God which cannot giue testimony to vntruth, should grant miracles & supernatural works, to proue that to be true, which euen in the light of reason is euidētly false. And those wonders which are attributed to some Pagans as to *Vespatiā* the Emperour as *Tacitus* & *Suetonius* report the healing of a sore head of one, & an eye of an other, & such others are confessed by the same Authors, that the Phisitiōs answered they might be healed by phisike, & so no miracles. And *Philostratus* their own writer is witnes, that *Apolonius Tyanæus* that great coniurer & friend of *Vespatian* was present, then who wil doubt by what art they

De consecr. d.2.c. Bereg. Bergom.hist. fol. 182. Tho.Waldē. to.2.

In vit. S. Ber.

*Neuer any miracles wrought since Christ to proue Religion, but by Catholikes, and for their faith.*

Iof.l.bell. Epiphan.de piscin.

Mahumet. in Alcoran.

*See* Cær.Bar. to 1. Annal. fol.752.753 Tacit l 4 hist. Sueton.in Vespatiā.c.7. philostr in Appol.l.5. Tacit.l.5. histor. Suet. super.cap. 4. Iof.lib. 7. bell.

they were don? And *Polibius* a famous author among those gentiles plainly confesseth that such strange things as were reported of their gods, as *Iupiter, Diana, Vesta*, and others were childish toyes or things vtterly vntrue.

Polib. lib. 16. histor.

Or if true miracles & supernatural workes had euer bene wrought by these men, that defend such absurdities as *Sozomenus* reporteth *Eutichianus* a nouatian heretike to had haue the gift of healing (which I neuer heard either of Iewe since Christ, Mahumetan, or Pagan recorded in any credible historie, or truly chalenged by them) yet if such a gift were granted to any Infidel or misbeleuer (which God is able to doe) it is impossible it should euer be practised to proue or maintaine their false and erronious opinions, but some other end, and purpose, as the manifesting the Iustice of God in puunishing offenders, or defence of the innocency of some falsly accused, detecting malefactors or the like. So murther hath often bin miraculously bewraied euen by the mā that was murthered, as of late at Vppingham in Rutland, the man murthered ten or forteene daies after his death bewraied the murder by opening one of his eies at the presence of this malefactor, as is credibly reported. And in this sence *Cayphas* a wicked enemy of Christ did prophesy, *That it was expedient one shoulde dye for the people*, for that proued the necesity of Christes Pasion. So God might heale infirmities by an hereticke, to shewe his mercy to people afflicted, and it was affirmed by some Pagans, that *Claudia* of Rome drewe with hirgirdle a Shippe that stucke in the sands of the Riuer Tiber, and a vestall Virgin drewe water in a siue forth of the same Riuer, to manifest their innocencie in some things wherein they were accused, although all these might be done by enchantments as euery Philosopher knoweth, none of them aboue the compasse of naturall causes. Wherfore to come to end of this dispute with external Infidels: As I haue proued in the former booke against all Atheistes and Irreligious, an absolute & vndeniable necessitie of a God and Religion due vnto him, in such order that by no possibilitie either the one or other can be vntrue: So in this it is manifest, against all misbeleeuers, that in particuler this Religion is that holy worship which was instituted and taught by Christ. To this all testimonies, diuine and humane assent. All authoritie that can be cited in such a cause agreeth, all people of renouned learning, or equall iudgment, ioyne in this sentence: all friendes allowe it: the chiefest grounds of our enemies themselues confirme it. All other worships by their owne confessions, are drowned in most profane and irreligious errors, euen against the light of nature it selfe, and such as depriue the professors of all title to true Religion. One Religion must needes be true, all others be both palpably erronious in themselues, & haue acknowledged

Sozom. l. 1. hist. c. 14.

Ioh. cap. 11. & 18.

not

not only in generall the veritie of this holy profeſsion, but haue giuen confirmation to thoſe priuat Articles which be the greateſt miſteries, & moſt ſecret difficulties in that worſhip. All witneſſe both of God and creatures all reaſon, naturall & aboue nature, haue ſo conſented. And euery article it defendeth, by infallible motiues hath bene reſolued into that moſt inerrable word and reuelation of God, who can neither be deceaued in himſelfe, or bring others into errour. Wherfore I will conclude with S. *Chriſoſtom*, that catholike faith is more certaine then any demonſtration, which Philoſophers knowe to be the moſt certaine knowledge. And approoue that ſaying of S. *Aguſtine*, that he would rather doubt whether he himſelfe liuing were aliue, then call any matter of that faith into queſtiō. For in naturall ſcience, the limited & deceitfull vnderſtanding of man whereon it is grounded, may be deceaued, but the infinite and vnſcrutable wiſdome of God, vpon which theſe truthes are builded, by no poſsibility can erre. And theſe ſhall ſuffice for externall Infidels. Concerning Proteſtants, and other Heretickes, and internall Enemies, I will proue Catholicke Romane Religion to be only true, and al others blaſphemous and damnable, by aboue an hundred Arguments in my next worke againſt them.

Chriſoſtom. hom. 8. in ep. ad Rom. Aug. lib. 7. confeſ. c. 10.

*THE ENDE OF THE FIRST PART*

of the Reſolution of Religion.

---

## A TABLE OF SVCH THINGS AS ARE CONTEYned in the firſt part of the Reſolution of Religion.

FINIS.